CRAFTS OF THE NORTH AMERICAN INDIANS
A CRAFTSMAN'S MANUAL

RICHARD C. SCHNEIDER

Published by:
    R. Schneider, Publishers
    312 Linwood Avenue
    Stevens Point, Wisconsin 54481

Library of Congress Cataloging in Publication Data

Schneider, Richard C   1929-
    Crafts of the North American Indians.

    Includes bibliographies.
    1. Indians of North America--Industries. I. Title.
E98.I5S36 1974   745.5'09701   73-13008
ISBN 0-936984-00-7 (pbk.) (formerly 0-442-27442-4)

DEDICATION

To my wife, Myrna, who gives love and encouragement above and beyond those of mari-
tal vows; and to the kids, Lora and Fritz,
who smilingly suffered through their father's
artistic temperament.

To the Native Americans, past and present,
without whom this book could not exist.

ABOUT THE AUTHOR

Richard C. Schneider is Professor
of Art at the University of Wisconsin - Stevens Point where he has
been teaching ceramics and other
arts since 1962. He was born in
1929 in Kenosha, Wisconsin and holds
graduate degrees from the univer-
sities at Milwaukee and Madison.
He has taught art in Wisconsin public schools at Antigo and Racine.
His pottery and sculptures have
been exhibited regionally and na-
tionally, and his work is found in
many private collections.

Schneider's interest in Indian artifacts originates from childhood,
but it was stimulated at the Milwaukee Public Museum with the encouragement of the Curator of Anthropology, Robert Ritzenthaler.
While taking coursework on the material culture of American Indians,
Schneider was not satisfied with the examination of specimens but
started experiments in the re-creation of ancient and modern techniques of manufacture. His homes in Stevens Point and nearby Big Bass
Lake are the sites of his research which explains why the crafts in
his book are primarily those of the Woodland peoples who originated
them. His research, wherever possible, was suggested by Native Americans who continue their crafts heritage today. In some cases, he
had to turn to scholarly writings and study of the artifacts themselves
in order to reconstruct the methodology of lost crafts.

A few years ago, Schneider began teaching a course on Indian crafts at
the university in Stevens Point where it may be the only course of its
kind which offers collegiate credit to students who learn about a culture through the re-creation of its artifacts.

Schneider's wife, Myrna, and children, Lora and Fritz, are also students
of Indian culture. Many of the crafts in this book result from their
experiences.

FORE-WORDS

The following chapters were originally conceived primarily as substitutes
for classroom lectures on Indian crafts. Most of the subjects are time-
consuming crafts which cannot be well demonstrated to a group of students
because (1) they may need to take place in several locations, especially
in the matter of gathering materials, (2) some materials may need to be
gathered at different times of the year, (3) the processes generally take
so much time or require necessary pauses that demonstrations must be
piece-meal to the degree that an observer seldom can witness the entire
process, and (4) some of these require close observation of fine detail
which is not possible in most classrooms. Motion pictures are a reasonable solution to these problems and are a good substitute for live demonstrations. There is, however, one shortcoming in motion pictures: the
viewer is too easily left with the assumption that he can tan a buckskin,
for instance, in a half-hour.

I have learned these crafts through a combination of book-study, observation, examination, conversation, and actual experimentation. I have writ-
ten my findings into these chapters which are, perhaps, overstated and
exaggerated, rather than condensed and simplified. All Indian crafts
seem to me to be simple and uncomplicated as one observes a skilled craftsman at work. In actual practice, one finds that there are numerous sub-
tleties and personal enlightenments which are difficult to observe and
may be more difficult to explain. So many times one hears such comments
as, "You have to know how to do this just right", or, "This has to be
done in a certain way", which indicates that there is no substitute for
experience. This book is about my experiences. In essence, it is not
simply *about* Indian crafts; it *is* Indian crafts.

Not all Indian native crafts are found on these pages. I have included
here only those in which I feel some expertise which are those which, for
some reason or other, have caught my fancy. I don't consider myself an
expert, for an expert knows all. When my skill reached a sufficient level,
I set down my experiences for others. I still can't guarantee that my
tanning will be perfect nor that my moccasins will fit, but I know that
I'll be close. Some crafts are absent in this book; these are on my list
for the future.

There is no Bibliography at the end of this book. Instead, where appli-
cable, I have included "References" at the close of chapters. These references have been useful to me in my initial experiments. They may also
be helpful to the serious student who is stimulated to work in greater

depth than my chapters offer.

I expect that the student is "educated" in one sense, but "ignorant" in
another. Most of us today have acquired intellectual knowledge about
many things, but we have lost the basic skills and imagination to trans-
form common raw materials into useful and delightful objects, although
we use hundreds of objects made by others. In other words, we are a
consumer culture, not a productive culture. This book attempts to encourage production. While I am pleased to discern a "back-to-nature"
movement on the part of some young people today, I cannot believe that
one can nor should return to the "good old days" of independent living
which may include disease, privation, and subsistence living. I do see,
in contemporary life, a real need for more frequent statements of *I
made this*", with accentuation on each word. What a wealth there is in
this short statement! Parenthetically, I place little value on ready-
made kits which erroneously encourage one to make such a statement. I
am not at all adverse to utilizing contemporary tools or materials
when their use diminishes the drudgery or improves the quality of the
product. I do feel concern about the step-by-step instructions which
accompany pre-cut and pre-stamped and pre-everything "craft kits" which
permit no individuality, but only result in an ability to follow directions.

On the succeeding pages, measurements are given in generalities; designs
and shapes are suggested; little, if anything, is precise. Indians, in
general, followed tribal codes or family preferences, but each craftsman
had idiosyncracies in sizes, designs, and techniques unique to himself.
I have tried to offer such generalities which seem universal, but your
own experiences will need to be your final guide.

Some chapters may seem repetitious because some people insist on reading
only those parts which have momentary interest. I urge that, prior to
trying any medium, one reads the entire chapter to gain a complete knowledge of the craft. I have tried to organize logically (which is so
dear to professors), but sometimes it was impossible to put everything
in sequence for all occasions. At the risk of encouraging too much
reading, I'd suggest that one read the related chapters before attempting
a project.

You will note that I tend to use the English idiom of the masculine pro-
noun in reference to crafts*men*. This is merely a matter of convenience,
for most of the craftsmen were, in fact, women. In typical hunting and
gathering cultures, hunting was a full-time male occupation. Without
frequent fresh meat, a group could not exist. Typical male crafts were
those directly concerned with hunting such as arrowhead flaking or those
which, even today, are associated with men such as whittling and carving.
Some very personal objects, such as pipes and drums, were, according to
custom and taboo, made by men. Objects associated with homemaking were
considered women's work although, by modern standards, they might be considered too heavy. Thus, in splint baskets, for instance, men might cut
the trees and whittle the handles, the women would split the splints and

do the actual basket weaving. In quillwork, men might hunt the porcupine,
but women would pluck, dye and do the quill embroidery. On this matter,
I preach no male chauvinism.

I claim little expertise in history, anthropology, or biology, all of
which pertain to the subject. Such information is best obtained elsewhere. I cannot help, however, to include bits of information from time
to time which seem to me to make the work easier or (intellectually, at
least) more profitable.

When trying some of these projects, I assume that you are willing to take
time, that you are willing to sweat some, and that you are willing to make
an attempt with no guarantee of success. (Few persons, for instance, will
tan a buckskin well on the first attempt.) Your attempts will increase
your awareness of the work of others, and you will probably be able to
recognize the superiority of the native product. Few people, except those
who have had similar experiences, will be able to share your pleasure in
the feeble results of your arduous efforts, but *you* will. Although you
will certainly take earned pride in a work well done, you can also take
pride in lesser quality work which represents the hours of preparation
and effort it took to create even poor work.

You will learn that these crafts are not financially profitable. It is
fairly accurately estimated that some two-thirds of the time involved in
a native craft is spent on the basic gathering and preparing of the raw
material. At a wage of a dollar or two per hour, you cannot make a living
wage. With the speed and quality which come from experience, it may become possible to eke out some extra income, but few buyers will come forward if you price the work high enough to make a profit.

The materials you'll use are (with the possible exception of glass beads)
cheap and (dependent upon your local situation) abundant if wisely used.
Most of the tools you'll need cannot be purchased so you'll have to save
money by making your own. Of course, if you only use them once, you'll
have the initial cost, but I expect that, once having made the tools and
tried the crafts, you'll continue.

While I do support the perpetuation and resurrection of crafts that are
dying or are lost, I do not advocate the creation of what are called, in
the language of anthropology, "fraudulent artifacts". There is an unfortunate market for unauthenticated historical wares which are sold to
collectors. In addition to being patently dishonest, such wares may also
lead to incorrect and improper conclusions about the history and sociology
which is largely deduced from artifacts.

I should also say that I am no advocate of competition with the few Native
American craftsmen who remain active. Compare your work to theirs, of
course, but make no effort to compete for the small market which still
exists. We are trying to gain understanding, appreciation, and sympathy
for the arts and skills of a people. Perhaps in this way we can also
generate similar feelings for the Native Americans themselves.

One last caution: I treat rather delicately the matter of artifacts which carry overtones of religious and spiritual significance such as drums, pipes, masks, and the like. While such projects may have interest to to-day's craftsman, the history of their use is such that one must question the validity of reproducing these today without a thorough and sympathetic understanding of their place. I do have strong reservations about the possible degeneration, for instance, for masks which may end up in Hallowe'en costumes.

As much as possible at this time, I have limited the scope of this book to the crafts of the Woodland Culture Area (which includes my home in central Wisconsin) for the obvious reason that many of the materials used in the old days are still available to me today I have offered, in my opinion, suggestions for reasonable substitutes which preserve the quality and experience of the originals. In cases where certain artifacts or technologies from other culture areas seemed appropriate, I have included these as well.

Finally, as an alien to the culture about which I write, I have tried to give a fair and honest relation. If I have, in ignorance, unintentionally offended anyone, I offer my sincere apologies; I would look forward to having these brought to my attention for correction. To the Native Americans who read this book, to those who gave information, I offer thanks. I have learned, but there is much to learn.

Students: read carefully, try hard, and use your heart as well as your hands.

                              R. Schneider
                              Big Bass Lake, Wisconsin
                              1972

TABLE OF CONTENTS

AN INDIAN CROOKED KNIFE

A very serviceable knife, now all but forgotten except in remote Indian
reservations and museum collections, is the once-popular "crooked knife"
(Fig. 1). These were traditionally used by men and are also commonly
known known as the "man's knife" to differentiate them from the "woman's
knife". The latter was made with a semi-circular blade fitted with a
T-shaped handle and which resemble some modern food choppers. Some
modern descendents are still called crooked knives, but they bear little
resemblance to the original designs.

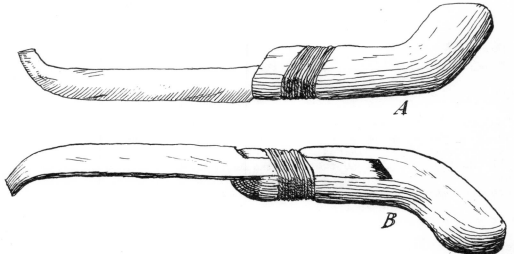

Fig. 1, Crooked knife with bent-tip blade. A, Top view. B, Bottom view.

Crooked knives were made either with a straight blade or bent at the tip
so that they could be used as a gouge as well as for straight cutting.
The name, however, seems to come primarily from the pistol-grip bent handle. Unlike most knives today, the crooked knife is used as a one-handed
draw-knife; that is, it is made to cut toward the body, not away from
it. The handle is grasped with the palm of the hand up with the fingers
closed over the top of the handle and the thumb along the outside of the
curve which points away from the user. Thus, the knife can be pulled
toward the user with the strong biceps muscle of the upper arm. This
technique is awkward to those of us who have been taught from childhood
to "cut always away from you", but, with practice, it is actually less
fatiguing and no more dangerous. Another unique feature of this knife
is that it is not an ambidexterous tool. All diagrams in this article
are given for a right-handed knife; southpaws, as usual, must reverse these.

The Blade

The Indians' source of steel was necessarily dependent upon the white
man. Knives were made of all kinds of scrap steel including old rifle
barrels. A small, old, flat file can provide the necessary metal for
your blade. Find a file about 8-10 inches long and about 3/4 inch wide.
Soften the metal by heating it to red heat and allowing it to cool slowly. Because of the differences in steels, this "annealing" process may
need to be done more than once. A small propane torch can do this, but
the heat is lost on one part of the metal almost as fast as it heats up
elsewhere. A quicker method is to ask someone in an auto body shop to
play an oxy-acetylene torch over it unless one has access to a forge.

When the file has cooled from the annealing, break off most of the thin
tang by clamping it in a vise and bending it until it breaks. This also
tells you how brittle the metal still is.

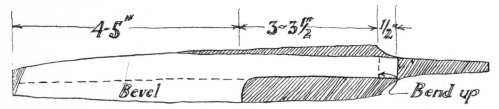

Fig. 2, Blade form. Cut away all shaded portions.

Grind away all the shaded parts in the diagram to make a rough blade form
(Fig. 2). Sizes and proportions are given in generalities, for these
knives were made by individual Indian craftsmen, sometimes with the aid
of blacksmiths, so that no two were exactly alike. There is no evidence
that these were ever produced commercially as trade items. You can,
therefore, make your own variations. Keep a can of water handy as you
grind in order to quench the metal when it becomes hot. Cool it as soon
as it begins to change color from the friction.

When the rough blank has been shaped, grind a smooth, long bevel on the
top of the blade only. Take your time to do a good job, for this is
slow work. The only way to speed this up is to forge this bevel which
requires equipment and skill not readily available to most craftsmen.
In this manner the knife edge is shaped like a wood chisel rather than
with a bevel on both sides as with a hunting knife, for instance. Grind
the back edge slightly round, and also round off the square edges of the
newly created tang. Grind the bottom surface flat and smooth and take
off the file teeth, if you wish, on the remaining portion of the top.

If you want a knife which can also be used as a gouge, heat the tip end
red hot and bend the last inch or so up in a smooth, even curve. The
tip can be left straight, if you prefer. Heat the tang end red hot and
quickly bend up about 1/4-1/2 inch. This, when imbedded in the handle,
keeps the blade from pulling out.

Now polish the entire blade with progressively finer grades of emery paper until you have a bright, clean metal surface. Heat the entire blade
slowly and evenly until you begin to see a straw-yellow color appear.
Continue to heat the blade cautiously as the color changes to brown and
finally becomes purple-blue. This indicates that the metal is now "tempered" to the proper hardness for cutting wood. As soon as it has reached this color, quench the entire blade, preferably in oil.

The Handle

Find a piece of wood about five inches long by two by one inch. You
might want to try an Indian-style handle from a bent branch so that the
wood grain goes with the curve of the handle. Shape this handle as
shown (Fig. 3) so that it fits comfortably in your hand as described
earlier.

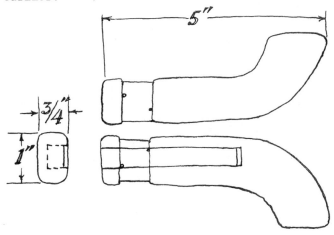

Groove the bottom of
the handle as shown to
receive the tang of the
blade and drill or chis-
el out a rectangular
hole for the bent end
of the tang. The tang
should fit snugly and
should be approximately
level with the bottom
of the handle.

File a low groove about
one inch wide all around
the handle about 1/2
inch from the end to re-
ceive the binding.

Fig. 3, Handle pattern.

Sandpaper the handle
smooth. Designs can be carved or incised into the handle at this time.
Some Indian knife handles were carved into animal shapes and other sculptural forms. Finish the handle with boiled linseed oil wiped on with a
rag.

The Assembly

Select some soft brass or copper wire, about 20 gauge in diameter, and
drill two holes of this diameter through the handle for the beginning
and end of this binding wire. Rawhide or cord was used in the past.

Insert the tang into the handle; shove the end of your wire through one
of the holes provided for it. Bend the wire sharply so that it stays in
the hole and then begin wrapping it evenly around and around in the groove.

When you have completed the wrapping and just before you cover up the second hole, push the free end through, and, with a pliers, pull it tight so that the coils are held in place. If the holes are just large enough to take the wire, this is all the fastening it needs.

Sharpening

The final touch is to sharpen the blade. This can be done the same as for a wood chisel: on the bevelled side only. The only exception to this is a few touches with a fine stone on the flat bottom in order to remove the burr or wire edge from sharpening. If you have made a blade with a curved end, this should also be sharpened on the bevelled side only, but you will need to use a curved stone called a "slip" which is designed for sharpening the inside of gouges. Sharpen the blade to suit yourself, but remember that a sharp knife which cuts when you expect it is safer than a dull one which may slip accidentally.

The Sheath

Because your knife is custom made, you will need to design a sheath especially for it. The diagram (Fig. 4) suggests an Indian-style pattern in which the knife slides well into the sheath for safety and not for a quick draw. Allow excess in your pattern for stitching the seams and also for the thickness of the handle. Tape a heavy paper pattern together for size before you cut any leather. The belt strap in the illustration is rivetted, and the rest of it is stitched. Some leathers, if dampened and wedged open, will hold a bulged shape upon drying so that the knife can slide in and out easily.

You will find, once you overcome your inexperience of a draw-stroke, that a well designed, sharp, crooked knife has many uses. It is fine for stripping bark and

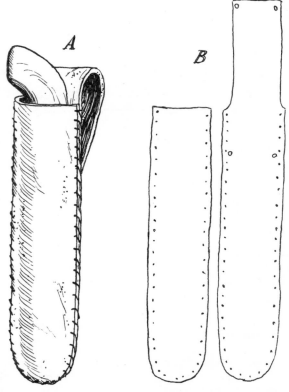

Fig. 4, Crooked knife sheath. A, Completed sheath. B, Front and back pattern.

paring down wood. I shaped many of the wooden parts of a canoe with mine. A straight-bladed model can notch out square holes such as mortises for

instance; and the curved blade model is fine for scooping out bowls.
The crooked knife has served the needs of many generations of men who
depended on it for their existence.

Fig. 5, Using the crooked knife.

AN ESKIMO-STYLE BOW DRILL

Several styles of drilling apparatus were used in aboriginal cultures all over the world and have served as prototypes for contemporary machinery. One of the earliest of these styles was probably a simple shaft, with some sort of a point, which was rotated back and forth between the open palms of the hand (Fig. 1). While this was fairly efficient inasmuch as the rotation principle was concerned, it had the obvious shortcoming of having minimal downward pressure. The hands were started at the top of the drill shaft and were pressed downward while rubbing back and forth. After five or six such rubs, one would have to pause in order to start at the top again.

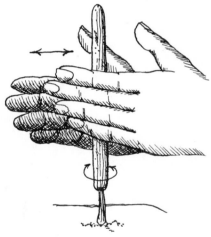

Fig. 1, Palm drill.

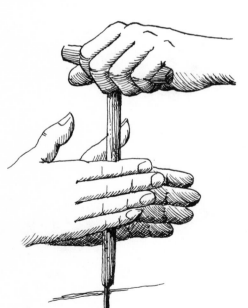

Fig. 2, Two-man palm drill.

This shortcoming may have resulted in the invention of a block or handle with a blind hole in the bottom-side to receive the bluntly pointed upper end of the drill shaft. Such a device would require two persons to operate: one to use both hands to rotate the drill and the other person to hold this "steady block" and, perhaps, to grip the work (Fig. 2).

One can imagine circumstances when a craftsman would find it necessary to work alone. Some sort of vise (his feet, perhaps) could be employed to grip the work, but three hands were

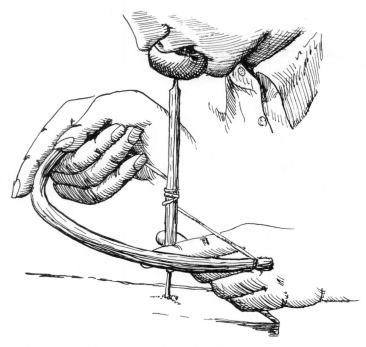

still necessary to operate the drill. This handicap eventually was overcome with the invention of a bow which, with its string wrapped around the drill shaft a few turns, could be drawn back and forth with one hand, thus rotating the drill with a speed and ease which was superior to the palm drill method. Assuming that the work could be held in some manner, the other hand could then hold the "steady block" with no dependence upon another individual.

Fig. 3, Eskimo-style bow drill.

The Eskimos were one people who created an additional refinement on this bow drill by re-designing the steady block so that it could be held in the teeth. Thus, one hand still moved the bow, but the other hand was freed to steady the work and hold the drill bit for starting the hole (Fig. 3).

The Bow

Select a straight-grained piece of wood about 15-20 inches long and at least 1/2 inch round or square. (No precise measurements will be given because each drill was unique.) I recommend hardwood such as ash or maple although any wood may be used. Eskimos, with little choice of wood, often made bows of bone (such as ribs) or even ivory (such as walrus tusks). A sapling can be used or you can split a piece from a larger log. In the former instance, you may be able to find a sapling or branch with a pronounced bow already naturally present. In either instance, pare the piece to a consistent thickness and smooth it by whittling and sandpapering. Notch or drill the ends to receive the bowstring.

If green wood has been used, bending may begin immediately, but slowly. Tie a stout cord on one end and create a slight bow by tying the cord firmly to the other end. Every few hours re-tie the cord to increase the bend until you achieve a bend about 3-5 inches from the center of the cord. (Make this too much, for you can expect to lose some when tension is released.)

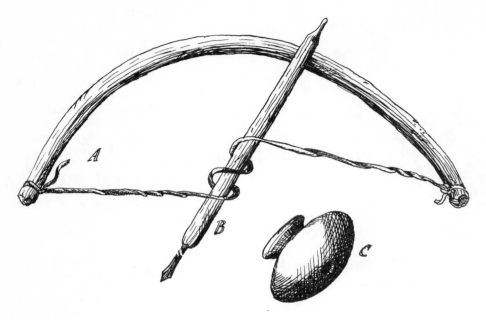

Fig. 4, Bow drill. A, Bow. B, Drill shaft. C, Mouthpiece.

If seasoned wood is to be used, soak it for a day. Bend the bow by im-
mersing it in boiling water or by pouring boiling water over it for 10
minutes or so. After this initial softening you may start the bend slowly with additional wettings as necessary. Don't let the wood dry or get
cold until you have finished the bend. Tie as above.

If a round sapling has been used, the bend can be made in any direction,
but you would be wise to utilize any natural curve which exists. If the
piece has been split from a larger billet, the heart grain side should
be to the inside of the bow.

If bending is awkward, the bow can be started by bending it around a
suitable form or template such as a tree trunk. Sometimes a bow will
kink if there are weaknesses in the wood or poor technique in the handling. The use of a template helps preclude this problem.

Put the bow aside for several days or a week, after which it should be
able to retain most of its bend after the tension cord is released.

Cut a length of buckskin (or other thin, supple leather) about 1/8-1/4
inch wide and longer than necessary to span the bow. Unlike the weapon,
this bow is never strung tightly; the string is tied so that it is about
2 inches too long (Fig. 4A). This excess is necessary to permit it to
be wrapped around the drill shaft. I like to twist the leather bow
string before it is tied so that it will have a somewhat round cross-section. A flat bow string may not wind and unwind smoothly.

Some Eskimo bows, especially those of bone or ivory, were exquisitely designed with incised decorative patterns and pictures. Try this if you
like, but be sure that the depth of incising does not weaken your bow excessively. Don't make the bow too heavy, though. Bear in mind that you
will tire more rapidly with a heavy bow than a light one.

The Mouthpiece

The mouthpiece or
steady block should
be made of hardwood
such as maple unless
you enjoy the taste
of pine pitch. The
grain should normally
run parallel to the
drill shaft. This
keeps the pivot hole
from wearing out un-
duly, and also keeps
the piece from split-
ting too easily. That
portion which is out-
side the mouth can be

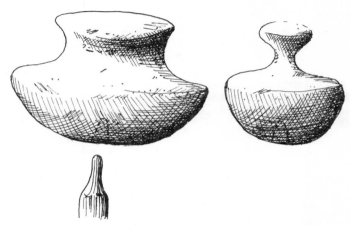

Fig. 5, Mouthpiece; side and end views.

'most any size and shape, but an oval shape about the size of the lips
is most frequently seen. The portion which fits inside the mouth should
approximate the inside shape of your teeth. This is smaller than you
think. Take a look at false teeth or take a bite out of a slice of
cheese to get an idea. The "neck" between the inside and outside portions (top and bottom as seen in Fig. 5) should be quite thin so that
you can clamp down with your teeth easily. Saw, whittle, and file the
piece to a size and shape which feels fairly comfortable. (It probably
will never feel really comfortable.) Sandpaper the block smooth and
wash off the sawdust.

In the center of the bottom bore a blind hole about 3/8-1/2 inch deep.
This should be a conical hole, so if a modern steel drill is used, twist
the drill around while drilling so that the sides of the hole taper toward the bottom (Fig. 5).

To finish the mouthpiece, grease this hole liberally. (Butter is O.K.,
but gets rancid.) A salad oil is satisfactory, and I don't get squeam-
ish after it soaks into the wood. Any grease or oil will need to be replenished from time to time.

Some Eskimo mouthpieces are made of bone or ivory, and the superiority
of this material for the pivot hole's bearing surface should be obvious.
Some wooden mouthpieces have been made with a bone or ivory insert containing the pivot hole inlaid into the bottom. Try this if you intend
to do a lot of drilling; otherwise, a good hardwood will soon acquire a
smooth polish for minimal friction.

The Drill

Find several clear, straight-grained saplings which, when de-barked, will
measure about 1/2 inch diameter by 8-10 inches long for the drill shafts.
Clean these well and sandpaper them smooth but not slick. Allow these
to season for several days. It is not necessary to pare these to an even
diameter; the wider butt end is fine for boring to receive the drill
point. Sharpen the opposite end to a rounded point about 1/4 inch in
diameter which is sufficient to keep it from breaking during use (Fig.
4B). This should fit a little tightly in the mouthpiece hole; ridges
will polish down to a loose fit when you start using it. Before setting
the shafts aside to season, check them for straightness by sighting along
their lengths. Bend them true and check from time to time during the
seasoning. While these need not be perfect, slight warping can cause
undesirable vibrations on your teeth later.

If you want to be really authentic, slot the end of a seasoned shaft and tie on a stone perforator (Fig. 6). Note
that such a point will drill a tapered hole which is one
characteristic of primitive drilling. The edge of the perforator is flaked as an arrowhead and, because the shaft
rotates in both directions, it cuts equally well in either
direction. (Remember this principle when you make any
points. A modern twist drill is unsatisfactory; it cuts in
one direction only.) If rawhide is used for lashing, check
the trueness of the point by twirling the shaft a few times
and make any necessary adjustments before the rawhide dries.

Steel points were used by Eskimos and Indians for over a
hundred years. Although any steel, such as from nails, can
be used, hardened tool steel will give better service.
Drill rod or old twist drills are sources of small diameter
stock. Anneal these by heating them red hot and allowing
them to cool slowly.

Fig. 6,
Flint per-
forator.

You will probably want to make several sized points, each
one of which will need to be driven into its own shaft. Figures 7A and
7B show two sizes for simple boring. Heat the point red hot and forge
it flat from both sides. Grind or file an obtuse angled point (90-120
degrees), but don't grind a knife edge. Just a simple flat surface on
each side is sufficient to make four cutting edges -- two for each direction of rotation. Re-heat the other end of the shaft and forge or grind
it square in cross-section. This, when forced into the shaft, will prevent the point from loosening.

Temper the steel to harden it by first polishing it with sandpaper or a
file so that bright, clean metal is exposed near the point. Now, re-
heat the piece *slowly* until a blue gun-metal color appears. Immediately
quench the piece in water. This should harden it sufficiently for many
holes. Further sharpening as required will not need annealing; simply
grind a new edge. Just watch that the angle on one side is equal to that

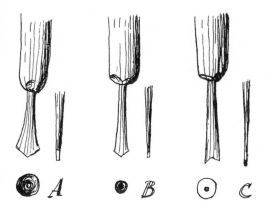

*Fig. 7, Steel points. A and B, per-
forators. C, Double-edged "bull's
eye" point.*

on the other; otherwise only **one**
edge does the cutting and then
only half efficiently.

A unique device for scoring a
circle around a shallow hole is
illustrated in Figure 7C. This
"bull's eye" is very popular in
Eskimo bone and ivory work as a
design element. To make this
point, proceed as above, but
sharpen the point opposite to
the above; i.e., file a V up into the end with one of the resulting points slightly longer
than the other. Touch up the
outer edges of the tip also to
make good cutting edges all a-
round. Temper as before. To
use this device, the longer point
creates a shallow center hole which acts as a pivot for the shorter point
which scores a circle around this center. Obviously, the distance between the points is the radius of the outer circle. This point normally
is not used as a perforator, but is drilled only deeply enough to score
the outside circle.

Use a modern drill to bore a hole in the center of the drill shaft slightly
smaller than the size of the squared end of the point. Clamp the point,
squared end up, in a vise, and tap the drill shaft down on top of it.
Besides wanting a separate shaft for each point, you will probably need
some spares when you crack a few here. The point needs to project only
about as far as the depth of holes you intend to drill. One of the lim-
itations of this drill was the depth of the hole, but, because most
holes were through fairly thin material, this was of small importance.
To drill thicker material, holes were often bored from opposing sides
which accounts for double-tapered holes found in many objects. Actually,
double-drilling makes a cleaner hole, for a drill breaking out the
opposite side tends to tear the material as it emerges.

Drilling

Try out the bow drill on a piece of hard wood or bone. (Soft pine, for
a contrary instance, will drill too quickly and jam the bit so that you
may loosen some teeth before you get the idea.) Take about three loops
with the bow string around the drill shaft at the middle of the shaft.
Put a little grease on the mouthpiece hole and the end of the shaft, and
put the two together. Place the work at a convenient height so that you
can bend your head over the shaft and create an even downward pressure
on the mouthpiece.

(From now on, my directions are for right-handed persons. Reverse these
if you are left-handed.) Clamp the mouthpiece in your teeth while

holding the mouthpiece and shaft in your left hand and the right end
of the bow in your right hand. Place the point where you wish to drill
and steady it with pressure on the mouthpiece. Change your left hand to
hold the point in place until the hole is started (Fig. 3). You may
also be able to use a few fingers to steady the work as well, and later,
let the shaft go completely in order to give a full grip on the work.
Be sure to hold the point in place especially on smooth work such as
polished bone.

While you grasp the end of the bow with thumb and fingers of the right
hand, position your little finger in such a way that it can create a
tension on the bow string. (Even with the three turns around the shaft,
there should still be some slack on the string.) This adjustable tension is an important shock absorber. You'll need enough tension on the
string so that the string can twirl the drill shaft, but it should be
loose enough to slip if the point gets stuck in the hole. You may otherwise receive a nasty shock in your mouth.

Draw the bow back and forth horizontally and slowly with your right hand
with just enough pressure to get the hole started. Speed can be increased with experience once the hole is started. Mouthpiece pressure
can also be increased.

If you intend to drill completely through the material, be very careful
just before the point breaks through. There is a tendency for the point
to become jammed just at that point.

Blow the hole clean frequently. You'll need to stop occasionally anyway
in order to spit. The mouthpiece will stimulate salivation which can
get rather messy after a few holes. Don't get too ambitious right away;
you will need to give your jaw a rest or risk an ache the next day.

A PUMP DRILL

Pump drills are still in use in some areas of our country, such as the Southwest, where they are used primarily for drilling turquoise for beads. The Cherokees of North Carolina use them to drill pipestone bowls. In most places, however, I suspect that modern geared hand drills are more popular today or, if electricity is available, portable power drills are used. These have some obvious advantages over primitive drills, but, until the recent invention of a variable-speed electric drill, most of them operated at speeds too high for many materials such as stone and shell. Also, until carbide-tipped drills are more common, carbon-steel drill bits burn up rapidly on mineral objects and are difficult to re-sharpen and re-temper. Pump drills are not entirely absent in contemporary White cultures. Not many years ago, factory-produced pump drills were listed in jeweler's catalogs where they could be purchased with special steel bits. The downward pressure of a pump drill in use is less likely to snap a fine bit than a geared drill which tends to wobble laterally as the handle is turned. I imagine that some of these are tucked away in drawers somewhere. Blunt wood pump drills are found in some fire-making kits which have frustrated Boy Scouts for years.

As with most primitive drilling devices, a pump drill alternates in rotation so that bits must be made to cut both clockwise and counterclockwise. Unlike an Eskimo-style bow drill, a pump drill cuts primarily with speed rather than pressure. Pressure comes from the weight of the whole drill and, minimally, from the downward thrust of the craftsman's hand.

Pump drills vary considerably in size, but even large ones can be easily disassembled for storage or transport. Measurements given here are average for general use. I'm sure that craftsmen will find individual preferences depending on the hardness and size of the material to be drilled. Certainly, one doesn't need a three foot drill for making necklace beads. In general, the larger the apparatus, the easier and more rapid the cut (given comparable drill bits). Too gross a size becomes awkward to manipulate; too small a size tends to be rather erratic and difficult to operate smoothly.

A pump drill is made of three parts: a drill *shaft* on which a string may twist and which is tipped with the drill bit; a *fly-wheel* which provides momentum after each downward thrust; and a *bow* and string which change vertical action to rotary action.

Drill Shaft

A slim, round shaft of well-seasoned hardwood 18-24 inches long is
needed for a drill shaft. A peeled sapling or shoot can be used, or it
can be whittled from a larger stick. Three-eighths inch diameter at the
top is good to taper to 1/2-3/4 inch at the bottom. A narrow shaft
gives more rotations to each "pump", but too narrow a shaft may bend or
wobble with each stroke. The upper end can be drilled to receive a bow
string (Fig 1A); a simple notch will do as well (Fig. 1B). If the notch
is narrow enough to pinch the bow string, it will stay in place well; a
notch makes the apparatus easier to disassemble as well without untying
the bow each time.

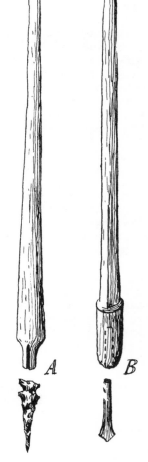

The bottom of the shaft must have a bit attached
to it which can cut in either rotation. (See:
"An Eskimo-style Bow Drill".) If you are in a
hurry, some hardware stores carry drill bits
for a modern "Yankee" pump screwdriver. Such
bits are available in diameters up to 1/4 inch
and are made to cut in two directions. If you
use a "Yankee" bit, you'll have to grind some
flats on that part which will be inserted into
the shaft to keep it from rotating in the shaft
instead of the work. The little notches which
are intended for the screwdriver tool just aren't
enough. By the way, don't bother with twist
drills which cut in a clockwise rotation only.

Some old jeweler's pump drills had a mechanical
"chuck" at the end which could be adjusted to
accept different sized bits. I haven't seen
one of these in years. If you will need different sized bits for your work, you'll need to
make a separate shaft for each one. Unless you
make each shaft the same diameter, you will also
have to make a separate fly wheel for each.

Stone points can be re-flaked right on the drill
shaft to re-sharpen them until not enough material remains for a good point. (You get a
free arrowhead then.) The same is true for a
steel point. In this context, remember that
primitive drills seldom were intended to bore
deeper than an inch and that holes often were
drilled from opposite sides to meet in the middle of the work. Mechanically precise diameters
were not important. Also remember that these

*Fig. 1, Drill shafts. A, round shaft with hole for bow string and
notched end to receive a stone perforator. B, Shouldered shaft with
squared section near bottom to prevent fly wheel twist and drilled to
receive flattened steel point.*

holes were usually conical, not cylindrical.

When you have completed a nicely tapered shaft, smooth it with sandpaper or rub it on sandstone for a nice finish. Check it for straightness by sighting along its length. Rolling it on a plane surface will also show up bends. Warm the warped area over heat and bend it true with your hands. If you hold it until it cools, it should retain this adjustment.

Fly Wheel

Fly wheels are made of stone, ceramic, or wood. The weight of stone is preferred, but the process of manufacture is more involved and is not worth the time unless you intend to put the drill to much use. Any type of stone can be used. Try to find a beach pebble which is already worn to a flat, circular, disc-shape. Peck or grind this to a true circle as much as possible. A stone 3-5 inches in diameter and less than an inch thick should give plenty of momentum to your drill. Clay is easy to shape but will need to be fired before use. A tree branch or small log can be sawed crosswise to produce a flat disc. A disc about 3/4 inch thick and 4-6 inches in diameter needs little refining to make good wheel. With cross-cut wood such as this you may have some problems with drying cracks. These will not diminish its function unless the wood cracks in half. In general, the size of the fly wheel is dependent upon the size of the drill and the weight of the material used.

Fig.2, Fly wheels. A, Wood sawed from cross section of log, with square center hole. B, Pecked stone. C, Fired ceramic.

Shape the fly wheel by whatever means is appropriate to the material you have selected to make it nearly perfect in shape and thickness. Drill a hole in its center large enough to receive the shaft. The fly wheel should slip down the shaft to a point close to the bit end -- a few inches from the tip. This is necessary to give a bottom-heavy weight to the shaft to keep it rotating without wobbling. Enlarge the hole or narrow the shaft accordingly. In any case, the fly wheel should be seated snugly so that the wheel and shaft rotate together. Twirl the shaft and wheel in your hands to see if any adjustment can be made on the flywheel to make it as balanced as possible. A wood wheel can be trimmed, and a stone one can be pecked a little more on the heavier portion to run more balanced. A wheel a little out of balance will run well, but not perfectly well. As much as possible, see that the wheel is at right angles to the shaft; i.e., horizontal. You may want to make the hole in the wheel and the section of the shaft oval or squared with a shoulder on the shaft below to keep the wheel from slipping too far

down (Fig. 1B, 2A).
In this way, the
flywheel can be
changed easily
from one shaft
to another with
little worry a-
bout it rotating
by itself.

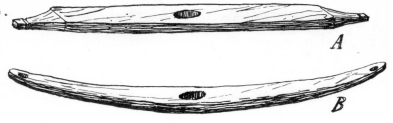

*Fig. 3, Bows. A, Rectangular "stick" bow with ends
tapered and notched for the string. B, Curved,
tapered bow with holes for the string.*

Bow

The bow needs no flexibility. It can be made of any wood or even a long
piece of bone. It can be quite short -- less than 8 inches -- or large --
2 or 3 feet. A convenient rule-of-thumb might be to make the bow half
the length of the drill shaft. Although a simple round stick can be
used bow-and-arrow fashion at the side of the shaft, a flat bow, about
1/2 by 1 inch in section, is better and can be drilled in the center with
a hole a little larger than the drill shaft above the flywheel. Thus,
the shaft is pushed up through the bow's hole so that the bow cannot
slip off during use. The ends of the bow can be notched or drilled to
receive the bow string. You'll not want to make this attachment permanently, for you'll probably need to make adjustments in tension from
time to time. A good craftsman will want to put a nice finish on the bow,
but a nice finish does not add to its function.

Any cord can be used for a bow string. Older pump drills used a buckskin
thong. If you use buckskin, cut it as evenly as possible. If you use
a cord, get a strong, thin one which is limp so that it can twine a-
round the shaft easily.

Tie one end of the bowstring on the bow, insert the shaft (with the fly
wheel in place) through the bow's hole, and put the string through the
hole or notch at the top of the shaft. The attachment of the string to
the top of the shaft should not be permanent to allow for adjustments
later. Tie the free end of the string to the other end of the bow so
that the bow can be suspended from the shaft about 2-3 inches above the
flywheel. The closer it is, the longer each pump-stroke can be, but,
if it is too close, you will find it difficult to operate the drill as
your fingers get in the way of the flywheel. Adjust the string in the
shaft top so that the bow is in a horizontal position. Slide the bow up
and down a few times to see that the shaft can twirl in the hole freely.

Operation

Hold the bow with the shaft between your fingers so that you can give
equal pressure on both ends of the bow (Fig. 4). With your other hand,
twirl the tip of the shaft so that the string winds up on the shaft and
thereby raises the bow as far as it can go. Clamp the shaft between

your your bow fingers and set the point in place with the other hand which is now free. You may need a few false starts to get a dent started. If you can't hold the drill point easily, hold the shaft above the point. You can usually allow the shaft to twirl in your fingers until the point has cut deeply enough to stay in its own hole.

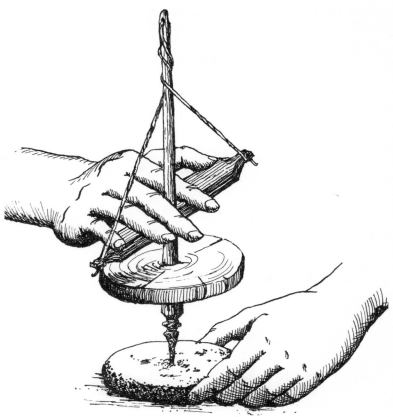

Press downward on the bow. This causes the string to unwind and rotate the shaft. Don't worry about in which direction. At the bottom of the stroke, ease up on the pressure and allow the bow to lift your hand back up. The string should rewind of its

Fig. 4, A pump drill in operation.

own accord as it is impelled by the momentum of the flywheel. When the bow reaches its highest position, press down again which will cause the shaft to rotate opposite to the first direction. It is a relatively simple matter to become accustomed to the pumping action. Let the drill do the cutting; don't give too great a downward effort. Listen for a rhythmic "whir-whir-whir" sound as the drill starts and stops and which indicates that the drill is working most efficiently.

I don't find that the pump drill has the power to drill large holes efficiently. One-fourth inch is a fair maximum. Of course, if you work with a four-foot shaft and a three-foot bow, you'll be able to get more power and thrust. For tiny holes -- in beads, for instance -- make a small, lightweight drill. If you need larger holes, ream them out with succesively larger bits or drill several holes and chip out the material between them.

Don't **neglect** the drill's potential for making fire. Try a blunt, wooden

point in a notched depression in softwood. If you can make hot, black,
charred dust collect in the notch, you may be able to blow it into flames
in tinder. If not, use matches, and keep the pump drill for holes.

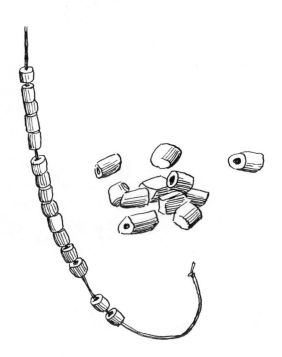

Fig. 5, Wampum shell beads.

PECKING A GROOVED STONE AX

A simple and tedious method of shaping stone is the process known as
"pecking". In essence, this involves crumbling the stone by pounding
two stones together so that one (usually both) are crushed a little
bit with each blow. With sufficient blows, a shape can be controlled.

Stone[1]

Some selection of raw materials must be made, but in areas of glaciation
or water erosion, this is not difficult. Stream beds and lake shores
are good hunting grounds for the nicely rounded smooth pebbles of a size
and shape which are desirable for pecking. Two stones are required --
one for the raw material for the tool to be made (in this case, an ax),
and one for the tool with which to make it (usually called a "hammerstone").

A preferred material for hammerstones is *quartzite*: a hard, dense, fine-
grained stone with little or no definite cleavage lines. Because quartzite was metamorphosed from sandstone, it may superficially show some
of the characteristics of the sedimentary rock, but true quartzite cannot be split into layers. As its name implies, it is almost pure quartz.
The sand particles from which it was formed are, perhaps, visible to
the naked eye, but, on close examination, quartzite breaks across the
grains of the sand, whereas sandstone breaks around the grains. Quartzite is normally white and has a glint of tiny crystals.

Other fine-grained, hard hammerstone material includes the varieties of
chalcedony such as agate, jasper, and flint. Soft stones, or those which
are quite coarse or subject to fracture easily, cannot be used. Search
out some rounded or oval pebbles in sizes of walnuts to the size of small
baseballs.

For the raw material for the ax itself, again, some hard, fine-grained
stone is necessary, normally a little "softer" than the hammerstone
material. The "Mohs Scale" of hardness is known to mineralogists as a
rating system of relative hardness of minerals. This ranges from 1 (talc
or steatite) to 10 (diamond). Most of the stones you will use will be
about 6 or 7 on this scale. I don't think that knowledge of the Mohs

---

[1]"Stone" is normally understood to be a piece of hard, non-metallic mineral which can be picked up. "Rock" is normally the term applied to a large mass of the same material; for instance, "a wall of
rock", which cannot be picked up. Occasional confusion comes when
some minerals usually include "stone" in their common names; for instance, "a sandstone rock".

Scale is important at this point, but it may become desirable if you get really involved in lapidary[2]. All you need to know at this time is which stone is harder than which: which crumbles when two stones are struck together. Stone varies slightly in hardness; mineralogists use precise names for these variations. The following names are general terms which refer to types of stone which have been used in the past. In the final choice, if Indians could not trade or win preferred materials in war or find them locally, they used whatever next best material was on hand.

One of the coarsest stones which has been used is *porphyry*. This term refers to a relatively fine-grained "groundmass" with larger crystals or "phenocrysts" imbedded in it. Porphyry reminds me of fruitcake in which the dough is likened to the groundmass and the cut-up fruits suggest the phenocrysts. Obviously, the hardness of the groundmass and phenocrysts differ so that porphyry is less suitable for an ax than for a rounded tool such as a club.

Granite is usually light-colored, but may vary from reddish to dark gray. Grains of other crystalline material in granite are readily visible to the naked eye. For all its popular reputation of strength, granite is relatively light weight. The coarseness of granite and its weight makes it also suitable primarily for clubs and mallets rather than good axes.

Gabbro is similar to granite, but is heavier for a given mass. It is usually dark gray or black and is finer-grained than granite. In my estimation, the difference is one of degree, and I don't usually worry about the proper name.

Diorite is dark gray or greenish and quite hard with small inclusions of feldspar and pyroxene.

Basalt is finer than any of the above and contains few phenocrysts. It is usually very dark and may be black. The minerals may not be visible to the naked eye.

Felsite is quite abundant. It is light in color and may even be white. It may have some porosity visible in the form of small holes which look like former air bubbles. Felsite is fine-grained.

Other rocks and minerals such as nephrite or jade have been used so that the above list should not be considered complete. Flint or chert makes fine cutting tools, but the process of manufacture is that of fracture, not pecking, so that these are not appropriate here. Typically, the best cutting edge in pecking would be obtained from fine-grained, hard stone while coarser stones will make clubs or mallets.

[2]Lapidary refers to the skill or science of stone cutting, shaping, or polishing.

The process to be described will be used to shape the stone implement, but, after the shaping, stone tools were further refined by "polishing" or abrading the surface. Such tools are normally spoken of as having been "pecked and polished". For polishing, you will need a block of some sandy-grained material, such as *sandstone*, on which the cementing of the sandy particles is incomplete so as to leave a sandy texture when the rock is cracked or broken. As mentioned earlier, sandstone breaks between the tiny particles and creates a rough texture. Some sandstone is so poorly cemented that it tends to crumble easily. This is OK unless it crumbles too much. If true sandstone is not available, any coarse-grained stone surface will do if you can find some fine-grained loose sand to use as an abrasive.

Stones which are unsuitable for pecking are those which fracture or split or are very soft. Examples of these are slate, limestone, conglomerate, and shist.

Pecking

Find a hammerstone which you can grasp easily
between thumb and first finger, and which is
perhaps 2 inches in diameter   (Fig. 1). Such
a stone will weigh less than a pound which is
a good weight to enable you to work for a while
without tiring too rapidly. A larger stone
does not necessarily work better. A nicely
rounded beach pebble is preferred for comfort,
and you'll find that you can change your grip
readily to present a new surface when one gets
worn away too much. Later, if you expect to
make a fairly deep groove in the ax, you will
need some hammerstones with pointed edges no
wider than the intended groove.

Fig. 1, Hammerstones.

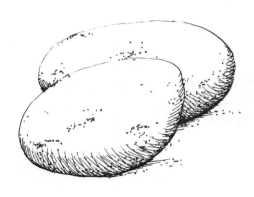

Fig. 2, Stone ax blanks.

Select a stone for the ax head which
is naturally about the size and shape
of the intended final product. Take
time for this selection or you may
lose interest quickly. You will be
able to peck down any size or shape
eventually, but it will take time.
Ideally, pick a piece about which you
can say, "This would make a nice ax."
(This may sound silly at this point,
but I daresay you'll find yourself saying it nevertheless after some experience.) A beginner might look for a
rounded stone perhaps 2-3 inches wide
by an inch or two thick by 5-6 inches

long (Fig. 2). Such a stone will
weigh about a pound or two.

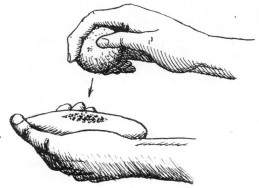

Although it's not necessary, you may
want a pair of gloves. A pair of
safety glasses is quite necessary.
You'll not be making chips which can
fly up into your eyes, but don't take
the chance until you become so skilled that there is no such possibility.

The process is simple enough, but
slow. Grasp the hammerstone between
the thumb and forefinger (and others,
as may be most comfortable) of your
favored hand (Fig. 3). Hold the ax-
stone in the palm of your other hand

*Fig. 3, Pecking with a hammer-
stone.*

in such a way that the surface you intend to strike is well exposed. If
you sit, rest your arm on your leg so that the hand is somewhat free to
bounce a bit as a shock absorber. The ax head must be cushioned below
each blow. If you place the ax head on a hard support or grasp it in such
a way that an air space is permitted beneath the point to be struck, you
take a chance on breaking it.

With free-swinging blows of the hammerstone, strike the ax head at the
place you intend to shape. This pecking process is aptly named, for it
is certainly reminiscent of a bird picking up seeds. Each blow of the
hammerstone will crumble the surface of the ax head just a little bit. A
light powder is evidence of this. Keep striking blows in a regular, comfortable rhythm to wear down the shape. After a few minutes, you should
discern the characteristic rough texture of a pecked surface. The hammerstone will show evidence of pecking, too.

Blows should be more-or-less at right angles to the ax head. Glancing
blows or those near the edge of the ax should be minimized to minimize
the chance of chipping or fracturing the edge. Be sure that the hand
supports the ax below the point of percussion. Turn the ax head as is
necessary to shape it all around. You may need to turn the hammerstone
from time to time, also.

The back or "poll" of the ax (unless it is to be a double-edged tool,
which is seldom the case) is, perhaps, the easiest to shape because it
is the thickest and, therefore, less subject to accidental breakage.
Near the cutting edge, however, blows should be directed slightly toward the poll end, especially right at the edge itself. Don't try to
peck a very thin edge for fear of fracturing it; leave this for the polishing process later.

Develop an easy rhythm of pecking. M'Guire, in his experiments, measured
the tempo at 140 blows per minute[3]. This is equal to the number of steps
per minute of a very fast walk.

[3]M'Guire, p. 167.

Blows are neither hard nor soft, but somewhere in between. Swing the hammerstone from your wrist and elbows so that it seems to bounce back up after each blow. Don't try to get done during the first few minutes. M'Guire needed 55 hours to complete the shaping, but this was on a very hard piece of nephrite[4]. On a piece of kersanite, the time including that of polishing, was two hours[5]. My own experiences mostly with quartzite hammerstones on basalt, show that a full day or more is not unusual.

A clear ring at each blow indicates that you have made a good selection of raw material. A hollow thud may mean that the stone has a weakness in it and might as well be discarded immediately. As a matter-of-fact, you might test stones on the spot in this manner during initial selection at your quarry site. Change hammerstones from time to time as may be needed as they wear down also.

When you judge that the ax head has reached a proper shape, begin pecking a groove. The head could be used as a hand-ax at this point, but a handle of some sort makes it more efficient. A groove is not necessary for the handle, but it makes a more permanent fastening.

Fig. 4, Pecked hand-ax with polished cutting edge. Length: 4 inches.

The poll of the ax is normally larger and, therefore, heavier than the cutting edge. To compensate for this, a groove near the poll end creates a balance to equalize the weight between the ends. Also, the longer cutting edge makes it function better by allowing a deeper "bite" into a tree when it is used.

The groove must be pecked with a pointed hammerstone shaped like a sharp egg (Fig. 5). Such a hammerstone must usually be replaced more rapidly than those used for shaping the body. Grooves are normally U-shaped rather than V-shaped. Axes are found with a full groove completely around the head; others are partially grooved. You'll probably settle for a partial groove unless you are remarkably persistent on your first attempt.

Some axes exhibit a raised area on either side of the groove. This trait permits a sturdy handle to be attached to a light ax. Probably, however, such a raised portion is indicative of an ax which, upon being dulled, was re-sharpened by further pecking on both the cutting portion and the poll

Fig. 5, Pecking a groove.

[4]*Ibid.*
[5]*Ibid.*, p. 168.

while the groove was left in its original depth.

The groove is normally rather shallow, especially on a thin ax, for fear
of cutting so deep that the ax is in danger of cracking. On larger axes,
the groove may be 1/2 inch deep or more. The width of the groove is determined by the width of the handle for which it is designed, but also
by the point of the hammerstones which are used. Obviously, the groove
must be wider than the width of the hammerstone point.

If you find yourself with a cracked ax partially finished, examine the
pieces to consider the wisdom of continuing. You may simply have to discard the pieces and begin on a new one. Work sites which have been ex-
cavated often disclose such fragments in various degrees of completion
which apparently have been broken in the process of manufacture.

Although I am aware that it is not an authentic technique, I have, on occasion, used a small steel hammer instead of a hammerstone for pecking
the groove. A half-pound cross-peen hammer head is ideally suited to
create a narrow, deep groove which is very difficult with hammerstones
alone. Try this, if you like, but probably at the expense of the steel
hammer.

The process of pecking persists to the present day, but primarily is used
by sculptors. A steel "bush hammer" is used which has a face of several
facetted points which crush the stone as does a hammerstone. I find it
difficult to differentiate between the surfaces created by each. I don't
find that the bush hammer is superior to the hammerstone, however.

In addition to shaping striking implements such as axes, mallets and
clubs, pecking is used for shaping other tools such as the *mano* and
metate or stone pestle and mortar, some of which are still preferred by
some people to the present day. The *mano* is often a naturally shaped
stone of a few pounds which is long and round and is large enough to be
held with one or both hands. The *metate* bowl is usually a stone with a
pecked depression to receive the *mano*. Both stones are coarse, granite-
like materials which present ideal grinding surfaces for corn meal and
the like. Careful pecking must have been used as the process for the
creation of effigies in hard stone, for no other lapidary processes were
available to the primitives which has the control of pecking. The "glyphs"
or low-relief sculptures in Central and South America were done by pecking, either directly with a hammerstone or indirectly by using a wooden
mallet on a stone chisel which crushed rather than cut the stone surfaces.
(Some "petroglyphs" or drawings in stone are found all over North America as the work of bygone peoples. Examination shows that these were not
pecked, but incised or abraded by rubbing sharp stones back and forth to
wear out a groove. Petroglyphs are usually created as linear outlines,
a concept which does not lend itself to pecking techniques.) Pecking
was also used to shape stone for masonry walls in Central and South
America. Some of these walls still amaze archaeologists and masons for

the accuracy of the joints and the time which must have been expended in
their manufacture.

Polishing

Don't expect to create a sharp cutting edge on a pecked ax. This implement functions more as a wedge which bruises its way into wood than as
a cutting tool which slices chips out. A blunt cutting edge can be pecked, but a better edge is created by an abrading or grinding process often known as "polishing". The entire head can be given a smooth surface
as in the case of well-crafted war clubs and the like. A purely functional cutting ax needs a polish only near the edge.

A slab of sandstone a half-foot square or so is good for a beginning.
This sedimentary rock often splits in level layers. Actually, a slight
depression in the surface will probably more nearly conform to the ax
head shape than will a plane surface. Search for sandstone with such a
concavity and set it firmly on the ground near a source of water. If
the weather is nice, you can get your feet wet and join the stone at the
water's edge. Otherwise, a pail of water should be handy.

Wet the sandstone and rub the ax head briskly back and forth on its surface (Fig. 6). Short-
ly, you should notice
a "slurry" of stone
dust and water mix-
ed with dislodged
sand from the sand-
stone. The texture
of the sandstone does
some polishing, but
the dislodged parti-
cles which roll back
and forth also help.
Some abrading is pos-
sible with dry
stones, but the lub-
rication of water
seems to speed up
the process. Pos-
sibly, the water
keeps the sandy

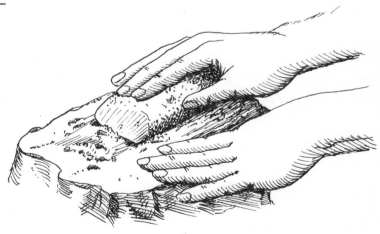

Fig. 6, Polishing.

particles between the grinding surfaces better. Also, the dust is washed
out partially with each stroke which keeps it from building up and reducing the abrasion. A little "mud" is desirable, therefore, but not a lot.
Keep adding water, either with your hands, or by dipping the ax occasionally.

Wash off the ax periodically, and you'll observe that the surface of it is taking on a smooth appearance which can also be felt.

If proper sandstone is not available, a good sand can be added between the ax and any stone slab. I like sandstone because it makes its own sand. In a pinch, the abrasive stone can be rubbed on the ax rather than vice-versa, but the chances of the abrasive stone slipping off just at the cutting edge and chipping it are such that the method described earlier seems to be far superior.

An hour of vigorous work may create a sufficient edge for you. More hours are required if you want a fine, smooth surface free from pecking pits. If you want a polish all over the surface of the head, you'll want some some sandstone surfaces which contain concave areas approximating the convex surfaces of the ax. The groove can be polished by rubbing it on a sharp broken edge of sandstone, but this is not necessary. You may be able to locate natural abrasive materials finer than sand to create a higher polish. Certain pulverized minerals can be made into a slurry to keep the fine particles in place; dry dust or too much water would push them out of the grinding zone. You may wish to experiment with abrasives on a buckskin scrap because the particles tend to imbed themselves in the leather instead of being washed out. A wooden surface may also give good results for you on the same principle.

When you have gone as far as you care to go, wash the ax well with water. Scrub it to remove the fine dust, and allow it to dry. I like to give a final polish with some grease or oil rubbed well in. Mere handling will do the same thing, but this takes a long time and the result is the same. Warming the ax *slowly* causes the grease or oil to impregnate the surface well. Once having acquired a nice finish in this manner, I'm sure that you'll fondle the ax frequently enough to perpetuate the finish with oil from your hands.

Hafting

A groove implies a need for a handle, although ungrooved heads were
hafted as well. The simplest (and
least aesthetically pleasing) method is to insert the head in a
forked or split branch with the
ends brought up over the top and
lashed together (Fig. 7). This
may include an X-wrapping at the
sides and some wrapping below the
head to keep the slot from opening further with use.

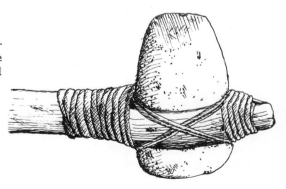

Fig. 7, *Partly grooved stone ax hafted into a split handle.*

A superior method would be to use a specially whittled shaft of ash, hickory, or some other strong hardwood which can be bent around the groove
to be fastened below the head. (Fig. 8). Determine the thickness of the

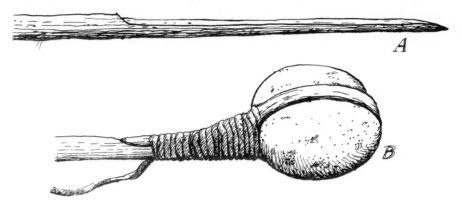

*Fig. 8A, Wooden handle shaft prepared for bending. B, Wood bent
around grooved club.*

handle you desire and the length. Add enough for the circumference of
the groove plus a few inches for overlap for wrapping. Whittle this additional portion to a curved cross-section which approximates the width
and depth of the groove. Steam or heat in boiling water this portion of
the handle until it is quite supple. Green wood may not need this treatment, but it helps. Bend this around the head in the groove gradually,
and reheat it as frequently as may be necessary. Don't try to make a
sharp bend all at once. When the wood has been bent completely around
the head, wrap the end to the shaft with well-soaked rawhide which should
shrink upon drying for a permanent fastening. You'll find that, if you
wrap from the handle upward, you'll be able to pull the parts together
more tightly than if you wrap from the head downward.

Some handles were attached to war clubs (where a little flexibility might
be desirable) with a band of heavy rawhide alone. This would not have
the strength required for repeated blows when chopping a tree, but it's
plenty for breaking a few bones.

Other wrappings include a partial or complete covering of rawhide sheets.
The sheet was soaked and cut to an approximate shape for the head and
handle. It was then made a permanent covering for not only the head, but
also the handle as well. Some "berry mashers", for pounding pemmican or
other foods, were so hafted to allow the pounding surfaces to remain un-
covered (Fig. 9).

Use

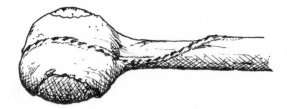

As mentioned before, unlike a modern steel ax, a stone ax did not cut out chips or flakes of wood with neat cuts. Small trees were felled by bending the tree so that the tension of the wood helped to separate the fibers as they were chopped so that they could be removed by hand. Down-

Fig. 9, "Berry masher" with rawhide-covered head and handle. Length of head: 2 1/2 inch.

ward strokes alone are best until the tree can be broken off the stump which is left looking somewhat frizzled. (Some people are known to rub dirt on the raw stump wood so that the scar in the forest is not so apparent.) Obviously, felling a large tree requires some effort. Often, a large tree might be ringed with wet clay or mud above the cut so that a fire built around the trunk would char the wood. This portion could be broken away with the ax. More fire could be built, and so on, until the cut was complete. Much wood "carving" was done in this way. Cutting and scraping tools were reserved for the final shaping and finishing.

Modern steel axes have heads which weigh about 3 1/2 pounds. Hatchets are less than two pounds. Stone axes usually are made for one-hand operation to free the other hand for gripping the work. Seldom does one find a stone ax which seems to be designed for two-hand work. I doubt if any hafting would hold tightly with the force of blows struck with both hands. Large stone heads have been found which measure 8-10 inches in length, but more abundant are those which average 5-6 inches and a few pounds in weight. Chopping axes can be heavy because each blow can be planned. Weapons can be slimmer and lighter for obvious reasons. A one-pound round stone on the end of a long shaft can inflict dreadful damage.

Cutting wood with a stone ax is slow work compared to a steel ax. Nevertheless, it is surprisingly rapid when one considers the competition. Indians would not cut trees unless specifically required for some purpose. Firewood, for instance, was picked up as dead branches and didn't require cutting. Unlike the White man who warms himself twice, (once when cutting wood and once when burning it), Indians normally used long pieces which were shoved into the fire as they burned away.

Philosophically, one does tend to ponder the need for cutting a tree longer than when one uses a steel ax or chain saw. Perhaps the stone ax still has some merits.

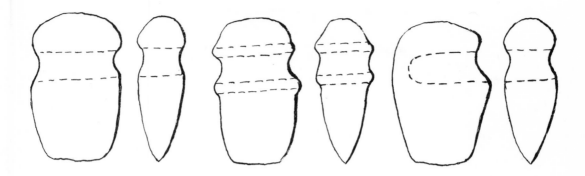

Fig. 10, Outline of typical pecked stone axes.

REFERENCES

Holmes, William H.   "The Lithic Industries", *Part I, Handbook on Abo-
                          riginal American Antiquities, Bureau of American
                          Ethnology, Bulletin* No. 60, 1919.

M'Guire, Joseph D.   "Materials, Apparatus, and Processes of the Aborig-
                          inal Lapidary", *American Anthropologist,* Vol. 5,
                          April, 1892.

Pond, Alonzo W.   "Primitive Methods of Working Stone", *Logan Museum
                          Bulletin,* Vol. II, No. 1, 1930.

*Fig. 10, Pecked and polished "bird stone".
Length: Approx. 2 1/2 inches.*

FLAKING A STONE POINT

Probably nothing intrigues the amateur more than the manufacture or collection of stone "arrowheads" (which are more appropriately called "points",
for one cannot be quite sure that all points were, indeed, affixed to arrow shafts). Flaked tools are of interest to professionals also, for,
unlike fugitive materials such as leather and wood, stone offers evidence
of cultures thousands of years old. A trained eye can make reasonable
judgements on processes of manufacture, materials, functions and design,
and thereby arrive at conclusions regarding the antiquity of a culture,
its habits, everyday life and relationships to other cultures. The abundance of both intact and broken or partially completed specimens adds
chapters to the history of early people.

Most farmers have a cigar box tucked away somewhere which contains finds
unearthed by the plow. Outdoorsmen with a perceptive eye also pick up
stone objects which show evidence of being worked by man. Unfortunately,
the provenance or origin of these items has not been determined; once
having been removed from the site, such objects can tell us very little
except in comparison with known objects.

It can be reasonably assumed that points which are notched near the base
were intended to be fastened to a shaft of some sort, although the lack
of a notch does not necessarily mean the contrary. A thin, light-weight
point less than, say, two inches long could be an arrow point when one
considers that the primitive archer was probably also skilled in stalk-
ing, and that the distance to his quarry was not great. Tiny points,
less than an inch long, are known today as "bird points", although this
size would be appropriate for any small game, not only birds. Larger,
therefore heavier, points must be assumed to be spear tips, for it is apparent that a bow could not throw such weights. Not all spear points can
be determined as heads for spears to be thrown; some are designed without
a barb so that they could well be hafted to lances which were intended
to be thrust into the prey and pulled out easily for another thrust.
Some large points might well have been used as knives with or without a
handle. Very long, slim points probably were perforators or drills, although they could function as weapon points as well. Scrapers, axes,
hoes, and the like, were flaked from stone, but their size and shape give
good indications as to their use. In all the lithic industries of primitive man, one must expect a flexibility and ability to improvise, both
in the use of stone tools and the materials and techniques used to make
such tools. Modern scientists have made remarkably precise analyses of
stone tools and their manufacture, but I shall not dwell on these here.
More important to this chapter is your willingness to experiment and your
persistence in improving your skill.

Nomenclature

Before the process of manufacture is considered, it might be well to es-
tablish the accepted nomenclature of stone points, because these terms
will need to be used later. (Fig. 1). The *point* or *tip* and the *edge*
are obvious terms. The *body* or *blade* refers to the
wide, generally triangular portion of the point. A
shoulder near the *base* narrows the blade to allow a
stem to remain as the part which will be lashed to
a shaft and is created by chipping away portions
on either side near the base. If the shoulder is
quite sharp, it may be spoken of as a *barb* created
by a *notch* which may eminate either at the side
or at the corners of the base. If the notches
are so made that the base is wide below them,
the projections on either side are called *tangs*
which keep the lashing from slipping off easily
and also prevent the point from pulling out
easily. Sometimes the base is ground or rubbed on another stone to dull it to prevent
the point from losing thrust by cutting backward into the shaft on impact. Some very
early points such as the Folsom or Clovis
type (types are today identified by the name
of the site or geographic area where they
were first found) have a concave *flute*
flaked off on either side of the body from
the base upward, a trait which makes these
types admirably designed for tipping a
thrusting weapon.

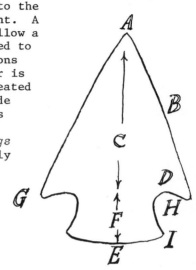

Fig. I, Point nomenclature
A, Point or tip. B, Edge.
C, Body or blade. D, Shoul-
der. E, Base. F, Stem.
G, Barb. H, Notch. I, Tang.

Cultures in a given time and place tended to create certain designs according to custom or tradition; many variations in type exist and will
not be defined here. For further identification, Robert Ritzenthaler's
"A Guide to Wisconsin Projectile Point Types" is a fine reference and
can be understood in layman's terms. Non-Wisconsin residents will find
it useful also, for most of the types illustrated therein are not unique
to Wisconsin.

Stone

Everyone knows that Indians used *flint* for arrowheads. What is not so
commonly known is that some people consider *chert* to be the proper term
for this stone. Definitions of origin hold that flint is formed as boul-
der-like nodules and is dark gray or black, while chert is formed in beds
or masses and is lighter colored. Most people use the terms synonomous-
ly; some timid ones say "flint or chert" to cover all bases. H. Holmes

Ellis, in his "Flint Working Techniques of the American Indians", settles for "flint" as an inclusive term which seems convenient to me.[1] Whichever term you like, flint or chert is a very fine-grained, hard, homogeneous stone which may be somewhat translucent and which varies from bone-white to red and black. The weathered surface of flint may be quite dull, but a fracture will show a lustrous vitreous finish similar to porcelain. Identity can also be established by the typical *conchoidal fracture* marks on a chipped surface (Fig. 2).

Flint found on the surface, where it has been subject to weathering, is usually so full of fractures that it cannot be used except, perhaps, for the smallest bird points. There is some controversy over the fact that groups of partially completed points have been unearthed

Fig. 2, Conchoidal fracture.

in caches. Some say that this was done to keep them "fresh" and point out that stone which is quarried from below the surface seems easier to work than stone collected on or near the surface. Specimens unearthed at quarry sites seem to show that Indians roughed out blanks for future work and carried them away instead of carrying large chunks. Ellis suggests, "Whether the Indians buried flint blanks because contact with the humid earth made them more workable, or whether these caches were simply for storage, or for ceremonial purposes is a matter for conjecture. The presence of buried blanks will, however, never be explained by the ingenious theory that 'the canoe carrying these blanks was tipped over'"[2]

Chalcedony and *agate* are also very fine-grained, hard, and exhibit conchoidal fractures. These run the spectrum of flint hues but are more translucent, even transparent. Chalcedony has a waxy surface when fractured. Agate tends to have banded colors, but other forms exist.

Quartz is found as large, transparent or translucent crystals. It looks like glass but is much harder; a sure test is that it will scratch common glass.

A natural glass is *obsidian*. This is found in areas of early volcanic activity. In every way it is like brown or black glass except that it is harder and seems less brittle. Obsidian is an ideal material for a beginner, but it is today considered a semi-precious stone and commands a price of 10-25 cents a pound at rock-hound shops here. It is not native to the Midwest, but local Indians apparently valued it sufficiently to receive it in trade (?) from such distances as the Yellowstone Park area. Obsidian is also plentiful in the Southwest and Mexico.

[1]Ellis, pp. 1-4.
[2]*Ibid.*, p. 5.

Quartzite is quite common and can be found in the form of beach pebbles.
It is somewhat translucent and is made from metamorphosed sandstone, the
crystals of which are readily seen. It is somewhat crystalline in its
rough texture and does not fracture conchoidally. I suspect that it was
used when more suitable stone was not available, for most quartzite points
are often poorly made. I find that it makes sturdy, but not delicate,
points.

Other materials such as petrified wood and onyx were used in the past.
Ideally, the stone should be very fine-grained or glassy and should be
homogeneous in texture in order to fracture well in any direction. Stone
should be as fresh as possible; buried material seems to flake better
than surface finds which have been air dried (even though the latter may
be re-buried).

Given no other material, I suggest that common *glass* can be a contemporary substitute. Quarter-inch window glass can be obtained as scraps
from any glazier and can be quickly cut with a glass-cutter into trian-
gular-shaped blanks for practice. Broken bottles and other glass objects often have thick portions which provide good raw materials. (I
find an especial delight in "re-cycling" blue Milk of Magnesia bottles.)
Thin bottles and common window glass are too thin. There are stories of
Australian and South American natives using glass electrical insulators
from utility poles as raw material, but these have today acquired antique
status and have become expensive. (Do I have to warn against taking them
from installations?) Through the courtesy of a local Telephone Company,
I was able to try some of these and made a fine pile of scraps.

I haven't tried it to a great degree, but hard *porcelain* is another modern
potential. It seems to be very much like flint in color and texture.
A broken toilet bowl should provide all the raw material you can use for
some time.

Heat and Water Fracture

One wonders how the popular myth of fracturing stone by heat and water
application originated. Ellis, in his customary thoroughness, has com-
piled several accounts of observers who claim witness to Indians who have
demonstrated this technique.[3] Various techniques are quoted -- from a
simple cooling process which "splits it into flakes" to a more credible
dripping water from a blade of grass or a feather onto hot stone to crack
off flakes. Heating may have been used in an initial quarrying to break
off chunks of rock, but, if so, it is not borne out by examination of
quarry sites. I find it difficult to believe that anyone supports the
theory of heat and water fracture after personal experimentation. The
stone will fracture, sure, but with no control in direction nor size, or,

[3]*Ibid.*

at least, much less control than with the processes described later.
Try it yourself on any piece of glass, for instance.

Safety Precautions

Get a supply of Band-Aids.

You can diminish the need for Band-Aids by using some heavy leather work
gloves at all times. These should be thin enough for sensitive work, but
heavy enough for good protection against the extremely sharp fragments
which are flaked off. I can usually flake a point or two safely without
gloves, but why take the chance? (Note: illustrations which follow in
the text are drawn without gloves for clarity.)

Safety glasses or goggles are a must! Tiny, sharp fragments are flicked
off and have a way of jumping some distance -- farther than the two feet
or so to your eyes. Without frightening a novice unduly, one should be
aware that a few winks with such a chip in one's eye will do permanent
damage. Did the Indian craftsman use goggles? No, but he also was capable of performing minor operations such as removing motes from eyes without the aid of a medical specialist. Were there any one-eyed or blind
Indians? Yes, probably, but a person who could not see well in a rigor-
ous life could not last long, either. *Don't permit anyone, including
yourself, to try stone flaking without adequate eye protection!*

Percussion Flaking -- Direct

Direct or primary percussion; i.e.,
striking blows directly on the object with a hammerstone, is the
simplest and least controllable
technique of flaking stone. This
technique alone is sufficient for
shaping large or rudely fashioned
implements such as axes and hoes.
With experience, it can be used
for smaller objects such as scrapers or for initial flaking in
preparation for later work. It
is possible, but difficult, to
shape a good point purely with
direct percussion.

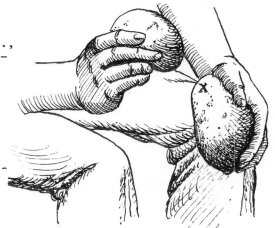

Fig. 3, Direct percussion.

Normally, a boulder or pebble
about the size of a melon and weighing several pounds is used for the raw
material. A quartzite hammerstone of about a pound or two is required
to strike the blows.

Grasp the boulder in one hand in such a way that, if you rest your wrist on your leg, the flake you intend to strike off will fall between your legs (Fig. 3). Hold the hammerstone comfortably in the other hand so that you can swing it freely from your elbow and wrist. Keep your fingers well back from the striking edge on both stones so that you don't catch yourself on a broken edge with the "follow-through" after the blow.

Strike the boulder more-or-less at right angles, but in such a way that the continuation of the blow will come through the edge of the boulder in an arc (Fig. 4).

A strong, sharp, hard blow is required, but not so much that you need to grunt with the effort. The fracture occurs mainly as a result of the proper angle of impact rather than extreme force. A blow struck too much head-on cannot be controlled; a blow struck too much at an angle will merely glance off. The exception to this is obsidian which requires a slightly glancing blow or else it will shatter or be crushed (Fig. 5).

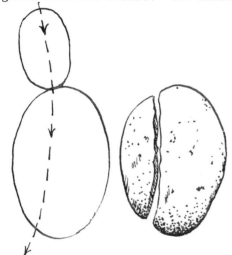

It will become apparent that different stones-- both raw material and hammerstone -- require slightly different angles and forces. There is no substitute for experience here. Given some experience, a few blows will shape a boulder into a serviceable hand-ax.

Direct percussion is also used to create blades to be used as blanks for smaller tools such as points. Examine the scraps from the above experience, and you may be surprised to find a few

Fig. 4, Direct percussion, angle of impact.

pieces in which you can imagine the potential for a point. To make good flakes or blades, first crack off the end from a large boulder (Fig. 6). For this cut, a slow and straight right-angle blow is struck with the longest axis of the boulder horizontal to the ground and resting on one's leg so that the portion to be broken off is not supported and can break off freely. With luck, this crack will result in a rather flat surface so that the boulder takes on an hemispherical appearance similar to a half-melon. This *striking platform* is quite necessary if you expect to make good blades.

Grasp the split boulder and hammerstone similar to that described earlier, but this time strike the blows near the edge of the boulder so as to break off a long, thin slightly curved, thin blade toward the rounded end of the boulder as if you were slicing off the skin of a fruit (Fig. 7). Once you get the hang of this, you should be able to flake off blades succesively around the circumference of the striking platform. Control of the angle of the stroke, point of percussion, and force of the blow are

Fig. 5, *Direct percussion on obsidian, angle of impact.*

Fig. 6, *Breaking off the end of a boulder to make a striking platform.*

Fig. 7, *Striking off blades from a core.*

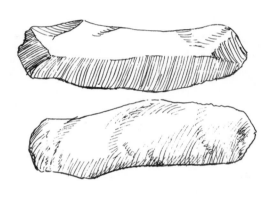

Fig. 8, *Front and back views of a flint blade. Length: 2 1/2 inches.*

required for good blades. These blades can be used as small knives just as they are, or they can be used as blanks for further shaping (Fig. 8). A dozen or more blades can be made from a single *core*, but one or two bad blows will destroy the striking platform so that no more are possible. Obsidian cores have been found which are as exquisite as a facetted cut-crystal pendant.

Flakes of larger size, as well as the blades just described, can be further shaped with direct percussion. If you don't have a glove, be sure to protect your hand with buckskin or other leather as you grasp the blank between thumb and fingers so that the edge to be struck is raised up with no part of your grip covering the zone from which you hope to strike the flake (Fig. 9). This chip is struck from the finger side of the blade; that is, the side closest to your body. A lighter hammerstone

Fig. 9, Shaping a point with direct percussion.

of a half-pound weight or so is used for this lighter work. Again, a swinging stroke is desired, but this time you should intend to fracture only a small flake across the surface of the blank. A lighter blow is sufficient. The angle of the impact is important. If the angle is somewhat at right angles to the edge of

the blank, a small, heavy chip will probably result (Fig. 10A). If the blow is more parallel to the face of the blade, a thinner, but longer, flake will be struck off (Fig. 10B). A sharp flip of the wrist is better that a full-elbow swing. With the exception of notches and a fine edge on the point, you can make a fair point with this technique. Lozenge-shaped blanks with convex bodies (called "turtlebacks" for the obvious similarity) were made this way at quarry-sites. These could be easily transported to the safety of a village for further flaking.

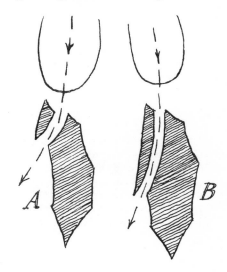

Fig. 10, Angle of percussion on a point (cross section). A, Small flake; too much of a right angle. B, Longer flake; angle of impact more in line with the blade.

Percussion flaking with the blank held in one hand is not always satisfactory. The smaller the blank, the more difficult it becomes to hold it satisfactorily to fracture off good flakes. You may wish to try a wooden "anvil" made from a stump stood on end at a convenient height. Although a hard anvil such as a stone may give support, it does not have the "give" as does wood or your hand, and the blank tends to crumble next to the stone anvil. On a wood stump, a half-inch deep groove sawed across the top can receive the blank in a vertical position with minimal support from the fingers. The blank can also be easily turned to present new edges for striking. If the groove is deep or fits the blank snugly, it may support the blank by itself. Obviously, the follow-through cannot be as complete as when the blank is held entirely in the hand, but it still can be enough to strike good flakes (Fig. 11).

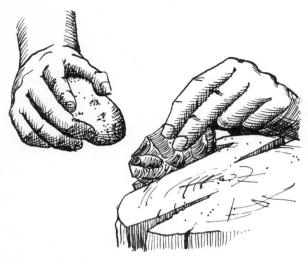

*Fig. 11,   Percussion flaking on a
wooden "anvil".*

Percussion flaked surfaces
have a unique splintery
quality which is quite unlike
pressure flaked surfaces as
will be described later. A
trained eye can discern the
differences, even on points
created thousands of years ago.

Other percussive techniques
may be tried. Instead of
striking the hammerstone on
the objective stone, reverse
the process. Place a large
hammerstone on the ground
and hit it with the objective
stone to knock a blade off
the latter. I find this technique somewhat less than satisfactory. Draw your own
conclusions.

I also shall not dwell on secondary or indirect percussive techniques
which involve the use of a hammerstone struck on a punch of bone or antler
which flakes off the chip. This can be done by holding the punch and
and objective stone cleverly with one hand so that the other hand is free
to use the hammerstone. This can also be done by two people: one to
hold the stone, and the other to hold the punch and hammerstone. Again,
I find that other techniques are superior in my opinion.

Defects

The intent of percussion is to throw off long, thin blades or flakes.
If you break off blades 3 inches long by 2 inches wide by about a half-
inch thick accurately and repeatedly, you don't need to read this. If,
as is more likely the case, you have some problems, the following may be
helpful.

Generally, the hammerstone should be lighter in weight
than the boulder to be flaked. As you work on smaller
and smaller pieces, you should have a supply of hammerstones handy and should make such changes as seem appropriate. Of course, when you are working on a
point, the hammerstone will have to be heavier than
the point, but this is an exception to the rule.

The conchoidal fracture will be quite apparent in most
of the raw materials you will use. These ripples are
not important except when they cause the flake to
break off suddenly before the logical end has been

*Fig. 12, Hinged
fracture.*

loosened (Fig. 12). This *hinged fracture* usually culminates in a rejected
blank unless a later flake takes it off. This is unlikely, because the
hinge is thicker and, therefore, stronger than the area surrounding it.
Hinged fractures may be the result of defects in the stone. They may
also be caused by lack of follow-through with the blow. They may also
be caused at the point where the fingers were gripping the blank when
the blow was struck so that the shock of impact could not travel through
the entire length of the stone. Maybe you're still too clumsy at this
point in your experience.

If your hand does not support the blank properly and completely all a-
round the area opposite the blow, you may break the blank. If you get
tired of holding and decide to support the blank on some hard surface,
you also take a good chance of breaking it, as the shock is reversed upward from the hard surface unless it is padded or made of wood which
absorbs the shock. Another cause of breaking the blank or shattering it
is that you may be striking too hard or too close to the center so that
it doesn't know which way to break.

If, when flaking across the blank to shape it further, you find that the
flakes are not long enough to go more than halfway across the body, you
will soon create a high ridge or peak near the center. If hinge fractures
are not the cause, you are probably striking at too much of an angle to
the surface. Direct the blows more in the direction you want the flake
to go. If you have already created a ridge or peak, you might as well
discard this blank, for there is no place to exert pressure on this area
to break it off. This problem should be resolved with experience.

One should be aware that the
direction of force through a
piece of glasseous material is
not in a straight line in the
direction of the blow, but
rather in an expanding cone
which radiates in all directions away from the point of
impact at an included angle of
about 100 degrees (Fig. 13A)
With this in mind, the blow
should be struck at an angle
so that a portion of this conical force near the edge of
the blank is in the direction
you wish the fracture
(Fig. 13B).

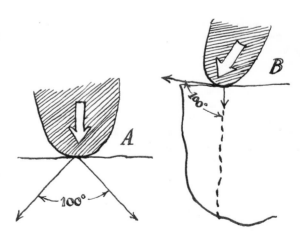

Fig. 13, Direction of force. A, Angle
through material on direct impact. B, Adjusted angle of impact to throw a vertical flake.

Percussion Flaking -- Baton

Instead of a hammerstone, a
baton or *billet* of wood or antler bone was used. Such a baton must be

lighter than a hammerstone, but it is, perhaps, more accurate and easier
to handle. It gets its power from the leverage of its handle rather than
the weight of stone. Batons may be just a few inches long up to a foot
or so. A shaft of hardwood, sometimes with a fortuitous knot at the end
and about 1 1/2 inches in diameter will make a good billet (Fig. 14A).
More common was a baton of deer antler which was cut at appropriate places
to make a blunt hammer head at the base with a slim handle toward the
tines (Fig. 14B). Sometimes a 2-3 inch length of antler set in or tied
to a wooden handle created a more contemporary-looking hammer-baton
(Fig. 14C). A hammerstone could be hafted as a stoneheaded club (Fig. 14D).

Some scientists hold that a baton
flake is noticeably different
than one made with direct blows
from a hammerstone. There may
be a difference between these,
but I can't see it. There is,
generally, the possibility for
longer and thinner flakes from a
wood or antler baton than from a
hammerstone, but this is seen
best in the process rather than
on the final product. Beginners
normally are more satisfied with
the result from a baton than from
a hammerstone, but if this is due
to a superior implement or to experience, I don't know. In any
case, be sure to try it.

The principles of percussion are
the same with either technique.
Those of us who have been
brought up with hammers and mallets may find the baton more
compatible to our conditioning.

Fig. 14, Batons. A, Hardwood. B, Deer
antler. C, Hafted antler. D, Hafted
hammerstone.

In the following, I shall consider only the use of a wooden or antler baton, because I consider the hafted stone mallet simply an extension of
the hammerstone. There does seem to be a difference in the result of
blows struck with batons made of organic material and those made of mineral material.

An old antler seems preferable to a fresh or "green" one. Fresh ones
seem to be greasier and slipperier than ones which have been weathered
to a dry surface. Old antlers "grab" the stone edge better so that the
force of the blow continues in the intended direction. If wood is used,
I suggest using a hard, heavy material such as walnut, ash, or hard maple.
Well-seasoned wood is preferable for the same reasons as for weathered
antlers.

The baton is not of much value in initial shaping or in striking blades

from a core; it just doesn't have the weight. It does provide good control in refining an edge already created by direct percussion. The blade
is normally held in one hand which may rest on your leg if you like.
The baton is held hammerlike in the other hand. With a sharp downward
blow, strike off a flake which will be dislodged below between the blade
and your hand (Fig. 15). A blow struck more toward the body of the blade will
crack off a longer flake.

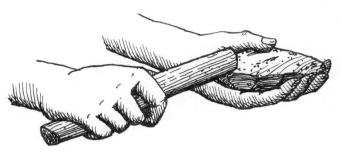

Fig. 15, Using a wooden baton.

An already thick edge may be thinned down with a baton if a thin edge is present as a beginning somewhere. Strike this thin edge in such a way that some of the thick edge is also struck. In this manner, an edge may
be thinned all around.

Small blades, too small to be grasped easily, may be supported on an anvil such as was used with primary percussion as illustrated in Fig. 11.

Pressure Flaking

I become more excited about pressure flaking, for this technique is necessary to create the perfectly shaped points which are sought by collectors. Not only is symmetry better controlled by pressure techniques,
but notches in a point are almost impossible without them.

There are several vari-
ations of pressure
flaking, but, basical-
ly, they are all con-
cerned with the com-
pression of the stone
and a shearing action
to dislodge the flake.
The most popular tool
for me is made of a
deer antler. (As men-
tioned before, a
weathered antler is
superior to a fresh
one.) An antler tine
can be used alone, but
I prefer one hafted to
a 6 or 8 inch shaft
(Fig. 16A). If you

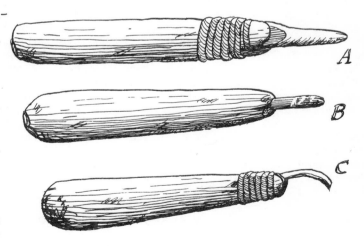

*Fig. 16, Hafted pressure-flaking tools. A, Antler
tip. B, Steel nail tip. C, Porcupine tooth tip.*

don't know a hunter who is willing to part with a "spike" or tine, a splinter of bone from a large mammal can be used, hafted or not. A contemporary Paiute used a nail to create the notches in an arrowhead[4]. I've always used nails, but I don't appreciate the groove pressed into my thumb after a few minutes. Common steel nails in sizes from 10-penny to 20-penny (3 to 4 inch, if you're not a carpenter) are fine. Just drive the nail into a shaft, and then file or grind off the head to a blunt point (Fig. 16B). (It doesn't hurt to drill a pilot hole for the nail first or you'll split many a handle.) Don't use hardened steel such as a screwdriver or awl; these merely slip off the stone. Soft steel, such as nails are made of, gets a better purchase on the stone edge so that one can press hard without slipping. For fine chipping, such as notching, antler, bone, or steel tips can be used. A tool used in the past was made from the curved incisor teeth of large rodents such as porcupine and beaver (Fig. 16C). These must be hafted firmly, for a curved tooth can easily come loose.

Wooden tipped tools can be used, but these wear down or split rapidly. Don't be limited, however. Almost any hard, strong material can be used. Northern Indians and Eskimos sometimes made flaking tools from ivory. (I have better uses for ivory.) Copper or brass are soft enough to get a good grip on the stone, but nails are so plentiful that I never get to trying these. Stone-on-stone is no good -- too slippery. In general, then, you need hard material for the tool tip, but not too hard. Flaking tools wear down with the small amount of abrasion required on each effort. Antlers may chip here and there. Don't be tempted to sharpen a tip. A point is desired, but not a pencil-point which will break off with the first push. If a tip becomes too blunted, just rub it on some rough stone to touch it up or use a file.

I've never gotten calluses heavy enough on the palms of my hands to survive the impact of a tool when a chip is dislodged to survive the cut of the chip itself. Indians probably used a pad of buckskin or rawhide for protection. In addition to a glove, a heavy leather pad is required to fit over the lower part of the palm of the hand which grips the blank. This should be made of *heavy* leather. Shoe sole or heavy belting is good. If thinner leather is all that's available, make it at least a double layer. Cut an oval or triangular piece about 6-8 inches long with a hole in one end large enough to slip over the thumb (with the glove on) (Fig. 17). While the thumb hole is not necessary, it sure helps hold the pad in place while you concentrate on the procedure. I'll guarantee that you'll cut yourself without such protection. Even with the pad in place, the fleshy part of your palm will become sore from acting as a backstop for the flaking tool. Watch that little flakes don't get inside your glove, too.

Choose a likely candidate from your supply of percussion-flaked blanks.

[4]Wheat, p. 71.

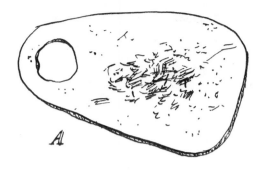

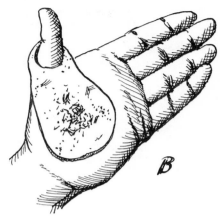

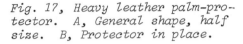

Fig. 17, Heavy leather palm-pro-
tector. A, General shape, half
size. B, Protector in place.

Hold it, on top of the leather pad, between your finger tips and the soft
part of your lower palm (Fig. 18). The edge nearest your wrist should
be tilted upward sufficiently so that a flake pressed off underneath
will come off cleanly with little interference from the pad. In other
words, the support of the palm is behind the area to be flaked. Rest
the back of your hand on your leg for added support. This is not necessary, but it keeps your arm from tiring quickly. Grasp the flaking tool
comfortably but firmly in your other hand and touch its tip on the top
of the edge of the blank closest to you. I like to rest the forward portion of the second knuckle of my first finger on the wrist of the other
hand as a fulcrum for better control.

Increase the pressure of
tip on the blank firmly
and steadily, not sudden-
ly, toward the edge of the
blade and downward, and,
at the same time, give a
little twist to the tool.
It helps to bring your elbow up as you bend your
wrist down. If the blunted tip of the tool has
found a good grip on the
stone edge so that it has
not slipped, you should be
pleasantly startled to hear
a satisfying "click" and

Fig. 18, Position of hands in pressure flak-
ing.

will discover that a small chip has been broken off below. You'll also
probably feel the less satisfying impact of the tool tip as it is stopped
by the leather pad.

Flake along this edge and turn the blank or move it as necessary to present a tilted-up zone at all times while you still maintain a firm but flexible grip on the blank. When you have finished this edge, flip the blank over to work from the other side. Turn it the other way to do likewise to the other edge. Try to throw flakes by working from a thinned part of the edge into thicker parts a little at a time. If an edge is already rather thick, it is difficult to thin it down except by working from an already thinned place.

Try to throw long flakes across the surface of the body of the blade -- at least half-way across. If you can't do this after some experience, try pressing the tip of the tool more *toward* the edge of the blank (Fig. 19B) rather than *downward* (Fig. 19A). Note in the illustrations that downward pressure tends to create a short, stubby flake, whereas pressure inward compresses the stone across the blade so that the twist can shear off a longer flake. Practice on broken glass before you try a harder stone. Sometimes, however, a piece of glass is cut in such a way

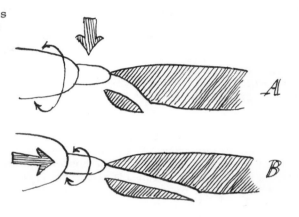

Fig. 19, Direction of thrust in pressure flaking. A, Improper: small flake. B, Proper: long flake.

that there is no real platform to give the tool a place on which to press. If this is the case, throw it out.

If the edge you are flaking just doesn't seem to respond with long flakes, perhaps the edge is not prepared properly. In this case, return to the hammerstone to try to thin it out with a fresh edge. Also watch that there is room below the point of pressure so that the flake can come off well toward the middle of the body below the blade. Be sure, nevertheless, that the entire length of the blade is held down firmly with as many fingers as are necessary to do the job. "Firmly", in this case, also means pressed down into the soft flesh of the palm so as to give support all along the length of the blade. (This should not sound like a contradiction). If the entire length is not supported evenly, pressure in the middle may cause it to crack in two. Hold the blade on the ham of your thumb rather than over the depression in the middle of your palm. If your ham gets sore, you are probably flaking in the right place.

When your practice has allowed you to create good, thin, triangular points, you are ready to try some notches. Switch to a narrower, more pointed tool and throw a good flake off the edge at the place where you want your notch to be. Depending on how well this was done, flake off two or three

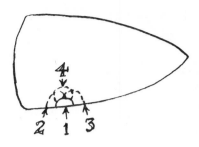

Fig. 20, Beginning sequence in chipping a notch.

more chips to open the notch more (Fig. 20). Turn the point over and enlarge the notch from the other side. Continue to turn and chip from alternating sides until the notch is as deep and as wide as you desire. Do likewise on the opposite edge. If you have not broken many points yet, this is a good time to begin; but, as with most skills, experience is the best teacher. Finally crumble the edge inside the notch with the tip of your tool or a small flake of stone so that the sharp edges are dulled. If you use the point as a weapon tip, this crumbling will keep the edge from cutting through the lashing which you'll need to keep the point in place. Crumble the base of the point for the same reason.

Other pressure flaking techniques have been used. For instance, the blank could be held against an "anvil" of sorts so that more pressure could be exerted than against your hand. Try this on the stump anvil as was used in percussion flaking. One amateur suggests a wide blade, like the end of a file, can be used with a rocking motion off one corner to give pressure with the other. Ellis cites a method of creating a lever "machine" used by the Potawatomi. He tried to reproduce this in the form of a simple arbor-press arrangement, but found it generally unsatisfactory[5].

For more pressure, try hafting the tool tip to a longer handle which can be tucked into the shoulder so that you can lean into the pressure with the upper body. If this process proves worthwhile, try attaching a T-handle to the end of the shaft -- more-or-less like a crutch -- so that you can lean into it in your arm pit. Experiment with the length of the tool and the placement of your work. It should be apparent that more support than your hand can give is necessary for the pressure possible with this tool. For instance, a firm support such as a padded rock or a wood stump anvil may be just the thing. Try kneeling as you support the work on the ground; stand, if you're working on a stump or table surface. In this way you can guide the tool tip with one hand as you hold the blade in position with the other (Fig. 21). You will probably get a sore shoulder, but what pressure! You may begin to try to flake off larger chips with this increased pressure, only to find that your antler is chipping or breaking instead. Try a soft steel tip made from a good spike. I am aware of one individual who claims proficiency in throwing off the long flutes on either side of a Folsom-type point by using a crutch-tool with a copper tip which is soft enough to get a good grip on the stone but won't chip or shatter like antler.

Take some precautions regarding the follow-through of such pressure. Un-

[5]Ellis, pp. 50-52.

like simple hand pressure, you
must try to halt the pressure
of your shoulder right after
the chip comes off. Pay attention to where the tool tip is
going to go after the chip
flakes off, or you may go over
on your ear.

You can imagine that it would
be a simple matter to extend
the length of the shaft so that
your chest can be used for pressure instead of an arm pit.
Use a larger, even padded, cross
bar to protect your sternum (the
vertical bone in the center of
your chest). If the blade is
rested on a support on the
ground and is grasped between
your feet or held by your toes,
both hands can be used to direct
the point of the tool, and you
can exert considerable pressure.
(This may be another point in

Fig. 21, Using a crutch-type pressure
tool on a padded stone anvil.

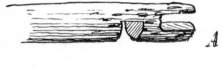

Fig. 22A, A deer antler notched
flaking tool. B, Using the
side notch for pressure.

favor of moccasins instead of shoes.)

Still other pressure techniques exist.
A notched antler, not unlike a notched
modern glass cutter, can be used (Fig.
22A). Notches of varying widths and
depths are desired to give a choice
which best fits the stone blank at the
point of pressure. These notches
should not be too deep for fear of
breaking the antler. This is one of
the hazards of a notch on the end, also.
Insert the edge of your blank into an
appropiate notch (Fig. 22B). Bend your
wrist (either up or down, as you wish),
and give it a little twist to shear
off the flake. In my experience, this
tool gives rather small flakes, and
I prefer the simple pressure tool described earlier as being more versatile.
The notched tool does, of course,
create a better purchase on the stone,
but the antler wears down rapidly if

it doesn't break first. A worn tool needs to be touched up frequently.
Actually, an old pliers will do almost as well for this technique.

Conclusions

I urge the practice on heavy plate glass or bottle glass as a raw material
for the beginner. It flakes well and is a little softer than most stones.

As has been described, a wide spectrum of tools and techniques is available. As you try these out, you will probably discover variations
which are best for you. Students often eagerly compare lengths of flakes
as they discuss the merits of the technique most amenable to them. If
you work primarily on points about 2 inches long, your chance of throwing a flake halfway across the body are good. As you improve, you can
work on more complicated or larger designs. You should also be able to
improve the rhythmic regularity of flakes which is covetted as the epit-
ome of craftsmanship. Try a small tool to create the saw-toothed serrated edge which is quite handsome and also quite functional in that it cuts
in readily. Incidentally, a dull point can be sharpened even though it
is attached to a shaft. Unless you are a masochist or have free dental
care, don't try the technique I once saw in photographs from Australia.
I still don't believe it, but here was a hunter blissfully flaking a new
edge with his teeth!

How long does it take to make a good projectile point? Given a good raw
material and a good blank made from it, perhaps five minutes. Fifteen
minutes is not a bad time to try for. I suspect that, from the quantities of rejects found at quarry sites, Indians took as much time in selecting blanks as they did in shaping them. Some writers suggest that
several hours were required. It seems to me that the abundance of points
tends to disprove this theory. My experiences support my contention.
So should yours.

REFERENCES

Bixby, Lawrence B.	"Flint Chipping", *American Antiquity*, Vol. X, 1945.
Ellis, H. Holmes	"Flint-Working Techniques of the Ameri-can Indians; An Experimental Study", Ohio State Museum, Columbus, 1940.
Holmes, William H.	"The Lithic Industries:, *Part I, Handbook on Aboriginal American Antiquities, Bureau of American Ethnology Bulletin* No. 60, 1919.
Howell, F. Clark	"Early Man", Time-Life Books, N.Y., 1965

Knowles, Francis H. S.   "The Manufacture of a Flint Arrow-head
                              by Quartzite Hammer-stone", *Occasional
                              Papers on Technology*, No. 1, Pitt Rivers
                              Museum, University of Oxford, 1944.

--------   "A Stone-Worker's Progress", *Occasional
                              Papers on Technology*, No. 6, Pitt Rivers
                              Museum, University of Oxford, 1953.

Olsen, Larry Dean   "Outdoor Survival Skills", Brigham Young
                              University, Provo, Utah, 1967.

Pond, Alonzo W.   "Primitive Methods of Working Stone",
                              Logan Museum Bulletin, Vol. II, No. 1,
                              Beloit, Wis., 1930

Ritzenthaler, Robert   "A Guide to Wisconsin Indian Projectile
                              Point Types", *Popular Science Series*,
                              No. 11, Milwaukee Public Museum, 1967.

Scheele, William E.   "The Earliest Americans", World, Cleveland,
                              1963.

Wheat, Margaret M.   "Survival Arts of the Primitive Paiutes",
                              University of Nevada, Reno, 1967.

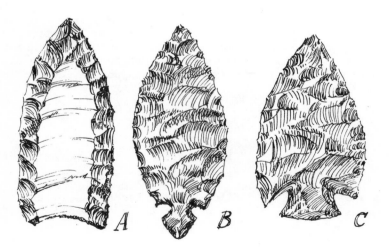

*Fig. 23, Typical stone point types. A, Folsom.
B, Turkeytail. C, Snyder.*

EINE SCHNITZELBANK

Why is a Whiteman's contraption found on the pages of a book on Indian crafts? First, although it does have a European ancestry and was a necessary piece of equipment for colonial craftsmen in this country, it was one of the many things adopted from the White culture by Indians, particularly eastern tribes, inasmuch as it made certain woodworking processes easier and quicker. Secondly, my own investigations into native crafts of this country have made me more aware of my own heritage from the "old country", and I find a personal delight in this marriage of the two cultures.

The *Schnitzelbank* (shnĭt́sél - bǎhngk) or "shaving horse" (the English name seems reminiscent of razors and stables) has passed out of contemporary shops along with the drawknife and spokeshave which were tools which naturally belonged with it. When reproducing Indian crafts one finds, by experience and research, that certain peeling, paring, and whittling operations were greatly expedited by using this simple clamping bench. Such jobs as carving canoe ribs, whittling basket handles, and paring snowshoe frames all are more easily done by returning to the early technology.

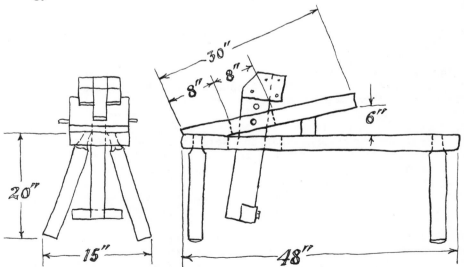

Fig. 1, An assembled Schnitzelbank. Measurements are approximate.

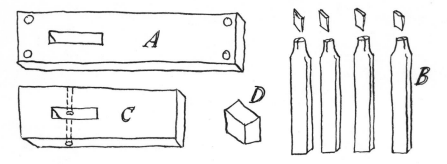

*Fig. 2, Bench. A, Seat. B, Legs and wedges. C, Upper
work surface. D, Spacing block.*

Schnitzelbank (I'll continue with the German word which is always capi-
talized) means carving, whittling, or cutting bench. Used with a draw-
knife or Indian man's crooked knife, it provides a convenient seat for
the worker and a surface and clamp for a variety of wooden shapes and
sizes, especially long and thin strips. Because a foot is used on a lever which grips the work, both hands are thus freed to grasp a tool.

Few tools are required. With a portable circle saw, power drill, hammer, and a few nails, I made one recently in about four hours. Only two
parts are necessary -- the bench and a hinged or pivotted lever-clamp.
The bench requires a piece of wood about 4 feet long for the seat (Fig.
2A), a shorter (30 inch) upper work surface which is tilted at a convenient angle (Fig. 2C), a block for spacing between the two (Fig. 2D), and
four 20-inch legs (Fig. 2B). All of the stock for mine was 2 x 8 inch
rough-sawed oak -- oak because it was handy. It could be made from any
2 inch wood.

The seat needs a rectangular slot in the center of the forward end (the
end farthest from the worker) about 6 inches from the end and about 10
inches long. Large holes can be drilled in the corners of this slot so
that the inside can be sawed or chiselled out. This slot is 2 inches
wide (or whatever width will be used for the lever-clamp). Then bore a
hole in each of the four corners of the seat at an angle of 10-20 degrees
so that the legs will spread outward for stability. These holes should
be drilled from the bottom side and can be "blind holes" which do not go
completely through to the other side. I think that the legs are sturdier if they do penetrate completely. The holes should be of any large
diameter -- 1 1/4-1 1/2 inch for strength.

Rip four 20-inch legs from 2-inch stock and whittle one end of each to
a diameter which fits the holes just drilled. (Such whittling is itself most easily done on a Schnitzelbank.) Saw a slot about 2 inches
deep in the center of the rounded end of each leg, and drive the legs
into their holes so that they project slightly out into the top surface.
A little tapping here and there will cause the seat to rest evenly on all

four legs -- if all legs are the same
length and all holes were drilled at
the same angle. I don't worry about
this too much because I usually work
outdoors and the legs dig into the
ground some anyway. Whittle four wedges
and drive one into each slot from the
top, thus wedging each leg permanently in place. Slice off the projecting portion of leg and wedge flush
with the surface.

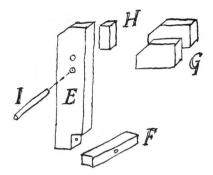

Cut the upper work surface plank about
30 inches long (which allows about 18
inches for sitting) and cut a rectangular slot 8 inches long about 8 inches
from the forward end. This slot
should also be about 2 inches wide.

*Fig. 3, Lever-clamp. E,
Lever. F, Footrest. G,
Clamp blocks. H, Spacer
block. I, Pivot pin.*

While it is not absolutely necessary, I like to bevel the bottom of the
forward end for a few inches so that it fits flat on the seat.

Make the bevelled spacing block about 4 inches high and test the three
pieces to fit. After making sure that they fit reasonably well, nail
them together with 3 1/2-4 inch nails.

Make the lever from a piece of 2 x 4 about 26 inches long (Fig. 3E).
Notch the bottom corner to receive a 2 x 2 x 12 at right angles for a
footrest, but don't assemble this yet (Fig. 3F). Nail two 5 inch long
pieces of 2 x 4 (Fig. 3G) with a short block between them (Fig. 3H) to
the lever in such a way that the excess sticks out on the same side as
the footrest notch. The back of this clamp assembly is usually bevelled
as shown, but this is not necessary.

Cut a piece of broomstick, rake handle, or dowel about 3/4-1 inch by 12
inches long. This will be the pivot pin. Holes to be drilled for this
pin should be slightly too large so that the pin can be removed.

Insert the lever-clamp from above into its slots and check it for fit.
It should be a little loose. Remove the lever-clamp temporarily to drill
the hole for the pin horizontally through the upper work plank in the
center of the slot. Reinsert the lever-clamp. With an ice-pick or screwdriver as a temporary pivot pin, move the lever-clamp up and down and
swing it forward and back to locate the proper place to drill its hole.
It should be located so that a forward thrust at the footrest will swing
the head down on the thinnest stock. Drill this hole. Also drill another hole about 2 inches below the first so that the clamp can be raised for thick work by changing the pin.

Now, with the clamp in place in the slots, screw on the footrest. I use
a large lag screw in case I want to disassemble it sometime. It could
be nailed.

Use a drawknife or rasp to round off edges on the bench, legs, and other areas which may get some wear. Round the seat portion especially if you intend to be sitting on it for some time.

Your Schnitzelbank is now ready to go! Sit on the back end so that you can work the footrest with either or both feet. One is usually sufficient. Pull the footrest toward you with your foot to open the clamp and insert your work on whichever side of the lever is convenient and close to the head. Your work space is then in the area between you and the clamp head. Push your foot forward which brings the clamp down and grips the wood against the upper work surface. Both hands are free to use a draw-knife or crooked knife both of which are used by pulling or drawing them toward the user. Short pieces can be turned end-for-end for working; long pieces can be pulled next to you between your arm and body or can be allowed to project in front, depending on the area on which you are working. If you need to work on thicker stock, pull the pin and raise the clamp to the lower hole. Simple!

Some pioneers added a thin, springy stick about a foot long into a hole at the center of the forward end so that it stuck out as a mast or an-tenna. A string was tied from the free end of this stick to the back of the top of the clamp head. In this way, the stick had enough tension on it when the clamp was closed so that it would be pulled open as soon as foot pressure was released. I don't think this is necessary unless you intend to shave a few hundred shingles.

After a year or two outdoors, my Schnitzelbank takes on a pleasant weathered and used look and yet, except for a little rust on the nails, is as good as new.

This project is of little value if you need to make only one basket handle. If you intend more production such as 40 or 50 canoe ribs, it's well worth the few hours.

"Ja, das ist ein' Schnitzelbank!"

Fig. 4, The Schnitzelbank in service for scraping a basketry splint.

THE USE OF BONE IN MAKING A SEWING KIT

An Eskimo-style kit composed of needle (and pin cushion), thimble, seam depressor, and case or container may be made from portions of bone from a leg of a medium-sized mammal such as a deer or calf.

The container or case (Fig. 1A) is made by sawing off the joint ends of the bone to create a 3 or 4 inch section. (Such a leg bone will not be perfectly round, but will rather be a somewhat U-shaped cross section.) The earlier Indian method would have been to saw back and forth with a chipped stone blade until the piece could be broken off. Steel tools were employed when available from white traders so a saw or file came into use in later times. Today, a meat saw, hack saw, or coping saw is quite satisfactory although any fine-toothed blade may be used.

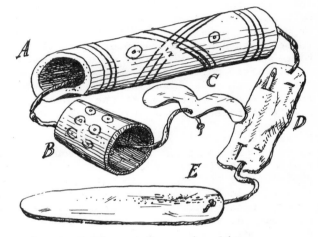

Fig. 1, Eskimo-style sewing kit.
A, Case. B, Thimble. C, Toggle.
D, Pin cushion. E, Seam depressor.
Length of case: 3 1/2 inches.

If a file is used, the triangular type is best to score a notch all around where the cut is to be made until the piece can be snapped off.

A fresh bone can be scraped clean inside and out, but a more expeditious way to remove the cartilaginous material on the exterior and the marrow on the interior is to boil the bone in water for a quarter-hour or so. The marrow can be then easily blown or sucked out, and a blade can be used to scrape off the cartilage, flesh, and fat which remains. While the bone may appear somewhat shiny immediately after boiling, this may be a result of the melted fat on its surface. If this fat remains, it will penetrate the bone and give it a yellowish cast. If it is well cleaned, the bone, when it cools, should have more of a dull white or ivory color.

Early Indian refining of the surface may have been to grind the surface where necessary with sand or sandstone and water as a lubricant. A simpler expedient today is to use common sandpaper in degrees from coarse to fine.

The finest grits of abrasive paper are usually made from black silicon carbide and may be obtained as a "Wet-or-Dry" type which can be used with water as a lubricant to float off fine bone particles which tend to clog dry sandpaper. Common flint sandpaper may be used but must be kept dry and is less satisfactory. The inside of the bone tube can be cleaned with a round file; and, although a high polish inside is not necessary, sandpaper can be wrapped around an appropriate twig for further refining.

Dependent upon the finest grit used above, the surface of the bone should now begin to take on a soft, waxy sheen, but a still higher polish can yet be applied. Indians used any locally-available fine material such as pumice. Possibly, however, some early pieces found in collections today may have acquired a polish from continued use. More recent bone work may be polished with a contemporary abrasive such as toothpaste or powder. A half inch or so of toothpaste on an area of bone can be rubbed with a damp buckskin or cloth for a high polish. With either paste or powder, some water should be used. Excess abrasive can be washed off after polishing is completed. In this chapter, the case is left open at both ends. Some needle cases were fitted with a permanent bottom and a removable plug at the top, but these were intended only for needle storage, not for an entire sewing kit.

Linear designs were scratched into the surface with a pointed stone tool called a *graver* or *burin*. Such a tool is characterized by a carefully flaked snout of triangular cross section at the cutting edge which is pushed along the surface of the bone to score it to a shallow depth of 1/64-1/32 inch. This depth can be tested with a fingernail in the groove. Several passes with the graver may be necessary for the desired depth to be achieved. In more recent times, steel tools were used. Such a tool can be made from a length of steel hafted to a convenient handle and sharpened to an appropriate point. The tip of a small file can be ground for a substitute. Indian and Eskimo designs tend to be often geometric and linear repeating designs: parallel lines, triangles, squares, diamonds, and the like. Occasionally the bow-drill would be used to make a design of tiny circles and bull's eyes. Eskimo designs on bone, but more often on ivory, frequently include pictorial representations (Fig. 2). Such pictures, especially those on ivory, became very intricate and exquisite and are highly prized collector's items today.

Fig. 2, Bone snowshoe needle with incised pictorial design. Length: 2 1/2 inches.

A final step in bone work with incised designs is to bring out the pattern by staining the design with some dark pigment rubbed into the grooves. Originally some dark material such as powdered hematite might be mixed with grease and rubbed over the bone surface. If a sufficient quantity was used, some was caught in the grooves while the polished surface of the bone could be wiped clean, thus giving a black line design on a white background. This method is similar to that of inking etched printing surfaces so that it has sometimes erroneously been referred to as etching. A more precise term is engraving as is done in certain printing processes or in metal surfaces. Today's method of darkening these lines is to rub in some dark paint, preferably flat black, but care must be taken that the paint does not unduly stain the polished surfaces as well as the grooves. If this happens, one must repeat the polishing process to regain the bone white. When a paint is to be chosen, I suggest that a sample be tried before working on a final piece.

Other parts of the sewing kit include an open-ended thimble which, when worn, requires that the needle be pushed against its side rather than against the top of the thimble such as often the practice when using modern closed thimbles (Fig. 1B). An inch section of large leg bone with an appropriate inside diameter (a ham bone is just about my size) is selected and cleaned as above. Because the inside diameter must fit the finger, the inside is reamed out with a round file to create a slightly tapering cylinder to fit the intended finger. The outside, irregular shape can be chopped, carved, filed, and sanded down to a corresponding shape allowing about 1/16-1/8 inch thickness of bone to remain as a wall. Because of the function of a thimble, the outer surface should be covered with a fine pattern of incising to catch the needle as it is pushed. Linear patterns may be used, but a series of shallow blind holes or bull's-eyes can be made with a bow drill. Other procedures are the same as for the case above.

A seam depressor measuring about 1/2 by 3 or 4 inches is also part of the kit (Fig. 1E). The thickness of the depressor is determined by the diameter of the hole in the bone case, for the depressor should fit cleanly inside for storage. The function of the depressor is to press down buckskin seams to give a finished, flat appearance to the sewn areas. (A contemporary tool called a bone folder may still be found in libraries where it is used to crease paper for binding.) Because of this function, applied design, if any, is not incised to the working end, but is reserved for the handle. A hole is bored in the handle so that it may be tied to the kit.

A final bone piece, a toggle, is needed to complete the kit in order to keep the parts from being lost (Fig. 1C). Simply, the toggle is a flat section of bone perhaps 1/8 inch thick and cut too large to pass through the case hole. This toggle may be a simple rectangle or may be sawed into a simplified double curve or W-shape with a hole bored in the center for tying.

A needle in early times could be made from a split section of bone or a thorn. It is probable, however, that a true needle was not used. Instead, an awl was used to puncture a hole, and the sinew or whatever was available for thread could be pushed through. If native copper was handy, a small nugget could be formed into a wire, pointed at one end, and flattened and pierced at the other. Indian women soon discovered the merits of traded steel needles which have been used to the present.

A fine buckskin thong or twisted sinew about 6 inches long is used to assemble the kit. The thong is tied to the depressor. A small piece of
skin is threaded on toward the center, and the toggle is tied to the opposite end. The piece of skin is used as a pin cushion for the needle
(Fig. 1D), and the thimble is threaded on at random. The depressor can
be pulled through the case tube so that the toggle and thimble remain
on the exterior while the depressor and pin cushion remain protected inside.

Other uses of bone (and antler and ivory) include awls of all sizes,
weaving needles (up to 12 inches or so), beads, bone knives, hair combs
or hair pieces, fish hooks, shamans' sucking tubes, projectile points
(especia°ly barbed fishing points) and even cribbage boards (these latter, of course, for trading).

REFERENCES

Brown, Charles E.   "Notes on the Occurance and Use of Bone, Shell,
                           Hematite, and Lead Implements in Wisconsin",
                           Wisconsin Archaeologist, V. 9, No. 1, 1910.

Lyford, Carrie   "Iroquois Crafts", U.S. Dep't. of Interior,
                           Bureau of Indian Affairs, 1945.

Penniman, T. K.   "Pictures of Ivory and Other Animal Teeth, Bone
                           and Antler", Pitt Rivers Museum, *University of
                           Oxford Occasional Papers on Technology*, No. 5,
                           1952.

Ray, Dorothy J.   "Graphic Arts of the Alaskan Eskimo", *Native
                           American Arts*, No. 2, U.S. Dep't. of Interior,
                           Indian Arts and Crafts Board, 1969.

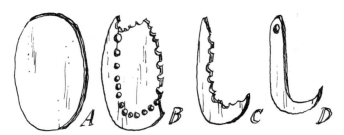

*Fig. 3, Making a bone fish hook. A, Disc of bone.
B, Center drilled out. C, A hook broken away from
the disc. D, A finished hook.*

RAWHIDE

Untanned skins and hides were used by Indians as a raw material for the manufacture of artifacts and as a binding lace for many other objects.

Compared to the process of soft-tanning, the work of making rawhide is relatively simple. Fleshing and de-hairing are really the only steps required to prepare a skin or hide for use. Actually, the steps or processes varied slightly from tribe to tribe and depended somewhat upon the skin being prepared. The process sequence described below is generally advisable.

First, of course, a skin must be provided. The Plains Indian rawhide came, quite naturally, from buffalo in most cases. Sources in other culture areas included deer, elk, caribou, and moose. Today, a reasonable substitute can be made from calfskin for thin rawhide, and cow or horse hide for heavier material. A calfskin may measure about 15-20 square feet. A full-sized cow hide is about 40-45 square feet. If the large hide is not needed in one piece for future use, I advise that it be cut in two pieces for ease in working. A complete cowhide when wet makes a clumsy bundle of better than 100 pounds.

As in most tanning processes, a fresh or "green" hide is desired, but a salted or dried hide may be used. A dried hide must be soaked in water for several days to soften it -- up to a week or more for a heavy hide such as a steer or buffalo. In addition, a salted hide must be rinsed daily to wash out the salt completely. A green hide needs only to be rinsed to remove hair, blood, leaves, and the like. (A good washing helps to kill some of the odor which may be offensive. I may add a little scented soap at times to serve both purposes.)

The hide should be wrung out now, if only to make it weigh less, but I find that the rinse water dripping down on me is somewhat disagreeable. If two persons are available, a simple twisting of the hide between them is usually sufficient. Working alone, the tanner may wrap the hide around the wrist of one hand and wring the hide out with the opposite hand.

The hide must be fleshed; i.e., all flesh or fatty tissue must be cut or scraped off. I prefer to do this while the hide is stretched, but it may also be done on the ground or with the hide draped over some suitable flat surface. Plains women pegged the hide out over the ground while Woodland women customarily used a stretching frame and worked in a stand-

ing position. I follow the latter -- it requires less back-breaking
bending.

A sturdy frame of posts of about 4 inch diameter is constructed so that
its rectangular opening is slightly larger than the stretched size of
the hide. Don't plan on the present size of the hide, for one can expect some enlarging as a result of the tension placed on it during the
work. Holes are punched with a knife or awl around the margins of the
hide -- 3-4 inches apart and about 3/4 inch from the edge of the hide.
Several long lengths of sturdy cord are used to lace the hide inside the
wooden frame so that the hide is suspended in the rectangle (Fig. 1).
Tension is adjusted so that the cords stretch the hide taut. The fleshing and de-hairing will require some hours of work so it is best to work
in a shady location. Even then, the hide may dry out during work and
may need to be dampened occasionally. Drying and dampening as well as
the pressure from tools will require additional adjusting of the cords
as needed to keep the tension even.

Fig. 1, Half a cowhide laced in a drying frame.

When the hide has been properly laced in place, flesh and fat are removed with a knife or a bone or steel scraper. Earlier, a stone scraper
was used for this purpose. A good curved flint scraper, with or without a handle, is still functional. Further, a new edge may be flaked
easily if the old one becomes dull. When all the flesh and fat have been
removed, the flesh side of the hide should have a bluish-white color and

a slimy, clammy surface, but not greasy. Be sure that all grease is
scraped or cut off.

The hide needs now to be de-haired. On a long-haired animal, it is advisable to shear some of the hair with a knife, taking care not to cut
into the skin itself. A small bundle of hair is pulled up with one hand
as the knife, wielded by the other, cuts the bundle off more or less
flush with the surface. If the hair has already begun to "slip", this
shearing may not be necessary.

A steel scraper made of a bent piece of strap steel about 1 inch wide is
ground or filed to a semi-circular cutting edge and is hafted with a
suitable wood handle. If the edge is fairly sharp (an extremely keen
edge may cut through the hide too easily), the hair can be shaved off
with firm downward strokes. Two hands are necessary. Two people can
work at once in this process if each one has a scraper. The scarf skin
will probably be removed along with the hair if the latter is difficult
to remove. These strokes tend to stretch the hide so that the cords may
need to be adjusted to keep the hide taut. A hide stretched too loosely may ripple up in front of the scraper blade which then can pierce the
hide accidentally. A half of a cowhide may take an afternoon for de-
hairing; a deer skin, about 2 hours.

It is almost impossible to flesh and de-hair the hide in the immediate
vicinity of the lacing and holes for fear of cutting the cords or dis-
tending the holes. This marginal area will be discarded later. When
the de-hairing is complete, the hide can be washed in the stretched position. A better job is accomplished if the hide is taken down, but it
means that it must be re-stretched afterward, which process is unduly
tedious. A good job of de-hairing and scraping should leave the hide
fairly clean anyway, and it is only the remaining scraps of tissue and
hair which need to be washed off. Because the hide is translucent to
a degree, it can also be checked for thickness according to the degree
of translucency. Excessively thick portions can be shaved down with
the scraper. This can also be done later as the hide becomes stiffer.
In the latter case, it is shaved almost as a plank would be planed except that the blade is curved rather than straight as on a wood plane.

Now the cords should be checked again, for the hide should have stretched quite a lot during these steps. For some rawhide construction, the
hide may be taken down for immediate use. I prefer to dry it stretched
out and to cut it later into usable shapes. The hide should be dried
slowly for 2-3 days. Some slight dampening may be needed if the weather
is dry. The shrinking of the drying hide necessitates a relieving of the
tension cords. The legendary strength of drying rawhide is such that it
may otherwise break the cords, rip out the holes, or even crack the frame
poles. If the hide is dried slowly and sufficient tension has been allowed, the hide should dry to an extremely hard surface more like sheet
metal than leather and with a brown or tan color. It may be translucent
or opaque.

Sometimes, during the drying period, the hide is sanded with a block of sandstone. If this is done when the hide is too damp, the sandstone surface becomes quickly clogged with tissue and must be cleaned off frequently. If the hide is too dry, it may already be so hard that the sand refuses to cut. The sanding, if done at the opportune time, evens out irregularities in thickness and removes bits of hanging tissue from the previous processes. Any nap or texture remaining from sanding can be smoothed with a light sponging. Coarse sandpaper can be used in place of sandstone, of course.

Some tribes cured rawhide with an application of urine. It is said that a washing in urine before drying creates a bleached white color. This has been called, by the French, *babiche*, when it is cut into lacing. In most journals, babiche and lace are terms used interchangeably with no reference to the urine treatment. I used a gallon of urine on a half cowhide recently, but with no noticeable results. The ammonia in the urine should act as a bleach, but in my experiment, it only made a smell.

When the hide is completely dry, it may be set aside for future use in a cool, dry place. Extreme humidity will cause the hide to wrinkle which may be bothersome later.

Making Babiche

One of the major uses of rawhide was for lacing. Green or wet rawhide is very flexible. It shrinks upon drying so that an extremely tight joint can be lashed. This joint has an advantage over nails and other fasteners in that the joint is slightly flexible, yet it is very sturdy. Many bone or stone tools were attached to handles with babiche. Pack frames and sleds could be made of relatively thin wood but still had sufficient flexibility to survive knocks in use. Harness for dogs, and, later, horses, were made of rawhide. Rawhide will remain flexible if impregnated with oil or grease. (So-called "rawhide" laces for shoes today are not really raw hide; rather they are oiled tanned leather.) It is almost impossible to conceive of snowshoes without considering rawhide webbing. Today, such webbing is usually painted with exterior varnish after the lace is dry to keep melted snow from softening it in use.

Dry rawhide is difficult to cut. I use a sturdy pair of tin snips for heavy hides such as cowhide. Dampened rawhide can be cut (slowly) with a sharp knife. Very thin rawhide can be cut with a scissors. Lace is most frequently cut from a disc rather than a straight edged piece. By using a disc and cutting a spiral of even width from the outside edge, a very long length of lace can be made. For instance, a disc of 4 inch diameter should yield a lace of over 8 feet if cut in an 1/8 inch spiral. The same size disc should make over 16 feet of 1/16 inch lacing, presuming that the width is even throughout. Larger, wider lace naturally requires a larger disc.

The brown dry rawhide should be soaked for several hours depending **upon** its thickness. Calf or deer rawhide may need only a few minutes. When sufficiently wet for cutting, the hide should be an opaque bluish-gray and fairly flexible. Very soft hide may be too floppy to cut well, so it should be a little stiff. Lace cut from this disc will probably require another hour of soaking before it should be used, especially if it is intended to shrink appreciably.

A sharp knife should be provided. Ideally, the blade should be thin with an edge honed keen as a razor. An old-fashioned razor strop gives a mirror-like finish on the blade which reduces the "drag" exerted on the metal by the hide during cutting.

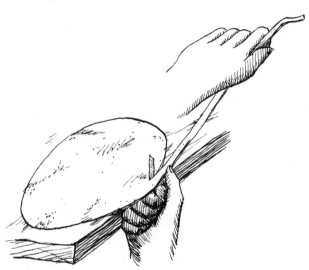

The simplest method of cutting is to lay the disc on a table or other flat surface. A slicing cut is made to begin the spiral on the circumference to the thickness of the lace desired. The right hand's fingers hold the knife blade erect as they press against the edge of the table for support. The thumb of the right hand becomes an adjustable gauge to guide the width of the lace (Fig. 2). The left hand grasps the beginning of the spiral and pulls it away from the body. The lace is cut from the disc as rapidly as the left hand pulls while the disc rotates

Fig. 2, Using the right thumb as a spacing guide against the edge of a table or board.

on the table. One can expect several uneven laces due to inexperience. One can also expect a blistered thumb if much lace is to be cut.

Another method also uses the thumb as a gauge, except that the knife is stabbed into a table or board for support (Fig. 3). Here the most appropriate cutting action is toward the body.

These two methods are a little rough on the thumb, especially if much lace is to be cut. A third method used by white Americans in early times is a little easier on the thumb, for it uses a notched piece of wood as a gauge for the rawhide to rub against (Fig. 4). The width of lace is determined by the distance of the blade to the under part of the notch. The height of the notch above the surface should be a little higher than the thickness of the rawhide. Again, the best direction of cut is toward the body.

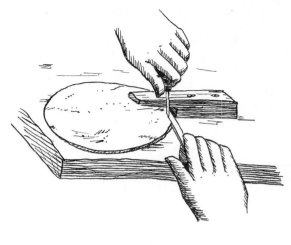

Fig. 3, *Using the right thumb as a spacing guide with knife stabbed into a board.*

Fig. 4, *Using a spacing block as a guide. Width of lace is determined by position of knife.*

Lacing thus cut can be used immediately, or it may need further soaking as described above. If lacing is made for future use, it can be wrapped in loose bundles for drying and storage.

Other Rawhide Uses

Lace, while important to Indian material culture, was not the only purpose to which rawhide was put. Some clubs -- both for pounding food and for pounding enemies -- were covered with sheets of rawhide cut to fit over the stone head and wooden handle and were stitched with babiche. Food pounders were covered only partially so that the actual stone pounding surface remained exposed.

Some food such as nuts, berries, and meat, might be pounded in a rawhide dish made of a disc and dried in a bowl-like form. The famous *pemmican* of the Plains was made by pulverizing dried meat and mixing it with crushed berries and fat. This mixture was made into patties and dried for future use.

Larger pieces of rawhide were used for moccasin soles, especially by the Plains Indians who normally wore footwear with hard soles and soft uppers. (Woodland Indians generally wore one-piece buckskin moccasins or the well-known puckered toe designs.)

Rawhide was also used for making saddles. The frame of the saddle **was** made from appropriately shaped bones and wood, and the whole was laced with wet rawhide. The entire assembly was then covered with wet **rawhide** sheet stitched over for a covering.

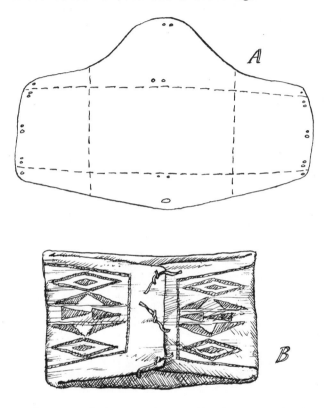

Plains Indians used containers of rawhide called *parfleches* (possibly French; *parer*, to ward off; *fleche*, feather or arrow. To ward off arrows, for rawhide was used for shields.) These suitcases or envelopes were of various sizes and designs and were the basic storage and moving containers of most Plains tribes. The shape varied slightly, but, in essence, it was a rectangle with two end flaps and a flap top and bottom which were folded over and tied (Fig. 5). The rawhide can be bent while damp, and, after drying, can be folded back and forth to remain partly flexible. Parfleches were usually painted with earth colors and other natural pigments. The typical geometric designs were painted by the women who made the parfleches. Pigment was mixed with water and glue and was picked up with a porous bone "brush". The pigment was then rubbed into the rawhide so that it was not merely applied to the surface.

Fig. 5, Plains-style parfleche. A, Typical pattern. B, Painted parfleche, folded and tied. Length folded: 15 inches.

Some Plains men made shields from the hide of the "hump" of the shoulder of a mature buffalo. This portion of the hide is naturally very thick -- over 3/8 inch raw. The hide was shrunk slowly over heat so that it thickened appreciably. It then was dried in a depression in the ground so that it took on a permanently dished form. This process took several months. Such a piece of hide is amazingly hard and would easily stop an arrow. Even a bullet, striking it at an angle, could be deflected. These shields were covered with a buckskin piece laced together on the concave side. Such lacing became the handle, and the buckskin cover was painted and otherwise decorated by the owner. Usually, this cover contained personal symbols of power given to the owner in his visionary ex-

periences. These supernatural devices had power to ward off harm and
amplified the strength of the rawhide shield.

Rawhide is ideally suited for drum heads because of its shrinking characteristics. As a matter of fact, it is still used in drums profession-
ally today. Several drum designs were used by Indians, but all had rawhide heads. Woodland tribes used a water drum in certain ceremonies.
This drum was made of a hollow section of log with a bottom fitted like
a barrel. The head was dampened and held in place with a hoop, much like
a barrel hoop, pressed over it and down the sides to hold the head taut.
The drum was tuned by pouring in a quantity of water through a hole in
the side which was plugged when the proper pitch was achieved. It is said
that this drum was not loud in its immediate vicinity, yet, when placed
on the ground, its sound carried for a considerable distance. Some Southwest tribes made drums by stretching rawhide over an appropriate pottery
shape. The head was held in place with a wrapping of lace. More familiar to the layman is the tambourine or "tom-tom". In the manufacture of
these, a hoop of split green wood about three inches wide was bent and
the overlapping ends laced together. Woodland tribes usually fitted
two heads over the hoop for a front and a back, and a handle was provided somewhere on the hoop. A drum was considered sacred to its owner who
painted the heads with personal symbols of magical powers. In addition,
some Woodland tambourines became a kind of trap drum, for several cords
were stretched inside beneath the head. Small pieces of wood were tied
on these strings so that a beat on the head vibrated the head but also
caused the wood to rattle inside. Plains tambourines usually had only
one head which was laced across the back or opposite side. These laces
provided a handhold for its use.

Oiled rawhide sewed together formed the exterior covering of Eskimo covered *kaiak* or the open boat called the *umiak*. The rawhide lashed frame
of thin wood with the rawhide cover was very light and remarkably re-
silient so that it could be bumped by ice floes and would spring back
into shape. Plains Indians made a *bulboat* of rawhide stretched over a
rude bowl-shaped framework of branches. The unwieldy craft were not very
seaworthy, but could be quickly constructed for crossing streams or riv-
ers and then dismantled to provide rawhide for other functions.

As long as it was kept dry, articles of rawhide were about as permanent
as could be desired. In arid climates, rawhide is still functional after many decades. Tools hafted with rawhide lace or covers permitted unusual shapes to be fitted with handles which otherwise are impossible to
assemble. Rawhide was used until it wore completely out. Old parfleches,
for instance, usually ended up as moccasin soles; some old moccasin soles
still show remnants of parfleche paint. Finally, during some of the dark
history of this nation, uncured rawhide was even made into a thin soup
by starving Indians.

REFERENCES

Griswold, Lester   "Handicraft", 8th Ed., Pub. by the author,
                            Colorado Springs, Colorado, 1942.

Mason, Bernard S.   "Book of Indian Crafts and Costumes", Barnes,
                            N.Y., 1946.

Seton, Julia M.   "American Indian Arts", Ronald Press, N.Y.,
                            1962.

Wissler, Clark   "North American Indians of the Plains",
                            Handbook Series No. 1, American Museum of
                            Natural History, N.Y., 1920.

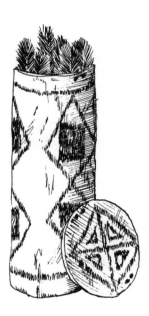

*Fig. 6, Rawhide feathered
headdress container.*

INDIAN-TANNING BUCKSKIN

The image of the American Indian brought to mind by most people today is that of the warrior costumed in fringed buckskin leggings and shirt, buckskin breechcloth and moccasins, and eagle-feather headdress. A maiden who accompanies him is dressed in a fringed white buckskin dress ornamented with beadwork.

This description of a typical American Indian is about as accurate as that which describes all European men as wearing *lederhosen* with suspenders and Tyrolean hats, and all women wearing wooden shoes and Dutch bonnets.

Actually, the men in many tribes wore leggings, but these varied in design and were not necessarily worn the year around. Shirts may have been used by some tribes, but a fur robe was often used in winter instead. The breechcloth was not even standard in all areas. Footwear varied -- a fact attested to by any motion picture cowboy skilled in tracking. ("Those are Cheyenne; I can tell by the footprints.") Women wore dresses at times, but not necessarily of buckskin; even so, they often went "topless". White buckskin was used, but the colored smoked buckskin was more common and functional. (It is interesting to note that the motion picture Indian's costume is always similar to that of current white fashions. Even the women's hemlines correspond to present day fads.)

Buckskin was, nonetheless, an important material for the manufacture of clothing almost universally in North American Indian cultures, but other animals such as elk, moose, and buffalo also yielded hides which were used for clothing. (By definition, a small animal has a "skin", and a larger one has a "hide". Thus a calf or smaller animal has a skin, but a cow or larger has a hide.)

The process of tanning skins or hides was similar with minor variations depending on the animal and the tribe and, sometimes, on the individual tanner. In the main, this paper will describe the tanning process of deer or buckskin by the Woodland culture area Indians.

Skins are often available from hunters, if inquiries are made, in the fall of the year. A skin may be given free to the craftsman, but on the market, a buckskin costs something like two or three "bucks" currently. A raw moose hide can bring ten dollars or more. The few buffalo which are slaughtered provide hides at about twenty-five dollars.

The Whitetail Deer (*Odocoileus virginianus borealis* Miller) is native to the Woodland area and is harvested in large numbers. Wisconsin's harvest has been in excess of 100,000 annually recently. The local newspaper here lists almost daily a car-deer collision, for deer do not obey road crossing signs and usually cross when light is poorest for the motorist. These "road-kill" deer can sometimes be obtained from wardens who have the responsibility of disposing of them. Wardens can also arrange the purchase of confiscated deer taken from over-eager hunters.

I first became excited about Indian tanning when I tried some beadwork sewed directly on commercially-tanned deerskin. After breaking several needles and searching for a man-sized thimble which is non-existent in department stores, I resorted to pulling the needle through with a pliers. I was rapidly acquiring a great respect for Indian seamstresses and mentioned this to a local Winnebago woman. "Oh," she said, "You must be using commercial-tanned skin. You need Indian-tanned skin." I soon discovered why.

Commercial-tanning is mostly a chemical process. The skin is fleshed and dehaired by machine and is split to a thickness of about 1/16 inch. The actual curing uses a chrome solution which penetrates the skin as the tanning agent. Commercial-tanning retains the "grain" of the hair side which forms the coveted "grain leather" of quality goods. Chrome-tanned leather is very durable and will not dry hard after wetting. It is soft, but extremely tough. When sewing, a special "glover's needle" with a triangular cross section and sharp cutting edges must be used, for a regular round needle seems to get caught or bound in its own hole.

Indian-tanning, on the other hand, is mainly a physical process. The suppleness of the skin is due mainly to the stretching and breaking of the cellular fibers which criss-cross each other and thus form the dermis which is the buckskin. These fibers are soft and flexible on the live skin, but, after skinning, dry together into a stiff layer which is rawhide. The physical effort of rubbing the skin to stretch and loosen these fibers requires a strong back and arms. The application of brains and a final smoking of the skin help to retain the velvety suppleness of well-worked leather and permits the skin to remain soft after wetting and drying in use.

Tanning is still considered woman's work. There are still some recognized specialists who tan skins for others. I recently purchased a pair of moccasins from a Schofield (Wisconsin) Winnebago woman who long ago ceased doing the tanning herself. She reported that the moccasins were the last pair she intended to make, because it was too difficult to find anyone to do it. Several Winnebagoes near Wisconsin Rapids still are proficient and use the buckskin mainly for backing for beaded necklaces or for small purses and wallets. One told me that she was considering the purchase of real estate on a river in order to have plenty of water for tanning. A Wisconsin Menomini once quoted me a price of $10.00 for tanning a skin (furnished by me). In this case, the person was male, so that it seems that not all Native Americans are bound by the tradition of sexual division of labor. More recently, I have heard of local prices up to $25.00 a skin. A Canadian trader's price list includes three unsmoked (white) Indian-tanned skins ranging from $17.50 to $27.50.

Ritzenthaler[1] gives a price of $2-4.00 per skin in 1947 and I presume this does not include the price of the skin. As in most Indian crafts, the work justifies a higher price, but buyers are not readily forthcoming if a higher hourly wage is used. This is another craft providing extra money rather than a full-time vocation. A nationally known commercial tannery specializes in deerskins tanned at $2-5.00, depending on the size. It can be seen, even at the $10.00 price, that Indian tanning is not competitive unless one sincerely desires the authentic process.

As aforementioned, skins can be obtained from hunters in late fall or from game wardens if arrangements can be made. One can, at times, purchase skins from jobbers. Many meat-hunters take advantage of the average price of 2 dollars a skin. Ritzenthaler reports that hides sold for "75¢ to $1.50 depending on size and condition."[2]

While a fresh skin is universally preferred, circumstances often require that a dried or salted hide be used. If the hide has simply been stretched and dried, it must be soaked for a few days to return it to the original softness. A fresh "green" hide does not require this. A common practice for temporary curing today is to rub about a pound of salt on the flesh side of a green skin and dry it in a bundle. Commercial tanneries require this step to keep the skin from rotting. If a salted skin is to be used for Indian tanning, it is important to rinse all of the salt out before proceeding. In addition to the several day's soak for a green hide, a salted one should be soaked up to a week and the water changed frequently.

In earlier times, deer could be hunted as needed and could be found. Today, with modern game management techniques, the harvest takes place only in the fall after the rutting season and, usually, bucks only are taken. Ritzenthaler notes that certain skins were considered easier to tan than others. "A fall or winter hide, for example, is thicker and harder to tan than a summer hide.... A buck hide is harder to tan than a doe hide, and a hide from an old animal harder than that of a young one."[3] "It is said that a summer hide, although thinner, is tougher than a winter hide, and was preferred for the making of clothing."[4]

Tools

The tools used are few and simple, but are designed well for their

[1]Ritzenthaler, p. 8.
[2]*Ibid.*
[3]*Ibid.*, pp. 8-9.
[4]*Ibid.*,p. 13.

specific tasks: a knife, a fleshing tool, a scraper, a beamer or de-hairing tool, a stretching frame and cord, and a stretching tool. A needle
and string are necessary for sewing holes and preparing the skin for the
smoking process.

Preparation

The tanning process involves fleshing, de-hairing, braining, stretching,
and smoking. The sequence of the first two may vary from tribe to tribe,
but both are, nevertheless, required. My experience shows that fleshing
is best done first. Work is done outdoors, but most processes can be
done inside if sufficient space is available, the floor can easily be
cleaned, and one does not mind the lingering aroma.

The first step is to wash the skin to remove blood, leaves, dirt, and
the like. A wet deerskin is quite heavy and clumsy to handle. (One
should not be disappointed when, later, the whole skin can be rolled into a bundle the size of a small melon.) It is wrung out by hand -- four
hands are better than two. Incidentally, two persons working together
make the work much lighter. Working by myself, I found that I take too
many "breaks" which could have been filled by a partner.

The several days' soaking and rinsing should cause the skin to expand
enough to allow the hair to "slip". This can be tested by pulling sharply on a small bundle (about a finger's diameter) which should rip out
fairly easily. The skin shouldn't be rotten so that the hair falls out.
Test several places; hair on the shoulders is rather tenacious. Seton[5]
suggests burying the skin in warm ground for up to six days until the
hair begins to slip. Cold does not help this process much. She also
suggests a quicker way using quicklime in a solution of 5 pounds of quicklime to 5 gallons of water. Half of this mixture is added to 20 gallons
of water to make a dilution in which to soak the skin. She says that
12 hours are sufficient to loosen the hair, but she cautions that neither
the skin nor the solution should be touched with bare hands. With this
method the skin should be washed in soap and water and then neutralized
in sal soda or ammonia. This process is, of course, not Indian. It is
said that some Indians spread wood ash on the hair side. This, mixed
with water to bring out the lye, will also cause the hair to slip. This
has been successful for me, but, unfortunately, it also may discolor the
skin -- especially if unsieved ashes are used. An Indian woman register-
ed shock at this method, however. "What are you trying to do, rot the
skin?" she asked. In any method, one needs to be ready to work when the
skin is ready to be worked. Note that the hair should come out cleanly
and should not merely be torn off. Test the hair especially at the shoulder where it seems most tenacious.

[5]Seton, p. 125.

Fleshing

The skin is draped over a flat board or log, and all the flesh and fatty
tissue remaining from skinning must now be removed. I have come to prefer a hunting knife with a thin, flat, sharp blade (Fig. 1). (The custom-

*Fig. 1, My fleshing knife. (Note thin cross-section.) Length
overall: 7 inches.*

ary large hunting knife is really a useless tool, except for chopping
wood.) A slicing cut with the blade held flat against the skin loosens
a bit of tissue so that it can be gripped with the fingernails of the
other hand. The knife continues to slice, in an area of about an inch,

as the opposite hand pulls up on the tissue.
Care should be exercised not to cut into the
skin itself. Such cuts can be immediately noticed and will provide difficulties later. The
completely fleshed side of the skin should have
a non-greasy, although slimy, white surface. If
it appears that the skin is drying as evidenced
by a yellow-tan color appearing, dampen it as
required. Be sure that all fat is removed, for
this will be absorbed into the skin as it dries
and will dry hard later. This caution is especially necessary in warm weather when the fat rapidly becomes soft. All tanning processes are
best done in the shade or on cool days.

A primitive flesher was made from the leg bone
(tibia) of a moose or bear (Fig. 2). A satisfactory substitute is a cow leg bone which is
about 1 1/2 inches wide. About 6-8 inches from
the knee joint the bone is chopped to a slant
edge which is serrated with a saw or file. The
bone, when fresh, can be shaped rather easily
with a hatchet and file. More recent fleshers,
showing white influence, are similar in design
but with a serrated steel blade. The joint end

Fig. 2, Bone fleshing   of the bone usually has a loop of buckskin which
tool. Length: 8 inches. is looped around the back of the wrist and held
                            against the tool in the palm of the hand in a
manner similar to that of holding a ski pole today. With this grip, a
downward chopping motion actually tightens the strap on the wrist so that
the tool is forced into the hand with each stroke. Densmore reports on
the use of this tool by the Chippewa:

"...The flesh next to the hide was removed by laying the hide over the top of a post so that it hung loosely all around. Four cuts were made in the fleshy tissue, these cuts being where the hide rested on top of the pole. Beginning at these cuts the tissue was worked loose by means of a bone implement, and entirely removed."[6]

The same design of tool is found all over North America. It was used by the Plains Indians except that the skin was stretched over the ground and the flesh removed in this position.

The knife, which I prefer, tends to make quite a smooth surface on the skin. The bone tool, used to hack or chop, creates a characteristic texture of shallow grooves from its serrations.

When fleshing is completed and the skin has achieved the clammy but not greasy surface mentioned above, it should be washed to remove clinging particles of tissue. It is then wrung out for beaming. A good fleshing job may take 2-3 hours depending on the skinning job.

Beaming

A *beaming* or *de-hairing post* is now required. The post is made from a log about 6-8 feet long or a piece of half-round slab wood sunk in the

Fig. 4, Beaming board. Length: 4 1/2 feet.

Fig. 3, Beaming post set into ground. Length above ground: 4 1/2 feet.

ground at about a 45 degree angle so that the projecting 4-5 feet portion is about belly high -- below the waist (Fig. 3). This post should be buried firmly, for there will be considerable downward pressure applied on it. A beaming board can be made instead from a half-round board about 2 x 8-10 inches and 4-5 feet long, and fitted with spread legs to hold it on an angle at the desired height (Fig. 4). In this case, the low end of the board may be shoved against a trunk or some solid object to keep it from

[6]Densmore, p. 164.

moving during the beaming process. Densmore observed and photographed a Chippewa woman who kneeled on the ground and held on her legs "a log which was braced against the root of a tree."[7] I'm sure that this simple, portable device has some merits, but I don't think that they outweigh the difficulty of kneeling for a few hours. I recently made a portable beaming board from a rounded piece of 2 x 10, 5 feet long and fitted on the bottom with two wedge-shaped blocks of wood on which were screwed two 3/4 inch pipe flanges (Fig. 5). The shape of the wooden wedges determine the spread and, therefore, the length of the legs. Black iron pipe was cut to appropriate lengths to be screwed into the flanges. These legs can be unscrewed again for storage or transport.

The wrung-out skin is draped, hair side up, over the top of the beaming post or board. The skin is held in place by leaning over the board from the projecting end and pinching the skin against the board with the tanner's belly. It will therefore be seen that the board or post should be rounded, and peeled or shaved smooth. It is important that this surface should not have pits or projections which may catch on the skin or cause the beamer to dig in. In addition, the projecting end of the post or board should be somewhat rounded to the same purpose.

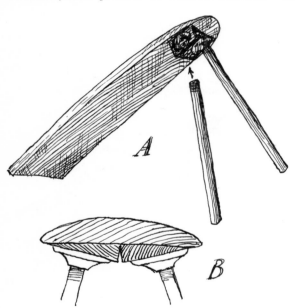

A

B

The *beamer* is a scraping tool made of a straight branch about 2-2 1/2 inches diameter and about 20 inches long. The diameter of the ends of this tool is determined somewhat by the diameter which is most comfortable for the tanner to grip. The scraper blade, earlier made from flint chips, is made by breaking off the handle from a common table knife and imbedding the blade into the center of the handle of the beamer. A hammer can be used to drive the blade in until about 1/4 inch remains exposed (Fig. 6). The blade is then filed smooth and square

Fig. 5, Portable beaming board with unscrewable pipe legs. B, Cross section at legs.

with slightly rounded ends. It is the pressure of the tool and its scraping action, not a sharp cutting edge, which removes the hair.

As the tanner leans forward over the board, she grips the beamer with

[7]*Ibid.*

Fig. 6, Beamer. Length: 20 inch, diameter: 2 1/2 inches.

both hands so that the blade, tilted slightly back, scrapes along the top of the board with a firm downward stroke (Fig. 7). (A waterproof apron is desirable. Clothes wet with tanning water are uncomfortable to the wearer and smelly to everyone else.) The hair is thus pushed off the skin in long strokes, always from the body downward. Take care that there are no ripples or folds, because these may catch the blade and cut the skin. Also be sure that the beamer is not slid sideways, for this is sure to slice into the skin. Although the skin stretches with the stroke, especially near the margins of the skin, it usually stays in place fairly well on the board. When the area on top of the board has been de-haired, the skin is re-positioned to present a new surface, and work continues. With hard work, and depending on how well the hair slips, it takes 2-5 hours to finish the job. Hair on an especially difficult hide can be sheared somewhat before beaming to facilitate the process.

Fig. 7, Using a beamer to de-hair a deerskin on a beaming board.

The *scarf skin* or *epidermis* is usually removed in Indian-tanning. Such skins have relatively little difference between the grain or hair side and the flesh side unlike commercially-tanned skins. Why the scarf skin is removed is not known except that some of this surface comes off with beaming and its entire removal may merely be a way to make the surface uniform. All of the scarf skin is scraped off, but care should be taken that the remaining skin is not scraped too thin or cut. Some care needs to be taken around bullet holes so that these are not stretched larger.

The by-product of this process, an amazingly large quantity of deer hair, today has no purpose and should be buried. Ritzenthaler[8] notes that this hair was formerly used as mattress stuffing and was preferred as stuffing for horse collars.

Some students have left a fresh skin go so long that they found that they could pull out almost all of the hair by hand; i.e., without a beamer and board. Try this, if you like, but you'll observe that the smell gets pretty strong. You'll still need to remove the scarf skin. One student left this on and his result was similar to a commercially tanned grain leather (which you can buy for less than your labor is worth.)

Braining

An important step in tanning is the addition of brainy matter to the skin. Earlier, the deer brain was available with the deerskin. Today, the brain is less accessible, especially if the skin was obtained from someone else. Ritzenthaler[9] states, "while beaver, rabbit, and pig were sometimes used, deer is by far the most common." I have found that a few meat markets carry veal brains in pound containers which quantity is about enough for an average skin.

Place the brains in a pan of water about enough to cover -- a quart or so. Simmer this for about a quarter hour or until they turn a grayish-white. The brain tissue should be mashed during the cooking. If possible, the creamy mixture should be strained to get rid of the lumps, but I seldom bother, because the lumps can be easily scraped off after the skin is stretched. Lyford[10] notes that a little fat is added to the mixture. Seton,[11] giving a Southwest or Plains method, states that liver, grease, powdered yucca and salt is added. Local Winnebagoes use brains alone. The cooked mixture is allowed to cool and is then ready for use. A recent innovation in braining has come to my attention without the opportunity to try it at this time. If brains are difficult to find, Wesson oil or a similar table oil has been used as a substitute. No precise amount was given, but, it seems to me, that about a cup would contain a quantity of oil close to that of a deer brain. I would expect that such "oil tanned" leather would be in some danger of getting rancid, so smoking becomes more of a necessity than just for color.

The fleshed and de-haired skin is washed, sometimes in soap and water, and rinsed. It is then

   "twisted into a rope. This skin is placed around a tree, the ends

[8]Ritzenthaler, p. 13.
[9]*Ibid.*, p. 9.
[10]Lyford, "Ojibwa Crafts", p. 98.
[11]Seton, p. 123.

overlapped and rolled together to secure them tightly and a stout, smooth, round stick about three feet in length is inserted and the roll is twisted tightly up to the tree, the stick being turned to one side, then to the other, wringing the moisture out of the skin and stretching it."[12] (Fig. 8).

Fig. 8, Wringing out the skin.

A smooth tree or pole should be chosen for wringing, or a protective covering should be wrapped around it. I use an ax handle or baseball bat for a wringing stick. The twisting action should be done with some strength. Don't worry about tearing the skin; it's too tough. The water may even spurt out under the pressure, but the skin is remarkably strong. Wring out the skin several times this way to remove as much liquid as possible.

An Alaskan method of wringing out the skin requires four holes to be cut on the rear end of the skin so that a 3-4 foot stick can be inserted through them. The other end is tied to a post and the stick is used to twist the skin. The stick is pulled as it is twisted so that the skin doesn't ball up right away. Regardless of how you wring it out after braining, it should be wrung as dry as possible before stretching.

The result of this twisting is a strange looking, stiff rag of skin which, when untwisted, still needs to be stretched. This can be accomplished by grabbing it with the fingers of both hands and pulling it apart. Certain wrung-out areas may have been squeezed semi-dry and may appear yellow compared to the rest of the skin which is still damp and bluish-white. Rubbing the skin together in these areas will even out the dampness so that the whole appears to be evenly white.

When the hand-stretching has returned the skin to a reasonably pliable condition, the skin is thoroughly immersed in the cooled brain mixture which is rubbed and kneaded into the skin. Ritzenthaler[12] says that the Chippewas leave it in this mixture for five minutes or even less. Lyford states that the mixture is "rubbed in with the hands and a smooth stone

[12]Ritzenthaler, p. 10.

until it is almost completely absorbed..., rolled up tightly, and left
overnight."[13] Ritzenthaler[14] says further that a winter hide would be
wrung out and re-brained. Local Winnebagoes do not leave it in overnight, but consider that five minutes is far from sufficient. I tend to
agree with the latter, but I usually leave the skin in overnight -- just
to be sure.

My experience has been that the oily brain mixture needs full penetration into the skin fibers. If this can be done, according to the tanner's judgement, one braining is sufficient. Otherwise, two are required.

The brained skin is again wrung out by hand and on the wringing pole to
remove excess moisture (and there is now much excess) and stretched by
hand again, all as described earlier.

Holes may now be stitched up with needle and sturdy thread or string, although this is not always done at this point. If holes are to be sewed
up, a sharp awl is very necessary, because the skin is quite slimy, very
tough, and almost impossible to shove a needle through. Awl holes make
this much easier.

Stretching

Four poles about 8 feet long and 4-5 inches in diameter are cut, peeled,
and smoothed. Two are set in the ground about 6 feet apart. The other
two are lashed horizontally onto these -- one at about knee level and
the other about 6-12 inches above the head. The rectangular opening between the poles should be larger than the estimated final size of the
skin. This frame is normally situated in a shady spot. If not placed
permanently, it may be moved against a firm support such as two trees.
A lot of pressure is exerted on this frame from both sides so it should
be as substantial as possible. It helps to lash the frame to the support or you may find the whole assembly will buckle later.

*Fig. 9, Ax handle stretching tool. Length: 32 inches. B, Alternate
pattern.*

[13]Lyford, "Ojibwa Crafts", p. 98-99.
[14]Ritzenthaler, p. 10.

A stretching tool also needs to be made. This can be made from an **ax** handle, the head of which has been whittled to a blunt point and made as smooth as possible so as not to tear the skin (Fig. 9A). A good hard-wood point will literally be polished by the stretching friction later. Some Indians prefer the customary flat end of the ax handle (Fig. 9B).

The skin may be draped over a surface such as the beaming board or held in the lap so that holes can be punched at intervals along the margin of the skin. So that they do not tear out, these holes should be about 3/4 inches apart. I tried an ice pick as an awl for this, but I found that the holes were too small for the cord I intended to use. I now use a knife to cut slits parallel to the skin margins. With a knife, how-ever, one should take care not to make these holes too large; they tend to stretch anyway.

Fig. 10, Preliminary lashing to stretch-ing frame.

Now a cord is passed in one hole and out the next. I found that a small diameter clothes line is fine for this purpose. The Winnebagoes like to use five cords for this purpose -- one for each side from neck to foreleg, one on each side from fore-leg to hind leg, and one across the tail from hind leg to hind leg (Fig. 10). The remaining ends of these cords are tied to the frame so as to hang the skin roughly in the center of the frame. Naturally, long enough cords need to be provid-ed. To hang the skin easily, one of the belly cords is tied to the top pole of the frame near a side pole. Then the cord from the other leg on the side is tied to the top pole so that the skin now hangs down, albeit bunched up. It mat-ters none if the neck of the skin is to right or left. The rear cords and top neck cord are now tied to the side poles, and the remaining cords are tied on the bottom pole complimentary to the first ones. The cords can now be loosened and retied so that the skin is suspended in the cen-ter of the frame. The skin should not be stretched too much at this time.

Finally a long cord, or several cords, is passed through the holes in the skin including the edge lacing cord already in the holes and around the poles in a continuous "whip stitch". In this method, any irregular-ities on the margins are given even tension as the final lacing goes through the holes, 'round the pole, through the holes, 'round the pole, and so on. The ends of this cord are, of course, fastened to the pole at appropriate points. Not every hole in the skin is laced; one or two

may be skipped at each interval, but I encourage using too many rather
than too few. By evening up the tension on these cords and adjusting
the tension on the primary cords, the skin can be stretched taut in the
frame.

This is now a good time to shave or scrape the skin to a
uniform thickness. A scraper is made with a steel blade
filed to a semicircular cutting edge bent at right angles
to the shaft which is lashed to a handle (Fig. 11). With
this tool the skin can be scraped in those areas, such as
the shoulders, which are quite thick. Indian buckskin is
generally quite even and thin throughout. One can judge
the thickness by observing the amount of translucency
of the skin. This scraping can be done from the flesh
and hair sides. In the latter case, because the scarf
skin has already been removed, such scraping does not
materially affect the surface. Loose bits of tissue can
still be removed from the flesh side with the knife.
Such scraping, done intermittently during the stretching
to come, produces the velvety nap characteristic of Indian
tanning.

Gripping the stretching tool with one hand near the butt
and one hand near the point, and standing somewhat at an
angle to the skin, the tanner now rubs the surface of the
skin vigorously (Fig. 12). I mean vigorously! Long, arc-
like sweeping strokes are used with some speed and pressure, and the skin stretches considerably under the pressure. Care is taken around the holes and near the margins. The best action is a back and forth cross-hatching
over the surface many times. Every minute portion of the
skin receives this treatment. The pressure of the tool
stretches and breaks the skin fibers. The rapid stroke
generates some friction which helps to dry the skin.

One should become ambidexterous here, for the arms tire
quickly. Two women normally work together taking turns.
I strongly urge this.

*Fig. 11,
Steel scrap-
er. Length:
14 inches.*

As the skin gradually returns to its original size, work
ceases long enough to adjust the cords to keep the skin
taut at all times. The frame may need to be braced or lashed because of
the tension on it. The skin, which was cold, clammy, and white begins
to feel merely cool, somewhat drier, more opaque, and begins to take on
an ivory cast.

Such work can proceed from both sides of the frame if it is mounted in
a vertical position. Some tribes like to tilt the frame at about 45 degrees so that stretching pressure is downward rather than sideways.
Plains tribes stretched the skin above the ground with pegs and worked
in this position. Some tribes used a frame which was placed above the

Fig. 12, Stretching the skin with an ax handle.

ground horizontally, combining the Woodland frame with the Plains position.

In any case, some time is involved in changing the skin to soft, white,
dry buckskin. Ritzenthaler says this requires "about an hour and a half,
depending upon the weather."[15] Lyford says this "may require two or
three hours."[16] Winnebago women told me that it takes two of them the
better part of a day to do this step. I tend to agree with them based
on my experience.

The weather does make a difference. As stated before, work usually takes
place in the shade. A dry, windy day is not considered best for stretching because the skin dries too fast. If this should happen the skin
should be dampened slightly so that the break-up of the tissue is not
hurried. If the skin dries hard, it may be taken down and re-brained,
and the process repeated. Rub and stretch the skin until it is *thoroughly* dry.

Experience in classes indicate that students do not always have the continuous time available for stringing a skin in a frame and stretching it
all in one sitting. Some students have found that they prefer to use a
stake (see "Tanning of Small Furs") which takes less space and, therefore, can be used indoors or out. The stake does not require the hour

[15]*Ibid.*, p. 11.
[16]Lyford, "Ojibwa Crafts", p. 100.

or so for punching holes and stringing up the skin. Also, if the skin
is not stretched completely dry at once, it can be wrapped in a plastic
bag temporarily so that work can easily continue. Don't let these per-
iods of pause continue too long; remember that putrification has begun
already.

Some persons like to use an unpointed or flat ax-handle or a canoe paddle for a stretching tool. Such wider blades allow one to rub over
small holes in the skin with less chance of ripping them open as does
a pointed stick.

The result of the effort is a skin which is soft, pliable, white, with
a felt-like surface from the scraping. It is then ready for smoking
and can be taken down by releasing the cords.

Smoking

Any holes should be sewed up with needle and thread or string. Stitching should be quite easy now that the skin is softened. Some skins are
left white as they come from the frame. More often the skins are smoked
which, it is said, permits them to return to a flexible state after they
have been wet. Also, the smoky odor tends to repel vermin.

The entire skin is next sewed up into a rude bag with a wide bottom of
about 15 inches diameter at the bottom and a small opening at the top to
permit smoke to escape. Which part of the skin is top or bottom is un-
important.

Some Indians sew a canvas or scrap buckskin cylinder about a foot high
at the bottom of the bag so that the new skin does not get too close to
the fire or become soiled.

A rather calm day is selected or smoking is done in a shelter. I tried
the garage once and nearly was overcome with smoke. Earlier, a fire was
built in a low pit and allowed to burn to coals. Now, some people use
an old steel can for this purpose. Charcoal is an excellent fuel for beginning a smudge fire.

Some smudge material is added on top of the coals to create a dense smoke.
The fire needs some oxygen to burn enough for smoke, but needs constant
control to keep it from flaming up. Smoke is required but not heat. The
smudge material varies according to tribe and the individual. Lyford
lists "soft inner bark of the pine tree, pine punk or other rotten wood,
chips of green wood, crushed cedar bark, or birch bark packed with cones
of Norway or white pine."[17] Ritzenthaler adds poplar wood to the list.[18]
Densmore[19] states that her informant used dry corncobs. Wisconsin
Winnebagoes prefer sumac twigs.

[17]*Ibid.*, p. 100-101.
[18]Ritzenthaler, p. 12.
[19]Densmore, p. 165.

Fig. 13, Smoking the skin suspended from a branch. Skin is stitched to a canvas cylinder which is placed over the fire in a metal pail.

With a good thick smoke billowing up, the skin bag is now suspended over the fire which is not flaming at all (Fig. 13). The bag can be hung from a branch if the fire is built beneath a tree. A pole can be set in the ground to lean over the fire to provide a place to tie the bag. Sometimes a stick tipi is made and the skin draped over it. If a pail is used for the fire, the skin can be hung around it, especially if the canvas cylinder has been stitched on the bottom of the bag. This keeps the skin from being burnt in contact with the hot metal. The bag can easily be lifted to examine the fire, add fuel, or allow air to enter. If the fire was built on the ground, the skin is pegged down with a shallow trough created to allow air to enter the fire. Sometimes an X is made with green twigs and inserted near the bottom to keep it spread open.

The rising smoke inside the bag stains the skin and permeates into its fibers. Smoke should issue from every minute opening in the bag. The color created varies from light cream to dark brown with a range of orange and tan in between dependent upon the smudge material and length of smoking. Each tanner claims that her choice is best. The bag needs to be adjusted from time to time to make sure that all areas inside are receiving an equal share of smoke; otherwise, the skin will come out uneven in color. If at any time a flame appears, the skin must *immediately* be removed and the flame smothered with more fuel. Even a finger of flame in contact with the skin will cause it to pucker up permanently. Lyford[20] states that a very thin skin may need only ten minutes. Ritzenthaler[21] reports that 15-20 minutes is required for a rather light smoking. For a rich orange, I have smoked a skin for over an hour. Heavy hide or a dark color requires up to three or four hours.

These times refer to the smoking of the inside of the bag. This needs now to be repeated for the other side. The bag is taken down, turned inside out and re-smoked until the new side receives a color comparable to

[20]Lyford, "Ojibwa Crafts", p. 101.
[21]Ritzenthaler, p. 13.

the previous side.

When both sides have been smoked sufficiently, the bag is taken down and the seams undone. String holding holes closed may also be cut open.

The skin may be folded or rolled up and set aside "to set the color." It may also be used immediately. Indian tanned skins have a typically pungent aroma which remains for years. Unless one is accustomed to the smell, it may be well to hang the skin outdoors for a few days to dispell some of the odor. Watch out for dogs! The skin is really smoked animal tissue and may seem to a dog to be nothing more than a flat summer sausage.

Conclusion

The buckskin is now ready for manufacture into useful articles. As mentioned before, the deerskin is not large as leathers go. A typical buck will measure about 6 square feet or so. A pair of leggings requires one skin per leg. A jacket or dress was made by sewing two large skins together so that the forelegs become rude sleeves and the neck is left open for the wearer's head. Two or three pairs of moccasins can be cut from one skin, depending on pattern and judicious layout. Some skins were tanned with the hair remaining. In this case, the tanning must proceed before the hair begins to slip. Processes are generally the same as above with the obvious omission of the de-hairing step. Such skins were used for robes, mats or blankets.

Besides clothing, skins were used for other artifacts. Bag containers were in common use. The beautifully beaded or quilled pipe bags are often superb examples of Indian art. Scraps of buckskin were cut into discs and cut "' round and 'round" in a spiral to produce lace or thongs of varied widths.

One will agree with me, after tanning a skin, that no piece of skin, however small, should be discarded as scrap.

REFERENCES

Densmore, Frances	"Chippewa Customs", *Bureau of American Ethnology Bulletin*, No. 86, 1929.
Hoffman, Walter J.	"The Menomini Indians", *Bureau of Ethnology, 14th Annual Report*, 1892-93.
Lyford, Frances	"Iroquois Crafts", Department of Interior, Bureau of Indian Affairs, 1945.
------	"Ojibwa Crafts", Department of Interior, Bureau of Indian Affairs, 1943.
Mason, Bernard S.	"Book of Indian Crafts and Costumes", Barnes, N.Y., 1946.
Ritzenthaler, Robert	"Chippewa Indian Method of Securing and Tanning Deerskin", *Wisconsin Archaeologist* (New Series), Vol. 28, No. 1., 1947.
Seton, Julia M.	"American Indian Arts", Ronald Press, N.Y., 1962.
Wissler, Clark	"North American Indians of the Plains", *Handbook Series*, No. 1, American Museum of Natural History, N.Y., 1920.

TANNING OF SMALL FURS

The following process may be helpful to those who wish to attempt tanning small furs at home rather than sending them to commercial tanneries. Although the tools are few and can be made by most handymen, and the chemicals are relatively inexpensive and readily available, the hours of effort that go into tanning and the quality of the end product are such that the expense of the commercial tannery is a better bargain than doing the work oneself. Certainly, a fine quality, rare pelt should not be practiced on, but, for those who have the time and inclination, and inexpensive pelts, here goes.

Tanning-Tawing

The process to be described here is technically not tanning at all, but "tawing", to be quite precise. Tanning, by definition, requires the use of tannic acid to soften and preserve the skin. The most common source of tannic acid or "tannin" today is the Live Oak tree (a specific species, not merely any living oak tree). The term, tannin, derives from the old name for oaks and firs (possibly the same root as the German *tannenbaum*). Tawing, on the other hand, refers more to curing skins with chemicals rather than tanning. Tawing seems best suited for furs while tanning is superior for leather. Common usage does not differentiate between these terms, so, for the sake of convenience if not accuracy, I shall use the term "tanning" interchangeably henceforth.

Tanning kits

Tanning kits are available from classified advertisers in sports magazines. Generally, however, the information given here is similar for procedures do not vary much. Chemicals offered in these kits usually are the same as can be purchased locally in super markets or drug stores, usually at a savings. Some kits may include chromium salts or alum, but the acid method described below appears superior for fur skins. Beware of "tanning secrets" ads. I just paid two dollars (in advance) for a single, neatly printed page which is no more secretive than a summary of what I give in detail.

Prices

The cost for a few skins tanned at home will probably be a dollar or two, depending on the quantities of chemicals purchased at one time. A rule-of-thumb average for most small skins would be about fifty cents. Commercial tanning prices today for small animals (squirrel, fox, rabbit) vary from about $2.00 to $7.50. Larger animals (coyote, bobcat) usually run over $10.00 per pelt and are best left to professionals. Prices, of course, do not include shipping. One would do well to practice on something small and inexpensive or poor quality. A run-of-the-mill muskrat skin may be worth less than a dollar, and squirrels may be obtained free from most hunters. Domestic rabbit skins are about ten cents from persons who raise them for meat.

Because a rabbit skin is so delicate, this is not a good beginning experiment (unless you don't mind small shreds). Don't start out on a deer-skin! Buckskin can be tanned, with the hair on or off, with this method; but until you know from experience what is involved, a buckskin can become an overwhelming frustration. Start small.

Supplies

The following materials are needed for tawing: a few ounces of *carbolic acid* (now called *phenol*) in either liquid or crystal form, a few ounces of *sulphuric acid*, some *borax* or bicarbonate of soda, a bottle of *neats-foot oil*, and several pounds of common *salt*. A gallon or two of *naptha, benzine*, or *"white" gasoline* is necessary for de-greasing as is a quart or so of *denatured alcohol*. (The latter may be sold as shellac solvent.)

Water is so obvious that it should not even be mentioned here, except that, traditionally, tanning water has been, literally, rain-water soft. I have no means of collecting rain-water, so I am forced to use tap-water from our well. This seems to work satisfactorily, but I have been able to make no comparison. The claim is made that rain-water is "pur-er" and that the chemicals work better in it.

Tools

Home tanning requires a few tools which can be made by an amateur and which should last a long time. Other tools are available locally.

Formerly, tanning liquids were put into enamelled or wooden containers to prevent contamination by contact with metals. Today, I find that a few small plastic garbage cans or pails are quite satisfactory and perhaps superior. Do be careful, however, to see that the plastic is not the kind which will soften in contact with your de-greasing solution.

A pair of rubber gloves is required for handling skins in the various solutions. A rubber or plastic apron might also prove useful.

A common spoon is often used by
trappers for scraping fresh skins.
A large tablespoon held in the
hand with one's thumb in the bowl
of the spoon works quite well.
I like to use a paint scraper
(Fig. 1) for scraping fat and
flesh away. A blade about 2
inches across is satisfactory.

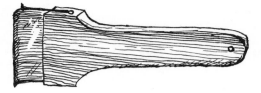

Fig. 1, Paint scraper.

Some trappers also use the old-fashioned zinc Mason jar lid as a scraper.

To shave the thickness of some heavy skins, a "skiving knife" may need
to be provided. A commercial one can be purchased for about $7.50, but
the one illustrated in Fig. 2 will be quite satisfactory and can be made

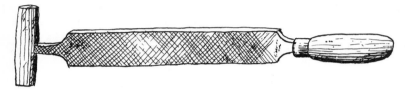

Fig. 2, Skiving knife made from a file.

from an old file by grinding or forging another tang at the blunt end
and affixing a T-handle. Grind off the teeth to create sharp, square
corners along all four edges. Any of these edges may be used as may be
convenient. The knife is used either as a pushing or drawing instrument depending on how the skin is held. The knife is pushed or pulled
across the surface of the skin with the blade at a slight tilt to scrape
or shave the surface. Both hands must be used. The T-handle helps to
keep the tilt of the blade constant. Keep the edges sharp. Some professional skiving knives are similar to a drawknife in that each edge
is bevelled to a knife-edge. Some knives also may be curved slightly into a crescent to match a curved fleshing board.

Fig. 3, Fleshing frames.

For small skins, a collection of fleshing boards should be provided.
Fig. 3 illustrates some representative shapes. Almost any wood will suffice, but the edges should be rounded and sanded smooth. The thickness
should be one inch or less for the smallest. The fox board measures
about 8" wide by about 4 ft. long. A weasel board may be 1 1/2" wide by
2 ft. and can be made from a 1/4" box slat. These are easy to make and
several should be available to account for variations in size. Skins
should stretch snugly, but not excessively. While these are necessary

to the tanner for fleshing, they can also double for drying stretchers when fresh or "green" skins are obtained. Normally, green skins are dried on such frames and are removed for storage or shipment. Incidentally, rust-proof wire frames are also used for the latter purpose. These boards are required only when skins are removed "cased" from the animal. A cased skin is stripped off with a single cut across the hind legs and through the anus. This allows the skin to be

Fig. 4, Fleshing board.

pulled off over the head, almost as in peeling a banana. Casing is standard for most furs, but some are skinned "open"; i.e., cut along the center of the belly so that the skin lies flat or open.

A floor fleshing board (Fig. 4) should be made for larger skins or those which have been skinned open. The rounded top end should be about as high as the waist of the tanner. The legs should be sturdy enough to resist some pressure. The top of the board should be planed and sanded to a smooth half-rounded contour. A 2 inch by 10 inch by 5 foot board makes a good fleshing board. This board is used by draping the skin, flesh side up over the rounded upper end and allowing the excess skin to hang down. The tanner pushes his belly against this end which holds the skin in place while he pushes the fleshing knife down and away from him. (It helps to wear a waterproof apron while fleshing with this board.)

A stretching stake or beamer is a necessity although the back of a chair will suffice in an emergency. A 2 x 8 board about 30 inches long is rounded at the top and is firmly attached to a sturdy base (Fig. 5A). The rounded top must be planed to about a 1/8-1/4 inch edge which is sanded very smooth. One of the last steps in tanning is to break the skin's fibers over this edge by rubbing it back and forth.

Another stake (Fig. 5B) may be made with a serrated metal edge insert which helps to break up tough fibers on heavy skins. For this stake a slot is sawed on the end to receive a semi-circular metal blade, the curve of which is filed into fine saw-teeth about 1/8 inch apart. These obviously are not very sharp lest they cut the skin to shreds. Sometimes, on a dried skin, the surface dries extremely hard, and the tanning liquid cannot penetrate this. A few pulls over the saw teeth break this surface up effectively. I have tried brass for this edge, but it apparently leaves a dirty stain of copper (?) on the leather. I now use steel which leaves no mark.

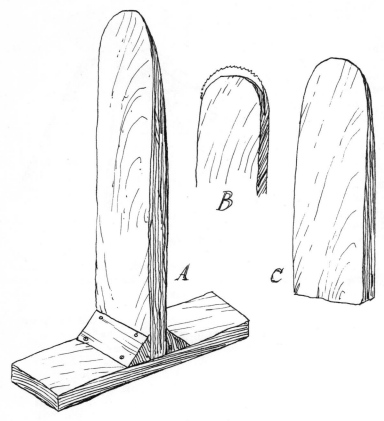

A plan is sug-
gested for a
small stake which
can be held in
a vise on a work
bench (Fig. 5C).
This can be made
of one inch lum-
ber, but should
be rounded and
tapered as with
the first stake.

If you like to
work outside
(which saves a
lot of sweeping
indoors as well
as a stinky
floor), the stake
can simply be
driven into the
ground to a con-
venient height.
Because there
is considerable
lateral pressure
on the end, this
stake should be
driven quite
deep. In a
pinch, a wooden

*Fig. 5, Stretching stakes or beamers. A, Standard
floor model. B, Metal saw-tooth insert. C, Vise
model.*

chair back can be used as a stake,
but, obviously, the process won't
improve the chair.

A dull metal or wooden blade called a "slicker" may be desired at
times to remove excess water from
rinsing (Fig. 6). This is used
as a squeegee with the skin flat
on a board. If this is used on
the hair side of a skin, be sure
to keep the strokes "with the grain" of the fur.

*Fig. 6, Slickers. A, Metal edge. B,
All wood.*

Handling Fresh Skins

Techniques of skinning are documented elsewhere. If in doubt, some treatise on taxidermy or zoology will probably provide help.

A fresh skin taken in the fall or winter usually needs only to be stretched flesh side out on a fleshing board so that excess fat and muscle tissue can be removed. If the skin is removed immediately after the animal
is killed, the skin often peels off with minimal cutting. Be sure to
get off all fat (which is especially difficult with a greasy animal such
as a 'coon), for this can "burn" the skin which then will not make good
leather. Animals with furry tails (not muskrat, for instance) usually
have the tails split open and are de-boned. Small animals, such as wea-
sels, usually are merely de-boned. Muskrat tails are simply cut off.

If tanning is not to proceed immediately, a wood or wire frame stretcher
is then used to hold the skin in shape as it dries. Some skins, such
as fox or coyote, are removed from the stretcher just before they are
completely stiff, turned right out (fur side out) and hung up to dry.
Smaller skins are usually dried flesh side out. If the skins are kept
in a cool, dry place, they usually will keep for several months. Be
sure, however, that there is no chance for mildew or for the skin to become rancid from getting too warm. Furs are never salted to preserve
them. Leather skins, such as deer or calf, which will be de-haired, usually are salted.

Softening

Prepare enough of the following to cover the skin:

    1 gal. water
    1 oz. (liquid) or 1 tbsp. (crystals) phenol (carbolic acid)

If the skin has been dried, immerse it slowly into the solution, taking
care not to crack it, until it is completely covered. A fresh (green)
skin can be placed in the solution immediately. The phenol solution re-
laxes the skin and makes it quite pliable. It may shrink the skin somewhat if it has been dried tightly stretched. Also important is the fact
that the phenol kills bacteria which, if allowed to remain, will rot the
skin and cause the hair to "slip" or pull out. (I know of one person who
went through all the remaining procedures only to have the hair slip at
the very end. Did you ever see a naked squirrel?)

I strongly advise using rubber gloves while handling skins in the solution because phenol can be absorbed directly through one's skin. Accidental splashes should be flushed with water and washed with soap.
Splashes in one's eyes may require treatment by a doctor. *Be careful!*

Twelve hours is sufficient for a small skin such as a muskrat. Heavier
skins may need a full day. The skin should be quite supple in any case.

A longer period is not objectionable. A green skin may not need the treatment, but I believe that the bacteria-killing bath is desirable for a few hours nevertheless.

Fleshing

When the skin is well softened, remove it from the phenol and rinse it well. This is also a good time to wash it with soap[1] and water to remove dirt and blood. Squeeze out the excess water; do not wring it out. If you have a slicker, this may be used here.

Stretch the skin out on an appropriate board. With a razor-sharp knife cut away any loose bits of flesh or fat which still remain. It should go without saying that these cuts should not go into the skin nor through it. Use the paint scraper, fleshing knife, or skiving knife to clean the skin further. (A good job of skinning in the first place cuts this job down to a minimum.) Be sure to get off as much fat as possible, for fat will interfere with the tanning solution. The fat comes off most easily when the skin is cold, so work in a cool room or outdoors if it is convenient. If the room becomes too warm, the fat becomes buttery and tends to be spread out rather than scraped off. Clean the scraper blade often.

Thick skins may need to be thinned down or "skived". Use the skiving knife, but carefully. A sliding cut will slice through rather than shave it off. Take care also not to skive too much to the point where the hairs appear on the flesh side.

Some tanners prefer to do this skiving earlier, when the skin is still stiff and dry. Try both methods. Small skins are often thin enough naturally and need not be skived at all, but, in general, the thinner the skin, the softer the leather.

Degreasing

Depending on the quality of your fleshing job and, to some extent, the amount of fat on the animal naturally, the skin may need to be degreased. A squirrel, for instance, may already be clean enough, while a raccoon is always too greasy.

Mix enough of the following to cover the skin:

    1 part alcohol
    2-3 parts benzine or naptha or "white" gasoline.

Do not use this fluid in an unventilated room! Better still, work out-

---

[1]"Soap" means a mild, bland soap such as Ivory. Don't use the modern detergents.

doors, for this is an extremely flammable liquid which even a spark **can** set off. The vapor is also dangerous to breathe.

The benzine will dissolve the grease in the skin. The alcohol combines well with both benzine and water. It therefore helps the benzine enter the skin and, later, helps evaporation of the mixture. Immerse the skin completely and work it around in the mixture. Again I recommend rubber gloves unless you don't mind degreased hands.

After a few minutes of this, strip off the excess liquid from the skin and whirl it around to remove more (outdoors, of course).

To dry the skin more, work it into a box or bag of fine sawdust. Hardwood sawdust is preferred. I imagine that the resins in conifer wood might also be dissolved in benzine and might combine with the skin. Some tanners use cornmeal or bran for this, but I'm too cheap to buy some. Clean, maple sawdust is fine; I've found that oak seems to stain the leather somewhat. Work the sawdust well into the fur and flesh sides several times and shake it out as completely as possible each time. The skin should now have lost its clammy feeling and should seem noticeably drier to the touch. Some additional scraping may be possible at this point.

If, judging by experience, the skin is sufficiently degreased so that the tanning fluid can penetrate well, work may proceed to the next step. If not, additional washings in the benzine solution may be required.

Some of the solution may be salvaged for future work. The clear liquid at the top of your container may be decanted into a container to be sealed and set aside. The grease is usually apparent at the bottom of the solution, and this must be discarded.

Tanning

Mix enough of the following solution to cover the skin:

> 1 gal. water
> 1 pound salt (Buy this in 5-pound bags. It's cheaper than 1-pound cartons.)
> 1/2-1 oz. sulphuric acid.

Add the salt to the water first and be sure that it is completely dissolved. This will probably produce a milky solution. Now add the acid slowly, stirring all the time. This usually returns the liquid to a clear state. Take care not to inhale fumes nor to get this solution on you or your clothing.

Place the softened, degreased skin in the solution so that it is completely covered and leave it in for from 1-3 days, depending on the thickness of the skin. Generally, a rabbit or weasel needs about 24 hours; a raccoon or fox, about twice that. It is better to over-soak than to remove the skin prematurely although a poor job may be re-tanned, if necessary. Stir the skin around frequently.

Then remove the skin and squeeze or slick out most of the liquid. Do not wring it out. Again, use rubber gloves. Rinse the skin well in a solution of 1 oz. borax or bicarbonate of soda to a gallon of water to neutralize the acid. If this is not done, the acid may continue to attack the leather and eventually cause it to weaken.

I do not recommend retaining the salt-acid solution for the future. It seems that the strength of the chemicals is diminished with use to the degree that further attempts with the same batch may be futile. Use a fresh batch each time.

Squeeze out all the rinse water possible. The slicker again may be helpful.

Oiling

Now hang the skin up or tack it out on a board, flesh side out, to dry partially. When it begins to dry somewhat (an arbitrary judgement), apply a thin coat of neatsfoot oil with your hands. Thin skins need very little of this; heavier skins may need more. Precisely how much to add is a matter of "feel" or experience and a fair determination can be made, unfortunately, only later in the process. Too much will result in an oily, smelly skin; too little, in a dry, stiff leather. Some excess, can, however, be later removed with an additional wash in the degreasing solution.

By applying the oil before the skin is entirely dry, the oil can enter the skin as the water evaporates. If the skin dries too much before application, the oil tends to stay only on the surface.

Staking or Stretching

Allow the oil to penetrate well and the skin to dry a bit more. Put the skin in a cool place so that it dries slowly. I usually allow it to dry almost stiff on the margins and then roll it up in plastic overnight to allow it to even out in dampness. Now comes another matter of judgement: when to begin staking. The best test I know is to fold the skin in a few places. If a white line appears on the crease, it's about time, but the skin should not be so dry that it cracks. If the white line appears, test further by pulling here and there. If the skin stretches noticeably and turns white in a larger area, you may proceed. If not, dry it more. If the skin gets too dry so that it won't stretch at all, dampen it with phenol solution and roll it up in plastic overnight to allow it dampen evenly.

Fig. 7, Staking.

Drape the skin, flesh side down (or outside, in the instance of a cased skin), over a stake. Grasp the skin with the hands about 8-12 inches apart with one hand on either side of the stake's rounded edge. Rub the skin back and forth rapidly in a manner similar to shining shoes (Fig. 7). Be especially cautious near the legs and tail and around the margins, especially with fragile skins, lest you tear the skin in your zeal. Change positions on the stake frequently to distribute the stretching and rubbing action all over the skin. You should notice an appreciable stretching of the shrunken skin, and it should be getting white all over. The heat generated by the friction and the rapid action drives the water from the skin. The bending or folding over the stake's edge loosens the fibers and the oil allows these fibers to move easily which creates the soft leather. Rub thoroughly, often an hour or more, until the skin is completely dry and white. The dryness can be tested by holding the skin against your cheek. If it is noticeably cool, this indicates that evaporation is still taking place and, therefore, there is still moisture present.

It is difficult to stake too much; most persons tire too quickly and don't stake enough. If it is necessary to stop temporarily, wrap the skin again in plastic. The staking must be done while the skin is damp, not after it has dried. In other words, it must be worked to a dry state. If the skin dries hard, even with proper staking, it should be re-dampened before staking again. This must sometimes be repeated as often as necessary.

Depending on the skin and your skill, the skin should not only be supple, but should also have a fluffy nap on the flesh side. This is the typical suede of commercially-tanned leathers. The serrated-edged steel blade stake helps to create a felt-like nap on heavier leathers.

Finishing

When the skin is soft and dry, it may be advisable to give it a quick bath in benzine again, especially if it appears to be still greasy or oily. Then work it around in the sawdust again and shake it out. If the fur seems greasy or sticky, as if it had too much hair tonic, clean the fur side with degreaser. It should be dry enough to be fluffy, but contain enough oil to give it the sheen of well-groomed fur. Some tanners advise beating the fur side with thin sticks such as willow twigs to remove the sawdust and raise the fur in a manner similar to beating a rug. Bran or cornmeal may be used instead of sawdust.

At this point I like to sandpaper the flesh side with an appropriate grade of sandpaper. Hold the skin on a flat surface or on a fleshing board and sand lightly toward the margins. Keep the skin stretched with one hand while the other does the sanding. Delicate skins such as weasel require fine sandpaper while heavier skins can accept coarser grits. Too fine a grit gets clogged up too rapidly; too coarse may cut the leather. Try several.

Sanding improves the pleasant felt-like suede. Sanding also is helpful in thinning down thick skins. This is useful on the mask or face portion of the skin. Sanding removes the "crumbs" of tissue which may be the result of poor scraping.

Finally, comb the fur gently with a coarse comb and, possibly, with a short wire brush which is sold for grooming house pets. Comb, obviously, in the direction of the natural "lay" of the hair.

If all has gone well, you should now be pleased with a soft, supple piece of leather with a lustrous, fluffy fur. If not, remember that tanning is not an exact science and try again.

REFERENCES

Moyer, John W.   "Practical Taxidermy", Ronald Press, N.Y., 1953.

Rogers, J. S., and Clarke, I. D.,   "Home Tanning of Leather and Small Fur Skins", *Farmers' Bulletin* No. 1334, U.S. Dept. of Agriculture, Washington, D.C., 1962.

Seton, Julia M.   "American Indian Crafts", Ronald Press, N.Y., 1962.

MITTENS

Both mittens and gloves seem to have arrived rather late on the North American continent. Possibly these were introduced by comfort-loving Whites. Indians and Eskimos, for the most part, went bare-handed and tucked their hands into the cuffs of opposite sleeves -- muff fashion -- to keep them warm. Beautifully beaded gauntlet gloves and mittens are today made of buckskin and moosehide for sale to tourists and sportsmen who value their durability.

When you have acquired a proficiency with buckskin to the degree that simple pouches and bags are too pedestrian, and you are not quite ready for the challenge of moccasins, a pair of mittens is a reasonable venture. A mitten has the simplicity of a bag in its basic shape but includes some complexity in the stitching of a thumb. Unlike moccasins, you can expect mittens to fit on your first attempt. I'm not prepared to give instructions on gloves because I think they are a problem for the graduate moccasin maker -- especially if you intend them to fit.

Leather

Indian-tanned buckskin should be considerd first. If you have tanned your own deerskin, you may be jealous of using so much leather (2-3 square feet) after your hard work. You can almost get a pair of moccasins from the same amount. Indian-style tannage is superior, however, in its stitching qualities, for a needle will pass through it quite readily and is worth the expense if it is available.

A second choice is commercially-tanned buckskin. This is just as supple as the native-tanned product and may be more even in thickness. To approximate the Indian-tanned surface, you could use the flesh or sueded side out. Some commercially-tanned leathers have been dyed to brown or tan close to the smoked color of Indian-tannage.

A last choice would be commercially-tanned garment suede of cow or calf in about 3-ounce thickness. While this does not have the stretch of buckskin, it is otherwise just as serviceable. It is, however, more difficult to stitch, and a pliers may be necessary to pull a needle through. When buying such suede, note the term, "garment", which indicates a soft, supple leather. Some suedes are split from the inside of grain leather and are so tanned that they have the surface finish but not the softness of garment leather. If possible, feel the leather before buying, and test it with a needle for ease in stitching.

Spread the skin out and try to determine the backbone of the animal.
This can serve as a base line from which you can cut the *tranks* or main
portion of the mitts. Try to cut both tranks at right angles to this
backbone (Fig. 1). Even the thumbs

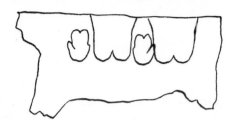

should be cut near to this area, for,
especially on deerskin, the perimeter
areas may have considerable variation
in thickness and stretch which can
seriously affect the fit. Don't cut
too close to any borders of skins.
You'll have to save these for small
bags and the like which don't require
a good fit.

*Fig. 1, Patterns laid out along
the backbone of a skin.*

Finally, for mittens, I don't recommend the typical thin glove leather
of about 2-ounce thickness which is used for dress gloves. It doesn't
seem wise to me to use such a fine material (and expensive!) for these
"chopper"-type mittens which will probably get some hard wear.

Measuring

Two measurements should be taken: length and width. The length can be
estimated by making a generous tracing of the general outline of the hand
with the thumb underneath (Fig. 2, Line A-A' around the fingertips). The

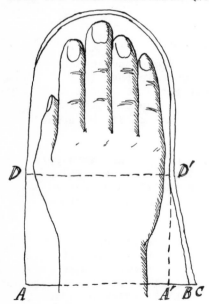

actual length of the mitt is a matter of
personal preference. An average length
would be to the wrist or longer. Enlarge
this tracing by about 1/2 inch all around
to allow for the thickness of the hand.

The second measurement should be taken with
a tape measure or a strip of stiff paper

*Fig. 2, Laying out the pat-
tern for the trank.*

*Fig. 3, Measuring the circumfer-
ence of the hand.*

wrapped around the hand below the knuckles, not including the thumb, **and** with the hand closed but not clenched (Fig. 3). Line D-D' on your tracing should equal one-half this circumference. If it doesn't, alter the pattern accordingly.

To allow for the added thickness of the thumb when the hand is inserted into the mitt, add a triangular section with a base of 1/2-3/4 inch to the right side of the pattern to create Line A-B. Add a seam allowance of 1/8-1/4 inch around the top and right side to create Line A-C which then forms one-half of the trank pattern. Cut this out. Retrace this on a larger sheet of paper, flip it over on A-D, and trace this to make the "butterfly" for the completed trank (Fig. 4).

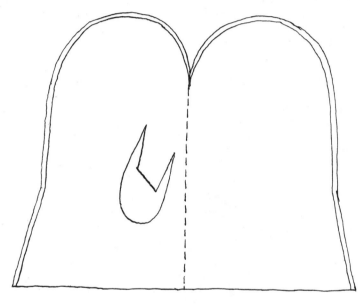

Note: The trank can be made in two pieces for each mitt so that the main seam will go completely around the top and both sides. This is sometimes done in order to utilize smaller pieces of leather. It is necessary if you wish to make a mitt of dissimilar leathers; e.g., a fur back and leather palm. In this case, be sure to add the seam allowance to the left side of the half-trank pattern.

Fig. 4, Basic typical full trank pattern for right hand "chopper" mitten.

This should give the basic shape for a mitt to be made from leather with a lot of stretch. If leather with little or no stretch or thick leather is to be used, add 1/4 inch more all around (1/2 inch total additional width). Because both mitts will be the same size, it is not necessary to measure each hand; merely reverse the pattern.

Such a pattern should make a loose-fitting mitt. If the mittens are to be worn with a knit, loose mitten liner, allow another 1/4 inch all around. The same is true if a lining, fur or cloth, is to be stitched permanently into the inside. Rabbit fur is real nice for a while but is notoriously weak. Also, it tends to shed. Other furs could be used, of course, but the problem of stitching fur without having a seam that looks as if it needs a shave is best left to experienced craftsmen. Fabrics such as

flannel or blanket cloth are fine. Mitten liners can be made separately (possibly on a sewing machine) and the cuff only stitched to the
leather later. It's possible to stitch the entire liner in place along
with the leather during assembly, but in this case I suggest that the
lining be rubber-cemented to the leather first. Personally, a separate
knit wool liner is superior. It can be replaced when worn out; when
wet, the liner and outer mitten can be dried separately. Also, a separate liner makes the stitching of the leather so much simpler.

Compare your pattern for size to the examples at the end of this chapter. Trace the *gouch* or thumb hole from the pattern which nearly approximates yours. Trace the thumb pattern for this size also, and be
precise. Cut out your patterns and mark the appropriate sides, "Right"
and "Left". It's easy to get mixed up, especially if you intend to sew
the mitts inside out. Lay the patterns out on your leather, trace, and
cut them out. Again, be precise, especially on the thumb parts.

Assembling

You may wish to assemble the mitt right side out in which case the
stitching will show. The 1/8 inch seam allowance is sufficient. For
a decorative effect, use a thread of contrasting color to the leather.
One disadvantage and one advantage: it's likely that the thread will
wear out more rapidly on the outside, but it can also be repaired more
easily.

On the other hand, you may
wish to stitch the mitt together inside out and turn
it right side out for wearing.
This puts quite a strain on
the stitching, and some irregularities in stitches
may show up more glaringly.
To preclude these deficien-
cies, use a 1/4-3/8 inch
wide *welt* between the two
pieces of leather (Fig. 5).
This means that you will
have to stitch through three

Fig. 5, Welting. A, Sewing the welt inside out. B, The completed seam turned
right side out.

pieces of leather which is a point to consider if the leather is tough.
The welt is easy to incorporate into the long curve around the trank
but is rather difficult along the complex thumb seam. It is, of course,
possible to stitch the trank seam inside out with a welt, and stitch the
thumb seam right side out without it.

Use heavy thread for these seams. Waxing the thread seems to strengthen
it. For Indian-tanned leather, a normal sewing needle is satisfactory.
Commercially-tanned leather may require the use of a three-sided "glover's needle" which slices its hole rather than merely punching it. For

some heavier leathers, you may need to make a glover's needle into a
handled awl to cut the hole; then a sewing needle can be used for
stitching.

Dress gloves exhibit several varieties of fancy stitches. For your
choppers, the whip stitch is sufficient. Holes should be about 1/8
inch from the edge and about 3/16 inch apart. The actual distance is
not as important as the regularity of the stitch. Pull the whip stitch
just enough so that they press snugly down into the leather. Don't pull
so hard that you distort the seam. Except for the welt business, whip
stitching is the same whether the stitching is to be exposed or on the
inside; just turn the later outside out when you're done.

During stitching, check the seam ahead every inch or so to see that the
two sides of the leather are still aligned. There is a tendency to
stretch the edge of the leather away from you so that it turns out to
be longer than the near side. You may find that the thumb is crooked
or that the trank seam ends up uneven. If you stitch with your right
hand, clamp the seam ahead with your left hand to keep the edges from
shifting as you stitch in a right-to-left direction.

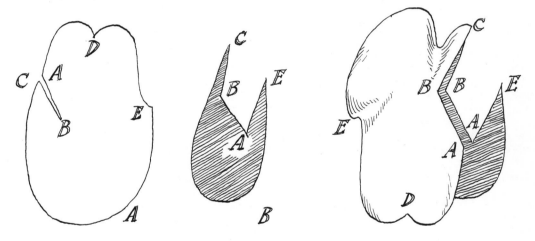

Fig. 6, Right hand thumb patterns.
A, Thumb. B, Gouch hole in trank.

Fig. 7, Aligning the thumb
and gouch.

Match the right thumb to the right gouch on the right trank. (Did you
mark these when they were cut?) Compare distance AB and BC (Fig. 6) on
the thumb to those on the gouch. They should be equal.

Tie a triple knot on the end of your thread and start on the inside of
the mitt to hide the knot. Begin at Point A and stitch to B. At point B
go through the same hole in the gouch twice as you go through the thumb
in two separate holes to "fan" the corner (Fig. 7). Continue sewing from
B to C and knot the end securely here.

Fold the thumb along its length and start a new thread at D. Take a
double stitch when you reach Point A to be sure that this weak place is
strengthened. You can now begin to see that, by twisting the thumb upward, the round base of the thumb can be aligned with the curved remainder of the gouch. You will be wise to pin or paperclip these together
temporarily to be sure that one edge does not slip while stitching further. Continue past Point A to E and thence around the curve back to C.
Knot off the thread at this point.

Before beginning to sew the thumb from D, you may want to try it on for
size. If necessary, the end of the thumb can be trimmed back into a new
curve if it is too long. After the thumb has been stitched into the
gouch, try it on again to check the length of the fingers. For warmth
(which is why you're making the mitts) this should be a loose fit. If
you intend to use a liner, keep this allowance in mind.

Now the easy one. Fold the trank along its center line. Begin stitching
at the fold just below the curve; stitch around the curve and down to
the cuff. Continue to check for alignment occasionally and make necessary adjustments to make the cuff come out even. Take a double stitch
at the cuff where it will receive some abuse from tugging the mitt on.

For class, fold the wrist over to the inside for a hem and stitch this
down on the inside, taking care that your stitches do not come through
to the outside. For real class, you could stitch on another piece of
leather for this hem. For extra high class, stitch on a strip of fur
about 1 or 2 inches wide along the cuff. Position this fur piece on the
inside of the cuff, fur side against the leather; i.e., the flesh side
of the fur exposed, and whip stitch this on along the cuff. Thus, when
the fur is pulled out, it becomes a barrier against cold air and snow.
It can also be rolled down on the outside of the mitt for a decorative
edge. If you wish, this can be permanently stitched down on the outside.

The mitten back can be beaded. Woodland floral designs without a beaded
background are quite nice. Use a nylon thread which will stretch as the
mitt is flexed. Don't bead so closely together that the leather is stiffened; you still need flexibility when you clench a fist. Indian women
probably would do the beading before the mitt is assembled for ease in
beading. I usually like to be sure that the mitt is finished first to
see that it's worth beading.

If you use a welt on the trank, this could be cut very wide for an inch
or so near the cuff so that, when it is turned right side out, you can
cut this into fringe. Fringes, however, seem out of place on a simple
mitten. If you really want a fringe, make an extra piece 4 or 6 inches
wide for a gauntlet cuff to be stitched to the cuff of the mitt. This
usually has a very wide opening to get the sleeve of your jacket inside.
This tapers to the size of the mitten opening. I expect that the pin-
nacle of class would be a fully beaded and fringed gauntlet cuff with
fur on the very end.

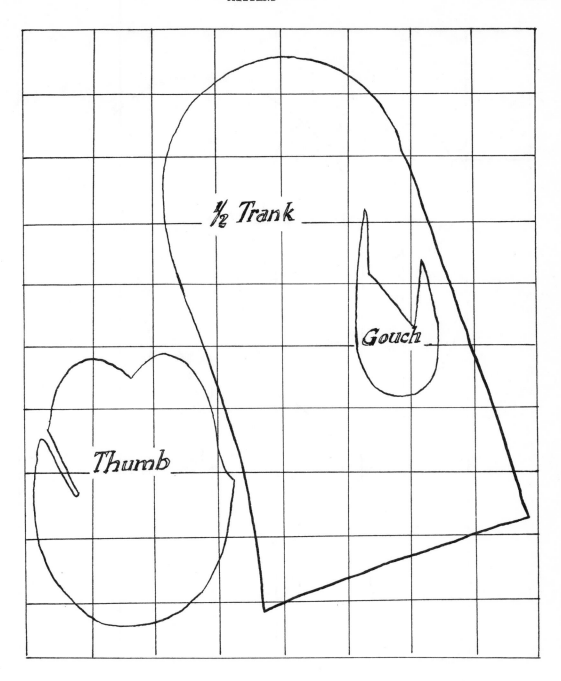

½ Trank

Gouch

Thumb

Fig. 8, 8-12 year old child's right hand pattern. (Enlarge
this diagram to one inch squares.)

Fig. 9, Teenager's or woman's right hand pattern.   (Enlarge this diagram to one inch squares.)

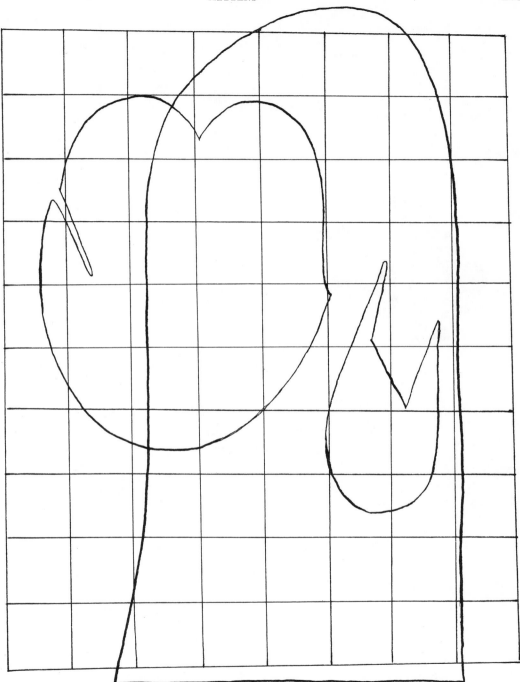

Fig. 10, Man's right hand pattern. (Enlarge this diagram to
one inch squares.)

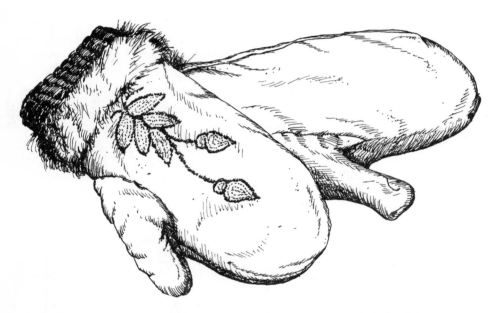

Fig. 11, Man's buckskin chopper mittens, stitched inside out.
Beaded back, rabbit fur cuff, and wool knit liner.

MOCCASINS

As with most nomadic primitive peoples, the American Indians probably
developed callused feet capable of withstanding abuse unknown to modern
Americans who cannot walk far without sturdy shoes or boots. Callused
feet alone, however, were not entirely sufficient. Even in the summer-
time, Indians customarily wore a foot covering of some kind.

Footwear was designed for the locale. The soft-soled buckskin Woodland
style was most useful in wooded areas for walking on pine needles,
leaves, or soft grass. It would not have been appropriate in rocky or
mountainous areas. Plains tribes also used soft-soled footwear, but
the most typical was the hard-soled Sioux style which gave better protection against the possibility of cuts from sharp prairie grasses. A
kind of sandal was sometimes worn by some southern tribes, but these
will be considered out of the scope of this chapter. Early Pueblo (Basketmaker) Indians and some Iroquois made a woven slipper from easily obtained materials -- the latter used corn husks or basswood fibers. Indians
harvesting wild rice such as the Menomini made a special high soft-soled
foot cover for the purpose of threshing the grain by treading on it.
The high sides, wrapped about the ankle, gave some protection from the
sharp husks of the rice which otherwise could slip inside. The high
boot of the Navaho gave protection to the lower leg in brush country.

Certain tribes tended to use unique patterns. Legend has it that clever
trackers could determine the tribe merely by exmining the footprints
made by unknown travellers. While the pattern of the footwear gives a
guide as to the tribe of the maker, it is far easier to tell the tribe
from the style of beaded or quilled decoration.

The most typical of Indian footwear has come to be known as a *moccasin*,
and this is the subject of this chapter. The moccasin, both in name and
type, is typically American Indian, and has been welcomed into contemporary culture as part of our native heritage. The spelling of the word
varies: *mocassin, makisin, mawkasin,* and others, with moccasin being preferred in most writings. Most Americans today recognize a "moccasin toe"
as referring to any shoe with a U-shaped puckered tongue over the instep.
The word itself is from the Ojibwa language which accounts for the variation in English spelling. A credible theory of the possible source of
the name "Ojibwa" comes from their word, *o-jib-ub-way,* which connotes
"puckered up" and thereby refers to "people of the puckered moccasin".
As will be seen, not all moccasins were puckered, nor U-shaped, nor soft-

sole; but the name will continue to be used both for some forms of cas-
ual contemporary footwear and for most types of Indian footwear.

Moccasins were most often made of buckskin or other soft-tanned leather
of elk, moose, or buffalo, the latter naturally being harder to cut and
sew but also lasting longer. Rawhide was used for sandals, but in this
chapter will be considered only as soles for the two-piece Plains-style
moccasin. Some of these were made of buffalo hide tanned with the hair
on which was turned to the inside for winter use. The Ojibwa used muskrat furs for liners for their winter moccasins. They also made a simple
"boot" of blanket cloth for the same purpose. Naturally, these winter
moccasins were made larger than normal to allow for the lining. Keep
this in mind if you design a moccasin to be worn with socks.

Indian-tanned buckskin is best to work with inasmuch as the tanning process makes it so soft that a needle passes through easily. Commercially-tanned buckskin seems just as soft, but needles seem to get stuck in
it. Any medium-weight soft leather may be used, but should be tested
with a needle to see how well it can be sewed. Sueded leather is similar in texture to Indian-tanned skin and is available at about a dollar
a square foot. Commercial grades of leather are sold in thicknesses
classed in "ounces" -- the weight of a square foot of leather. This
can be translated roughly in 64ths of an inch. Buckskin will grade about
3-ounce or 3/64 inch. Thinner leathers are not very practical; stick
to 3 or 4 ounce. Heavier leathers are too thick to be worked and
stitched easily, although factory-produced shoes may be 5-6 ounce weight.
Use some judgement in placing patterns on the skin before cutting. Ideally, pieces should be matched on either side of the backbone of the skin
(if it was tanned in one piece). In general, patterns should have the
"grain" of the leather going in the same direction. (I have a tendency
to be stingy and arrange the patterns to utilize all available areas.
I also have a tendency to produce irregular moccasins.)

Moccasins are always assembled inside-out so that the stitching is done
on the exterior flesh side which will be turned right side out when
stitching is completed. Seams are usually pressed (not with a hot iron,
however!) or pounded (gently) flat, especially in puckered areas. Some
moccasins, particularly those with beading, were lined inside with a
cloth or canvas lining to protect the area somewhat and to provide stiffness. The U-shaped tongue of certain Woodland moccasins was sometimes
made of velvet with beadwork, and in this case the lining protected the
stitches which, of course, came through on the inside. Beading on buckskin normally did not use stitching which penetrated to the inside.
Some modern examples now use felt as a substitute for velvet. Bead and
quillwork, and moosehair embroidery was normally done before the moccasin was assembled. (I recommend that the assembly be completed first to
see if the result is worth decorating until one becomes more proficient
as a cobbler.) If lining is used, this should be cut out along with
the leather pattern and stitched in during assembly.

Woodland moccasins were often decorated on the instep or tongue portion.
The flap around the ankle was decorated also, and an extra width of flap

or cuff might be stitched in place for just such a decorative area. This
ankle flap could be worn upright by wrapping it with thongs, but with a
beaded flap, it was always worn in a down position to expose the design.
This flap might also be made of or covered with velvet as a background
for beading. Woodland moccasins were seldom fully beaded; i.e., the
beadwork did not extend down the sides; and designs used usually allowed the buckskin or velvet to become a background for the design elements. Recently, fancy moccasins with fox, muskrat, or beaver fur cuffs
have become available.

An old custom of the Menomini was to cut a hole in a child's moccasins.
A legend held that if an evil spirit came to take the child, he would
see that the soles were "worn out" and therefore would not take the child
away with him.

Plains Indian designs sometimes allowed the buckskin to be used for bead
or quillwork designs. Motifs were embroidered on the instep portion and
around the circumference near the sole. The flap was seldom decorated.
Plains designs sometimes covered the entire top of moccasins from heel
to toe. Fine Sioux examples are found in most large collections as are
examples from the Blackfoot, Cheyenne, and Crow. An old custom of some
peoples required that burial moccasins be beaded on the soles as well as
the uppers so that the deceased person would be well clothed in the next
world. Such fully beaded moccasins are, naturally, extremely rare today.

Indians were the first Americans with the (now) New England adage of
"fix it up, wear it out, etc.", and moccasins were a good example of this.
Old moccasins were taken apart and repaired with new pieces as required.
Fully beaded uppers often received new rawhide soles. Unlike shoes today, one worn-out moccasin did not require that a new pair be acquired,
for only one was needed. Further, many moccasins were made the same for
both feet so that they were interchangeable. As a matter-of-fact, these
were exchanged daily to keep one from wearing out before the other.

Moccasins did wear out, of course. Preparations for a journey included
making spare footwear. A war party normally carried extras, but warriors
were not adverse to stopping long enough to make some on the spot, if necessary. A man could carry along sewing gear although clothing-making
in camp was strictly women's work.

Moccasins were usually stitched with sinew which is still preferred if
one wants to do a really good job. Holes were punched with an awl of
bone for the sinew which was inserted without benefit of a needle. With
the sinew knotted at the thickest end (sinew usually tapered in diameter
slightly). the narrow end could be pushed through the awl hole, and,
when pulled up, would actually fill the hole more tightly than an even-
diameter modern thread. Knots were kept on the outside of the moccasin;
such a tiny knob could wear sore against one's foot if it was on the inside. The sinew was dampened for flexiblity and shrank slightly on drying to make a tight seam. Sinew usually lasted longer than the thread
used today. Few Indians now use sinew in favor of needle and thread.
Heavy waxed thread is preferred -- either linen or nylon. Such thread

is not the heavy weight commonly associated with commercial shoes, but
is really only a seamstress' thread of about 40 weight as sold in shops.
If the leather is soft and the thread is pulled tight, the thread press-
es into the seam in such a way that it is almost hidden and thus receives
little wear. I prefer a stronger thread usually known as "extra heavy".
White is frequently used by Indians, but I try to find a brown hue to
match the color of the leather. In addition to needle, thread, and scissors as basic tools, a beginner may want an awl made from a needle, and
a thimble. Depending on the thickness and tannage of the leather, a
pliers may become necessary for pulling a stuck needle through a hole.

On Stitching

Most moccasins exhibit
the simple whip stitch
(Fig. 1A) done when
the seam is inside out.
This is satisfactory
for many seams, if
stitches are taken a-
bout 1/8 inch apart
and tightly sewed.
It does, however,
tend to make a bulging
seam on leather, or,
if pressed flat, allows
the stitching to show
some (Fig. 1B).

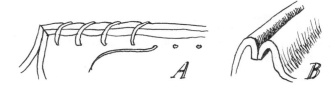

Fig. 1, Whip Stitch. A, Sewing inside
out. B, Seam shown right-side out.

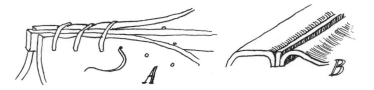

Most well-made mocca-
sins are whip stitch-
ed with a "welt" a-
bout 1/4 inch wide
and as long as the
seam requires (Fig. 2A). This is superior
to the simple whip stitch inasmuch as the
welt tends to hide some of the stitching
when the seam is turned right-side out
(Fig. 2B). It is also stronger, for it
puts less strain on the thread.

Fig. 2, Whip stitch and welt. A, Sewing inside
out. B, Seam shown right-side out.

When a whip stitch is impossible, as sometimes when a fringe is part of the seam,
a running stitch is used (Fig. 3A). A
double running stitch gives more strength
and a smoother seam (Fig. 3B). Running

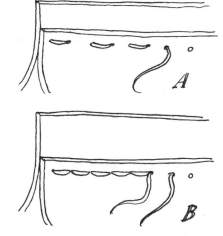

Fig. 3, Running stitches. A, Single running stitch. B, Double running stitch.

stitches may also be used with a welt.

A puckered seam is often required and a
good one is difficult to do. An otherwise
fine moccasin may be disfigured by a poor
pucker. One way to accomplish a seam is
to stitch into the flat side of the seam
1/8 inch apart as you stitch into the portion to be puckered for a larger distance,
say, 3/16 inch (Fig. 4). (If the leather
thickness
is heavy, the

*Fig. 4, Stitching a pucker;
estimating the interval by eye.*

stitches need to be proportionately larger;
of course, the interval gathered into puckers
is then larger also.) This procedure causes
ripples or pleats in the latter section as
the stitches are pulled tight. The problem
is to judge the amount of pucker required to
make the seam come out even at the end of the
puckering. A good seamstress could, probably,
begin at one side of a toe, for instance, and
come out with an even-intervalled pucker by
estimating by eye the amount required for each
stitch. I recommend that the seam be basted
in place first at the toe and on either side
and that pencil marks be made at appropriate
places on both sides of the seam to act as
guides. You might also begin at the
center of the pucker (of a toe, for instance) and stitch in opposite directions to help you come out evenly (Fig.
5). You may wish to try the "seamstress
gather" which is started by stitching
a single running thread through the
side to be puckered -- as many stitches
as necessary for the completed edge
(Fig. 6A). When this thread is tightened and the leather slid together a-
long it, the material is pleated much
as what happens when draw drapes are
opened (Fig. 6B). The convenience here
is that the amount of gathering can be
pre-determined and adjusted to fit the
non-puckered edge. To sew this together,
stitches are taken through the original
holes in the pucker and then to corresponding holes in the non-puckered edge
(Fig. 6C). While puckers are required
for the soft-sole Woodland style moccasin, the same principle applies to, for

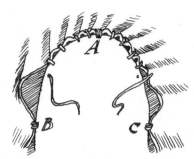

*Fig. 5, Beginning a puck-
ered toe at the center
and stitching toward both
sides. Note basting at
A, B, and C.*

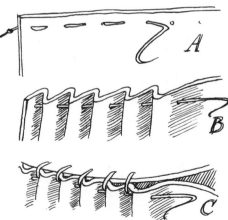

*Fig. 6, Creating a "seamstress
gather". A, Running stitch.
B, Gathering the pucker. C,
Stitching the pucker to the
flat edge.*

instance, the toe area
of a Plains style hard-
sole piece. I suggest
that you try a few
puckered seams on scrap
leather before you at-
tempt it on a good moc-
casin.

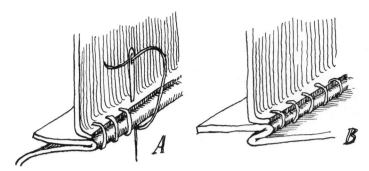

Certain heel seams pre-
sent unusual problems.
After the long verti-
cal seam is stitched
(inside out, of course),
the small flap on the
base is folded back so

*Fig. 7, Stitching a heel seam with flap. A, Sew-
ing inside out. B, Seam turned right-side out;
heel flap projects outside toward the left.*

that three layers of leather need to be stitched together (Fig. 7A). Thus,
when the shoe is turned right-side out, the flap appears on the exterior
(Fig. 7B) and can be left as is, cut into a small fringe, or bent upward
to be stitched on.

Pattern Making

First, don't expect to make yourself a pair of moccasins which will fit
perfectly on your very first attempt. Too many variables exist which experienced women compensated for as they worked. However, study the ac-
companying directions carefully, and you will be able to make a reasonable
facsimile.

The best way to make a pattern is to take apart an old moccasin. Indian
patterns were made this way to assure a reasonable fit, but the construction and material permitted some leeway in sizes. A loose moccasin could
be tightened with the thongs usually wound around the ankles. A tight
fit stretched somewhat in use. Most soft-sole moccasins were not made
in pairs, but were stretched to fit either foot. Hard-sole moccasins
were made in right and left shapes.

Without an old moccasin as a guide, one must develop a pattern on a flat
piece of leather which will result in the proper three-dimensional size
and shape. I strongly suggest experimenting with paper patterns first.
These can be taped together sufficiently so that one can get a semblance
of the final shape. If this turns out well, it can be taken apart and
transferred to cloth which can be basted together to give the student
some experience in stitching and to enable him to try on the moccasin.
Adjustments can be made on both paper and cloth patterns before the final
tracing on the actual leather.

Generally, light-weight buckskin can be designed to fit snugly and will
have some "stretch" in the final fit. Heavier leathers do not have this
quality and will need to be designed slightly larger.

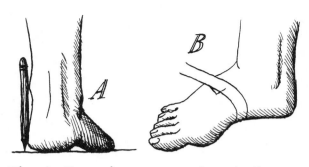

Fig. 8, Moccasin measurements. A, Tracing a foot pattern. B, Measuring the instep circumference.

On all seams, allow about 1/8-1/4 inch extra for stitching. Obviously, this presupposes that you will make your stitches a like amount from the edge. A greater allowance must be made for heavier leathers which cannot bend easily along a seam. Remember that moccasins were not made in exact sizes such as 7 1/2 D, but rather in a more general range such as 7-8 B-E, more or less.

Take time to design your pattern. The foot pattern is made by tracing its outline as in Fig. 8A. Be sure that the pencil is held vertically or you will be inaccurate. The weight of the body should be on the foot during tracing just as one normally steps on a new shoe to test its fit.

One other measurement is critical; the circumference of the instep. Take this measurement with a tape or strip of leather (Fig. 8B). This measurement will be indicated on my pattern drawings in the future as length "X". In most adult moccasins, this length will probably be about 8-10 inches. On one-piece moccasins, this distance can often be measured straight across the pattern. On two-piece designs, the width of the foot pattern gives part of this distance and the upper must be wide enough for the remainder of this distance.

Woodland "Stocking" Moccasins

The Ojibwa made a simple form of moccasin worn chiefly by small children and old women. This was made with two pieces of leather roughly conforming to the profile of the foot allowing enough for three-dimensional expansion and seams (Fig. 9). This was stitched down the heel, along the bottom or sole, and up the instep in a single seam. This style was also made of blanket cloth and, as such, was used as a liner for puckered moccasins in winter much as one would wear a stocking. These were made in quantity, and a supply was normally kept on hand[1]. Such moccasins had an uncomfortable seam right on the center of

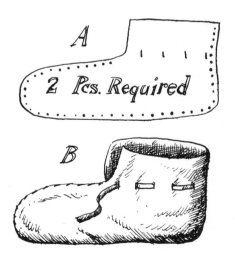

Fig. 9, Woodland two-piece "stocking" moccasin. A, Patterns. B, Finished moccasin.

[1]Densmore, p. 34.

the sole so they were not used alone if one had to walk far. These are not seen any longer.

A second style of "stocking" moccasin is shown in Fig. 10. It has the advantage of not having a seam on the sole while still being one of the simplest foot coverings used by Indians. Its disadvantage is that a much larger single piece of material must be used. (It is always easier to find two small pieces than one large one.) The toe is stitched from the bottom up over the instep, and the heel is stitched up the back. The semi-circular sections at each side are left to be folded down as flaps.

Ojibwa One-Piece "Partridge" Moccasin

Another moccasin made for children was the "partridge" style of the Ojibwa[2], which was so-named because of the

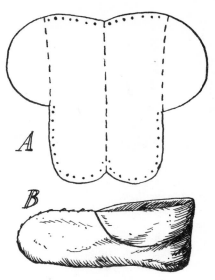

Fig. 10, Woodland one-piece "stocking" moccasin. A, Pattern. B, Finished moccasin.

straight puckered seam across the toe which was somewhat reminiscent of the fan-tail of a partridge. The heel was stitched together with a short fringe which dragged on the ground. The seam up the instep also was made into a fringe. This moccasin was lined with rabbit fur, dry moss, or hay for warmth in winter. It is seldom made today and is never found as a trade item any longer.

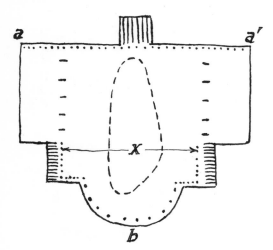

Trace an outline of the foot. Draw *Line a–a'* about 1/2 inch above the heel and at right angles to the foot (Fig. 11). The length of this line is up to the individual; you might try about 6 inches toward either side for an average cuff. Point *b* at the toe should be about 2 inches from the traced toe. Distance *X* is the diameter of the instep. The length of fringe is arbitrary.

Fig. 11, Ojibwa one-piece "partridge" moccasin pattern.

[2]*Ibid.*

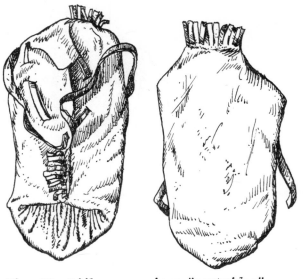

*Fig. 12, Ojibwa one-piece "partridge"
moccasin. (After Densmore).*

It is best not to cut these fringes until after the moccasin is assembled; otherwise, they tend to get mixed into the stitching. When the pattern seems correct, transfer this to the flesh side of the leather and cut it out. Assemble it by stitching first across the long, straight instep seam with the leather right-side out. A running stitch must be used and should be reinforced with additional stitches at the ankle opening. Turn the leather inside out for the puckered toe. The heel seam is brought together over the fringe portion, and the heel is stitched together in a T-shaped seam with the bottom of the sides folded outward to meet the fringe on either side. Because this sewing is also done inside out, the fringe flap should be to the inside at this point.

Reinforce with extra stitches the ends of the seams where they are subject to most stress. Turn the moccasin right-side out and cut the fringes. A buckskin thong about 1/2 inch by 2 feet long is cut and is threaded through holes punched in the flap. This thong is often wrapped around the ankle before being tied. Seams are pressed flat or pounded gently on a flat surface.

Woodland One-Piece Soft-Soled Moccasin

An old style of moccasin was made with a straight puckered seam up the front and a plain seam up the heel. This style was typical of the Ojibwa, Winnebago, and Iroquois tribes, and was often made from one piece of leather. It is seldom made today in favor of the round toe style described later. The one-piece moccasin had a characteristic pointed toe. Again, right and left foot patterns are the same.

Trace a foot pattern as above and develop a flat pattern as shown in Fig. 13A. Distance X between b–b' should be the circumference of the instep. The distance from the heel tracing to heel flap d is about 1 inch. The distance from the toe tracing to point e is about 1 1/2 inches. Trace the pattern onto the leather and cut it out. If the pattern is cut this way, the added cuff flaps will normally have the flesh side of the leather outside if the cuffs are worn in a "down" position. Sometimes, these cuffs were cut separately and attached at the dotted lines so that the

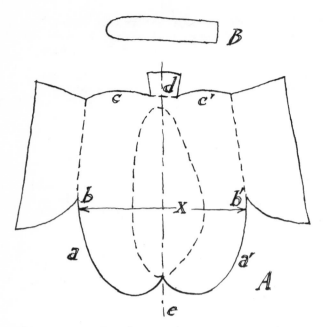

Fig. 13, Woodland one-piece soft-soled
moccasin pattern. A, Sole, upper, and
cuff pattern. B, Optional narrow tongue.

Fig. 14, Woodland one-
piece soft-soled moc-
casin.

grain side could appear both on the moccasin proper and on the cuffs.
This could also be done if one were short of material large enough
for one piece. Iroquois women's moccasins were assembled without a cuff
which was attached later as one long piece. Men's moccasins were separated at the back seam so that the cuffs then laid flat on both sides
of the foot.[3]

The front edge of the pattern (a-a') was sometimes cut with zig-zags, as
if with a pinking shears, so that the puckers could be gathered closely.
The moccasin is folded inside out along a center line (d-e). This curved
line is stitched together with stitches about 1/8 inch apart by joining
b-b'. Sew toward the toe which is pulled up with puckers.

Sometimes a narrow strip (Fig. 13B) was stitched to both sides of the seam
rather than stitching one side directly to the other. If this narrow
tongue is used, be sure to diminish distance X to allow for this extra
width. This flat area between the seams often was beaded or quilled.

The heel seam (c-c') is stitched together with the heel flap (d) on the
inside as the moccasin is inside out. Two thongs are attach-
ed at points b and b', and the moccasin is turned right-side out.   The

[3]Lyford, "Iroquois Crafts", p. 29.

heel flap now should be on the exterior.

Bead and quillwork was often done along and on either side of the toe
seam. Such decoration is too irregular if it extends much into the
puckered areas. The cuff was sometimes fringed, but more often was decorated with beads, quills, or ribbon piping. The cuff might also be
made of or covered with velvet.

When this moccasin was worn, the two tie thongs were usually crossed in
front and tied behind the heel.

Woodland Two-Piece Soft-Soled Tongued Moccasin

Most common and well-known
of the moccasins today
is the two-piece or tongued
moccasin of the Woodlands.
Actually, this is usually
made of three pieces; the
sole and upper, the
tongue, and the cuff flap;
but the moccasin proper
is, indeed, made with
only the first two parts.

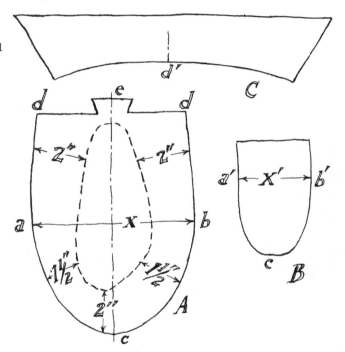

Again, the pattern is be-
gun with a foot tracing
(Fig. 15). Develop this
pattern by drawing an e-
longated semicircle about
2 inches all around ex-
cept at the foot's great-
est width (*a-b*) where it
should be about 1 1/2
inches. A small tab or
flap (*e*) is left at the
heel. Tongue patterns
vary all the way from a
rounded triangle to an
oval, with the most of-
ten seen flat-ended
oval form as in Fig. 15B.

*Fig. 15, Woodland two-piece soft-soled tongued
moccasin pattern. A, Sole and upper. B,
Tongue. C, Cuff flap.*

An estimation of correct size can be gotten from the top of one's foot
by drawing an oval to conform roughly to the shape of the top of the
instep. Distance X on the foot pattern and X' on the tongue pattern
should equal the total instep circumference plus seam allowances. The
cuff flap is made of a single long piece of leather long enough to go
almost completely around the ankle. (Note the different lengths in Fig.
16.) The edge along d' (Fig. 15) is curved slightly; the two ends are
cut diagonally which makes the curved line shorter. The curved line is
the edge which will be stitched to the moccasin.

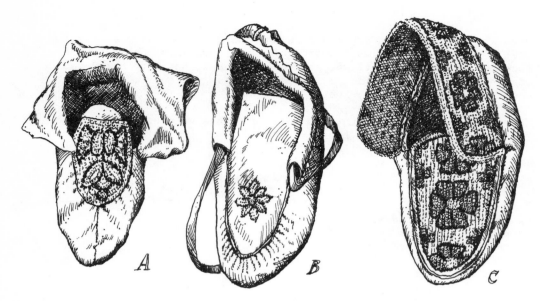

Fig. 16, Woodland two-piece soft-soled moccasins. A, Transitional type
including both a straight toe seam and a tongue. B, Modern Winnebago.
C, Modern Cree with beaded and lined cuff.

To assemble the moccasin, baste the sole A to the tongue B at the points
a-a', b-b', and c-c' with the flesh side out. Use whip stitches about
1/8 inch apart to stitch the seam as you pucker the sole piece as evenly
as possible. The tongue is not puckered. When the toe is completed,
try the moccasin on the front of your foot while you pull the heel together (Fig. 17). Adjust the pattern to fit better, if necessary, and
sew up the heel seam. The cuff seam
is begun at the center of the heel
(d-d') and then is sewed around the
top of the moccasin in both directions to point a and b where the
tongue joins the sole. Turn the
moccasin right-side out to sew the
heel flap up on the outside, or you
may leave it loose as is, or you
may trim it off entirely.

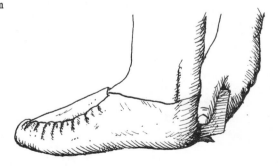

Fig. 17, Testing a partially assembled moccasin for fit.

Seams are pounded flat, especially
the puckered area. The seam joining the cuff and upper is usually
left as a roll. A thong about 2
feet long is attached under the
cuff at the heel so that it can be brought across the ankle in front from
both sides to return to the rear to be tied under the cuff. Such a thong
may also be threaded through punched holes.

Fig. 16A shows a transitional type of moccasin design with both the
straight toe seam and a small puckered tongue. This example has quite
a large cuff and also a velvet insert on top of the oval tongue. Note
that the leather tongue is longer than the insert.

A modern Winnebago moccasin with a large tongue and light beading is
shown in Fig. 16B. The cuff is stitched up to form a tube for the
lace thong and then is folded back down to be cut on a scalloped edge
on the exterior. I purchased this pair recently for $12.00 from a wo-
man who claimed that this was the last pair she intended to make.
She had not done her own tanning for several years, she told me, and
Indian-tanned skins were getting too hard to get any more. The illustration shows clearly the use of a welt in the toe and heel seams. Most
moccasins I have purchased recently use a welted seam.

A modern Cree moccasin made of moosehide is illustrated in Fig. 16C.
The cuff is lined to help it stand up so that the beaded exterior is
visible when it is worn. These moccasins have a large beaded tongue
which extends to the toenail so that minimal puckers are needed.

Plains One-Piece Soft-Soled Moccasin

On the northern plains, possibly
through influence from the eastern Woodland tribes, a soft-
soled moccasin was often used
by such tribes as the Flathead
and Blackfoot. Such moccasins
could be made of leather with
the hair left on the inside
for winter use. This moccasin was made in several variations, but, in general, all
patterns show the sole and upper side-by-side. The pattern,
when folded, made one long
seam along one side of the foot
only (on a left moccasin, for
instance, along the left outside), and up the heel. Be
sure to flip the pattern over
to cut the pattern for the
other foot; right and left
moccasins are made opposite
to each other.

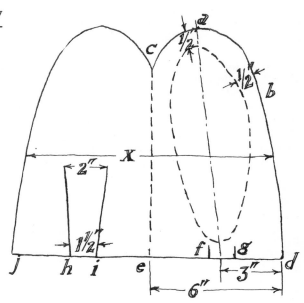

Fig. 18, Plains one-piece soft-soled moccasin pattern.

To develop this pattern, trace
the outline of the foot and add 1/2 inch all around. Cut out this enlarged foot and make a new pattern by turning the original slightly askew
as indicated by the center line on Fig. 18. Make points *a*, *b*, and *c*

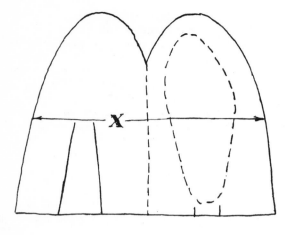

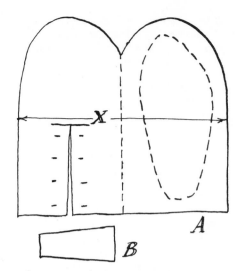

*Fig. 19, Plains one-piece moccasin
variation with long tongue.*

*Fig. 20, Plains one-piece moc-
casin variation with separate
tongue.*

about 1/2 inch from the foot. Mark point *d* about 3 inches from the center line and about 1/2 inch below the heel. Draw a curve connecting *cabd*.
Draw line *de* for the heel at an angle to the center line of the foot.
Dotted line *ce* now becomes the center line of the pattern and should not
be cut. Cut out the curve and heel lines and fold it over on *ce*. Trace
the two cut lines onto the other half and cut this out also to make a
symmetrical pattern. Mark the heel slits (*g* and *f*) equidistant from *d*
and *e*, and cut these. On the other half of the pattern, which will become the upper, mark and cut the tongue slits (*h* and *i*) about 1 1/2
inches apart at the heel and 2 inches apart at about the center of the
moccasin's length. (These can be cut longer later, if necessary.) This
should make *jh*, *ie*, *ef*, and *gd* approximately equal.

Cut this pattern from leather and fold it, flesh side out, along *ce*.
Stitch the curve of the upper (*cj*) to the curve of the sole (*cd*). No
puckers are required for this moccasin. Now attach *h* and *i*, leaving the
tongue loose in between. Stitch *hjdg* to *ief* thus forming the heel seam.
Turn the moccasin right-side out and stitch the heel flap (*fg*) over this
vertical seam. Sometimes this flap was left hanging free, and might even
be fringed.

This style of moccasin might be considered to be too low, so sometimes
another piece, about 2 inches wide, was cut long enough to go around the
top from one side of the tongue, around the heel, to the other side of
the tongue in order to become a cuff. If this cuff was turned down and
stitched down on the bottom as well, it created a tube for a tie thong.
The thong could also be simply passed around the ankle to be tied in
front. In some cases, the thong was laced through holes provided for it
as in the pattern (Fig. 20) or the illustration (Fig. 21A).

Fig. 20 shows a pattern variation on the first design in
that a slot is cut for the foot
rather than a tongue. A separate tongue (Fig. 20B) should
be cut with the narrow end attached to the end of the slit
when it is opened up. Fig. 19
shows another variation in that
the tongue is cut with a long
reversed taper. In general,
all principles of design for
the first pattern apply to
these variations; namely, that
the pattern is made by folding the sole half to form the
upper, distance X is the instep circumference, and the
four short distances on the
heel line are roughly equal.

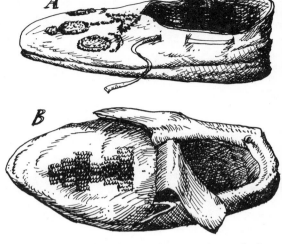

*Fig. 21, Plains one-piece soft-soled
moccasin. A, Cuffless, with floral
beadwork. B, Cuffed with Plains beadwork.*

*Plains Two-Piece Hard-Soled
Moccasin*

Tribes of the Plains area usually made a two-piece moccasin with a soft
leather upper and a hard rawhide sole.

The rawhide was usually made of buffalo hide, but cowhide may be used instead. Such rawhide varies from 1/8 to 1/4 inch in thickness when fresh
or wet; this shrinks to about 1/16 to 1/8 inch upon drying. If the rawhide is dry, it can be cut with a tin snips; a knife will work with difficulty. Rawhide can be cut more easily when wet. I suggest that the
sole pattern be marked on dry rawhide regardless of when it is to be cut.
If wet or fresh rawhide must be used, some allowance must be made for
this shrinkage. The rawhide must be softened for stitching by soaking
it in water until it becomes grayish and somewhat swollen in thickness.
Thick rawhide may require an overnight soaking. Fresh rawhide may, of
course, be used immediately. In the absence of genuine rawhide, some
other leather, about 5-6oz. may be used. Use heavy "shoemaker's" waxed
thread for the sole seam.

Make a foot tracing and cut it out about 1/4 inch larger all around. Use
this shape as a basis for the upper pattern which is made 1/2 inch longer
at toe and heel as in Fig. 22A. The length of the straight line for the
heel seam should be about 8 to 10 inches. The width of the foot at its
widest part (X') plus the length X from a to b should total the circumference of the instep plus a seam allowance. Cut line gd about half the
length of the pattern. Cut line ce about 3 inches long at the end of line
gd to make a T-shaped opening. Transfer this upper pattern to soft leather and cut it out. Transfer the dotted line foot pattern (Fig. 22C) to
rawhide and cut it out. As with the one-piece Plains patterns, these

patterns are for one foot only and must be flipped over for the other foot. The tongue (Fig. 22B) should be as wide as line *ce* and may taper to about 2 inches. The length of the tongue is about 4 inches.

Soft rawhide or other heavy leather is difficult to stitch, even with a sharp needle and thimble. One may even need a pliers to pull the needle through. An awl is almost a necessity for punching guide holes for each stitch. Stitches are made with the upper and sole back to back, inside out, and with

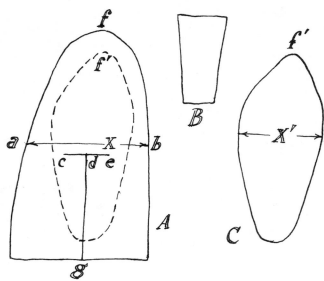

Fig. 22, *Plains two-piece hard-soled moccasin pattern variation.*

the soft leather of the upper slightly pulled around the sole (Fig. 23A). Use a whip stitch at an angle so that the needle pierces the rawhide in the middle of its thickness (Fig. 23B). In this way, the stitching is visible somewhat from the exterior of the moccasin when it is turned right-side out.

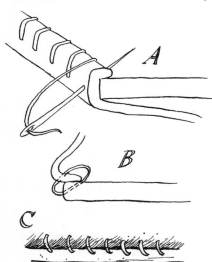

Fig. 23, *Stitching a rawhide sole. A, Upper leather bent around sole for stitching. B, Cross-section of seam. C, Exterior of finished seam.*

Attach the center of the upper (f) to the center of the sole (f') at the toe. Stitch the upper to the sole from f-f' backward toward the heel on each side. Pucker the upper leather slightly around the toe to give height for the tips of your toes. (Some of these moccasins were made a little too long so that one's toe did not come all the way to the toe of the moccasin. Such moccasins were almost flat at the tip.) The stitching on either side below the ankle does not require puckering. Check the heel for fit. Sew the heel seam after making any necessary adjustments. Stitch the tongue in place and turn the moccasin right-side out. Lace a thong through holes punched along the top of the upper about an inch below line gd. The thong should be outside the leather at the heel so that it does not rub on one's heel.

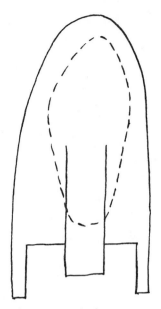

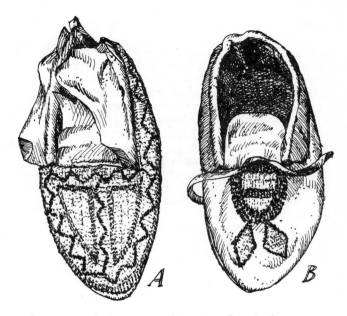

Fig. 24, *Plains two-*
piece hard-soled moc-
casin pattern varia-
tion.

Fig. 25, *Plains two-piece hard-soled mocca-*
sins. A, Northern Plains style. B, Crow
style with turned-down cuff.

Such laces were optional.

Sometimes an additional cuff was added to the top. A longer thong could
then be wrapped around the moccasin at the ankle and then up the leg to
hold the cuff up. When worn with leggings which also were wrapped, the
entire leg was then protected from the knees down. The tongue was usually left hanging down in front on top of the instep. Designs were beaded or quilled on top of the instep (Fig. 25A and B). Sometimes the entire upper was decorated all around down to the sole seam with the cuff
area excepted.

A variation of this pattern is shown in Fig. 24. This has a self-tongue
and requires an added cuff. Measurements are developed as above. This
pattern includes two tabs or strips at the heel which were knotted at the
outside and which dragged behind as the moccasin was worn. Sometimes a
large fringe was made at this point, supposedly to destroy the footprints
as one walked.

I suggest that one wear the moccasins immediately upon completion until
the rawhide dries sufficiently to hold its shape which then conform exactly to the wearer's feet. If allowed to dry freely, the rawhide may
wrinkle improperly.

Navajo Two-Piece Hard-Soled Moccasin

A boot type of moccasin was used by the
Navajo and other tribes in the arid
country of the Southwest. The Pueblo
Indians and others used sandals at times;
it is possible that this moccasin was
a refinement of the thongs on top of
these sandals. With the button fastening of the Navajo boot, it is also possible to imagine that this design originated with White man's shoes. The
moccasin had a turned-up rawhide sole
which made the side seam come not so
close to the ground as it was with the
Plains styles. The turned-up sole made
it more practical in country of sharp
rocks and tough brush.

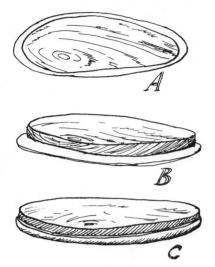

Fig. 26, Navajo sole construc-
tion. A, Marking the sole.
B, Lining up block and sole.
C, Sole bent up for drying.

An accurate pattern of the foot is
traced and is transferred to a block
of wood to be sawed out. A larger foot
pattern is made from the first to be cut
out 1/2 inch larger all around. This
latter pattern is used for the sole and to help lay out the upper pattern.
Cut a piece of rawhide or heavy leather to the shape of this pattern. If
leather is to be used, it must be "oak tanned" or "carving" leather

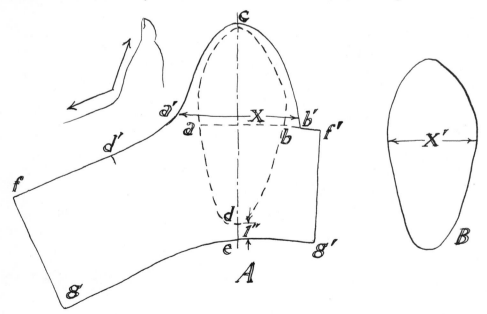

Fig. 27, Navajo two-piece hard-soled moccasin pattern. A, Upper pattern. B, Sole pattern.

which is vegetable-tanned in such a method that it can be bent when
wet and will retain its bent form upon drying as will rawhide. Thoroughly wet the sole (The leather takes only a few minutes; rawhide may need
an overnight soaking.), and lay it against the foot block (Fig. 26A and
B). Coax the overlapping edges over the edges of the block by smoothing
it with the hand until all margins have been bent (Fig. 26C). Allow it
to dry partially until it can hold this shape. In the case of rawhide
especially, do not permit it to dry completely or you will not be able
to sew through it. Leather may be damp or dry. Another sole is required for the other foot; this may be easily done by using the opposite
side of the foot block. It is said that a primitive method of forming
the sole was to press the foot into soft clay which was allowed to dry
hard. The soft rawhide was then pressed into this depression, thus
conforming to the shape of the foot which made it.[4]

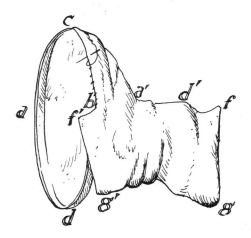

*Fig. 28, Stitching the Navajo
moccasin.*

Develop the pattern of the upper by
laying the foot pattern on a sheet
of paper and drawing a center line
as in Fig. 27. Lay out distance X
on the paper by subtracting distance
X' on the sole from the total circumference of your instep. Draw curve
$a'cb'$ with c being the toe of the
pattern. Distance de is about 1 inch.
Locate point f' about 1 inch to the
right of b'. Draw line $f'g'$ parallel
to the center line. Draw line eg'
perpendicular to the center line.
Find length $fd'a'$ by measuring around
the sole from point a around d to b.
Mark point f so that line $fd'a'$ will
be at an angle roughly similar to
that shown as the angle of the leg
to the top of the foot. Draw a perpendicular to line $fd'a'$ from f and

and mark off length $f'g'$ to locate corner g. Draw line ge to blend into
line eg'. (How did the Navajos ever figure this out in the first place;
or was pattern-making inherited?) This pattern now is cut out and is
transferred to the leather for cutting. As in some previous patterns,
this one must be flipped over for the other foot.

Begin stitching the upper to the sole at bb'. You can try stitching inside out as was done with the Plains style hard-sole moccasin (Fig. 23).
Otherwise, assemble it right-side out with a whip stitch diagonally
through the upper and the edge of the sole as in Fig. 29A. Note that
the upper is on the inside of the curved sole (Fig. 29B). This latter
method is quite simple up to point c. It then gets more difficult until
the sewing reaches aa'. Bend the upper to join dd' and fb'. Corner f'
is left hanging. Stitch along the sole (line adb) so that geg' stands

[4]Miles, p. 117.

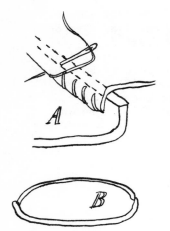

up as a cuff. Corner f' is stitched inside of f. Corner g now becomes a flap which can be pulled around the ankle to the side.

Cut a buttonhole about 1/2-1 inch from corner g' and try on the moccasin. Pull the flap around your ankle and mark through the buttonhole to the leather underneath which marks the location for a button. Formerly, any button was used as could be found or made from bone or the like. Recently, Mexican "conchos" of silver have been substituted for less pretentious buttons. Another button is sometimes placed lower down; sometimes this latter button is alone.

As with the Plains style hard-sole moccasin, let the sole dry while you wear this moccasin to help it retain its shape.

Fig. 29, Stitching the sole seam. A, view from inside. B, Cross-section.

Conclusion

While the above styles include those with the widest distribution, there were still many styles of footwear of the American Indian which were not mentioned. These run the spectrum from simple sandals to high, boot-type moccasins and legging-moccasins. A variety of hybrids were sired by the basic styles. Variations occurred between tribes using the same style; straight or curved cuffs, high or low cuffs, fringed and plain tongues, different methods of tying, styles of decoration,

Fig. 30, Navajo two-piece hard-soled moccasin.

etc. Indentification of illustrated examples as having been made by certain tribes is accurate, but I'm sure that I will find contemporary members of the tribe who will take exception with, "We don't make moccasins this way." I've tried to give generalizations, but I expect that individual preferences will prevail in actual construction today.

Moccasins are seldom worn today except by the old folks. There are probably more moccasins of the shoe-store variety worn by Whites today than there are Indians who still wear their authentic designs. Modern Indians usually use the White man's shoes (which are more practical on concrete walks and streets) although some wear "sneakers" or soft "bedroom slippers" as reasonable substitutes. Few moccasins are made today in the old ways, for White buyers want a sole of rubber to walk their straight and narrow concrete paths.

A few moccasins are still offered for sale on or near reservations in
the United States and Canada. These sell for 10-25 dollars a pair, depending on the quality and decoration. Seldom does one see a pair with
full beading or quillwork. Some makers have given up tanning in favor
of commercial suede-type leathers. The work expended on a pair of moccasins is seldom sufficiently valued in sales so, perhaps, the finest
modern work is done for use by the family of the maker. Very few people,
for instance, can understand the love and patience which must go into
the making of a fully beaded pair of child's burial moccasins.

REFERENCES

Douglas, F. H., and
Marriott, Alice L.

"Plains Indian Clothing", *Denver Art
Museum Leaflet* No. 24, 1931.

Densmore, Frances

"Chippewa Customs", *Bureau of American
Ethnology Bulletin* No. 86, 1929.

Griswold, Lester

"Handicraft" (8th Edition), Pub. by the
author, Colorado Springs, Colorado, 1942.

Lyford, Carrie A.

"Iroquois Crafts", Bureau of Indian Affairs, U. S. Department of Interior,
1945.

"Ojibwa Crafts", Bureau of Indian Affairs,
U. S. Department of Interior, 1943.

Miles, Charles

"Indian and Eskimo Artifacts of North
America", Henry Regnery, Chicago, 1963.

Seton, Julia M.

"American Indian Arts", Ronald Press,
N. Y., 1962.

Wissler, Clark

"North American Indians of the Plains",
Handbook Series No. 1, American Museum
of Natural History, N. Y., 1920.

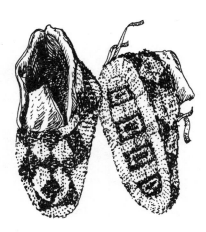

*Fig. 31, Plains two-piece child's burial
moccasins.*

ON DRUMS

Ceremonial and social dances, chants, and rhythms are a universal trait
of all peoples. Indians developed this trait to the degree where, even
today, almost any situation, emotion, or circumstance has its traditional and impromptu songs and dances appropriate to the occasion. Certain tribes used other musical instruments such as flutes, whistles, re-
sonators, and rattles, but every tribe seems to include one or several
forms of drums. Some of these were strictly ceremonial, and their use
was specifically prescribed as to time and place, purpose, and even to
the person who was permitted to play them. In effect, such drums were
highly personal and were thought to have a spirit or life of their own.
Thus, some drums became heirlooms which could not be abused or have their
ownership transferred lightly, any more than one would consider giving
away his brother or child. The owner of a good drum (one which had attributed to it certain powers as proven by past experience) was a res-
pected individual. Such drums were not used on purely social occasions.

Such a drum, associated with healing ceremonies, was the Woodland-style
water drum. Here a basswood or cedar log about 10-12 inches in diameter
by about 18 inches in length was hollowed out to create a thin-walled cylinder. A water-tight bottom was attached, possibly with an outer ring
of root or split wood to keep it intact. A hole was bored or burned in
the side so that water could be poured in and, therefore, change the tone,
depending upon the depth of the water. A thin rawhide of deerskin was
stretched over the top by pressing down another ring, much as a modern
embroidery hoop functions. If you must make a drum such as this, recall
its medicinal history and don't abuse the drum with frivolous behavior.

Other drums were made, sometimes several feet in diameter from such frames
as wooden wash tubs. More recently, modern White man's drums are being
used. Some were one-sided or single-headed; some, double-headed. Pueblo
potters made bowls which were made into drums. (If you try one of these,
be sure that the tension from drying rawhide doesn't crack the bowl.)

The Frame

More to the point of this chapter is the one- or two-headed flat drum or
"tom-tom" type which, in one form or another, is now used almost all over.
An adequate rim can be made from several modern containers. Nail kegs
seldom are seen anymore, but occasionally one can be found at a rummage
sale. These are a nice size as is, but they can be cut down, if one
wishes. One student made a fine drum from a well-weathered herring keg.

Wood veneer cheese boxes are still used by some Wisconsin creameries.
These can also be used as is, or the box can be taken apart and reassem-
bled with rawhide lace. Someone who is clever with a circle saw may
be able to rip a thin piece from a suitable plank which can be bent after
thorough steaming in boiling water.

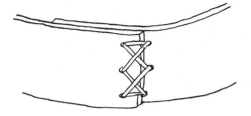

*Fig. 1, Method of lacing a
wooden drum frame.*

For strength and, it appears to me,
honesty to the craft, I like to use
wide black ash splints which came off
too thick for baskets. Split white
cedar is good, too. A piece perhaps
3-4 inches wide (it can, of course,
be more or less) is bent to a 12-18
inch diameter with about a 3-4 inch
overlap. You'll need a strip some 40
inches long for the lesser diameter;
use πd formula for larger sizes. If
fresh wood is used, it probably will

take such a bend easily. Otherwise, it may need to be softened in boiling water. The outer end may be shaved somewhat so that the overlap does
not appear so evident. A C-clamp can be used to hold the joint together
while 1/4 inch holes are drilled for sewing. Some heavy cowhide rawhide
lace is stitched through as a shoe is laced and is pulled as tight as possible (Fig. 1). If you lack confidence in your lacing, you may wish to
spread some glue in the joint first. Before the wood takes a set, check
the frame for symmetry and make necessary adjustments. Dry the wood and
lace for a few days and remove the clamp. Sandpaper or whittle the rims
round and smooth. Although the wood by itself is a good surface, especially after it gets a little wear, I like to cover the outside of the
frame with a strip of birch bark, brown side out. This hides the overlap and seems to me to enhance the drum. Birch bark scraped designs are
appropriate on such a surface. If bark is used, you may need to drill
and lace more holes for the overlap of this cover.

The Drum Head

Your drum can be made one-headed after a Plains style, or it can have two
heads as was custom in some Woodland cultures such as the Ojibwa. Select
a deerskin or calf rawhide which has been dried flat and stretched. For
a small drum of this size, heavy hide such as cow is too thick and doesn't
permit the reverberations of a thinner head. Place the drum frame on the
rawhide and trace the outline. I can't find any preference, but it seems
to me that what was the hair side of the hide should be out on the surface of the drum. To follow my instructions above, place the hair side
of the hide down with the frame on top on the flesh side. Mark another
line an inch out from the traced line to allow for a hem to drape over
the rim of the frame for lacing holes. Obviously, if you intend to make
a double-headed drum, you'll need two such pieces.

Cut out the rawhide head(s). Scribe a guide line about 1/2 inch from the
outside for hole placement. Mark an even number of points along this

line. (For the two-hole technique of lacing, an even number not divis-
ible by 4 is required: 14, 18, 22. For the single-hole technique, a
simple even number is all that is necessary.) No more than 1 1/2 inches
should be allowed between holes or you will create undesirable pleats
later; one inch intervals are about right. The interval need not be precise but should be roughly equidistant. I think that too much precision
makes the drum appear mechanical and spoils the uniqueness of each piece.
Punch these holes with an awl or a leather punch, and make these large
enough for easy insertion of the lacing. If two heads are to be used,
place the heads back to back and punch through both simultaneously. This
is to assure that the lacing will be aligned. You may want to number the
holes, in either instance, to aid you in lacing. For any markings, see
that these are on the reverse side of the head, and use something which
will not bleed through to the good side.

Soak several yards of rawhide lace or *babiche* for a few hours. Estimate
the length by multiplying the number of crossings by the diameter of the
frame. You want this to be soft and stretchy. Depending on the thickness of the head, soak it for an hour or a few minutes. You don't want
this to become too floppy, but you want it soft enough to stretch well.

A Single-Headed Drum

Lay the drum head face
down on a smooth surface,
and center the frame on
it. Lace through two
holes on one side. Pull
one end through about a
foot so that you'll have
plenty left for a knot.
Cross the other end over
to the appropriate hole
to the appropriate hole

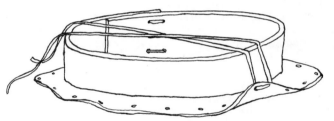

*Fig. 2, Beginning the two-hole method of lac-
ing a single-headed drum.*

on the opposite side (Fig. 2). Center the frame as you do so. Lace into the adjacent hole and return to the first side again. Pull this a
little tight and again check for centering. Continue lacing as in Fig.
3.

If more rawhide lace is needed to complete the job, make a splice by
slitting the two ends to be joined (Fig. 4A), and slip one inside the
other and bring its other end through (Fig. 4B). Pull this tight (Fig.
4C). This makes the strongest splice for rawhide except for the limita-
tion of the half-thickness at the slits. It is very difficult to tie a
non-slip splice with normal knots in rawhide. Such splices should be
made at the crossing of the laces where they are not as apparent as elsewhere.

Make final adjustments as may be necessary to center the head on the
frame and pull all lace tight. Not too tight -- you don't want to tear
out the holes. Bring both loose ends toward the center crossing, and

tie them several times over this so as to
group all the strings in a hub. If you
make several turns around and end in a square
knot, this should hold upon drying. Don't
worry if the drum sounds "dead". It will
tighten considerably in a day. Check the
head hem near the lacing and smooth out as
many pleats or ripples as you can in the
early stages of drying. Small ripples will
often stretch themselves out.

If holes tear out in early stages of lacing,
take out the lace and begin over. If holes
tear out later, you may decide just to introduce another piece of lace. If holes
seem to tear out rather easily, you may
have a rotten rawhide, or you're simply too
strong. In the former case, use another
head. In the latter, don't pull so hard;
let the rawhide do some tightening of its
own.

A single-headed drum such as this is usually
gripped over the center hub by shoving the
fingers of one hand through appropriate
spaces. This gives a clearer sound than

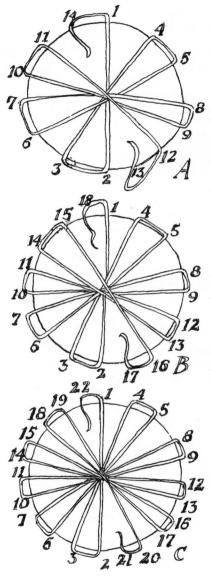

Fig. 3, Two-hole lacing
method. A, 14 holes, B,
18 holes. C, 22 holes.

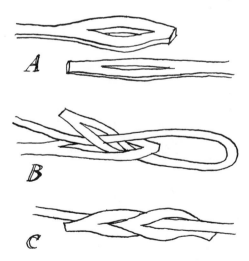

Fig. 4, Rawhide splice. A, Slit
ends. B, Inserting ends. C,
Pulling together.

setting it on the ground or gripping
it by the rim.

A variation of the two-hole lacing
method is to punch the holes in
pairs around the hem (Fig. 5).
This seems to make less of a ripple
between holes when the lace is pulled tight. A one-inch interval is
maintained between pairs.

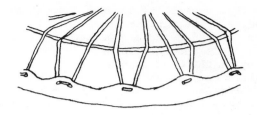
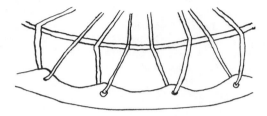

*Fig. 5, Close spacing on two-
hole lacing.*

A simpler way of lacing is to go
through one hole at a time and
thence to a hole on the opposite
side (Fig. 6). This may not bring
the strings together as a hub naturally, but this can be done with
the terminal knot. This single-
hole technique is best suited for
double-heads or heads which are
laced to pegs.

Fig. 6, Single-hole lacing.

Double-Headed Drums

Begin as above by centering the frame on a dampened head. Lay the second head on top to get an idea of how much hem and how much bare frame
is available on the sides. Some very narrow-framed (less than one inch
high) drums are simply stitched together so that no frame shows at all.
For this type, I suggest that you cut the heads a bit too large so that
they can be trimmed as necessary as you stitch (Fig. 7).

*Fig. 7, Double-headed drum with
heads stitched together.*

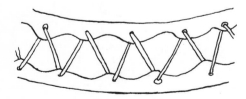

*Fig. 8, Double-headed drum,
single-hole lacing.*

A higher frame is usually laced with
about an inch of hem pulled over the
edge of the rims all around. To do
this well, rotate the upper head
slightly so that its holes are centered over the spaces between holes
on the lower head (Fig. 8). Lace the
heads together with single-hole stitch.
The juxtaposition of the two heads
makes a pleasant diagonal pattern.
A two-hole method may, of course, be
used instead. In any case, try to
keep the heads centered and the lacing fairly even in pattern.

Tie the loose ends together with two
square knots. If the knot is made
near a hem, the loose ends can be
tucked underneath to hide them. Smooth

the wrinkles and set the drum aside to dry as before.

Pegging

Single-headed drums with thick wooden sides can be laced to pegs. Keg frames, for instance, can be laced in this way to conserve lace.

Drill 1/4 inch holes a few inches below the edge of the head hem. These holes should be at an angle upward so that the pegs will project downward. Whittle enough pegs from dry saplings. (Green wood will shrink later and become loose.) Make one end of each peg slightly less than 1/4 inch and the other end slightly more so that the smaller end can be driven in. Drive each peg in snugly, but not so much that the frame is split. Cut off each peg to allow 1/2 inch to project. If you're accurate at whittling, you can cut these to length before the pegs are driven in.

Use either single- or double-hole technique for lacing. See that you make the right number of holes for pegs. Note also the position of the head so that the lacing forms a nice pattern (Fig. 9).

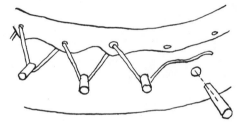

Fig. 9, Single-headed drum with pegged single-hole lacing.

Snare Drum

Some drums were made to give a sound similar to a modern snare drum. Before the head was laced on, holes were drilled in the frame near the rim. Small sticks or bones were tied to lace which was then stretched between these holes in such a way that the sticks could wobble just below the head. The head was laced on as above. When the head was struck, the sticks bounced on the underside and gave a secondary sound. Such drums could be made single- or double-headed.

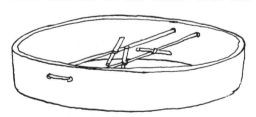

Fig. 10, Drum frame with snares in place.

Some double-headed drums were, in fact, made into tambourines by putting small pebbles inside before the heads were laced completely. This type could be struck and rattled as well.

Handles

Although this subject hardly requires a paragraph, it should be noted
that double-headed drums normally had a rawhide or buckskin loop attached to the lace somewhere which could be grasped as a handle. A piece
of leather about an inch wide and a foot long makes a good loop and allows for a knot for tying on.

Although I have been here concerned primarily with hand-held "personal"
drums, larger drums used for dances were placed directly on the ground.
It is said that placement caused the drum to be heard for a mile. Other
large dance drums were attached to frames or stakes in such a way that
they were suspended above the ground. Such drums have several players,
all beating in unison.

Decorations

A most frequently found form of decoration was painting upon the rawhide
head. Because many drums had, as aforementioned, spiritual significance,
designs were highly subjective and often were determined as the result
of dreams or visions. The Ojibwa Midewiwin drum was painted red and
black according to tradition[1]. I suggest that you not paint any designs
until you have some reason.

For any painting, don't use water-soluble media such as tempera or poster
paints which will blur or run if you dampen the rawhide. Oil-based paint
can be used, but please thin it out with turpentine first so that it acts
primarily as a stain. Nothing is worse on a fine drum than a glossy oil
paint globbed on. And while I'm at it -- please, no Indian chiefs or
trout stream scenes. Keep the portraits and landscapes for framed pictures. Drums require more symbolic colors and shapes. Also, don't use
oil paints on damp rawhide; be sure that it is completely dry first.

Guard against bright, foreign colors. Keep the hues soft, even dulled.
Diluting helps. Although Indian drums may have been painted brightly
most of these hues, in the course of time and use, became dulled -- for
the better, I think. You might try natural dyes or pigments. Information
on the former can be obtained elsewhere. For the latter, try clays and
earths: white, brown, red, yellow. Charcoal will, of course, be a fine
source for black. If you can't find natural hematite, scrape some rust
off old iron -- it's the same chemically, anyway. Such pigments should
be ground fine between two flat stones. By mixing this with some grease,
it can be painted (rubbed) on with a porous bone, stick, or your fingers.
Not too much grease, though; don't make oiled rawhide. After a while,
such colors will permeate the rawhide to give a pleasant surface. For
any kind of painted decoration, try out a sample of rawhide before you

[1]Lyford, p. 36.

start on the drum.

Bells (jingle, small cow-bells, thimbles, tin cones) were used on drums.
The number of bells ranged from few to many. Some bells, such as the
former two, rang with any movement. Others, such as the latter two,
rang only when struck by adjacent bells. Any of these can be tied at appropriate places to the lacing. Dew claws from deer were cleaned and
polished. These were drilled to be hung from the drum to act as rattles.

Buckskin thongs can be tied on and allowed to hang as fringes. Fur
bunches seem appropriate to the marriage of wood and rawhide and can be
sewed on. Feathers also seem to belong -- small fluffy tufts or long
wing or tail feathers. Take some care where these are located so that
normal use does not harm them.

If you can keep track during the business of lacing, Crow beads can be
strung on the lace as an integral part of the drum. You may also be
able to devise other ways of applying beads of all kinds.

In summary, decorations, as we would call them, were often very personal
and had subjective or ritualistic significance. What some persons see
merely as "pretties" on a drum probably meant something quite precise to
its owner. Thus, a feather might commemorate a worthy feat as was the
basis for the Plains-style "war bonnet" on which each feather represented some brave accomplishment. A colored bead might be a reminder of
some thought or experience which occured at the time as may be the case
when an odd-colored bead seems out of place on a woven belt.

Drum Sticks or Beaters

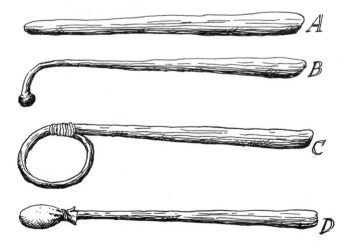

Drums were often played
with the hand directly
on the head. A different
sound is made with a
beater of some sort, and
these varied as much as
drum designs did. Beat-
ers were often consider-
ed to have a "life" simi-
lar to that of the drum
itself so that the two
were necessary components
of the whole instrument.

Fig. 11, Drum sticks.   A, Straight stick. B,
Knobbed Woodland stick. C, Southern Plains
hoop stick. D, Padded straight stick.

The simplest beater was
a single stick much like
modern drums require (Fig.
11A). A stick 1/2 inch in
diameter and a foot long
will suffice for this
when it is smoothed and

polished.

A bit more complex was a Woodland style drum stick made from a knobbed
stick which was bent at right angles (Fig. 11B). This was held so that
the knob portion hit the head at right angles[2]. This bounces off the
head very satisfyingly.

The Apache and Navaho were known to use a stick bent into a complete circle (Fig. 11C)[3]. This can be made from a fresh sapling about 1/2 inch
in diameter by 2 feet long. Heat the last foot in hot water and bend it
slowly. Tie securely.

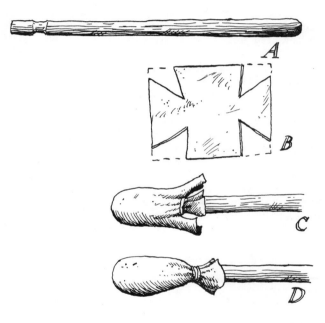

Straight sticks often had
a padded head which makes
a more booming sound than
a wooden head. This beater can be made with a stick
about 1/2 inch in diameter
by notching the end one
inch down (Fig. 12A).
Don't notch too deeply or
the remainder may break
off while playing. Cut a
piece of soft buckskin
about 4-6 inches square as
shown in Fig. 12B. Wrap
this around the end of the
stick as you include some
sort of padding. (Rags
are OK.) Tie this at the
notch with sturdy thread
or thin string so that the
leather is pressed into the
notch to prevent the whole
from slipping off (Fig. 12C
and D). Some heads were
spherical, but some were
made as elongated ovals.
These padded sticks were

*Fig. 12, Padded drum stick. A, Notched
stick. B, Buckskin pattern. C, First
tie. D, Completed head.*

often used for large medicine drums which gave a booming sound anyway because of their size.

Most drumsticks were made of wood, but the desire for lightness and flexibility has led to unusual variations. I recently examined a Winnebago
drum stick made from a piece of fiberglass fishing rod!

[2]Conn, p. 115.
[3]*Ibid.*

Beater Decorations

As a "sister" to a drum, the beater was frequently highly decorated.
Similar use of paint, bells, fringed handles, and beads were used, but
not necessarily in the contemporary notion of a "matched set". Stitched beadwork known as Mohawk, Ute, or Peyote stitching, lends itself
nicely to the round handle shaft. Be sure that a leather or thread wrapping is firmly attached to the wood and that the beadwork is frequently
stitched down to keep it from slipping.

Conclusions

Drums are still very much in use today. Although not highly publicized,
medicine ceremonies usually require the rhythm of a drum and an experienced player. Religious chants of all sorts are often accompanied by a drum.
In fact, a drum might be considered to be the primary instrument and the
vocal to be the accompaniment.

Humidity changes the "voice" of drums of rawhide. A damp day lowers the
sound. It is not unusual for a drum head to be heated briefly over a
fire to bring it to proper pitch; nor is it unusual for a dance to pause
while the head is re-heated.

While writing this chapter, I was continually plagued with the search for
a proper verb to describe making a drum sound. "Playing" seems frivolous,
but perhaps this is adequate when one refers to a primarily social dance.
"Pounding" may be too crude and powerful a word, and yet it may be appropriate in the joy of, say, a victory celebration or feast. "Beating"
sounds cruel, but what about a dance in preparation for combat? I think
that I've used all terms interchangeably, depending on my mood at the
moment. Come to think of it, maybe this is most accurate anyway for a
subject which also speaks with different "voices", depending on the mood
at the moment.

You will note that I have made no mention of the souvenir-type drum made
by stretching a piece of inner tube rubber over a large tin can covered
with birch bark. Drums of which I have spoken are not toys any more
than is the violin in the hands of a master. The instrument is to be
treated as an individual and should be, as Julia Seton puts it, "treated
with reverence, or at least respect."[4]

[4]Seton, p. 207.

REFERENCES

Conn, Richard G.,   "Indian Musical and Noise-making Instru-
                            ments", *Denver Art Museum Leaflet*, No. 29,
                            1931.

Griswold, Lester,   "Handicraft", 8th Ed., Pub. by the Author,
                            Colorado Springs, Colorado, 1942.

Lyford, Carrie A.,   "Ojibwa Crafts", Bureau of Indian Affairs,
                            Dept. of Interior, 1943.

Seton, Julia M.,   "American Indian Arts", Ronald Press, N. Y.,
                            1962.

BEADWORK

Beadwork has become irrevocably associated with American Indian crafts
to the degree that some persons harbor the erroneous opinion that, some-
how, Indians always did beadwork. While it is true that pre-historical
Indians used beads of bone, stone, shell, and seed, only the Hidatsa
of the Plains ever learned the craft of glass bead making,[1] and then
only by melting the trade beads in order to create their own. Nevertheless, it is the introduction of European glass beads which provided the
medium which we recognize as authentic American craftwork today.

Historically, beadwork came into use in the mid-16th century in the south,
and, in the east and north in the 18th and 19th centuries, respectively.
It is said that porcupine quillwork probably antedated beadwork. Certainly designs used by Indians for quillwork were found readily adaptable to
beadwork with some adjustments for technique. On many older pieces,
quillwork and beadwork exist side-by-side. Beadwork still is practiced
today, but quillwork has almost entirely ceased as a contemporary craft.

The work of plucking quills, dying them, and stitching a design is more
difficult and time-consuming than trading or buying beads and stitching
them. The glossy, bright colors of beads must have been immediately
coveted over quills the first time they were made available in trade.
Beads are indestructible compared to quills; even if the backing on which
they are used is destroyed, the beads can be salvaged and re-used. There
is one small drawback of beadwork -- its weight. On a heavily beaded
item of clothing, for instance, several pounds of beads may be used, and
the garments were used only on special occasions, apparently the added
weight was not considered that important. Beadwork rapidly became popular as soon as it was introduced. Because it was usually associated
with decorative clothing, it began and stayed a woman's work. After ex-
periencing the effort of preparing and using quills, it is easy to imagine an Indian woman inducing her husband to acquire the White man's
beads when they were offered in trade.

Beads were traded by the Spanish in the Southwest as early as 1540. In
eastern North America, beads were probably not introduced by Dutch, English and French traders until sometime around 1750. Beads did not reach
the Plains until about 1800. The historian uses the introduction of certain types and colors of beads to help determine the extent of White con-

[1]Douglas, p. 90.

tact with Indian groups, for it is possible to trace the use of beads by tribes to the White trade of the period in question and back to Europe from whence they came.

Ceramic and metal beads were traded along with glass ones, but the latter have become more typical of Indian work than the former ones. Tiny beads, particularly with the rich color and smooth finish of glass, must have held a peculiar attraction for the aborigine who, only with diligent effort and patience, could produce a poorer quality with local materials.

It seems reasonable that the early Indian woman, aware of the comparatively drab colors she was forced to use and seeing the merits of an exciting medium and simpler techniques, would be enthusiastic about acquiring trade beads. The trader, too, would have quickly found that several pounds of easily transported beads would glean greater returns in furs than a like weight of brass kettles, flour, fabric, or firearms. Early beads normally came from the manufacturer strung on threads of a given length. These lengths or hanks soon became a medium of exchange. Some companies today still sell their beads at a price per string or hank rather than per pound.

The first beads in this country probably came from Venice which is still known today for its glass industry. Later, beads were and still are produced in Czecho-Slovakia. Besides these "Bohemian" beads, some came also from France, England, and Holland, and, more recently, Japan and Germany. The Czecho-Slovakian beads of today are still considered the best in the qualities of even sizes, color, and center holes. These sell today for about 6-7 dollars a pound. Less expensive beads are probably imported from Japan and retail for about $2.50 a pound. A good job of beadwork of the latter variety usually requires some culling out of uneven sizes.

Bead Making

Several ways of manufacturing the glass beads are known. In Venice the technique of "drawing" beads is an extension of glass-blowing in that the worker blows a heavy, hollow, pear-shaped bubble of molten glass of the desired color. A helper pulls the lump of soft glass into a long, very fine tube, sometimes over 100 feet long, in a manner as an exaggerated taffy-pull. Glass is amazingly ductile if it is worked at the appropriate temperature.

This long tube is cut into small lengths which are cut later into the size of the beads. Each tiny bit still has a perforation left from the original bubble as it was stretched into a tube so it is not necessary to perforate for a center hole. Cylindrical beads, known today as *bugles* are completed this way.

If rounded edges are desired, as in the case of most beads, the bits of glass are put in a heated drum of iron along with a finely puverized re-

fractory mixture of sand and ashes or clay. This drum is rotated, much
the same as a cement mixer, and kept hot to soften the glass slightly.
The bits roll against each other with the mixture acting as a polishing
abrasive until the sharp broken edges are worn off and a spherical form
is achieved. The mixture also helps to keep them from sticking together.[2]
The mixture is washed off when the drum has cooled; some beads may have
this white, dusty powder still clinging to the inside hole.

Beads can thus be made of opaque or clear glass. Iroquoian pieces show
much evidence of the latter, while most Plains work was done with opaque
beads. Some drawn beads were made of tinted transparent glass over a
white core. These were made by drawing a white glass bubble and rolling
it over a plate of molten, colored, clear glass or dipping it in a pot
of this so that a surface of the colored glass is distributed all over
the original bubble. When this is drawn out into a tube, it creates a
bead with a core of white with a transparent colored coating which has
a richness and depth which only glass can give. These are still available today and are used by some local Indians. They have never been
popular, however, and, when used, they seem to have a cheap, gaudy, quality which is not as pleasant as that created by the simple use of transparent or opaque beads alone.

Wound beads require an earlier technique which will be seen to be a much
more tedious process. To "wind" a bead, a single lump of molten glass
is pulled out into a long, thin rod (not a tube). Then the cool rod is
broken into lengths of few feet long. Individual workers now soften one
end of a rod and wrap or wind it around a copper or iron wire of small
diameter until a complete turn is made with the glass. This is further
heated to fuse the glass together. When several more turns have been
wound on and fused, the bead and wire is allowed to cool. The metal
shrinks more on cooling than the glass so that the wire can be with-
drawn. Wound beads are typically large and may be identified sometimes
by the layers which are evident on close examination. These beads were
seldom traded because factories were set up to produce the drawn beads
at far less cost.

Some drawn beads were decorated with strips or contrasting colored glass.
Strings of glass were fused to the surface of the bubble. When this was
drawn out, these created very fine stripes parallel to the hole. These
were left as bugles or rounded by tumbling in the drum.[3]

Bead Sizes

By far the most important beads used by the American Indians were the
small, opaque white and colored, spherical glass beads. Larger wound
beads and bugles were traded and used, but the first beads of wide dis-

[2]*Ibid.*, p. 96.
[3]Van der Sleen, pp. 22-27.

tribution and use were the so-called *pony beads*, so named because they were often carried in by the trader's ponies. These beads were about 1/8 inch in diameter with a fairly large hole which made sinew-sewing quite easy. Pony beads vary in size. If one attempts to do a large pattern with this type of bead, one needs often to make a careful selection for uniform size. Pony beads were used on the Plains from about 1800 to 1850. Today, these sell for about 50¢ an ounce or $5.00 a pound, depending on actual size and quality.

The next beads to be introduced were the so-called *seed beads* of glass which are not to be confused with beads made of real seeds. The glass seed beads are about half the size of pony beads, but these also varied in size. Today, these are classed by size numbers from 10 to 13 with the largest numbers being the smallest. Size 10 is about 3/32 inch in diameter; size 13 is almost down to 1/16 inch. Seed beads are most typical of Indian work and are universally used today for almost all work. They are available in transparent colors, white, or opaque colors. The earliest colors appear to be opaque white and medium blue. Other colors appeared later. Some tribes had favorite color combinations, often with symbolic significance. These sell today for from $3.00–$7.00 a pound and 15–25¢ a glass tube full, depending on color and quality again. In small lots, a 20-inch string of beads may be obtained for 10¢ from some suppliers.

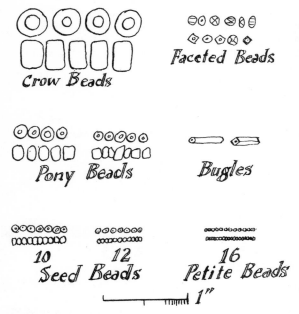

Fig. 1, Bead sizes and shapes.

Some extremely tiny beads were also used. These *petite beads* are today sold as size 16 and are less than 1/16 inch in diameter. These are customarily used only on the finest work, for they are so small as to make the job very tedious and hard on the eyes. Examples are found in some collections where they are decorative artifacts of some importance or siginificance. They are seldom used today. They can be obtained from a few suppliers today at a price somewhat higher than seed beads.

After 1885, some other bead forms were introduced in the Plains area. These were the metal or glass angular beads; i.e., instead of being rounded, they were cut or faceted, a quality which gives them an unusual flash or sparkle as light reflects from the many flat, mirror-like surfaces on a beaded piece. These were known as *cut beads* or *faceted beads* in some areas and are today quite expensive.

Another type of glass bead, known commonly as *Crow beads* (although **they** are not unique to the Crow Indians), are quite large -- over 1/4 inch in diameter. These are sold today in fewer colors than seed or pony beads and are not much used by modern craftsmen. They are found mostly on strings for necklaces and other such items where a few beads are used for colorful accents. Crow beads were not normally used for weaving or stitching on buckskin for design motifs. Crow beads today sell for about 75¢ a hundred beads.

Early trade beads varied considerably in size. Some early work show this unevenness as it appears quite crude and irregular in pattern or texture. Finer quality work required that the worker select even sizes -- a process which resulted in a quantity of culls or left-over beads which would have to be used elsewhere. Commercial beads today generally do not have such variations in size, but beads are still sold on the basis of evenness of length and diameter.

The worker today should seek such evenness in size when purchasing beads whether by the pound or by the string. Many colors are available -- one dealer lists some thirty hues, each in several different numbered sizes. One should take care that the beads are purchased all of one size or a peculiar irregularity will result over larger surfaces. A good job of even size has a pleasant uniformly textured surface. Some dealers will furnish a sample card or chart of actual beads at a small cost so that one can actually see what is being ordered. When ordering a quantity, especially for a large area of background color (even white), one should order enough for the entire piece, for colors do vary in given lots -- much as dye lots in yarns.

Needles

Special bead needles are available today in packages of about 5 for 15¢. Needles commonly sold are size 16 which are the thinnest and are intended for use with size 16 petite beads. These are quite suitable for woven beadwork with larger bead sizes where the needle must pass through the bead hole twice. Since most "hobby" beadwork is woven on a loom, these thin needles are usually avaiable in local hobby shops. Larger needles may be obtained from certain suppliers in smaller size numbers to size 10. The smaller the size number, the larger the needle diameter. Ordinary sewing needles are not small enough for most seed beads; for Crow beads and some pony beads, however, small common needles may be adequate.

Beading needles are typically longer than common needles because in many cases, several beads are taken up at one time and may be held on the needle shaft rather than on the thread. Also, in woven beadwork, the length of the needle is often the determining factor of the width of the weaving. This is not always true, but it is considerably easier to weave when the width of the work is less than the length of the needle.

A beading needle typically has a long eye. Even so, it is difficult to thread one. I use, in frustration, a modern needle threader, if I can

find one fine enough. Some beading needles are sold with a threader included in the package.

One needle will usually last for a long time if it is used only for bead
weaving, for there is little abuse of the needle in this technique. Beading on buckskin is harder on the needle as it must sew into the skin itself. Such work may cause the needle to bend in use and finally break.
Sewing on Indian tanned buckskin is relatively easy while sewing on commercially tanned skin is almost impossible and is very hard on needles.
On the latter, a thimble is usually required; perhaps a pliers needs to
be used to pull the needle through.

Thread

Before needles and thread were traded to them, the Indians used a sinew
thread pushed through a hole punched by a bone or thorn awl. Later
steel awls were made from nails appropriately sharpened. Sinew-sewed
buckskin is remarkably sturdy -- pieces made with this can be fairly
serviceable even up to 100 years old.

Until a few years ago, silk thread was most popular for beadwork because
of its superior strength even when the thread was twisted into an extremely fine thread. Today, twisted nylon sewing thread is more commonly a-
vailable. As a matter of fact, it is almost impossible today to buy silk
thread.

Some suppliers can furnish several sizes of fine silk and nylon thread
and can, on request, recommend certain sizes for certain sized beads.
Size D, for instance, is suggested for size 11 beads. The thinner size
A is fine enough for petite beads. Size F (sometimes called size 100)
is used for pony beads. Seamstress size 50 thread is available in department stores but is too heavy for seed beads. This can, however, be
used for the warp in bead weaving. This size is too thick to pass through
the needle eye, or, even so, to pass through the bead hole. Department
stores normally do not carry the finer sizes, but they can sometimes be
purchased at sporting goods stores which handle fly-tying supplies. Most
stores sell, simply, "beading thread." Because manufacturer's size de-
signations vary, some experimentation and experience is necessary and is
dependent upon the size and quality of beads used as well as the method
of beading.

A few Indians today have taken to using nylon monofilament (a single
thickness, not twisted). Monofilament, now very popular as a fishing
line, can be obtained in a fine 2-1b. test fishing line. Recently, an
even finer sewing thread has come on the market. It is practically color-
less and so becomes almost invisible where it is used. Monofilament, however, requires special knots where such are necessary; customary square
knots and the like will quickly loosen and the work will fall apart. My
judgment is that the problem of knotting is greater than the questionable
advantage of an invisible thread. Some heavy monofilament is now being

used in chains and weaving and, although it is flexible, it is also stiff
enough to be used without a needle, i.e., the monofilament itself is pushed through the beads.

Cotton thread is seldom used in beadwork. It just doesn't have the
strength of silk or nylon. One appropriate use, nevertheless, is as warp
for woven beadwork, for heavier thread can be used here. I don't think
that the slightly lesser cost justifies its use, even here.

Some beadworkers use the seamstress method of trailing one long end of
thread from the needle and sewing with just this one thickness. As the
length is used up, the shorter end is further shortened to lengthen the
former. This is done periodically, as required until the entire thread
is almost all used. The end is then fastened, the needle removed, and
a new length is started. Some workers prefer to use both trailing ends
at the same length so that, in effect, a double thread is being used as
one. Normally, one thread length is about 6 feet long -- as much as can
comfortably be used at one time.

A cake of beeswax is sometimes used to add stiffness and strength to the
thread. This is quite necessary on silk and cotton, but is questionable
on nylon. Still, I always use wax on any thread. A good habit, I guess.
Wax can be obtained from drug stores for about 25¢ an ounce. Beeswax is
desired over other waxes for its stickiness. The wax is easily distributed on the thread, after it is on the needle (or on the loom), by rubbing the cake rapidly up and down the thread. The friction melts the
wax sufficiently so that the liquid impregnates the thread's intercises.

Spreader Plate Loom

Bead weaving lends itself to bands, belts, and other long rectangular
shapes. Such weaving is usually done on a loom of some sort. Warp
threads are normally stretched on this frame while another thread, the
weft, carrying the beads is woven in from side to side.

Densmore describes what is probably the original loom -- a simple and
quite portable expedient for holding warp threads:

> "...Threads were kept in position by passing them through a double
> piece of birch bark. Holes were made for each thread by passing a
> needle through the birch bark, and the threads were tied in a knot
> at each end. These warp threads were kept taut by fastening one
> knotted end to a post or other stationary object and fastening the
> other end to a stick placed beneath the woman's knee or to a cord
> tied around her waist."[4]

[4]Densmore, p. 192.

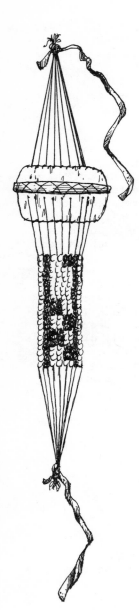

Such a method of stretching warp threads for beading
is closely associated with the method of stretching
heavier warp strings for sash weaving (Fig. 2).
The same principle of using the body to create the
tension on the warp is still practiced by certain
Africans in their technique of weaving long bands
of fabrics.

Fairly heavy thread is used for this warp which
should be evenly tied at both ends so that the tension is evenly distributed. One more thread is always necessary than the number of beads to be woven
across the warp. For instance, a band 21 beads wide
will need 22 threads. This is a standard rule on
all weaving. Sometimes an additional double thread
is used as one thread for the right and left margins of the warp. This *selvedge* strengthening is
typical on all fabric weaving, but is not common on
beadwork.

The holes in the birch bark spreader plate (for it
is not truly a loom) are in line, and a uniform
distance apart. These holes are normally spaced
farther apart than a bead width so that the bark is
not weakened. The excess width at the plate is not
of great concern because the weaving will shrink to
the appropriate size when beading commences. A
small stick is lashed to the spreader plate to give
necessary stiffness to the bark.

A thong is tied to each end of the knotted warp so
that one thong can be tied to a firm support and
the other thong to the weaver's body as described
above.

The spreader is kept a few inches from the weaving
which is started on the end closest to the worker.
As weaving fills in the area, the spreader is moved
farther away up the warp until no more warp can be
used or the piece is finished. There is always
some waste at the end of any piece of weaving. The
process of weaving and finishing the ends will be
described later.

*Fig. 2, Ojibwa
birch bark warp
holder or spread-
er plate (after
Densmore).*

Although no mention is made of this, a modern hand-
weaver's technique can be used to facilitate the beginning. Two very thin sticks or stiff reeds can
be woven in at that point where weaving is intended
to begin. One stick is woven over-under-over, etc.
each warp thread. The other stick is woven under-
over-under, etc., just opposite to the first. These weft sticks help separate the warp until several rows of beading take over this function.

The sticks can then be slid out.

Beading Techniques

There are two basic techniques
which were practiced by Indians
since they began beadwork. No
one seems to know exactly how
the techniques were developed –
whether by native ingenuity or
by trader's tutoring but they
are still used today with some
newer techniques being recently adopted. The first of these
techniques, but probably not
the first to be developed historically, is beadwork woven
on the loom. The second to be
discussed is beadwork stitched on a foundation fabric,
usually buckskin. More recent

*Fig. 3, Bow loom with weft sticks in
place.*

techniques include interlaced beadwork on a round foundation such as a
handle, and lace techniques which have become popular in contemporary
work.

Bow Loom

Whereas a loom is basically a device for holding warp strings, the most
primitive of these is made of a single branch or stick which is curved
like a bow with the warp strings from end to end in the manner of a group
of bow strings (Fig. 3).

A stick about the diameter of one's finger and with a more or less noticeable bend is selected and cut somewhat longer than the piece which is to
be woven on it. Without a suitable bowed stick, a straight green one
may be cut and tied with a temporary stout cord in a bowed shape. When
dry in a few days, it will retain most of this curve and the cord may be
removed.

A number of warp threads, one more than the number of beads to be woven
as weft, are cut a few inches longer than the distance from one end of
the stick to the other. These warp threads are knotted together at each
end and those ends can be tied to the ends of the bow. Some tension is
desired, but not so much that the warp strings break. If each thread
carries its share of tension, a goodly amount of pull can be exerted on
the group -- more so than one thread can take singly. To facilitate
tying, the bow stick may be notched at each end as if for a real bow
string.

Some threads, particularly those
in the center of the warp, may
be slightly loose when weaving
commences, but this should even
out as work progresses.

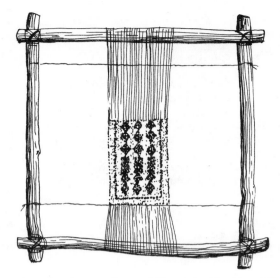

This loom can be held parallel to
and between the legs in such a
fashion that the stick is held
firmly, but the ends project upward and hold the warp above the
legs. Weaving normally starts
near the body and proceeds to the
far end.

Before beginning bead weaving,
a few weft sticks can be inserted as described for the spreader plate loom.

*Fig. 4, Frame loom (first method) with
unfinished band and showing spreader
strings in place.*

Frame Looms

A slightly more complex loom was
made by lashing four sticks together in a crude rectangular frame which,
incidentally, is the basic form for most primitive weaving -- beaded or
otherwise. Sticks are up to one inch in diameter and are fastened with
the bottom and top sticks on top of the two side pieces as one views
the frame from above (Fig. 4). Normally, an X-lashing is used. More
recently, a few nails are used for fastening, but the lashing really
helps to keep the frame in a rectangular shape. Even more recently, the
frame is made of sawed and planed lumber slats about one inch by one
inch. Some of these are fastened with half-lap or tenoned joints. While
the stick frame was made as necessary, the slat looms were often smoothed and polished to be used over and over as a permanent piece of equipment.

Two methods of warping and weaving are known, and, to some extent, require different sizes of frame.

For the first of these, the frame is made a few inches larger all around
than the piece to be woven. The warp thread is tied a little to the
side of the center on the top stick and then is wrapped 'round and 'round
the top and bottom sticks about one beadwidth apart. Each complete wrap
is counted as two warp strings, and enough are added, plus one, as the
number of beads to be used across the band. The end is cut and tied to
the nearest end of the frame. An odd number of threads means that the
end is tied on the bottom stick (presuming that one started at the top);
an even number will end at the top. A double layer of warp threads is
now on the loom separated by the thickness of the stick at each end.
Because the layers are to be used as one, a slim stick is woven in near

the bottom as described earlier. Some workers weave in a heavier string instead of weft sticks, and such strings are tied to each side of the frame. These are left in place until the piece is completed and removed from the loom. With the worker seated on the ground, the bottom of the frame is held in her lap and the top is leaned against a post or some other support at about a 45 degree angle. The same effect can be gained today if one is seated in a chair with the top of the frame leaning on a table edge.

For the second style of loom, where long bands are customarily made, the warp is started by temporarily tying it to the top of the loom. It is again wrapped 'round and 'round from top to bottom and return, and so on, one bead apart. The difference here is that each complete wrapping will be considered only one warp thread, or, a thread on only one side. Again, the extra-thread principle is in effect. After wrapping the required number of strings plus one, the beginning and ending are tied together, thus forming a continuous warp belt. On this loom, beading is woven only on one side and proceeds away from the worker until it becomes awkward to reach farther (Fig. 5). By slipping the continuous belt of warp downward

Fig. 5, Frame loom (Second method) with continuous belt warp.

toward the worker, the woven part is brought around the bottom end of the frame which necessarily brings new warp up from the underneath side and down from the top. This continues until the piece is completed or so little warp remains that more weaving would be impractical. It will be seen that the string with the knot on it will lie diagonally across the warp and that the diagonal becomes more acute as the weaving is completed, so a few inches are wasted at this point. For a given length of band, the frame needs to be slightly more than half the final length of the band. This loom was often used by the Ojibwa and others for making "chains" which were narrow bands to be worn around the neck and not chains in the true sense of the word. A single warp can be used for several short bands if a strip or two of cardboard is woven in at the end of one section of beadwork as a spacer before the next piece is started. This cardboard is removed later to create a short space between the weavings so that, when the pieces are cut apart, enough remains of the warp to be knotted together to keep them from unravelling the weaving.

Box Looms

Some recent looms are
made by removing the
lid from a small wooden
box (Fig. 6). Some-
times the bottom is re-
moved also to make a
frame similar to the
other looms. The box
loom differs from
these looms in that
small slots are sawed,

Fig. 6, Box Loom.

filed, or cut one bead apart at right angles to each end on the top surface of each end. A nail or peg is driven in the outer surface of each
end, and this becomes a post on which the warp threads are fastened. A
warp thread is fastened on one of these posts, hooked on, and returned
in a new slot to the beginning, for the required number of times, plus
one. Sometimes all the warp threads are knotted together first and
hooked on the posts as a group. In actual practice, however, the first
method is far more satisfactory in the convenience of getting each warp
thread in its appropriate slot. Also, the tension is distributed more
uniformly among the strings.

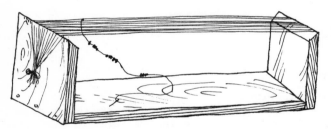

Fig. 7, Scrap Lumber Box Loom.

A similar loom can be made
of scrap lumber with a bottom and two sides of one
inch thick lumber (Fig. 7).
The two ends may be bevel-
ed to make the slots easier to cut and thread. The
absence of sides facili-
tates weaving as may be
seen later. The simpli-
city of such looms allows
one to construct several

of different sizes for different sizes of finished work. These looms are
often used today for they are ideal for working on a table surface. Some
fancier ones are made with a roller at one or both ends so that a long
warp can be rolled up in the beginning and unrolled as needed.

Modern Bead Looms

The simplicity of any of the preceding looms is such that few people need
to purchase a commercially made loom, but some good ones are available.
These are quite foolproof and well designed; also inexpensive -- about
$1.50 (Fig. 8). Most of these are made of a continuous steel rod made
into a bent frame with a roller at each end. These rollers are customarily provided with a thumbscrew and a peg so that the roller can be
held in position when the warp is tied to the peg. The top ends are
provided with a coil spring with a spiral just open enough to allow a

thread to fit in each coil
one bead apart. About 6-
10 inches of beading may be
done if the loom is strung as
a box loom. The rollers allow several feet of warp to
be rolled up on one roller.
Finished work can be rolled
up on the other end while
more warp is unrolled from
the first to replace it. On
a textile loom, the first
would be known as the "warp
beam" and the other, for
finished work, as the "cloth

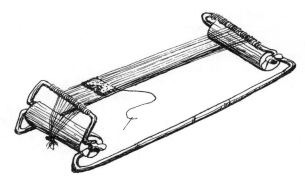

Fig. 8, Modern Commercial Loom.

beam." If these beams are to be used with several feet of warp, some
thin sticks should be rolled up under the threads to keep the threads
from piling up unevenly and thus creating an uneven tension. Sometimes
the cloth beam becomes too full to be rolled up further so the finished
work needs to be cut off and the remaining warp re-tied to the cloth
beam. Some workers have been known to saw this loom apart across the
center of the bottom. These two ends are then fastened on a longer
board so that the distance between the ends is increased. Commercial
looms are made for tabletop work, but the board bottom also can be balanced on one leg as one prefers.

Weaving Techniques

After a loom has been chosen and constructed, one must decide on the
actual method of weaving. Some methods include true weaving; i.e., the
weft thread goes over one warp thread, under one, over one, and so on.
This is known as *single weft* weaving. In more frequently used methods,
the weaving is really a simple back-and-forth winding of the weft thread
with the beads hanging between the weft threads. This method is called
double weft weaving. Some variations on these are still possible and
can be investigated by the student after the basic knowledge is gained.

A pattern is determined. Today, a student can make designs on graph
paper with about 1/8 inch squares. Such patterns should be used only as
guides, for one is forewarned that beads are not the perfect square shapes
as are found on the graph paper. Special bead graph papers are used for
more accurate designs. (See end of this chapter.)

Weaving techniques require geometric designs -- squares, straight lines,
triangles, diamonds, rectangles, and the like. Weaving is generally not
suitable for curved motifs as are typical of Woodland designs; but some
of these have been adapted, more or less successfully, to woven beadwork.
Horizontals and verticals are ideal; diagonals must be designed as a stepped line.

Colors are selected for the design and a quantity of beads of each necessary color are poured into a shallow dish. I like a saucer if I'm working at a table; but when I need to hold the bead dish on my lap or place
it on the ground, a saucer tends to spill too easily. A shallow soup
bowl, not so small that I can't comfortably get my hand with the needle
in it, is then better. Some persons suggest an ice cube tray, but this
is too large for me. If only colored beads are used, a white bowl is
best to show off the colors. If white is dominant in the color mixture,
a dark bowl is best to show the colors and bead holes. A deep cup is
useless, for it is almost impossible to scoop out beads with the needle.
It's also a good idea to keep dark blue beads separate and in another
dish from black beads. In poor light it becomes very difficult to select the proper color.

Single Weft Weaving

The loom is strung with the proper
number of warp threads. In addition
to the extra thread always required
for weaving, single weft work requires two more threads at either margin for a double-thread selvedge. A
proper needle is threaded with weft
which is tied to one pair of selvedge
threads. Most weaving is done beginning on the warp nearest the worker,
so this knot should be at the bottom of the loom. The weft is waxed.
(Wax is replenished occasionally as
work progresses.)

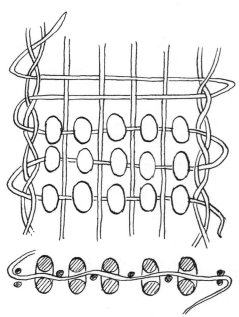

The proper number of beads is picked
up with the needle in proper color
sequence, one bead for each space
between threads. In single weft
weaving, the needle is woven in and
out of the warp threads -- over one,

Fig. 9, Single Weft Weaving.

under one, and so on -- and then is passed through the selvedge threads
(Fig. 9). (Incidentally, in the illustrations, the beads and threads
are expanded to make the elements more readily visible. It should be
obvious that these are quite close together in the actual work.)

Another group of beads is strung on the weft and is woven over and under
in opposition to the first row to return to the same side from whence it
came. The same twisted warp is created again, and the process is continued. In this method, it can be seen that, if the beads are cut away,
the weft does form a woven fabric, albeit loosely. The selvedge threads
cannot be twisted in the same spiral indefinitely, so this twist changes
occasionally -- right, then left, then right, and so on.

If the weft thread is insufficiently long to complete the piece, weaving should stop some 6-10 inches from the needle. The end is knotted to the selvedge, and the remaining loose end is woven back in the previous beadwork to hide it. Any excess still remaining is snipped off. I like to tie the new weft on one row back from the last so that the weft goes through the last row before starting the new one. The loose end of the new weft is woven back into the previous beadwork as with the old end (Fig. 11). Work continues until the piece is completed.

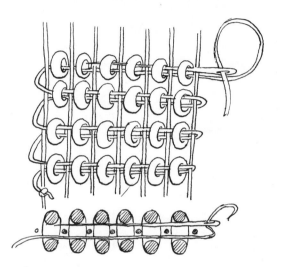

Fig. 10, Double Weft Weaving.

Double Weft Weaving

For double weft weaving, the double selvedge may be used for extra strength, but it is not necessary. If it is used, the double thread is treated as one. The end of a threaded weft is tied to one selvedge. Enough should be left at the knot so that the "tail" can be woven back in later to hide this ending. Enough beads are picked up with the needle for the first line of the design and are slid down to the knot. If one starts at the left, as do most right-handed persons, the needle is passed under the warp from left to right, and the right hand now pulls the needle gently upward. The beads are now hanging under the warp. The left forefinger can press the beads upward, each bead into its proper space between the warp threads (Fig. 12). By pressing gently thus, the beads are held in place while the right hand slips the needle back through the aligned bead holes -- but this time the needle and thread are on top of the warp threads (Fig. 10).

The needle is again brought from the left under the warp; another group of beads is picked up, pressed into place; and the needle is returned from right to left on top of the warp. This continues until the piece is completed. It can be seen that the beads are themselves structurally important, for, if they were removed, the weft would appear to be merely wrapped around the warp strings. New weft threads are tied on as needed, and the tail ends hidden as before. For double weft weaving, it is desirable to start the new weft from the same side of the weaving each time (Fig. 11).

It will be observed as weaving proceeds that one selvedge appears to be whip-stitched -- this is the left side from which the weaving was started. The right side has just small loops where the weft is returned back through the same bead holes.

Take enough care to notice that the
returning thread is always on top of
the warp threads, for it is easy accidentally to slip the needle below
them. If this happens, the beads on
either side will hang down from their
neighbors and spoil the fine mosaic-
like effect of woven beadwork. If
this mistake is noticed early, one can
backtrack to that point and repair
the error. If not, an extra weft
can be tied on locally near the area
and be stitched properly through the
beads in addition to the original
threads.

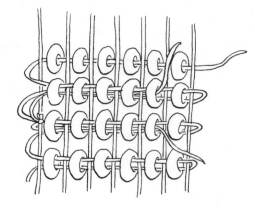

Split Weaving

Fig. 11, *Ending old weft and beginning new weft. Method of
hiding tail endings.*

Recently some Indians have produced
woven neck pieces for sale. Such a neck piece is wide where it hangs
down on the breast, but is then split with half passing around each side
of the neck. Simply to cut the band lengthwise would cause the entire
piece to fall apart. This split can be done if the warp is split into
halves toward the end of the weaving, and each is treated as a separate
band. One can use the existing warp threads, but if the split is to appear even, an extra piece of warp must be tied on at the split or allowed in the beginning to provide the extra warp thread which is always
required (Fig. 13).

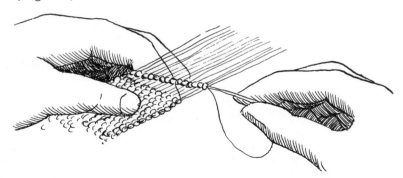

Fig. 12, *Left forefinger pressing beads up from beneath
warp.*

When the piece is removed from the loom after completion, the two ends
must be woven or stitched together in such a way that the band appears
to be continuous.

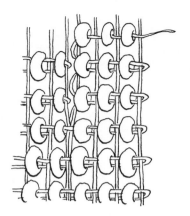

Fig. 13, *Split Weaving.*

The same effect as on the preceding page can be achieved by weaving a belt half as wide as will be necessary for the pendant portion and stitching these together side by side after the piece is taken from the loom. Naturally, in this latter method, a design should be chosen which is conducive to this kind of joining or else the seam becomes too apparent.

Tapered Weaving

At times a pointed end is desired instead of the normal squared end. In this case, the weaving continues as before, except the one warp thread is left at either side of the selvedge each time a new row of beads is woven in (Fig. 14). By varying the number of warp threads to remain each time or the number of rows to be woven before another pair of warp threads is omitted, one can vary the taper. The warp ends which remain after the piece is finished are woven back in much the same method as that of finishing a weft end.

Edging

A nice method of hiding the selvedge threads is to string on each selvedge a group of beads of sufficient quantity to make a string as long as the intended piece. In this case, the weft thread does not go around each selvedge, but rather passes through the hole

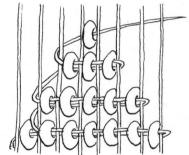

Fig. 14, *Tapered Weaving.*

of these selvedge beads (Fig. 15). Because beads are normally smaller in thickness than they are in diameter, more selvedge beads are required than woven rows. To compensate for this, occasionally two selvedge beads are threaded instead of one, or a bead is permitted to stay loose between rows of weaving. Some judgment must be made as to how many times this is necessary as beading proceeds.

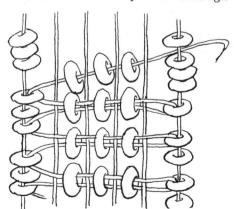

Fig. 15, *Beaded Selvedge Edge.*

It is well to string too many beads on the selvedges originally as the warp threads are strung. Extra beads can be slid off when the piece is removed from the loom. If necessary,

a pliers can be used to break beads to remove them, but this procedure
always carries with it the chance of cutting the thread as well. Besides, it is just wasteful. If additional beads are required, the respective warp thread must be untied, strung with more beads, and retied.
One might just as well overdo it in the first place and slide the extras
off later.

Although a design can be worked into this edging by varying colors, the
problem of aligning them with the woven rows is not worth the effort.
A single color on the edge is quite nice in any case.

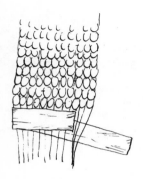

Ending

When a piece is finished, it must be removed from
the loom. This is done simply by cutting the warp
strings near the points of attachment on the loom.
A few inches is normally left at either end in the
process of weaving anyway.

If the band is to be stitched to leather or some
other foundation, a piece of adhesive tape can be
wrapped around the warp ends immediately adjacent
to the beadwork (Fig. 16). When the band is stitched to the leather, this taped portion is folded underneath out of sight. If tape is to be used, the
taping is best done before the warp is cut from the
loom.

Fig. 16, Taped End.

In some cases, some additional
weft thread without beads is woven
in and out of the warp threads in
a true weaving technique to help
hold the warp and weft together
(Fig. 17). This method is not
entirely satisfactory without some
additional fastening.

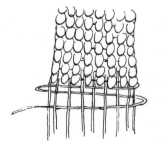

Another method of ending is suggested by the split weaving technique. For this ending several
splits are made in the warp --
each split only a few beads wide.

Fig. 17, Woven end.

*Fig. 18, Knot-
ted Fringe End.*

Each of these groups is beaded as a separate band so the result is a beaded band fringe. For a fuller fringe, some extra warp threads need to be
tied on the last row of beading.

A basic method of finishing any weaving is that of tying a fringe. Normally, in this method, a group of three to five warp threads are tied together with the knot placed close to the beaded edge (Fig. 18).

For a further decoration, these groups of warp may be pushed through a larger bead such as a pony bead to cover most of the knot; then a larger knot is tied below this bead to keep it from slipping off. Several beads may, of course, be strung on a group of warp threads.

Another fringe technique has become popular today. Each warp end is threaded
on a needle and is strung with a group of
beads in a color pattern appropriate to
the main body of the work (Fig. 19). The
end is then knotted to keep the beads
from slipping off. To hide this still
better, the loose end is sometimes worked
back into the bead holes. Sometimes, instead of making a single string of beads
for each thread, the thread may be doubled
back to the main body of work, thus forming a beaded loop. Such beaded fringes
are often used by beadworkers today for
the bottoms of pendants.

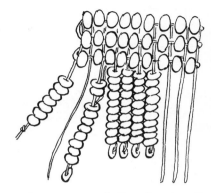

Fig. 19, Beaded Fringe End.

Other appendages may be added as desired -- metal beads, metal cones, buckskin fringes, hair -- almost anything that strikes the worker's fan-cy or which she has handy.

Some work, mainly arm and head bands and decorative belts and garters, are finished with a buckskin thong at each end so that the band can be tied in place on the body. A thong fastening is indispensable in that it is almost infinitely adjustable. In this case, a knotting of groups of warp near the beading is sufficient, and the same knot that holds the groups of warp together also holds the thong.

A tapered end may be finished if the
warp has shrunk as the beadwork was
tapered. Thus all the warp threads
come together in the center of the taper
anyway so these can be braided or twisted and threaded through pony or crow
beads to be held in place with a ter-
minating knot (Fig. 20). Another method is to weave in some of the warp
threads back into the main beadwork
while the last remaining ones are
threaded through a dropper of beads.
Sometimes these droppers are re-thread-
ed several times before the end of the
thread is fastened so that the beads
are stiffened with this heavy core of
thread.

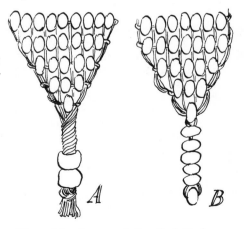

Fig. 20, Tapered Beaded Ends.
A, Use of Crow beads. B, Use
of seed beads.

If all other methods fail, simply tie every two warp threads together
with a knot right at the end of the last row of beadwork. Re-thread this
end on a needle and weave it back and forth across a few rows of weaving
through the bead holes.

Continuous belt necklaces can be joined by placing them end to end and
stitiching a weft through the last few rows of beading on one end, then
over into the adjoining end for a few rows, tie it off, and hide the end.
This effectively hides the joint if the design has been well chosen at
this point.

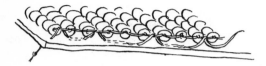

*Fig. 21, Stitching a woven belt
to buckskin.*

For a sturdy beaded belt, the beadwork must be stitched to leather or
some other fabric. If the leather
is soft, such as buckskin, the perimeter of the beadwork is whip-stitched along its edge with a heavy thread
which normally does not pass completely through the skin to the back side
(Fig. 21). Such stitches are strong-
er if they are taken over each row of beads, but jumping two or three is
permissible if done carefully. If the leather is heavier, such as belt
or strap leather, holes must be awl punched completely through at 1/4-3/8
inch intervals. These holes are best punched all at once, instead of as
necessary. If one has a good cobbler friend or a sturdy sewing machine,
these holes can be easily punched by machine without thread in the needle.
Don't try to stitch the beadwork itself by machine; the needle may break
or you may break the beads. Stitching on a belt starts on the under side
of the leather, up through the beadwork on top, over the selvedge, and
back into the same hole. It then goes to the next hole on the underside
and the process is repeated there, and so on (Fig. 22). A sharp needle
should not be used here; such a needle may pierce the thread rather than
slide past it. If a belt is made of stiff leather, allow a little looseness on the beadwork to permit it to stretch when the belt is worn; otherwise it may break or be distorted. For a real fine job, cut a fine groove
on the backside of the belt from hole to hole. This partially hides the
thread and also protects it somewhat from wear.

Buckskin tabs are sometimes added
to each of a band to be affixed with
snaps or buckles. These tabs are
usually double thick with a thickness
covering a row or two on top or bottom of the beadwork. Stitching
usually goes completely through one
layer of leather, through the beadwork, and out the leather on the
other side.

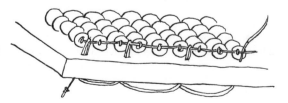

Fig. 22, Stitching to heavy leather.

Contemporary pieces are showing some departures from old methods of finishing although designs and colors still may be traditional. Some of
these departures are honest attempts to make them "better;" others are

necessitated by demand of purchaser or by the desire to cut down the
time of production. Recently, imports from Asia have been introduced in
this country. While designs are different, these are still beadwork, and
the layman purchaser does not know or appreciate the difference. The
Asian wares are generally much cheaper in price than the Indian work.
Hence, the Indian must educate his public or cut his prices which are already below subsistence level for a full-time vocation.

Beading On Buckskin

Probably the first method of beading developed by American Indian was
that of stitching beads directly on buckskin. Several methods of stitching were used -- some more favored by certain tribes than others.

On a beaded garment, the rougher flesh
side of the buckskin was often turned to
the outside. Stitches holding the beads
in place did not go completely through
the skin so the inside, next to the
wearer's body, was quite smooth. The
unique method of Indian tanning in which
the skin's fibers are broken and loosened
makes this buckskin easy to stitch. Commercially tanned buckskin or other leathers, being vegetable- or chemical-tanned
are too close-fibered to permit a needle
to pass through as easily. If commercially tanned leathers must be used, skins
should be chosen to be quite thin and
supple, and, if possible, should be tested with a needle to see how easy it can
be stitched through. Beadwork stitches
on buckskin normally do not go entirely
through the buckskin; i.e., stitches
are not visible from the reverse side.
Instead, stitches are made just below
the surface.

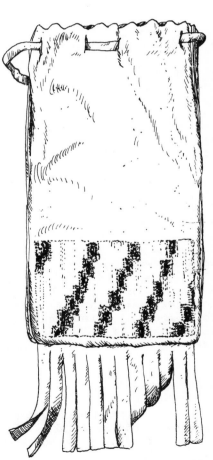

Later work to be developed, especially
in eastern America, was stitching on
cloth. Some Ojibwa designs, for instance,
were simply linear pattern outlines using
the cloth itself as a background. Later
yet, another line was stitched inside
the first, thus making a double outline.
Finally, up until the present time, the
entire inside was filled with beads and
the surrounding background was also
covered.

*Fig. 23, Contemporary Canadian
Sioux bag, overlaid stitch.
5 inches by 7 inches overall.*

When available, velvet was used as the background -- often red or black or blue and green. In the case of velvet, the fabric was first basted to calico or buckskin to give it stiffness.

Early Ojibwa designs were cut from bark and were outlined on the material with white thread. Densmore[5] notes that in 1929 the Ojibwa used flour paste (a mixture of flour and water) to trace the patterns on velvet. The design kit included a birch bark container for the paste, an applicator stick, and a stiff feather to brush away unwanted paste (after it dried) outside the design. Beadwork on velvet customarily did not completely cover the velvet background.

On light colored buckskin, the design might be scored with an awl to indicate outlines. Today, I expect that most beadworkers use pencil. Don't try ball point pens; they smear.

Some old designs were drawn on paper which was basted directly on the material, and the stitching went through the paper which was left underneath. A recent Sioux bag I obtained still has the paper intact (Fig. 23). The paper backing also gives a little stiffness to the beaded portion of the piece.

Canvas (the loose variety, not the very stiff and heavy tarpaulin) is much used today. As is the case with beading on any fabric, stitches go completely through the canvas with each stitch so that the reverse side of the beadwork is covered with a multitude of short threads. Work on canvas is normally intended to be sewn later on buckskin articles, such as bags and purses for sale. In these cases, the beaded portion of the canvas is made slightly smaller than is required so that, after it is stitched in place, a single row of border beads effectively hides the canvas edge. Other stitches may, of course, be used for this purpose.

Woodland Styles

Possibly because of the Woodland Indian's earlier use of beads, they developed several methods of stitching not normally found on the Plains. Also, because the Plains designs were usually geometric, one or two styles of stitching sufficed, whereas the Woodland floral motifs required methods which could be used for curved lines.

Overlay (Overlaid) Stitch[6]

As stated earlier, beads were sold in strings or hanks of 10-20 inches in length -- one color to a string. The overlay stitch makes use of this situation, because two threads are needed; one on which the beads

[5]*Ibid.*, p. 191.
[6]Some writers refer to this also as the spot or couched stitch.

are strung, and the other to stitch the former to the buckskin surface.
Of course, when patterns were to be worked in, the beads had to be re-
strung on the first thread.

With the design sketched on the skin, the
worker would string the beads (if not already
strung) on a thread, the number of beads varying with the length of line to be made. A
long thread could be loosely strung with more
beads than might be required for the first
line on the design. Left-over strung beads
would then be available for future work. The
loose stringing allowed the thread to be cut
as required while stitching was done and still
allowed enough to be threaded on a needle for
starting and ending another beaded line or
two. This length of strung beads was wound

Fig. 24, Strung beads
on a cloth roll.

on a roll of cloth to keep it from knotting or just plain getting in the
way (Fig. 24). The thread could be unrolled as needed, much as a knitter
works from a ball of yarn and pulls off as much as is convenient to work
with. Thread for bead stringing is as thick as can conveniently be used
to go through the beads; the thicker the better for a nice, even line
on the pattern. A thorough waxing is also desired to add stiffness to
the thread.

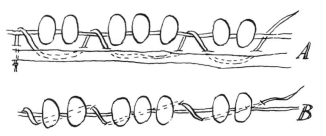

Fig. 25, Overlay Stitch. A, Side view.
B, Top view.

The end of this beaded
thread is threaded on a
needle which then was
stitched to an appro-
priate line ending on the
pattern. The needle was
removed and the thread
knotted to the skin sur-
face. The string of beads
rolled on the cloth was
now unrolled a few inches
to be stitched on. An-
other needle (not neces-

sarily a beading needle, for a regular fine sewing needle would suffice)
was threaded with fine thread (not necessarily bead thread, for a regular fine sewing thread would suffice) and was fastened to the pattern
on the buckskin near the knotted end of the bead string. This thread
was used to hold the bead thread to the surface. A single spiralling
stitch was used, in intervals of two or three beads, to sew the first
thread down (Fig. 25). The student will quickly develop a favored direction of stitch -- I like to go right to left so that I can hold the
rolled beads in my left hand and keep the string in place with the fingers while I stitch with the right -- so that the work may need to be
rotated occasionally as the pattern line changes directions. (Interestingly, many beaded designs look quite nice from any side with no important top and bottom orientation.) By bending the skin slightly to make

a hump along the line, one can stitch just below the surface of the skin without going completely through to the back side. As mentioned before, this was not of concern on cloth beading; as a matter-of-fact, it is well-nigh impossible. On cloth, nevertheless, it still is desirable to hump the cloth so that one stitch goes in and out the same side at once rather than to take two separate stitches each time. These stitches normally were close to right angles to the beaded line with the parallel portion of the stitch going beneath the surface of the skin below the bead line. If the beaded line is kept quite tightly strung and the beads press against each other, the overlaid thread is quite difficult to see. When the line of a color is completed, the bead string must be cut. If enough thread is allowed -- about 6 inches or so -- this can be threaded on a needle and stitched off into the skin to be knotted down and the end snipped off. The overlaid thread is likewise fastened down and cut off.

Overlaid stitch lends itself to either straight lines and curves. A well-made piece is stitched so tightly that it is difficult to determine what stitch has been used.

Normally, the design portion to be done in one color is stitched on the motif outline and then successive rows are stitched on the inside in ever-decreasing areas until the area is completely covered. A well stitched area has a lovely mosaic-like texture which is pleasant even without color. Allow just a little space between rows of beads so that the beaded surface still is flexible. Too tight a spacing creates a stiff beaded area.

While it is impossible today to determine the source of beadwork exactly, some differences are apparent if one allows exceptions. Modern Ojibwa beadwork normally uses stylized floral patterns, but the Minnesota Ojibwa frequently outline an area in one color and use a slightly different color to fill the enclosed area. Wisconsin Ojibwa often stitch several rows of outline with a small linear pattern near the center of an area. For instance, the Minnesota leaf design may be outlined in yellow and filled with green, while a Wisconsin design will be green with yellow veins in the leaf. In both geographic areas, white, either opaque or translucent, is favored to fill in the background.

Spot Stitch

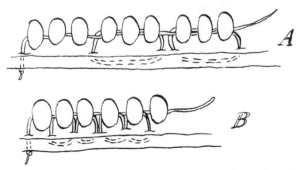

Another method of sewing which can be used for either straight or curved lines is the spot stitch. In this and succeeding methods only one thread is used, and the needle and thread must be fine enough to pass through the bead holes twice. A thread is knotted to the surface to be beaded at one end of the

Fig. 26, Spot Stitches. A, Three-bead stitch. B, One-bead stitch.

pattern line. A few beads -- from one to three normally, (but up to five) are picked up with the needle. A short backward-pointing stitch is taken a short distance away from the knot. The length of this stitch varies, of course, with the number of beads on the string each time. If a sharp curve or corner is desired, only one bead at a time is used; a straight line may be made with 3-5 beads at once. The needle goes through the last bead or two; more beads are picked up; and the backstitch is repeated. Thus the thread, while stitching the beads to the surface, also forms a more-or-less continuous line through the bead holes.

The spot stitch is convenient in small areas. One thread is easier to manipulate than two, and the problem of knotting down the ends is cut in two. The main problem is that one must use a bead needle through the leather while in the overlaid stitch one may use a heavier needle. The overlaid stitch normally gives a more uniformly continuous line although a good job of spot stitching can be just as fine.

A word of caution: if several beads are used for each stitch, the result may be a series of rather floppy loops. If these are pulled tight to make the beads lay close to the buckskin, the leather surface may begin to pucker beneath the beads as a result of the tension. Two beads per stitch seems best to me, and I return the thread through only the last bead in the series rather than through both of them.

Couched Stitch[7]

The couched stitch gets its name from the curved cushion-like surface associated with an upholstered couch seat. It was used with excellent results in the past, notably by the Iroquoian tribes. A well-done portion of a floral pattern beaded with this stitch has a pleasant three-dimensional relief surface similar to embossing techniques in other media.

A bead is knotted to the surface of a design and a group of 6-10 beads is picked up with the bead needle. Unlike previous stitches, however, couched stitches do not follow the outline of the pattern. Rather, they go across the design somewhat laterally, something like the fibers of a feather. In this manner, the stitch is similar to the satin stitch of embroiderers or the same stitch in quill embroidery on birch bark. The length of the stitch is slightly less than the combined length of the beads on the thread so that when the stitch is pulled snug to the surface of the skin, the beads cannot lie flat, but are forced to bulge upward slightly with a low convex surface (Fig. 27). A series of such stitches are taken back and forth across the surface of the design, each one bulged upward about equally. This makes the beaded area seem to be thicker than it actually is. The number of beads varies according to the distance to be covered, but at no time is the number over 10-12.

---

[7]This stitch is variously referred to as embossing, loop, or pile stitches.

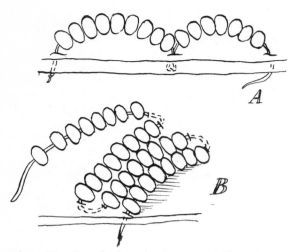

*Fig. 27, Couched Stitch. A, Side view.
B, Top view.*

More than this number would
be too loose or would pucker
the skin underneath rather
than curve the bead loop.
Rows are stitched together as
closely as possible so that
they press against and thus
reinforce each other. If an
area is to be covered which
is more than this maximum
number of beads, two or more
stitches are taken instead
of one large, long one. Designs are normally created
with this in mind so that
leaves or petals, for instance,
are no great distance across.
Rows are not necessarily
stitched at right angles to
the main axis of a design motif, but usually are at an
angle which enhances the form. Iroquoian work often uses two groups of
beads of different related colors in one loop or stitch so that, in addition to the curve of the beads, there appears to be an additional shading
from the colors. Sometimes padding was added beneath the beadwork to
hold it up and increase the three-dimensional quality.

The couched stitch is not used in linear designs, for the loops thus
formed would be prone to be caught in twigs and the like and might too
easily pull loose. Further, the loops do not lend themselves well to
a continuous line.

Plains Styles

Plains Indian designs usually were geometric although floral patterns
were introduced from the east and are found occasionally. In these cases
the overlaid stitch could also be used to create rows of beadwork as in
weaving so this method was also used in the geometric patterns.

Lazy Stitch

The most common stitch used on the Plains is known today as the lazy
stitch. It is perhaps the quickest method of beading on buckskin of the
methods practiced by Indians. Here again, the thread is fastened to the
surface of the skin and a group of 6-12 beads is strung on this thread.
The needle takes a stitch in the surface of the skin, but again does not
pass completely through the surface on the backside. The length of the
stitch is roughly equal to the length of the beads on the string. When
this is pulled fairly tight, the string of beads is held flat on the surface of the skin. Another row of beads, the same length as the first is

picked up on the thread and
is stitched down back toward
the starting point and parallel to the first (Fig. 28).
The pattern of beads is
created by rows of beads in
stitches of short straight
lines which are stitched
down only at the ends of each
short line.

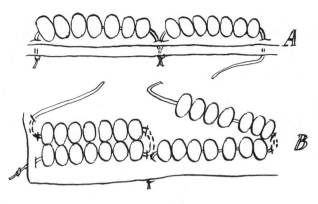

This method of beading resulted in a series of horizontal bead lines which
could be varied in color,
but, as in the case of weaving for a diagonal pattern,

Fig. 28, Lazy Stitch. A, Side view. B, Top view.

lines might be partly one color and partly another. The lazy stitch is
very similar to the couched stitch and varies mainly in that no effort
was made to curve the beads upward. This embossed effect, however, is,
to a degree, a natural result of the lazy stitch, especially when the
stitches are pulled up tightly. A gentler tension is desired so that
the skin underneath the rows does not pucker up. The ridged effect of
several rows of beading is typical of the lazy stitch which is easy to
recognize in most Plains work. The lazy stitch also differs from the
couched stitch in that the stitches are at right angles to the design
row rather than at a diagonal.

It is said that the lazy stitch is less firm than the overlaid stitch,
but became widespread in usage because work progressed more rapidly. Experience proves that it is a simpler stitch and, generally, areas of the
pattern are completely covered much more easily and quickly. The overlaid stitch holds the string of beads in place every few beads apart, so
damage to a beaded area would mean that the overlaid thread would have
to be broken as well as the thread upon which the beads are strung. One
stitch pulling out or broken on a lazy stitch would result in a loop hanging free or spilling the beads from the thread.

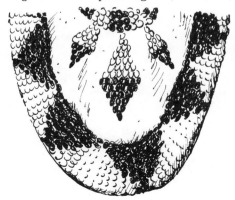

To stitch a curve with the lazy stitch
such as might be needed around the toe
of a moccasin, the band of beads was
made of rows of lazy stitches which ra-
diated from the inner curve of the design so that the outer margin was
spread apart slightly (Fig. 29).

Fig. 29, Sioux moccasin toe lazy stitch.

The beauty of the lazy stitch comes mainly from its regularity of patterned rows in a gently ridged texture. The thread should be as heavy as possible so that each row is firm. To this end, the thread should be waxed frequently, for the wax is partly removed at each stitch by the friction of sewing. Unlike bead weaving, where one bead must be in each warp space, the lazy stitch permits varied numbers of beads to be used; if beads differ slightly in thickness, one may pick up a different number of beads for each stitch and still keep the same length for each line.

Rosettes

Rosettes or round discs of beadwork vary in diameter from about 1 1/2 inch up to about 4 inches. Such pieces are often sold today as pendants or are sewed on costumes and are known also as targets and bull's-eyes in some areas. Earlier, they probably got their start as round discs placed at intervals on wide beaded bands called *blanket strips*. Blanket strips were stitched to blanket borders, of course, but were also fastened to leggings, shirts, and horse trappings.

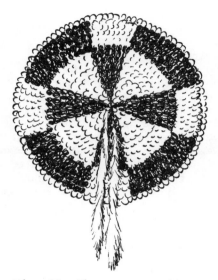

Rosettes normally are beaded on buckskin, but the work of tanning skins has caused many contemporary beadworkers to turn instead to felt as a foundation fabric. Today, most workers merely cut a disc of the desired size and begin beading directly on it. Earlier, the disc might

Fig. 30, Cheyenne rosette with fur strips.

be lashed to a wooden hoop and stretched taut as an embroiderer who uses an embroidery hoop to stretch a fabric. Today some women like to back these rosettes with stiff interfacing material such as is used to stiffen jacket collars and the like. In this case, the stitching normally goes through both the felt and interfacing.

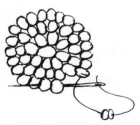

Fig. 31, Beading a rosette, spot stitch.

Two or perhaps three methods of beading rosettes are known today. The simplest one is the spot stitch described above. One bead is stitched in the center of the disc, then four or six are spot-stitched singly around this center bead (Fig. 31). The next concentric circle contains about twice as many as the previous row, but this principle does not apply further. Each row increases in number, naturally, but not twice as many each time.

If the design is built of complete concentric circles, it is a little easier to work in a pattern of color. Some rosettes are stitched in the form of a continuous spiral where color beginnings and endings are awkward in the

design. Rosettes are normally symmetrical in design, and the ending of
the spiral tends to confuse the symmetry.

The rosette usually is built up to the desired diameter by concentric
beaded rings. As the diameter increases, the number of beads on each
loop of the stitch may increase as well. The concentric ring stitching
lends itself nicely to balanced designs.

Another method used to bead rosettes is the overlaid stitch. Because
the color design changes rapidly, especially in the first circles, only
as many beads are strung as will be used for a few stitches at a time.
The first circles should be overlaid between each bead until a large
diameter is created; then, two or three beads may be jumped at once.
The overlaid stitch lends itself to a spiral design as the bead thread
is continuous. If concentric rings are desired, the bead string should
pass through the first few beads in each ring when the beginning point
is reached again each time. Then the bead string can be stitched out to
the next ring before more beads are strung on again.

Another method of beading was an interlocking threading which forms a
lace-like pattern of beads, albeit close together. This is the same
technique which will be described later as the Peyote stitch method for
beading rabbit's feet. The only difference for the rosette is that occasionally the stitch is taken into the leather to anchor the beadwork.
Otherwise, the lace disc will be held only at the center bead. The main
objection to this method is due to the technique of putting each new row
of beads partially in between beads of the previous row. The problem
occurs inasmuch as more and more of the foundation leather shows through
as the diameter increases. Either the rosette is kept small or a break
in the pattern must be made to introduce extra beads, two at a time, instead of one, in the spaces between beads or the previous row.

Rosettes are usually backed with another disc of buckskin with the "good
side" out. This covers the stitches on the backside if canvas or felt
was used, and also serves to stiffen the disc. The backing is stitched
to the beadwork along with a beaded edging to be described later.

Earlier rosettes were often enhanced with a pendant of hair, fur, or
buckskin thongs attached to the very center. Such embellishments might
also be affixed to the circumference.

Some rosettes are imported today from Hong Kong to meet the "need" of
souvenir shops and Boy Scout costumes. I recently purchased a few of
these 3 inches in diameter at $1.39 a pair. These are quite well made
although of ugly color combinations and with psuedo-Indian designs. At
this price, no American Indian can afford to buy beads and other materials and spend the hour or two required to make a rosette, especially
when one realizes that the quoted price is retail, and the return to the
worker is about half that. These Hong Kong rosettes are beaded in concentric circles over printed paper patterns using an overlaid stitch
which jumps up to eight beads in the larger circular rows. The back is
covered with a thin leather, probably calf, and the edge is hidden with

a beaded edge stitch. These imports are usually indentified with a label, but, unfortunately, entrepeneurs are peddling these to Indians who
remove the label and sell them as local work.

Edging Methods

Margins of buckskin and cloth articles were often trimmed with beaded
edging. In eastern areas, beaded edging superseded the earlier fringed trim. Sometimes the edge was cut in a scallop which made a handsome
edge with beading. Edging is decorative, but when it is used to cover
a seam of pieces of material, it could also be called functional. Further, the edging received the wear rather than the fabric itself. Edging
was quite common in Woodland beading where it persists today, but was
not often used in Plains work.

Edging -- Basic Stitch

The most common edge is found made of beads so arranged that every other
bead sticks out at right angles to beads along the edge of the material.
A bead is stitched to the edge of the material and the thread returns
outward through the bead hole.
Two more beads are picked up
and are stitched down near to
the first. The first of these
beads is allowed to remain in
an upright position at right
angles to the edge while the
thread is returned through the
second's hole so as to make

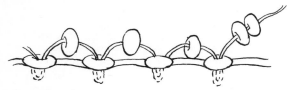

Fig. 32, Basic Stitch.

it lie flat to the surface of the edge. By continuing the method, alternating vertical and horizontal single beads create the basic stitch
(Fig. 32).

Edging -- Looped Stitch

What I choose to call a looped
stitch is, in principle, the
same as the basic stitch, except
that more than two beads are
picked up each time and more
distance is allowed between
stitches (Fig. 33). In this

Fig. 33, Looped Stitch.

method, two or more beads, more-or-less vertical to the edge are put in
place while one bead still is horizontal and contains the thread where
it is stitched to the material. More than three or four beads in this
method results in a floppy series of loops which is not very practical.
The added bead or two allows one to sew the edge more rapidly than the
simple basic stitch alone, for fewer actual stitches are required per
inch.

Edging -- Lace Stitch

A lace-like stitch is also based
on the basic stitch. In this method, two beads are sewed to the
fabric with the thread returning
outward through the holes in both
beads. Three more beads are
picked up and stitched down as
in the basic stitch except that
the thread returns through the

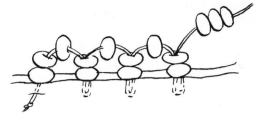

Fig. 34, Lace Stitch.

last two beads each time. This results in alternating beads of two horizontal or parallel to the fabric and one vertical in between them each
time.

It can be easily imagined that several variations on the basic stitch are
possible in addition to those described above. The basic criteria should
be to determine what is appropriate to the design of the article which
is being made, and what kind of stitch is best from the point of view of
the function to which the article will be put.

Edging -- Spot Stitch

Beads can be stitched entirely vertically to the edge by using the spot
stitch described earlier. In some cases, especially where corners or
where sharp corners are required, only one bead is picked up to be stitched down at a time. The thread in this case usually runs horizontal to
the edge, but beneath the surface so that it remains hidden. Also the
thread may return through the last entire group of beads each time for
strength, whereas the spot stitch on a flat pattern requires that the
thread be returned only through the last bead or so of the previous group.

Edging -- Overlaid Stitch

The overlaid stitch is still the strongest stitch, and, as such, is entirely suitable for edging. The method has been described earlier.

Edging -- Couched Stitch

A couched type of edging can be
used to hide the edge of a seam.
This method, where several
beads are stitched across the
seam from one side to the other,
and back through to the original side, is especially useful
where the seam is quite thick
(of two or more thicknesses

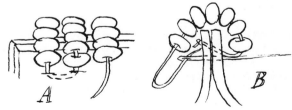

Fig. 35, Couched Stitch. A, Side view.
B, End view.

of material, or where the material is thick of itself) (Fig. 35). Many

more beads are needed for this stitch than any of the above, but occasionally the accentuated thickness is desirable and worth the effort.
A couched or lazy stitch is started on one side of the edge, a short
distance from the edge, and a string of 6-8 beads is draped over to the
opposite side where it is stitched down. Another group of beads is
picked up and is stitched back to the original side. A variation of
this stitch can be made by stitching the beads at a slant or bias to the
edge so that the couching is seen as a series of parallel diagonals.

Beading On Other Foundations

Beadwork was also done on foundations other than buckskin or cloth to
make decorations in three-dimensions. These include beading on a thong,
on a round foundation, and woven beaded pendants.

Beading On A Thong

Probably the simplest method of applying beads to a surface is that of
wrapping a string of beads on a thong or strap of buckskin or, sometimes,
softened rawhide. These "hangers" could be fastened to feathered bonnets
or clothing as decorations. A fringe of buckskin could also be covered
with beads in this method. If
the handle of a club, quirt, or
pipe was covered with skin, this
method could be used over a hard
center core.

If a single thong is to be beaded,
a piece of buckskin is cut to the
desired length, allowing some
material to be left unbeaded for
fastening to the finished object.
Naturally, the narrower the thong,
the narrower the beadwork will
be. A wide thong will be pinched
or folded lengthwise in the
beading process so that a wide,
flat thong will become merely
a larger diameter hanger.

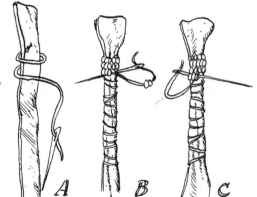

Fig. 36, Beading a thong, spot stitch.
A, Wrapping the thong. B, Stitching
on the beads. C, Returning the stitch.

A needle is threaded and is knot-
ted to the thong a short distance from the end. Sometimes at this time
the thread would be wrapped around the thong several times to make a
round core. This would be stitched through the core several times as
well to hold the wrapping in place.

Now a dozen or so beads are picked up on the thread, pushed up tightly
to the knot at the top, and wrapped tightly around the core as far as it
will go with the wrapping as close together as possible. The thread is
stitched through the core and is brought back near the end of the beads

to return out the last few beads in the method of continuing a spot stitch (Fig. 36). Another group of beads is picked up and is stitched in place. The process continues until the thong has received the desired amount of beads. The projecting end of buckskin might be further fringed to add to the decoration. If the thong is stretched between two points during the wrapping, a better job will usually result. The relaxing of tension when the wrapping is complete may create a little internal pressure to help hold the beads firmly in place. Such a beaded thong, depending upon its thickness, will not be very flexible.

Thongs beaded in this manner do not permit much designing, but bands of color are easy to create if the spiralling is not objectionable. Careful counting of the number of beads in the circumference will permit some vertical stripes to be made.

If buckskin is wrapped around a wooden core such as a quirt handle, this method can be used. In this case the stitches must be made tangent to the surface rather than directly through the center as above.

The Ojibwa made round pendants or globes in a similar manner as the beaded thongs. A ball was made of some soft material and the thread was wrapped 'round and 'round and stitched down as above. Beads were sometimes wrapped laterally, sometimes longitudinally as gores on a pumpkin. Occasionally, a buckskin loop was provided as a hanger before the beading was begun.

Round Foundation -- Peyote Stitch

An attractive surface can be applied to cylindrical objects with a woven or interlaced stitch known as the *Mohawk*, or *Ute* stitch, depending on locale. This stitch has also recently been called *Peyote* beading, because it has been used frequently on the handles of gourd rattles used in the Peyote ceremonies. This method can be used on handles, pipes, and other small diameter rods. On a flat surface, it can be used to bead small rosettes by starting at the center and beading outward. It is seen today as the main way of beading rabbit's feet and small dolls which are always salable in souvenir shops.

I will describe the beading of a rabbit's foot, but the method is the same on any other foundation. The foot is completely dried for several weeks. There is little actual flesh or fat in the lower leg of the rabbit. The foot is cut off about two inches long. Most contemporary rabbits' feet are, in actuality, rabbits' toes. The feet of the snowshoe rabbit (Varying hare [*Lepus americanus phaeonotus* J. A. Allen]) are so large that a single claw with fur attached is sufficient. When dry, these feet may be easily split into the single toes or claws. Simply dried rabbits' feet (or toes) are O.K., but you might want to pickle them in salt to be sure that vermin do not get started in the flesh.

A narrow buckskin thong is fastened to the cut end of the foot by wrapping it with thread. This becomes a loop handle.

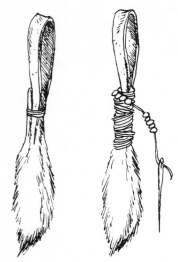

Fig. 37, Starting a rabbit's foot.

The bead thread (or a larger thread for now) is knotted to the top near the loop, and is wrapped firmly around the foot for about an inch. A bead thread is again knotted near the loop and is strung with enough beads to go halfway around this diameter (Fig. 37). One wrap is made around the top and the thread is stretched and knotted in place. The reason for the half-length of beads now becomes apparent. Space the beads equally around the circumference, one bead-space apart, along this wrapped thread.

Now the slow part starts. One, by one, beads are added by stitching through one of the beads on the first row, then through a new bead, then into the next bead in the first row, then a new bead, and so on (Figs. 38 & 39). Each new bead is pulled up halfway into the space between the strung beads in the first row. When the second row of beads is complete, another row is started which will place beads directly below the first row. The fourth row of beads will be directly below the second, and so on in sequence. The idea is to pull each new bead up into the space provided by the preceding row with the thread maintaining a zig-zag course through both old and new beads. A thread passes through each bead hole twice. Some folks like to put on the total number of beads for the complete circumference. In effect, this creates both the first and second rows of beads at once. To make the third row, every other bead is used from this original bead wrapping. It should be apparent that an even number of beads is required for the original wrapping.

The beads thus woven together need not be held down more than to be stitched down at the end of the beading. If the thread is pulled tight each time, there is sufficient pressure to hold the total web in place, even on a wooden rod foundation. The rabbit's foot is usually beaded for about an inch so that the claws of the animal are not covered. To be sure, however, I take a stitch through the wrapping every so often.

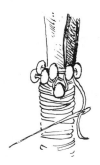

Fig. 38, Beading a rabbit's foot.

If beading is done directly on a wooden core without a leather covering, the end of the beadwork may be wrapped a few times with the thread to provide a surface for stitching down and knotting the end.

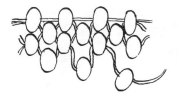

Fig. 39, Detail of
stitch.

Fig. 40, Stitching a
rosette.

Fig. 41, Beaded doll,
1 3/4 inches high.
Peyote stitch top,
lace stitch skirt.

The Peyote stitch is generally not suited for
irregular cores -- those which vary in diameter.
However, some adjustment is possible by introducing two new beads at the opportune time rather than just one. Beads can be omitted in
order to reduce the diameter, also.

This method is ideal for colored bands or stripes,
and, in addition, is one of the few methods
suitable for designs with a spiral base line
as in a barber pole. As in other weaving methods, geometric patterns of diamonds and triangles may be beaded into this stitch.

Recent rabbit's feet have degenerated into
poorly designed Indian "chiefs" and "squaws"
by beading black hair, brown skin, red lips,
and other colors for clothing (Fig. 41). Some
recent work has added other stitches upward
for a "war bonnet" or downward for a "skirt."
Modern beadworkers now make these as dolls
without a rabbit's foot at all. The foundation is usually made of white felt strips
which give enough stiffness so that the doll
can stand by itself. These recent pieces have
lost any tribal significance in color or pattern.

Woven Pendant

The Ojibwa formerly made a woven pendant which
has not been seen recently (Fig. 42). For
this pendant, diamonds were woven on a loom
with a single bead as a connection between the
four which are required for this piece. When
the diamonds were woven in correct sequence,
an unwoven triangle appeared between the middle ones (Fig. 43A). Actually, the shapes are
not truly diamonds, but parallelograms.

When the diamonds had been woven, the band was
removed from the loom. The warp threads (because they are not actually
held firmly in place) were carefully drawn together, thus forming a zig-
zagged shape with the side of the diamonds adjacent to each other (Fig.
43B). By sewing the opposite sides together, this formed a little four-
sided beaded bag which would be stuffed with some soft material. The
open side was then stitched shut so that the warp ends were hidden inside.

This method may be the most complicated and tedious to make, but it is
one of the most interesting pendants and can be used whenever added embellishments are desired. I expect to see some of these again appear-

Fig. 42,   *Fig. 43, Woven band of diamonds for pendant. A, Belt cut*
Ojibwa   *from loom. B, Diamonds pulled close together and prepared*
pendant.   *for joining.*

ing as earrings and pendants soon.

I suggest that, after the warp threads are pulled tight to form the flat
bag pattern, the loose warp ends be taped and folded in out of the way.
Needless to say, one must take care not to stitch the warp thread accidentally during the weaving.

Beading a Strap -- Zig-Zag Beading

A seldom seen and yet very simple and rapid technique of making a brace-
let or collar is what I shall call zig-zag beading. This has been seen
recently used with Crow beads; it will not be appropriate with seed beads
because of their small size. A buckskin strap about 3/8 inch wide is
cut about twice as long as the intended beadwork. A few large beads are
pressed into alternating folds of the strap (Fig. 44A) and a sturdy cord
is knotted to one end and thence through the strap, bead, strap, bead,
and so on (Fig. 44B). More beads are pushed in place and stitching continues as before to the end when the cord is knotted off. It would be
possible to make a continuous band by stitching the ends together, but
I have seen these made with sufficient strap left at each end to permit
them to be tied together.

Fig. 44, Zig-zag beading. A,
Aligning the beads and strap.
B, Stitching with a single cord.

Beading Without a Foundation

Two or three methods of beading without a foundation have come into use
in this century. The first of these I call lace beading because its
openwork is suggestive of cloth lace. Another method uses wire instead
of thread; and a possible third is best made from fine rawhide.

Lace Beading -- Flat or Mat

By using beads such as Crow beads or other large beads, one can make rectangular or hexagonal flat mats which may serve as hot pads and the like.
Narrow bands can be made as chains for necklaces. Although the first method to be described is not truly lace openwork, the procedure is similar
enough to be grouped in this classification (Fig. 45).

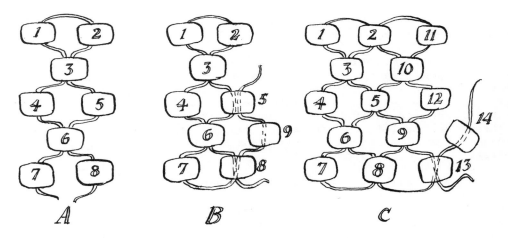

*Fig. 45, Flat or mat lace beading. A, First step. B, Second step.
C, Third step.*

A thread appropriate to the size bead being used is threaded with a
needle at both ends. Two beads (1 and 2) are strung and are centered on
the thread. Both needles pass through a hole in the third bead (3).
Each needle now goes through separate beads (4 and 5). Both needles
again pass through another bead (6), and separately, through another pair
(7 and 8). This alternating two and one bead method is continued for the
length of the chain or mat. At this point, the chain may be used for a
fine necklace by attaching a catch at each end.

To widen the piece, another row of beads is added at one side by threading one needle through the hole in an adjacent bead (9) and back into
the bead above it (5). To continue, another new bead is strung (10) and
the thread goes into another old bead (2). Another bead is added (11)
and the string returns to an old bead (10) and so on up and down the
chain. Alternating needles are used each time.

It should be pointed out that the beads are pulled together by tugging on the thread as beading progresses.

A long band of any width can be woven in this manner and can be used as an arm band, garter, or necklace with appropriate fastenings at the ends. Hexagonal sides on a flat mat can be created by omitting the beads which would otherwise normally make the square corners of a mat.

A tube can be created with such a mat by joining the outside edges of a rectangle if the mat has an even number of beads on one edge and an uneven number on the other that they mesh together.

It can be seen that this method is similar to the Peyote stitch. The difference is that the former progresses up and downward, whereas the latter progresses horizontally around a core.

Lace Beading -- Two-Needle Necklace Chain

In addition to the above description, a chain can be made on the same principle by adding two or more beads each time instead of single beads. The space between the strings caused by the use of multiple beads gives this stitch an open diamond pattern, especially if the threads are pulled tight (Figs. 46, 47). This technique is popular today as necklace chains for rosettes.

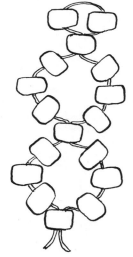

The first three beads are strung as before, but now three or more beads are picked up by each needle. Again a common bead is pierced by both needles, and another group of three each is picked up by each needle. It may help the beginner to use a bead of a different color for the common bead. Additional rows may be woven in at each side as above if desired to widen the band. This method is commonly used for the "skirts" on beaded dolls. If the group of beads are odd in number one is assured of having a common bead for additional rows. Of course, if a single chain is sufficient, the beads may be any small number.

Fig. 46, Necklace chain, three-bead multiples.

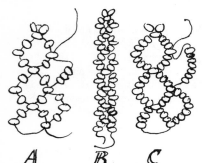

Fig. 47, Multiple bead chains. A, Three-bead multiples. B, Three-bead chain pulled tight. C, Seven-bead multiples.

Lace Beading -- One-Needle Chain

To begin a single needle chain, tie on a
single bead on the end of your thread.
Determine the number of beads you desire
in the zig-zag in the center of the chain;
i.e., three in Fig. 48. Thread on three
times this number, plus the one already
tied on, i.e., ten in Fig. 48. Return
the thread through the first bead. Add
seven more beads and return the thread
through the seventh bead in the first loop.
Add another seven and return through the
middle (fourth) bead in the previous loop,
and so on. When this is pulled together,
the result is a double parallel line
with a zig-zag in between the two. For
ease in stitching, make every center
(common) bead a contrasting color. This
helps to pick it out easier and also
makes a colorful pattern in the chain.

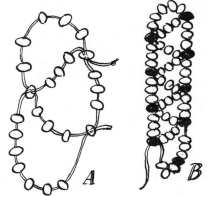

Fig. 48, Single-needle chain.
A, Method of stitching for
seven-bead loops. B, The
seven-bead loops pulled tight.
The dark bead indicates the
common bead for each loop.

This practice may be used with other numbers of beads except that it
should be an odd number to assure the presence of a common bead each
time.

Lace Beadwork -- Collar

A wider collar or choker type of necklace can be made by first stringing enough beads on a double thread (this will be the thread which
holds the whole together) to form the length desired to go around the
the neck. Allow extra length for attaching a clasp.

Start a new thread by knotting it to one end of the string of beads.
String on some beads in multiples of four (8, 12, 16, for instance),
and make a loop by going back through the first bead on this string in
the direction opposite to the thread at first. Run the thread through
some beads on the original string and out (Fig. 49). The number of
beads chosen determines the shape of the diamonds to be created below.
A rule of thumb is to use the same number of beads as are on one side
of the diamond loop. (A 12-bead loop will have four sides of 3 beads
each. Therefore pass the thread through 3 beads in the original string.)

Now begin a new loop by stringing as many beads as would be on one side
of the first diamond. (In the 12-bead loop, this would be 3 beads.)
Go through the corner bead of the first diamond (the 4th bead) and pick
up the remaining number of beads to complete the loop (8 more beads).
Remember that the common bead in the first diamond is counted in the
total of the second loop. The thread now goes through the first bead
on this loop as in the first diamond, and then through the original

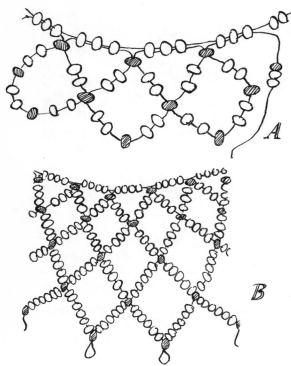

string as before. This method continues until the
first row is complete with
diamond loops at regular intervals.

Another row of loops is created below the first by using
the bottom bead of each loop
in sequence. Succeeding rows
of loops may vary in number
of beads to create varieties
of diamond shapes. Larger
loops will cause the necklace
to expand at the bottom so
that it will flare outward
nicely when it is worn.
Sometimes a large bead or
"pearl" is attached at the
bottom of the final row as
a "dropper" for a termination
of the necklace (Fig. 49B).

A clasp is finally attached
to the original string with
the ends which were left for
this purpose. If stiff,
waxed string was used and
the loops were pulled fairly
snugly together, the piece
should take on a stiffness
similar to starched lace.

*Fig. 49, Lace Collar. A, Stitching the
first row of diamonds. B, Section of
finished collar with expanding size near
bottom. Dark bead indicates common bead.*

This method has no real history, but it is being made by some Indians
today in an attempt to modernize the craft for contemporary tastes.

Beaded Rings

About thirty years ago, a fine wire started being used for certain pieces
of beadwork instead of thread. Rings, especially those with parallel
sides and made with wire, are made with one of the easiest of beading
methods. Fine wire, about 30 gauge and made of stainless steel or tin-
ned steel is chosen for this purpose. This is often sold as, simply,
"beading wire." Normally, seed beads are used, but bugles and other
special beads are sometimes added as "stones" in the center of the ring.
The wire must be fine enough to pass through the bead hole with three
thicknesses.

Start with a wire about a foot long. String some beads -- say, 6 -- on
the center of this length. String another 6 beads and push the other end

of the wire through their holes
so both wires go through in
different directions (Fig. 50A).
Pull the wires tight and adjust
the kinks, if any, to make two
parallel rows of beads. Be careful of kinks in this fine wire;
they may cause the wire to
break. Continue to string 6
beads at a time to complete a
band as long as is required by
the size of the finger it is
intended to fit over. (Note
that a ring must pass over the
knuckles and not merely fit the
fleshy part of the finger.)
The proper length can be tested
by wrapping it temporarily on

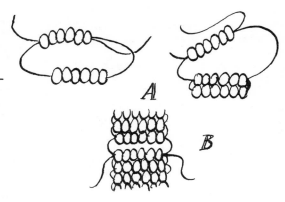

Fig. 50, Beaded Ring. A, Starting a
ring. B, Ending a ring.

the finger. Narrower or wider bands can be easily made by decreasing or
increasing the number of beads in each row.

To increase the width of a given band, add one more bead in each row when
the band is about half the intended length. This permits the band to be
connected later on the "back" side. Increase the number until the proper width is achieved and decrease accordingly to return to the original
width. Bugles and other large beads may be woven in at the maximum width
as is done with stones on metal rings.

When the proper length has been made, the ring is closed by bending it
into a ring and pushing both remaining wire ends through the first row
which was made, each wire again in opposite directions (Fig. 50B). Do
this for a few more rows, and cut off the ends so that they cannot puncture the skin. Each row of beads should be pulled tight each time.
Beads are held by the stiffness of the wire and are fastened only at the
margins.

Armbands

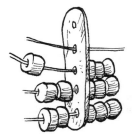

Armbands, necklaces, and other collar-like cylinders
can be made with large beads such as Crow beads and
heavy leather or rawhide.

Several spacer straps are made of leather or softened
rawhide about the diameter of the beads to be used and
as long as the intended width of the band. These are
punched with holes, one hole for each row of beads
(Fig. 51). Leather or soft rawhide thongs are cut
somewhat longer than the circumference of the piece.
These are threaded singly through the spacer holes.

Fig. 51, Rawhide
strap.

An equal number of beads is strung on each thong, and another spacer is
added to keep the rows of beads separate and parallel. More beads and

spacers are added until the length
is completed. Spacers are roughly
equidistant to each other. Enough
should be used, normally four, to
keep the rows even. One does not
need to be added at each end, for
the first one will suffice when
the band is tied into a ring (Fig.
52).

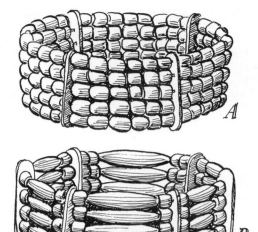

If the piece is to be permanently
joined the thong ends are knotted
for each row so that the knot is
somewhat hidden in a bead hole. If
the band is to be tied each time
it is used, soft leather thongs
should be used for construction or
should be added later for this purpose.

If rawhide is used, it should be   *Fig. 52, Armbands. A, Crow bead*
well soaked to make it pliable.   *armband. B, Hair-pipe bead choker.*
Surprisingly thick thongs can be
pulled through bead holes if the end is cut narrow to get through initial-
ly. If the band is knotted permanently, the rawhide, when dry, will make
a strong knot and the band itself will have some stiffness. Further,
the natural shrinkage of the rawhide on drying will help to draw the beads
snugly together.

Diagonal Beading

Almost forgotten today is a marriage of finger weaving and beading techniques called diagonal beading or what Orchard calls "bias weaving."[8]
This is found in old collections, but I know of no Indians who practice
this today. I consider it to be the most complicated of all beadwork,
but the result is not true evidence of the work that goes into it. Possibly this is why it has disappeared in favor of simpler techniques.

To begin, a number of double warp threads are knotted about a bead-width
apart to a strap of buckskin which is tied to a support so that the many
strands can hang down for work. To make the work simpler, thread the
ends of each double warp on a needle, i.e., a separate needle for each
pair. Do not wax these strings, for they will need to be separated often later. Thread a bead on the needle to the right and direct the thread
horizontally toward the left side so that the bead is next to the second
double warp on the right. Thread this second double warp through the

[8]Orchard, p. 112-116.

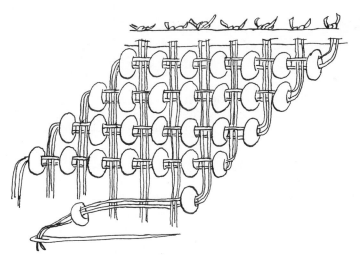

first double threads and put on a new bead on the first set. Continue in this fashion until you have put on the last thread toward the left (Fig. 53). It should be seen that this weaving technique is very similar to that of finger weaving in that successive warp threads from the right become weft threads across the surface and then become warp threads again at the left.

Fig. 53, *Diagonal or bias bead weaving.*

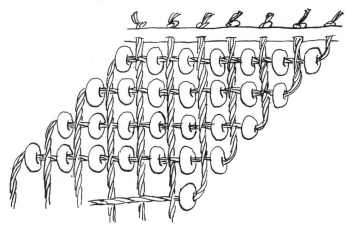

The main problem in this weave, I think, outside of the tedium of putting on one bead at a time, is the problem of keeping the warp thread ends separated as they hang downward. I suggest that the beginner keep the number of beads small for practice -- six or eight at first. I don't recommend this technique for those with little patience. Only a few connoisseurs will appreciate it, anyway.

Fig. 54, *Diagonal or bias bead weaving using Crow beads and 3-ply twisted cord.*

If you want to be a bit more authentic, try long horsehairs instead of thread and needles. The horsehair is stiff enough to be its own needle; it also will make a rather stiff band of beads. An innovation created by a student suggests that a 3-ply twisted cord can be used with Crow beads for a handsome, but heavy, belt. In this case, he used a single cord for each warp thread rather than the double ones described above. Instead of parting the cord as it was brought toward the left, he pushed it between the plies of the vertical warps between each bead (Fig. 54). While a 3-ply cord was used in this example, it would seem to me that a 2-ply cord would function just as well.

Errors

Occasionally a student nears completion of a piece of beadwork only to
notice that a bead of the wrong color has been inserted improperly in
his design. Examination of authentic work also gives evidence of what
appear to be similar errors. At the same time, one is impressed by the
craftsmanship which is such that it is difficult to excuse such a single
mistake in comparison to the degree of skill required for the excellent
quality elsewhere. A young Mohawk man here was questioned about this
and responded that such odd beads, at times, might indeed be mistakes.
"However," he added, "sometimes we put a bead in like that to remind us
of something that happened while we were beading. For instance, if
Grandmother came to visit just then, we might put in a bead that doesn't
fit the design to help us remember that." This explanation seems plaus-
ible to me and successfully reconciles the contradiction of "mistakes"
by a skilled craftsman.

One difficulty in student work is caused by using up one color of beads
in a pattern before the entire area is completed. Sometimes it is discovered too late that the new batch of beads purchased to finish the
area are slightly different in hue or tint than the original portion.
Beads are colored by matching a new lot to an existing color, but the
match is not always perfect. One may also acquire batches of near-
matching colors from different suppliers. These may seem exact in the
container, but, on the actual beadwork, it becomes apparent that there
is a deviation. Such changes appear also in native workmanship from time
to time. The best way to preclude such problems is to purchase too many
beads than are needed for a project and to use the left-overs for small
artifacts such as rabbit's feet and the like. Another possibility is to
mix two near-perfect batches together to create random irregularities
which are superior to sudden changes in color -- particularly in large
areas of the same color. It will be noticed on early beadwork that the
technology of glass bead manufacturing was such that individual batches
had slight irregularities in color. I think these nuances add charm
and authenticity to the work. As a matter-of-fact, the older beads
generally are less intense in color
than contemporary ones -- they have
an antique, faded look which also adds
to the harmony of patterns and combinations of colors.

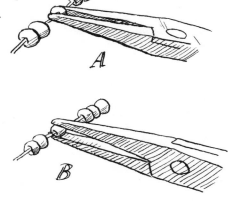

If a disturbing error of bead omission
is discovered, it is a relatively easy
matter to thread on a stitch with an
additional bead or two. If an objec-

Fig. 55, Breaking an undesirable bead.
A, Correct method; pliers' jaws are a-
bove the thread. B, Incorrect method;
jaws will cut the thread when the
bead cracks.

tionable bead must be removed, it is simpler to break it completely than
to try to go back to that point. A narrow-nosed pliers can be used to
break the bead (Fig. 55A). Note in the illustration that the bead is
broken in such a way that it cannot cut the thread. Don't break it so
that the pliers can damage the thread which then may create more problems (Fig. 55B).

Beadwork Design

No other medium used by the American Indians, with the possible exception
of ceramics, or West Coast woodcarving, has resulted in such a variety
of expressions in line and color as glass beadwork. No other medium has
become so synonymous with Indian crafts as beadwork. No other medium has
become so completely assimilated in Indian culture and yet the product
is still honestly and ethnically Indian.

While some degree of individualism was present in the conservative Indian
society, most patterns and use of color were traditional, if not in actual copying of designs, then in perpetuation of design principles. The
ties of tradition were strong enough in tribes so that some generalizations may safely be made, even to the degree that early historical work
may be identified as unique to a specific tribe or even sub-tribes. On
the other hand, the identification of a "style" does not prohibit the
possibility that this could be a style common to several tribes. More
recent work has become more cosmopolitan, but one still hears such re-
marks as, "We always made these designs," or, "That didn't come from us.
We don't make designs that way."

While beadwork was and is practiced by most Indians in North America,
the Woodland and Plains tribes reached a zenith, both in quality and
quantity, in beadwork production. Generally, because I can't possibly
cite every deviant, Woodland woven designs were geometric, and stitched
designs were curvilinear and floral; and Plains designs in any technique
were geometric.

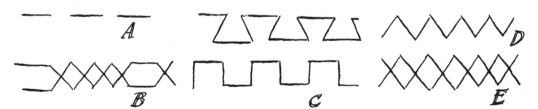

*Fig. 56, Woodland linear designs. A, Jumping. B, Ottertrail. C, Block.
D, Sawtooth. E, Diamond.*

Fig. 57, Sioux design patterns (after Lyford).

Fig. 58, Ojibwa design patterns (after Lyford). Top: head bands, Lac du Flambeau, Bottom: moccasin designs.

Fig. 59, *Ojibwa cut-out design patterns (after Densmore).*

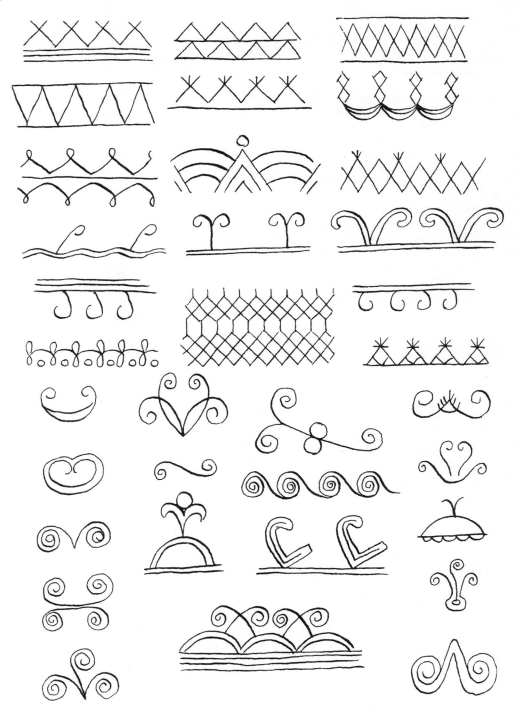

Fig. 60, Iroquois design patterns (after Lyford).

Woodland Designs

Informants agree that the geometric linear patterns are older
than floral patterns and probably
began with porcupine quill embroidery designs. For the Ojibwa,
"the simplest was an interrupted
straight line in which the beaded portions and open portions
were of equal length, three or
four beads being commonly used
in such a pattern."[9] This was
called the "jumping pattern."
A double jumping pattern, connected with diagonal lines became a "block pattern." Diagonal lines alone became a saw-
tooth or diamond repetition.
Extending some of the diamonds
resulted in the "ottertrail,"
so called because it is supposed to resemble the tracks of
the otter. Still other combinations were used.[10]

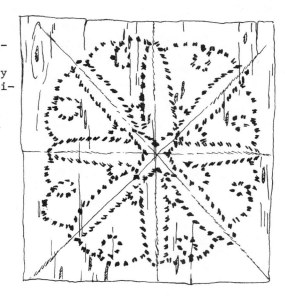

Fig. 61, Canadian bitten pattern.
4 by 3 inches.

Ojibwa patterns at times were suggested by birch bark bitten patterns
now called "dental pictographs." These were made by folding a thin
split of birch bark and biting along its edges. When such a piece is
unfolded, a star or cruciform design results (Fig. 61). The star was
a favorite symbol in dreams and for decoration. Bitten patterns are
ideal as beginnings for beadwork. Although pencilled designs today are
common, it is said that in earlier times women were more free with scissors in making designs, and a good scissors was a highly valued tool.
Still earlier, these Indians pricked out designs in birch bark with an
awl, and the design could then be torn out as would be a perforated postage stamp today.

Iroquois designs were similar to the Ojibwa lines as just described. In
addition, a "celestial tree" design was made of reversed curves which
was repeated and embellished in many ways.

> "A popular design unit consisted of an inverted semi-circle resting
> upon two parallel, horizontal lines, having at one top two diver-
> gent curved lines each springing from the same point and curving
> outward like the end of a split dandelion stalk. The semi-circle

[9]Densmore, pp. 183-184
[10]*Ibid.*

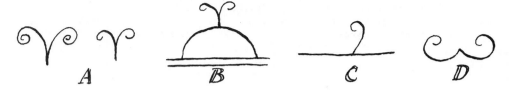

Fig. 62, Iroquois linear designs. A, Celestial Tree. B, Celestial tree, earth, sky dome. C, Pot hook. D, Double curve.

represented the sky dome, the parallel lines, the earth, and the curved lines represented one celestial tree."[11]

Another favorite motif was the "pot hook" or "scorpion". The circle was known as the symbol of life which was a common symbol in many cultures (Fig. 62). The unbroken circle represents the continuation of life in the world beyond. (In the Southwest, an interrupted circle around a pot is symbolic of the life of the pot; i.e., the life line is not complete, therefore the pot is still alive -- it is not complete or finished).

The Ojibwa early conventionalized flower and leaf forms and related them to both woven and stitched beadwork. In later years, these designs became more imitative of nature. The wild rose is an abundant flower in the land of the Ojibwa and is a favorite design. Feather, cranberry, and grape designs appeared as well as later "claw" designs which could have been suggested by crawfish claws.

In this century, the designs have become more realistic to include recognizable roses, blue bells, lilies, morning glories, maple, oak, and grape leaves, pine cones, and acorns. French fabric influences may account for the pictorial representation of bouquets in flower pots. No botanist's accuracy was considered necessary in these designs as rose flowers were added to grape leaves or thistles to oak leaves. It appears that the beadworkers selected cut patterns of birch bark or paper and included tracings of certain motifs, but the juxtaposition was unique each time.

Both the Ojibwa and Iroquois utilized the "double-curve" motif as a basic element in many designs. This line is found in almost all Woodland beading on buckskin. There seems to be an innate desire for symmetry beginning with the double-curve motif and expanding into a highly complicated pattern. Interestingly, the desire for balance did not require an exact symmetry of right-center-left mirror designs, for, at times, the right and left elements, while related, were not exactly the same. Weavings seem to be designed for half the length of a band, and then reversed for the remaining half so that each woven design seems to have a center.

[11]Lyford, "Ojibwa Crafts," p. 76.

Ojibwa colors included the entire spectrum, but bright red and orange
were not often used in old designs although they are quite popular today. Rather a dark red or pink was used. Violet hues were very popular. Several greens and blues were found in floral designs, possibly
because they approximate the local color of leaves. Generally, however,
there was no requirement to reproduce the actual color of the subjects.

Earliest designs were made with white bead outlines alone with colors introduced later as the inside of the outlined patterns was beaded. Black
seems to have been used early in the form of dyed buckskin or velvet as
a background color with beaded black used later. Today, black or white
is most often used on fully beaded articles. The Iroquois also used
white beads only in the early linear patterns. Ojibwa designs often used
contrasting hues while later Iroquois beadwork avoided strong contrasts
in favor of harmonizing hues. Iroquois designs were often beaded in
transparent beads while much other Woodland work was done in opaque beads.

Plains Designs

As with the Woodland
tribes, Plains designs
were borrowed, traded,
and, in the case of war-
fare, stolen so that
acculturation occurred
in designs as well as
other cultural traits.
Also, as with the Wood-
land cultures, designs
were conventionalized
by tradition which
persists to the pre-
sent day, and certain

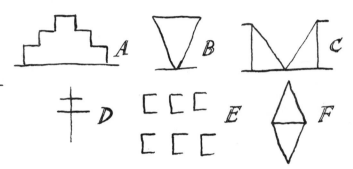

Fig. 63, Sioux designs. A, Mountain. B, Leaf.
C, Cloud. D, Dragon Fly. E, Horse Tracks.
F, Feather.

colors were favored over others. Designs may once have had real symbolic
significance, but that significance was lost a long time ago. Today, a
name given to a motif is a descriptive name only and not indicative of
a true symbol. (Designs, when truly symbolic, appear in the personal
art of religious painting on shields, robes, and the like.) A pattern
in beadwork has no more significance than does a pattern of tear drops,
for instance, on a contemporary woman's dress indicate that she is in
mourning. Some of the patterns with descriptive names include the mountain, leaf, cloud, dragon fly, horse tracks, and feather of Sioux origin
(Fig. 63).

Earliest designs on the Plains consisted mainly of large triangles, diamonds, sawtooth bands, and rectangles. In the latter half of the 19th
Century, designs became more complex, with Siouan designs using more
delicate linear patterns running through. While the dominant technique
of Plains beadwork was that of the lazy stitch with its requirement of
geometric patterns, floral patterns were not uncommon. Today, there
seems to be about as much floral work done as the earlier geometric designs.

White and light blue beads appear to be some of the first colors to be
traded to the Plains tribes, and many early pieces were beautifully designed with these two colors alone. Sometimes a dark red or black was
included in lesser quantity. Typically, Siouan designs would be red,
white, and blue, but interestingly, these never seem to be patriotically
"American," but remain uniquely and honestly, "Indian."

Colors had symbolic meaning, especially in body painting and dream designs. Black is almost universally the color of death; red, the color
of blood or wounds. Symbolic of the four directions, four races of man-
kind, four seasons, are white (north), yellow (east), red (south), and
black (west). Beadwork, however, seems to be done with favorite, rather
than symbolic, colors.

Designs common to most Plains tribes in the early period included solid
triangles, hour glass shapes of triangles, terraced diagonals, crosses,
and rectangles. These were used by 1870. Later designs developed into more identifiable "styles," although the term "style" here means that
such designs were in use by many groups but were directly associated
with the tribe giving it the most usage.

Sioux Styles

Similar shapes to the above were employed but with a lighter and more
spread-out area that the old style block patterns. White is favored
as a background color and medium and light blue next most common. Reds
and blues formed most of the design elements, with some green and yellow. Outlining was not done as the color contrast itself was sufficient
to make the elements show up. Thus, the Sioux style utilizes mainly
the primary colors with few other colors appearing at all.

The fine lines were introduced in designs about the time that White settlers became established on the Plains. Some writers attempt to show,
with compelling clarity, the relationship of some Sioux motifs to certain Oriental rug designs, particularly those of the Daghestan type.
It is quite possible that, as the White man has adapted the Indian *swas-
tika* or winged cross, the red man could have adapted the Asian rug designs which he saw at White settlements. The design similarity is quite
striking for those who pursue this theory of acculturation. Regardless
of the theoretical source or influence, the designs did change in the
latter 19th Century and the beaded fact remains.

The Sioux style of beadwork, as with the majority of Plains beadwork,
was stitched directly on buckskin. The lazy stitch alone was used.

Crow Style

The style used by the Crow and Shoshoni Indians included more massive
blocks of design reminiscent of the old style work -- triangles, rectangles, and diamonds. These were normally elongated or made tall and

did not include the linear work of the later Sioux.

White was seldom used except as an outline. Light blue and lavender were popular colors with dark blue, green, and yellow also being used. Red and other colors were not common.

The overlay stitch was most common in the Crow style.

Blackfoot Style

This style is typically made of small squared or rectangles or several beads across and built into terraced or stepped triangles, squares, and diamonds. Larger blocks or patterns are usually made of one color with other colors used on the margins.

White was used as background beading with other colors used for the design elements. A wide spectrum of colors was used, and all beading was done with the overlaid stitch.

The Craft Today

In 1870 on the Plains, eight hanks of beads (a hank here referred to 10 strings of beads, each string being 8 inches long) was worth a good buffalo robe. At today's prices for beads, these beads would be valued at about $2.50. Such a robe today could bring $25.00 or more, if it would be available. (Actually, a raw buffalo hide sells for about $25.00 and commercial tanning comes to an additional $50.00 or more.)

Bead prices really have not increased appreciably over these many years. I estimate that the above example of quantity is about a half pound which, in size 10 beads would cover an area about 8 by 10 inches. Such an area of beadwork might, dependent upon many variables, bring the worker approximately 10 to 15 dollars, if a buyer could be found. If such a price were paid by a trader, the piece would then be on the market at $25.00, an unattractive price for anything in a souvenir shop. A rosette purchased from a local Indian costs 2 to 3 dollars with a beaded necklace. A beaded rabbit's foot may bring up to a dollar.

A chapter on techniques and design should not be concluded with a summary of mercenary considerations, but these considerations today are basic to any craft. Completely beaded moccasins, bags and some costumes have just about disappeared from the contemporary scene. Partly beaded work is now offered only from isolated areas of the United States and Canada. More westernized Indians on reservations or those residing outside of their borders have continued the craft, if at all, in the making of small, rapidly made, inexpensive trinkets such as pendants, earrings, coin purses, dolls, and the like. Even at that, an Indian must work quickly, and long hours, to make a subsistence living from this craft. This is still mostly women's work and is used mainly to supplement other income. Now the presence of Asian imports threatens even

this token continuation of the craft. The indiscriminate layman souvenir buyer associates any beadwork with Indian beadwork and is willing
to pay the least possible for a trinket to be discarded later along with
the slides of his vacation.

The American Indian has accepted the European glass bead and has made
with it one of the highest achievements of his many crafts. The stronger sinew, formerly used for stitching, has given way to the steel needle
and nylon thread which are much simpler to use. Tediously tanned buckskin has been replaced by velvet, canvas, and other fabrics. Still,
this is a hand craft.

Designs which have slowly evolved in several generations have degenerated into "cute" pictorial stereotypes strongly influenced by white concepts, colors, and buying practices.

A few agencies, funded by the government or organized as cooperatives,
still maintain a high caliber of work and offer it for sale, but the
largest quantity of work today still is purchased by white traders for
white buyers.

The status of the craft at this time appears to be low; the future is
dark indeed. It appears that beadwork will continue in museums of the
past and in "kiddie-craft" of the future, but not in the vital work of
those whose ancestors brought it to a culmination. Hope for the future
persists in that some craftsmen continue to make beautifully designed
and tediously crafted pieces for personal and ceremonial use. Another
positive sign is the growth of the informed and sympathetic white buyer
who is being educated to appreciate the traditional designs and who is
willing to pay an honest price for the craft.

BEADWORK

REFERENCES

Densmore, Frances   "Chippewa Customs", *Bureau of American Ethnology, Bulletin* No. 86, 1929.

Douglas, F. H.   "Plains Beads and Beadwork Designs", *Denver Art Museum Leaflet* No. 73-74, 1936.

Ewers, John C.   "Blackfeet Crafts", Bureau of Indian Affairs, U.S. Dept. of Interior, 1945.

Griswold, Lester   "Handicraft" (8th edition), Publ. by the author, Colorado Springs, Colo., 1942.

Jeancon, Jean A. &   "North American Plains Indian Hide Dressing
Douglas, F. H.   and Bead Sewing Techniques", *Denver Art Museum Leaflet* No. 2, 1930.

Lyford, Carrie A.   "Iroquois Crafts", Bureau of Indian Affairs, U.S. Dept. of Interior, 1948.

--------   "Ojibwa Crafts", Bureau of Indian Affairs, U.S. Dept. of Interior, 1943.

--------   "Quill and Beadwork of the Western Sioux", Bureau of Indian Affairs, U.S. Dept. of Interior, 1940.

Seton, Julia M.   "American Indian Arts", Ronald Press, N.Y., 1962.

Tanner, Clara Lee   "Southwest Indian Craft Arts", University of Arizona Press, Tuscon, 1968.

Van Der Sleen, W. G. N.   "A Handbook of Beads", *Musee du Verre,* Liege, 1967.

Wissler, Clark   "North American Indians of the Plains", *Handbook Series* No. 1, Museum of Natural History, N.Y., 1920.

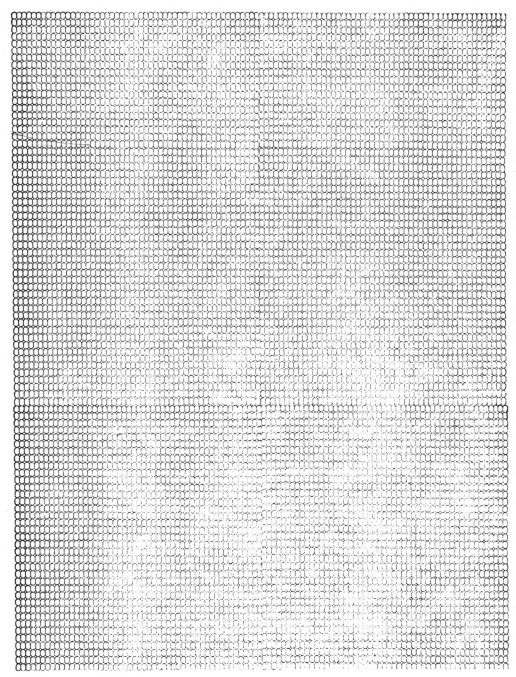

Fig. 64, Bead graph for size 11 beads.

CONTAINERS OF BIRCH BARK

A trait common to most Woodland tribes living in the arboreal zone of
the birch tree is the construction of bark containers. The white covering of the paper birch (canoe birch, white birch) (*Betula papyrifera*
Marsh.) is unique in its qualities of flexibility, size, thickness, and
endurance, and is admirably suited for the manufacture of containers of
many sizes and shapes as well as the renowned birch bark canoe. The
paper birch is found in many parts of North America, particularly in
Canada, Alaska, and central and northeastern United States. Contrary
to common opinion, birch bark was not used by all Indians. There was
some evidence of trade of good canoe bark, but otherwise its use was
entirely limited to the range of the tree. Even then, not all Indians
in its range made wide use of it.

The paper birch is readily identified by its snow white or silver outer
bark which becomes evident when the tree reaches about ten years of age.
This bark is in sharp contrast to the reddish color of young trees and
twigs on mature trees. Decorative birch trees in yards, parks, and other
private and public places are *not* a proper source of bark. In northern
Wisconsin and other heavily wooded areas, however, the birch is a common source for pulpwood, firewood, and, occasionally, lumber. No birch
tree should be disfigured merely to obtain bark today, even though the
careful removal of layers of the white bark will not kill the tree if
the inner, coarse, dark bark is left undisturbed. One can, on occasion,
locate groves of birch which are scheduled to be cut for some purpose.
Such trees are a legitimate source of bark if permission is granted by
the owner. Public lands are not such legitimate sources. Fresh bark
is best for craftwork, but if none is available, bark from birch firewood or from down trees can be used.

Selection is made of the clean white bark which normally grows above the
average winter snow line. Certain trees, particularly those which are
reaching old age or have grown in extremely shaded areas tend to be
scored with fine superficial lines on the surface of the bark. The
cleaner bark is preferred. One should also try to find bark which will
be relatively free from the black scars of knots or twigs. These will
appear as holes or "eyes" when the bark is removed. While the clearer
bark is preferred, bark with small scars should not be discarded. Indeed, many Indian artifacts of birch have several such scars on finely
crafted pieces -- indicating that the Indian used all that was available
to him. For making the relatively small articles described below, small
pieces -- one or two feet square -- are sufficient and are abundant.
Larger pieces are required for canoes or wigwam coverings, but this is

outside the scope of this paper. No taboos are associated with the gathering of the bark although one Indian reported that one should not eat
the lumps in corn meal mush on the day one intends to harvest the bark.
Eating them would result in excessive "eyes" in the bark. The informant
contended that this idea was really superstition, but added that he never
ate the lumps -- just to be sure.

Gathering bark, which may involve cutting the tree, was formerly man's
work. Cutting and stitching -- household work -- was done by the women.
Today, these lines are not as precise as earlier. The bark is generally harvested in the warmth of spring or early summer. Bark peeled in a
winter thaw, early summer or spring or late in the fall tends to peel off
the dark inner rind of the bark along with the outer white layers. This
bark seems to be more solid than bark gathered at other times. This inner rind becomes quite dark in time. If the dark brown is scraped off
in design motifs, a pleasant light-dark pattern is created. Therefore
this "winter bark" is prized.[1] In contrast, the "summer bark" separates
into layers more easily and tends to be more yellow in appearance. For
containers, especially those where no scraped designs are intended, the
summer bark is satisfactory. One informant, an Ojibwa in Ontario, states
that the best time for peeling is in spring, even into June, at such a
time when a vertical incision in the bark results in the bark almost
peeling itself off. It is readily seen, when peeling a tree, that the
natural tendency of the bark to curl is exactly opposite to the way it
is found on the tree. This should be borne in mind when objects are
made from the bark, for the outer, whiter layer is turned to the inside
while the darker layer from the inside then faces the outside of the object. A bark canoe, for example, is white on the inside and brown on
the outer side, never the opposite.

Small pieces of bark may be stripped from standing trees. Because most
source trees should be identified as ready to cut anyhow, it is simpler
to cut the tree first and to peel it slowly as it lies on the ground or
on sawhorses. Large, heavy pieces of bark were stripped with wooden
wedges. Occasionally hot water poured into the separation helped the
peeling process. Small pieces usually can be peeled without such devices.

Pieces of bark are rolled inside out for transportation, but should be
separated soon thereafter for pressing. Small sheets may be stacked and
pressed on a flat surface with a board and weight on top. Check occasionally to see that mildew does not invade the bark and destroy its color.

The resinous bark of the birch does not rot easily, but dark blotches of
mildew are unsightly on finished products. It is this resinous quality
also which causes the pleasant odor and crackle when birch logs are burned in a fireplace. Although it does not rot easily, it does become brittle with age. It is almost impossible to bend without cracking after a

[1]Adney, pp. 14-15.

few years. The fresh bark is somewhat elastic so that holes punched
with an awl tend to shrink slightly and make quite a tight joint.

The bark should not be allowed to dry out completely before using it.
Work should be kept damp or, at least, in the shade. Some Indians
stretched a canvas over the canoe they were working on and objected when
it had to be removed to permit sufficient light for photographs to be
taken of it during construction.

Spruce Root Lacing

The material most commonly used for sewing the seams of bark objects is
the root of the black spruce (*Picea mariana* [Mill.] B.S.P.) which is
found in much of the range of the paper birch. The roots of this species
are long, but small in diameter and, when split, make an agreeably tough
and flexible lacing material. The tree grows well in moist soil and the
roots are near the surface of the ground. They can be dug up with a
stick or pulled up by hand. A good place to gather such roots is where
they are already exposed by stream erosion or by road excavation. In
any case, not so many should be taken from any one tree that it would
endanger the life of the tree. Adney[2] reports that white cedar, tamarack, and jack pine were also used, but were considered inferior to the
black spruce. My experience has shown that jack pine (*Pinus banksiana*
Lamb.) roots are quite a reasonable substitute and are more easily obtained because the jack pine is a highland tree. The harvest of black
spruce usually requires the use of hip boots.

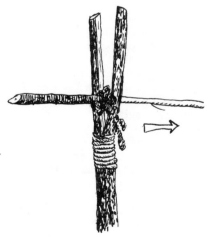

Although she describes the Tlingit's use
of the Sitka spruce which does not grow
native to the Woodland area, Paul's description of the preparation of the roots
is similar to that used for the black
spruce.[3] The roots are gathered in the
spring and are sunk in water for some
days. These are then removed, scraped
and split. She describes the use of a
split stick to strip the root bark:
   "...The bark is stripped off by drawing the pieces of root through a
   split stick called an eena (Fig. 1).
   The base of the eena is stuck firmly
   in the ground and the split shaft
   is tied with a string midway to the
   top. The end of the...root is inserted just above the string bind-
   ing and drawn through with the right   *Fig. 1, Tlingit eena.*
   hand while the fingers of the left

2*Ibid.*, p. 16.
3Paul, pp. 13-15.

hand regulate the pressure exerted by the jaws of the eena....**Too little pressure on the jaws of the eena fails to remove the bark and too much pressure destroyed the prized luster of the outer surface.**"[4]

While it is possible to peel the fresh wet bark with the fingers, I have found that a board notched with a narrow V-cut into it serves well as an eena. If another block of wood (with a sharp edge) is pressed against the root as it is pulled through the V, the bark is stripped off quite neatly. This last block then serves as the pressure-regulating device (Fig. 2).

Paul describes how the bark is split.
"The knife is used to make the first cut in the larger end of the section. Then the root is taken between the front teeth just where the split begins, and is held taut throughout the separation process by shifting the position of the teeth lower down the root wherever necessary. The splitting is

Fig. 2, Contemporary V-board.

done by means of the thumb and forefinger of the right hand which holds the root just below the cut, the thumb underneath. The thumbnail forces the separation and regulates the speed while the left hand draws away the strand being worked off and keeps the work taut."[5]
Needless to say, a good thumbnail is required.

A knife can be used, but should be employed only as a wedge rather than as a cutting tool. Too sharp a knife cuts the fibers and there is a strong tendency to split off to one side or the other. Knife or no, three hands seem to be necessary; one to hold the end, one to split with, and one to pull off the split piece. One's teeth are substituted for the first function. I am just not proficient in splitting roots into thirds. Because I always split one third completely off anyway, I now split them into halves which is far simpler.

Thick roots are split again. When used, the smooth exterior of the root is always stitched to the visible outside and the coarser inner portion is relegated to the inside. For most of the construction described in this paper, widths of 1/8 inch or so are used. Larger splits are used for heavier construction such as canoes.

[4]*Ibid.*
[5]*Ibid.*

The split roots are coiled and bound in loose bundles containing similar sizes to be laid away for future use. When needed, the roots are soaked for a day or two to make them pliable once more.

Roots may be dyed at almost any time after they are split. Natural dyes were used in early times, but recent work is dyed with commercial dyes which, unfortunately, are quite strong in color and artificial-appearing, and are generally not compatible with the natural brown of the bark.

Basswood Cordage

Another sewing material, the basic cord of the Woodland tribes, is made from the inner bark of the basswood or linden tree (*Tilia americana* L.). This tree, fortunately, is a prolific sprouter so that one can usually cut one or two sprouts of about 4-6 inch diameter while allowing others in the group to remain. (Incidentally, the wood, although classed as deciduous or "hardwood", is actually quite soft and even grained. It is prized for whittling and carving even today.) Some use should be found for the wood, for stripping the bark for cordage destroys the tree. As with many native materials, the inner bark of the basswood is gathered in the springtime when it can be stripped off the rough outer bark after the whole bark is pulled from the trunk. Strips several feet long are pulled longitudinally in contrast to the harvest of birch bark which is peeled around the circumference of the tree. Strips a few inches wide peel off with fairly parallel edges. Thongs may be split out immediately, but to make a quantity of cordage, the bark is soaked from two weeks to a month until the soft tissues rot away leaving the tougher fibrous strands. This "retting" is hastened by adding hardwood ashes to the water as the lye from the ash hastens the process. Hoffman[6] notes that, in addition to the wood ashes, the process is accelerated by boiling the bark in the mixture. (Amateurs should beware of too much handling of the material in wood ash. The lye is harmful to the skin.) The lye is then thoroughly rinsed out. He states that a hole of an inch diameter is bored through a deer shoulder blade bone or similar, and the fibers are pulled back and forth through this hole to remove splinters and soften it.

Hoffman describes the process of rolling cordage in a relatively simple technique. Actually this is about as simple as spinning wool by hand. There's not much to it -- once you know how.
> "The manner of making twine...is by holding in the left the fiber
> as it is pulled from a hank, and separating it into two parts which
> are laid across the thigh. The palm of the right hand is then rol-
> led forward over both, so as to tightly twist the pair of strands
> when they are permitted to unite and twist into a cord. The twisted
> end being pushed a little to the right, the next continuous portion

[6]Hoffman, p. 260.

of the united strands also are twisted to form a single cord."[7]

The forward push or roll creates a tensile twist on the two strands and the return roll joining them results in a reverse tension which holds the two cords together as one -- the same principle as that in all cord making, ancient or modern.

For longer cord, new bunches are added into the first without knotting. The twisting action is all that is necessary. Basswood cord thus made can be produced in a diameter of 1/16 inch or less, but can be made into heavier ropes as well. This cord is superior to modern cordage in several ways -- it is soft when working with it and does not injure the hands as does jute; it does not kink when dry; and it is supposed to be stronger, diameter for diameter, than other natural fiber ropes. While it has a good wet-strength, I prefer to use it slightly moistened, but not wet. It seems to stitch more snugly.

Seamless Pan

The simplest bark container probably is the seamless maple sap dish or pan used by such tribes as the Ojibwa and Menomini for gathering sap in the making of maple sugar, a staple in the diet of these tribes. Hoffman[8] states that these were 7-10 inches wide, 20 inches long, and about 8 inches deep. Of course, these expedient dishes could be made to any dimensions as the need arose. Bark containers were used for cooking by the addition of hot stones dropped into the dish until the meal was cooked. It is said that as long as the flames of a fire do not reach above the liquid level inside the container, a meal can be cooked over the fire in a birch vessel.

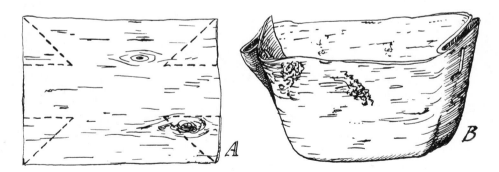

Fig. 3. Seamless pan. A, Pattern. B, Finished.

[7]*Ibid.*
[8]*Ibid.*, pp. 288-289.

Folding the edges or corners in a V-angle results in a seamless, therefore waterproof, container which was quickly and simply fastened with a
few stitches of cord or spruce root or a pin of wood (Fig. 3). Hoffman
notes that "a woman in good circumstances might possess as many as 1,200
to 1,500 birchbark vessels, all of which would be in constant use during
the season of sugar making."[9] Lyford[10] states that as many as 900 "taps"
were made in a sugar camp, and one would expect that at least two containers -- one filling, one being emptied -- would be required for each
"tap".

Makak

The *wigwassi makak* (Ojibwa: *wigwass*, birch bark; *makak*, pail or container)[11] type of pail or box requires a little more complex pattern and usually was made with some care to last several seasons. A makak can be
described as a deep container with a square or rectangular bottom and inward sloping sides which form a circular or oval rim opening. It is
usually reinforced around the rim and may or may not have a lid or handles
(Fig. 4). These were made in various sizes, averaging 5-10 inches at the
bottom, 4-10 inches deep, and 4-8 inches across the top. Makaks for storing sugar might store only about a pound or two while pails might be
over a foot high.

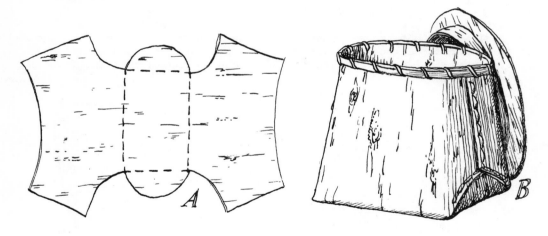

Fig. 4, Makak. A, Pattern. B, Finished, with lid.

[9]*Ibid.*
[10]Lyford, "Ojibwa Crafts", p. 25.
[11]Alternate spelling: *mocock, makuk, macock,* etc.

A piece of bark of sufficient size is laid white side up on a flat **sur-**
face. Small makaks are made from split bark, larger ones from heavier
thicknesses. Although it can be laid out directly on the bark, the amateur would do well to experiment with paper or cardboard patterns. This
pattern is made to allow for overlapping seams and an awl is used to
scribe the outline on the bark. Bark which is dry should be soaked in
warm water briefly at this point to make it more flexible. Too long a
soak will merely cause the bark to curl up into a tight scroll which is
almost impossible to flatten out again. Heating over a low fire softens
the natural resins and allows the bark to be bent without cracking. The
bark, when cool, tends to hold the shape it had while warm.

Most makaks are made with the grain of the bark parallel to the long
axis of the pattern, up the sides. For a rather sharp angled bend, a
line scored with a dull awl helps the accuracy of the bend. This can
be done at this point.

I find that a sturdy scissors cuts the bark quite well. For heavier
bark, I need a tin snips. A knife can be used, but this needs to be quite
sharp, for the wedge shape of a knife blade has a tendency to split the
bark parallel to the grain. I expect that a stone knife was used in pre-
White times, but frankly, I don't have much confidence in this.

When the pattern has been cut and scored (if desired), fold up
the two flaps on the bottom to about a right angle. Next
bend the ends around so that they overlap each other and the
flap as well.

The two ends are stitched to the respective ends. If spruce
root is used, an awl is required to make the holes through
the bark, and the sharpened end of a root is pushed through
the holes. The same priniciple is involved if basswood cord
is used. I find it easier to use a large needle threaded
with the cord although it still is a good plan to punch a
guide hole with a steel awl. An awl point filed to a triangular cross-section tip, or made from a glover's needle
which has this design, cuts well through the bark (Fig. 5).
A simple round awl point has a tendency to split older bark.

Stitches: Running Stitch

A basic stitch, known today as the running stitch, is the
easiest form of sewing (Fig. 6).

Fig. 5,
Triangular
pointed awl.

As in the case of all stitching, the first stitch is taken
from the inside to the outside so that the end is hidden
inside. In a well-crafted piece, the ends are hidden between the two
pieces to be joined, and pressure from later stitches holds these in
place. No knots are used; the loose end is simply caught underneath succeeding stitches. The stitch continues in one hole and out the next, in

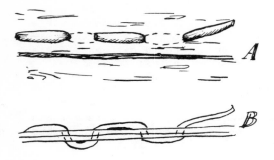

Fig. 6, Running stitch.   A, Top view. B, Side cross section view.

Stitches: Double Stitch

A stronger and neater stitch is the double stitch which is really a double running stitch using two fibers which are stitched through each hole so that the fibers pass each other in opposite directions in each hole, and the surface stitching seems to be a continuous series of short lines (Fig. 7). A good method of beginning the double stitch is to pull half the length of fiber through the first hole and then to use both the beginning and

sequence, for the necessary distance. It is well to punch awl holes as needed rather than to punch them all ahead of time. Stitches are about 3/8 to 1/2 inch apart. If a length of lace or cord is too short to finish, the old end and new end are overlapped for a few stitches, again with the endings hidden inside. When dry, loose ends are snipped off. On the makak, the vertical seams are sewed and then the bottom flaps are stitched on.

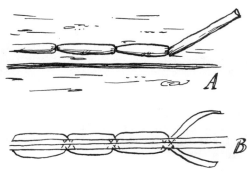

Fig. 7, Double stitch.   A, Top view. B, Side cross section view.

ending as if they were beginnings of two separate fibers. If spruce root is used in this method, the inner length must be given a half twist so that the smooth exterior appears outside.

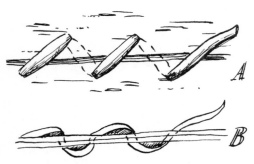

Fig. 8, Diagonal stitch.   A, Top view. B, Side cross section view.

Stitches: Diagonal Stitch

Another simple stitch is the diagonal stitch which is useful in that it helps to hold the edges of a seam down as well as sewing the pieces together (Fig. 8). The diagonal stitch starts on one side of a seam and goes back in on the other side so that the stitching appears to be a series of parallel diagonal lines. Often the diagonal stitch goes through only one layer of bark in each stitch rather than piercing both as in the previous technique.

Stitches: Cross Stitch

A cross stitch is a double diagonal stitch and makes for a decorative as well as a sturdy
fastening (Fig. 9). As in the
double stitch, two fibers are used
in each hole, forming a zig-zag
line. If these stitches are staggered, they cross each other and
the stitch appears as a series of
X's similar to a laced shoe.

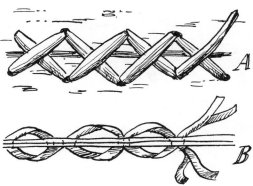

*Fig. 9, Cross stitch.   A, Top view.
B, Side cross section view.*

Stitches: Parallel Stitch

The parallel stitch is a variation
of the diagonal stitch so that the
exterior, visible portion of the
fibers are at right angles to the
seam (Fig. 10). The inside portion of the stitch appears as a
simple diagonal.

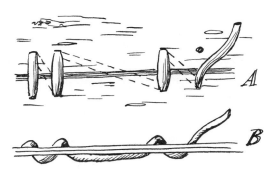

*Fig. 10, Parallel stitch. A, Top
view. B, Side cross section view.*

It will be seen from experience
that several possibilities of dec-
orative stitching are possible. Dyed fibers offer further possibilities.
Indeed, many bark objects were stitched with purely decorative patterns
on the surfaces where no functional stitching is necessary.

Makak, Continued

When the makak has been sewed completely, and the loose ends hidden, a
strip split from black ash or some similar wood is lashed to the outside of the rim of the container. This strip is approximately 1/8 inch
thick by 1/2 inch wide by a few inches longer than the outer measurements of the rim. Naturally, for a larger or a smaller makak, these
measurements would increase or decrease respectively. The bark rim is
trimmed, if necessary, to make it level. The reinforcing strip can then
be bent to conform to the general circular or oval rim shape. Where
the seam overlap appears, both ends of the strip are shaved to a long
wedge shape so that the overlapped joint is no thicker than the strip
itself. A clothespin helps hold this strip in place during lashing.
A simple diagonal stitch (or whip stitch, now) is used to bind the reinforcing strip to the rim. Spruce root is the preferred lacing. The
diagonal stitch is sufficient to bind the strip, but it is made strong-

Fig. 11, Binding rim reinforcement (whip stitch).

er and nicer in appearance if the root is stitched very close together in parallel stitches which cover the strip entirely. Because the holes in the bark are so close together, they were often staggered or stepped in long and short stitches in some regular sequence which gave an added decorative effect (Fig. 11). As before, the beginning and end of the lace is hidden between the strip and the bark.

Makak Lids

Makaks for storage of sugar or wild rice often had bark lids which were stitched directly on the rim. Here, an oval or circle the size and shape of the rim was cut and fastened with a diagonal stitch all around after the makak was filled.

A removable lid is made by cutting a bark piece about 1/4-3/8 inch larger all around than the rim. Another piece of bark, often with the grain running against the length, is cut about 1/2 inch wide by the length of the circumference of the rim. This is overlapped to make it slightly less than the inner measurement of the rim and stitched to the lid piece, allowing a slight clearance inside with the 1/4-3/8 extra as an overhang to the outside. Spruce root is not useful here unless it be extremely fine. Basswood cord is better, but recent lids are stitched with black thread. Black is traditional, although brown would be less visible.

Because the stitches are visible on the top, and to add stiffness to the top, a second lid piece is cut the same size as the first. Where the first piece should be stitched so that the white bark is up when the lid is in place, this second piece is laid on top so that the white side is down and is then stitched together around the margin with a diagonal stitch. To hide this seam and to provide a pleasant border, a small strip of sweetgrass or other fiber may be stitched into place as a coil around the edge. In the absence of sweetgrass, I use readily available cedar inner bark.

The normal flexibility of the makak and lid are such that it should stay in place with friction alone. Occasionally, a short cord of basswood is knotted and pushed through the center of the lid from the bottom and then is joined to the makak.

Makak Handles

Some makaks, particularly those to be used as pails, are fitted with
handles of root, cord, or black ash which are fastened in various ways
to the sides of the container. If a lid is also provided, the handle
must be open enough to provide clearance to remove the lid.

Bowl

Birch bark is used for other vessels. A winnowing tray some 20 inches
across was used to remove the chaff from wild rice after threshing.
Other smaller bowls were made for general use and later, with decorations, for trading.

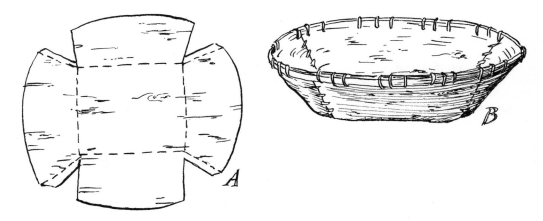

Fig. 12, Bowl. A, Pattern. B, Finished.

Such low bowls were made by laying out a pattern, circular or oval, and
cutting a slot in each quarter (Fig. 12). The width of this slot and
its depth determine the size of the bottom and the angle or slope of
the sides. Naturally, not so much bark is cut out that insufficient remains for overlapping seams.

The four sides are bent upward and the seams are stitched together.
The rim is customarily reinforced as above.

Scraped Patterns

The dark "winter bark" is prized for designs scraped into the exterior
surfaces of containers. Actually, even canoes were sometimes decorated
with this technique.

The typical floral patterns of the Woodland Indians were the basis for
scraped designs. Every woman had a supply of her favorite cut-out bark

patterns of leaves and flowers (Fig. 13). These were
traced in a symmetrical arrangement on the exterior.
An awl was used for tracing
rather than a pencil. The
scored line from an awl gives
a precise margin to the design when it is scraped.

Scraped designs are classed
as positive or negative.
The positive method is
simplest and most direct.
It includes simply tracing
the design and scraping out
the inner areas. The scraping is done with a knife
blade, and only a layer or
two of bark is removed. This
removal should provide a
contrasting color of lighter
hued bark. The design then
appears as light color on a
darker brown background.
Dampening the surface of the
bark during scraping may be
beneficial. In general,
these areas are not dis-
turbed.

Fig. 13, Birch bark patterns (after
Densmore).

Negative scraping is the
opposite of the above and is the technique of scraping the background
or negative areas of the design. This may or may not be more difficult
depending upon the complexity of the design.

Pitching

It is surprising how tight a well-made birch bark seam can be if it is
stitched properly. However, containers such as sap or water pails or
cooking utensils need to be sealed with gum to make their seams really
water-tight.

Gashes are made in spruce or pine trees, but not so placed nor so deep
as to kill the tree. The gum or pitch collects in these wounds and can
be collected periodically. (For the amateur, turpentine can be used to
remove the pitch from hands and clothing.) The pitch is collected in a
can and can be softened over a low heat. Take care, because this can
be a fire hazard! The hot pitch becomes quite fluid and can be daubed
over seams or cracks with a stick. If necessary, the bark area can be

warmed over heat also, or with a birch bark roll made into a torch, to
make the pitch penetrate the seam better.

For canoe making, especially, the pitch is mixed with pulverized charcoal. This changes the naturally clear amber of the pitch to an opaque
black. This author is not sure of the purpose of this, but it seems
reasonable that the black would give a true indication of the amount
of pitch on a seam. The clearer natural color could be deceptive in
this respect. On pitched containers, the black seam is not considered
objectionable. The charcoal also seems to give some stability to the
hot pitch to keep it from flaming too much.

Other Bark Artifacts

Many other articles were made of birch bark. The Ojibwas were known as
"birch bark Indians" because of their many uses of this material. Artifacts include porcupine quilled boxes, moose caller trumpets, envelopes,
wigwam coverings. Less well known are the mnemonic devices or memory
aids of the Medicine Society of the Ojibwa (*Midewiwin*). These aids were
pieced scrolls which were drawn with pictographs to indicate certain
ritualistic procedures of the society -- dances, songs, etc.

The only purely decorative art of the Woodland tribes is the bitten patterns or dental pictographs (see "Beadwork"). These charming little
designs are still available in Canada today. They are made by folding
a single thickness of bark several times through the center. A linear
pattern is bitten through the folded layers with the canine teeth of
the artist. This unusual art is done primarily by "feel", for the woman
cannot see where she is biting while she proceeds. Several lines are
bitten, and, when the bark is unfolded, a symmetrical design appears
which is especially visible when held up to the light. The process is
similar to that used by primary school children when stars and snowflakes
are cut from a folded paper.

REFERENCES

Adney, Edwin T., and
Chapelle, Howard I.

"The Bark Canoes and Skin Boats of North America", *U.S. National Museum Bulletin* No. 230, 1964.

Butler, Eva L.

"Uses of Birch Bark in the Northeast", *Robert Abbe Museum Bulletin* No. VII, Bar Harbor, Maine, 1957.

Densmore, Frances

"Chippewa Customs", *Bureau of American Ethnology Bulletin* No. 86, 1929.

Douglas, Frederick

"Birchbark and the Indian", *Denver Art Museum Leaflet* No. 102, 1941.

Harlow, William M.

"Trees of Eastern and Central United States and Canada", Dover, N.Y., 1957.

Hoffman, Walter J.

"The Menomini Indians", *Bureau of Ethnology 14th Annual Report,* 1892-93.

Lyford, Carrie A.

"Iroquois Crafts", U.S. Department of Interior, Bureau of Indian Affairs, 1943.

"Ojibwa Crafts", U.S. Department of Interior, Bureau of Indian Affairs, 1943.

Paul, Frances

"Spruce Root Basketry of the Alaska Tlingit", U.S. Department of Interior, Bureau of Indian Affairs, 1944.

Speck, Frank G.

"River Desert Indians of Quebec", *Indian Notes,* Vol. IV, Museum of American Indian (Heye Foundation), 1927.

PORCUPINE QUILL EMBROIDERY ON BIRCH BARK

Porcupine quill embroidery on birch bark is a craft naturally resultant from the coincidence of the normal habitat of the Eastern Porcupine (*Erithizon dorsatum dorsatum* Linnaeus) and the range of the paper birch (*Betula papyrifera* Marsh.) and the Woodland Indians' use of available materials for the construction and decoration of artifacts.

The Woodland tribes generally found abundant quantities of birch, for the range of this tree is from New England and the Maritime Province of Canada westerly into the Great Lakes states and northerly into the interior of Canada and parts of Alaska. All Woodland tribes used both bark and quills for various articles, but not all selected the paper birch for containers nor decorated them with porcupine quills. This curious craft is of minor importance. The Iroquois, for instance, did little of this while the excellence of Micmac quilled boxes sets the standard for the craft. The Ottowa and Ojibwa became quite proficient, and most quilled boxes today come from isolated groups such as the Ojibwa in Canadian reserves.

It seems probable that quillwork on birch bark is a relatively recent craft. Examples documented and more than 100 years of age are virtually non-existent, but then the quilled boxes are, by their very nature, fragile pieces. The bark itself is subject to splitting along the grain, especially as it becomes old and brittle. The many holes in the bark -- two for each quilled stitch -- are often very close together and aligned which tends to make an old piece of quillwork about as strong as a sheet of perforated postage stamps of the same age. The quills also become brittle with age. Almost any old piece subject to past use has several splits or lost quills.

It may be that the tribes practicing this craft used the boxes for storage, but the holes from quilling made them relatively useless for food storage. Further, common containers were not given the hours of work required for quilling even a small box. It is quite apparent that the boxes did not lend themselves to the semi-nomadic existence of their makers.

Watkins suggests that the Ottowa became proficient in the craft as they became more agriculture-oriented as early as 1850. Probably the greatest stimulation to the craft in the past came with the development of Niagra Falls as a tourist attraction. Souvenir seekers provided a market for Indian crafts, and the quilled boxes were purchased by many visitors in the early decades of the present century. Johnson(1929)

notes that the Ojibwa and Potowatomi of Parry Island began this craft
about fifty years prior to his writing. A fine collection of some
eighty quilled boxes was acquired by the Southwest Museum in Los Angeles.
These were identified as being made before 1920. The quality and complexity of workmanship and design indicates that this was a well-estab-
lished craft by that time.

Examples may be purchased in Canada today where they are found occasionally, but never in great quantity, in trading posts and souvenir shops.
I know of no Indians still actively engaged in quilling on birch bark in
the United States. One Menomini woman in Wisconsin still has a reputation for this craft but has not accomplished any recently. The oft-heard
complaint of the older women is that the young folks just don't care to
learn or are unwilling to spend the time required for the return gained.

In Ontario, pieces may be purchased from an Indian trader at a price of
about three to four dollars for a cylindrical quilled box of about three
inches diameter. I have acquired some larger pieces for up to seven and
a half dollars and have seen a few masterpieces selling at fifteen dollars. Needless to say, these latter do not sell readily. As recently
as 1962, a modest award was offered for quill decorated boxes at a Nova
Scotian Indian crafts exhibit. Some rectangular "cigarette boxes" sell
for as little as two dollars today, but these are quite poorly and quickly made and with minimum design. My personal experience with this craft
has been that it cannot be a full-time occupation. For instance, at a
dollar an hour, my smallest experiment would need to be sold at fifteen
to twenty dollars, which price does not include preparing the bark and
quills. Purchasers are not abundant at this price. Today it is considered an avocation by the women, and it can seldom be depended upon as the
major source of income.

It is generally accepted that quillwork pre-dates the time of the White
traders whose beads became more popular than quills. Plains Indians'
quillwork stands supreme in most examples of quilled buckskin. (Some
quillwork on buckskin still continues in both Canada and the United
States.) Quilled buckskin is quite well-known, and most museums have
collections of clothing, bags, horse trappings, and other artifacts in
this medium. There are some significant differences between quilled
buckskin and the lesser-known work on birch bark. Most quills on skin
are held onto the surface with stitches of sinew or, later, thread. On
bark, the quills are inserted completely through holes in the bark and
are folded underneath on the inside surface -- similar to the manner of
a staple through paper. On skin, one quill nay be folded over the sinew or thread for several short stitches. On bark, one quill is usually
used for each stitch which may average an inch in length. Thick quills
can be used effectively on skin. Thick quills on bark require holes so
large that the tendency is to split and destroy the bark. In both crafts,
however, the thinner quills are selected for quality work, and the woman
takes extra pride in such time-consuming work. Frequently, the design
on the lid of a box is done with fine quills and thicker ones are allowed
on the sides. I have seldom seen the thickest quills yielded by the porcupine used at all on boxes. I've tried some myself. They are clumsy

to work with and result in a crude design. Both types of quillwork employ natural and dyed quills, but the preference in Plains work is toward the colored ones.

Tools

The tools used today are a bone
marker or pencil for tracing designs, a bone, thorn or steel awl,
thread, tweezers, scissors, cut-
out birch bark patterns, and
pouches or bladders for storage
of quills. A slightly dulled
bone marker or steel awl is used
to score the outline of patterns.
A hard pencil may be used as a
contemporary equivalent. The
scored line of the marker appears

*Fig. 1, Quillworker's awls. Typical
length: 3 inches overall.*

better than a pencil line when the bark becomes damp as work progresses.
Steel awls are in common use today. These are made by driving a needle
into a wooden handle. Some handles are designed with a button carved into the end much like a clothespin so that the awl can be slipped between
the fingers and out of the way when it is not needed and yet is quickly
at hand (Fig. 1). This device obviates the necessity to set it down and
pick it up each time. Several such awls of different diameters should
be handy for a selection when different sized holes are desired. Thread
is used to assemble the boxes and also to attach the customary sweetgrass (*Hierochloe odorata* [L.] Beauv.) borders to the rims. The Ontario
Ojibwa prefer No. 40 black cotton thread. A tweezers is necessary to
pull the quills through the bark. Only a small fraction of an inch projects through as the quill is inserted -- seldom enough to grasp with
the fingers. Some boxes are too small to reach inside for this purpose.
Also, the extreme sharpness of the quills is such that it is unwise to
attempt to reach inside with the fingers. I use a commercially made
eyebrow tweezers, or, on occasion, a small needle-nosed pliers. An informant on Manitoulin Island, Ontario, showed me her tweezers, about 1/2
inch wide by 3 inches long and made from a bent metal strap. Other literature is notably lacking in mentioning this tool, but experience proves
that it is indispensable. No one seems to know what was used in earlier
times. A small scissors is used to snip off the sharp quill ends after
embroidery is completed. A larger pair is useful for cutting the bark
parts although a knife could be used. Each woman has a supply of birch
bark patterns from which she selects those to be used for patterns on
the box. In earlier times, bladders were used for storage of quills.
Today, tin cans or boxes are in more common use. I prefer envelopes.

Box Design

Men usually peeled the bark from the tree in spring and early summer.
The Manitoulin Island Indians gave the first two weeks in June as the
best time for harvest. With care, the white bark may be removed from
the tree as it stands. We have all seen unfortunate evidence of decorative birch trees in yards and parks or along roads which have been gir-
dled by the removal of bark bands. Although the tree can continue to
grow if the inner rough bark is not damaged, the white bark will never
return to that portion. A source should be found where trees are intended to be cut anyway or from down trees.

The silver white of the outer bark becomes the inside of the box. The
bark has a normal tendency to curl in a direction opposite from the way
it formed on the tree. The bark is composed of many thin layers which
may be split with care into lightweight sheets for the manufacture of
small items. These "splits" are light tan or brown with the characteristic cork-like velvety texture and bark pattern of the white exterior,
but with less of its peeling nature. Although the men chose bark which
contained few "eyes" or scars, they apparently made no effort to select
entirely blemish-free pieces once the bark had been peeled. Nevertheless, some bark is just too uneven or loaded with eyes to be used. For
large objects such as the famous birch bark canoe, the entire thickness
of bark was used in as large a sheet as possible.

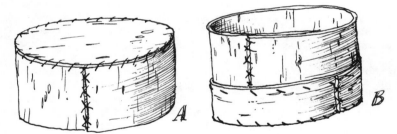

*Fig. 2, Cylindrical box assembled for quilling. A, Lid.
B, Bottom. Typical size: 3 inch diameter.*

Smaller objects can be cut by selecting portions of larger sheets and
splitting them to the desired thickness. A thin split liner affixed to
the inside of a box after embroidery adds stiffness later. Quillworker's
bark is usually cut into handy-sized pieces of a foot or two square and
is pressed after harvest so that it does not curl unduly. Fresh bark is
quite flexible and can be bent easily without cracking. Split bark bends
more easily than thick bark. Old bark or any bark difficult to bend may
be dampened or heated. Bark heated over a low flame or coals becomes
quite soft and will hold its shape after it cools. Excessive heat or
dampening may cause the bark to curl too much.

Anything associated with sewing is traditionally woman's work. The
Indian women continue the craft from this point.

No pattern for quilled boxes is noted in the literature although Butler
and Hadlock illustrated patterns for makaks and other containers. Most
boxes today are cylindrical with removable lids (Fig. 2). A disc is cut
for the top of the cylinder and a long rectangle is cut for the side wall.
A judgment of length of the latter can be made with the $2\pi r$ formula, but
these seem apparently to have been made by trial and error measurements
as the occasion arose. Most cylindrical boxes are about 3 inches in diameter and about 2 inches high. They vary from about 2 1/2 inches in diameter to 8 inches and 8 inches high. The direction of the grain on the
disc is immaterial, of course. The direction on the sides of the cylinder varies according to the craftsman. I have seen examples on which
the grain runs parallel to the vertical, to the horizontal, and, in one
example, even to a diagonal. The craftsman apparently decides which has
least problems; the natural curl of the bark or its tendency to split.

A goodly number of "cigarette
boxes" are made today and correspond roughly to the measurements of a pack of cigarettes
(Fig. 3). Larger rectangular
boxes are no longer popular,
but some were made up to 10
inches long. There are some
examples of boxes with a convex "pirate's chest" lid, probably patterned after trader's
storage chests. A rectangular box bottom could be made
of a single piece of bark cut
so that the four sides are
from it. More often, however,

*Fig. 3, Quilled "cigarette" box with sweet-
grass covered seams.*

the bottom and four sides are made separately and assembled. The tops
of cigarette boxes are made with a single flat sheet attached with bark,
sweetgrass, or thread hinges.

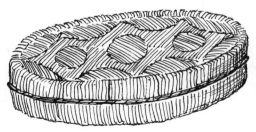

*Fig. 4, "Needle case" decorated
with undyed quills. Length: 5
inches.*

Other boxes have been made in the
past but are not common in contemporary manufacture. Small, oval boxes
are known as "needle cases" and may
have been designed for that function
(Fig. 4). Larger oval boxes are called "glove boxes" and are apparently
the result of tourist-buyer influence. An occasional makak and tray
are quilled. Some heart-shaped boxes
were made earlier also.

A few boxes are made of thin pine
covered with quilled bark. Others may have wooden tops and bottoms,
but these are uncommon.

Box Construction

After a pattern was developed and cut out, it was assembled with needle
and thread. Although I use a steel needle, it still seems wise to punch
a guide hole with an awl first for each stitch. I found no examples
stitched with basswood cordage. I tried some myself with satisfactory
results, but I found the cotton thread as used on Indian examples to be
simpler.

With the exception of quilled lids, the box needs to be assembled before
embroidery is begun. Most methods of decorating the sides of a round
box require that the quills be stuck into both the bottom and the sides.
The lid design is usually quilled first and then the sides assembled for
further quilling. Rectangular box sides may be quilled before assembly.

The vertical joint of a cylindrical side is joined by simply butting
them together. A stronger joint is made by overlapping the two ends, in
which case the area to be overlapped is usually shaved in thickness. A
simple running stitch or X-stitch is used to fasten the joint.

The top rests on the rim of the cylinder and is held in place with a whip
stitch.   I tried this too, but I prefer the buttonhole or catch stitch.
The bottom is attached to its side walls in the same manner. Occasionally, an extra, shorter cylinder of bark is stitched to the exterior of
the bottom cylinder so that its diameter coincides with the diameter of
the lid when the two are put together. A slight tolerance is allowed so
that the lid can be removed yet has enough friction to keep it in place.
Allowance should also be made for the thickness of the quill ends inside
as well as the liner to be added later.

Some containers, expecially round bowl shapes, were made of coiled sweetgrass with only a lid and base of bark. In those specimens, only the
lid has embroidery.

Preparation of Quills

Probably because it involved hunting or trapping, the acquistion of a
porcupine was left to the men. Occasionally, the men might also help
in plucking the quills. The quilling was exclusively women's work.

Porcupines are active almost the year around. They tend to hibernate
during extremely cold weather, but warmer winter days bring them out
once more. Porcupine quills should not be taken in the hot months. An
Ojibwa informant states that during these times the quills seem to fill
with a liquid which, during quilling, may be discharged and spoil the
work.

It is said that a cap thrown at the animal (from a safe distance, even
though the "porky" cannot literally throw his quills) will usually pick
up a quantity of them -- if the cap can be retrieved. "Road kills"
are a good source of dead animals, for porkies are notably slow in cross-

ing highways. In Wisconsin, the porcupine is considered a pest with no
closed hunting season. He can be shot from treetops where he feeds on
buds and twigs or found in burrows. If one gets close to him on the
ground, a well-placed blow on the nose with a club will usually dispatch
him. Professional foresters can also provide a carcass. The porky's reputation for destroying pine trees results in a perpetual vendetta between him and forest management personnel.

A word of caution in handling this formidable beast is hardly necessary,
but the best way to carry him is by a claw -- after he is dead. No quills
grow on the belly, but don't rub him on the flanks. Actually, the porcupine can be petted (some hardy persons keep them as pets) but only from
head to tail, never in the opposite direction. Even with the utmost caution, a quill or two gets stuck in tender places and should be removed
immediately. If allowed to remain, they can result in infection. *Be
sure also that the barb is not broken off below the skin.* Gloves are of
little value. They are clumsy and provide no real barrier against the
needle-sharp quills. The best precaution, in the last analysis, is utmost care and a bottle of antiseptic.

Stroke the quills down in one area, and, very carefully, separate some
of them into a part, as in combing the hair. Grasp a small bundle of
quills (don't worry about the fur at a time like this) and jerk them
out sharply. Once a small area has been cleared, work can proceed more
leisurely, but still with only a finger-sized bundle at a time. (Incidentally, the long "guard hairs" -- brown with tan tips -- can be plucked at this time also. These should be saved for the construction of a
roach headdress.)

Fig. 5, Porcupine quills

The most useful quills are about
2 to 2 1/2 inches long and less
than 1/16 inch diameter (Fig. 5).
These come from the shoulders and
and flanks. If one anticipates
really fine work, more delicate ones
come from behind the head and surrounding area. Larger quills come from
the back and tail. These are generally too thick for bark embroidery,
but can be saved for buckskin work. In any case, separate the quills as
they are plucked, into similar sizes in piles. In one afternoon, the
porky should become rather bald. An average porcupine may contain some
40,000 quills which, when sorted out, should fill several cans or boxes.
If necessary, the carcass can be frozen, because only the surface needs
to be thawed for plucking. Especially in warm weather, however, don't
wait too long before the plucking is completed.

Dyeing the Quills

Indians employed the dye potential of various plants in pre-white times,
but quickly adopted the trader's dyes because of their strength, variety,
and ease of preparation. Seton had no problems in dyeing quills with one
dye lot, but a later batch did not work well at all. She tried wood ash

lye as a mordant, but this softened the quills into a jellified mess.
Finally, while awaiting advice from the dye manufacturer, she received
word from a Sioux woman who told her to add a quarter cup of sugar to
the dye. This unlikely addition solved the problem.[1]

I found that commercial Rit dye was quite satisfactory if used richer
than the instructions provided -- a whole package to about a quart or
two of water. The quills are rather waxy and a strong solution is necessary. I simmered the quills, stirring frequently, for about 15-30
minutes to a shade darker than desired for the final color. An enamel
dish should be used to avoid contamination when the dye comes in contact with bare metal. I avoided boiling the quills, for I did not wish
to cook them. The quills were rinsed in cold water until the water ran
clear. A common kitchen sieve can be used to this end. A light hue,
such as yellow, needs a longer dye time than most, but, in general, about
30 minutes is sufficient for rich colors. Pale, less intense colors are
achieved simply by dyeing for a shorter time.

Although secondary hues can be purchased or mixed, I preferred to keep
dyes to a minimum and unadulterated. (To mix a color, always add the
darker dye to the lighter one; i.e., add red to yellow to make orange.)
I achieved a pleasant orange by redyeing yellow quills briefly in red dye.
Some Indian examples exist which use the bright pinks, lavenders, and
chartreuses of "Easterbasket" genre, but these are quite inappropriate
with the natural bark color. Old Indian pieces are, for the most part,
quite subtle in coloration. Upon examination, it is discovered that
these gentle colors are the result of bleaching through the years. The
colors were much more vivid originally.

After the quills were rinsed, I dried them on newspaper. Some of the fur
mixed in with them can be removed at this time. When dry, I stored the
quills by color and size in envelopes. An envelope-full lasts a long
time.

Design

In most cases, cut-out stencils or patterns are used even today. These
are traced with the marker or awl.

Most Indian designs are built from smaller pattern elements. Changes in
design are accomplished by varying the position of the elements. The ex-
actness of certain repeated shapes clearly illustrates such a method.
Some free-hand drawing was done, but by far the greatest amount of designing was according to symmetrical pattern arrangements. Typical Woodland floral elements include the heart, cloverleaf, daisy, rose, and
thistle stylized forms. (See "Beadwork" and "Containers of Birch Bark"
for typical designs.) Contemporary Canadian pieces now show tourist
influences with the use of maple leaves and silhouettes of bears and

[1]Seton, pp. 160-161.

deer. Interestingly, no one yet has used a porcupine as a design element. Each woman has a collection of favorite patterns. My Ojibwa informant reported that she may cut out shapes which she finds in newspa-
pers.

Some designs go back to the very early geometric patterns which may cover
the top and sides. Depending on the technique of stitching, some of
these are quite effective in natural white quills.

Sometimes a design may be found utilizing the darker portion of the quills
as shading in floral motifs. The dark part of the quills is usually co-
incident with the side rim of the box, thus allowing the pure white portion to be seen from the top (or bottom).

Embroidery Procedures

The technique of stitching the quills to the bark is a relatively simple
skill which can be acquired rapidly. The excellence of embroidery is
perfected with practice combined with some caution, selection and much
patience.

Quills are first soaked (they float) for about 5 minutes in a pail of
warm water. Hot water leaches out the color on dyed quills and is no
real advantage over warm water. It seems that both warmth and wet are
required for the desired flexibility. When the water becomes cold, the
quills crease and crack easily. Long soaks in cold water make no appreciable change. Earlier, quills were kept in the mouth to this end, but
I feared the possible toxic effect of the dyestuff, to say nothing of
the sharp quills. Also, the porcupine is prone to have a bad case of
fleas and lice.

An awl is selected with a diameter slightly smaller than the diameter of
the quills selected for use. A hole is punched on the margin of the design and a quill is inserted, brown end first, from the backside of the
bark. This dark tip works best for this purpose, for it is smooth,
stiff, and tapers gradually. Still, a tweezers must be used to pull it
through the hole until only 1/4 to 3/8 inch of the butt remains on the
underside. If the quill is properly warmed and wetted, it should return
immediately to its original shape after being squeezed through the hole.
Then another hole is punched on the opposite side of the design and the
quill inserted, this time from the design top side. The tweezers again
pulls the tip through to the inside until the design side of the quill
is laid smooth and flat against the bark. Quill stitches continue thus,
two holes for each quill, to fill in the design. The tip and butt ends
are bent under on the inside as is a metal paper staple. These ends are
snipped off from time to time as they interfere with future quilling.
These should be cut off so that about 1/16 to 1/8 inch remains. If they
are cut off too close to the bark, they may pop loose. The softened
quill is compressed in the hole and expands to original size as it comes
out. The bark shrinks somewhat also. If the quills are bent inside,
these three factors are all that is required to keep them in place. No

thread or glue is used.

Stitches may or may not cover the entire box. The inexpensive cigarette box contains a minimum of quills in a scattered design on the center areas of top and sides. Round boxes are typically quilled around the top and bottom rims to hide the joint. These latter quills may number more than the top design. In my collection, an old Micmac box of 8 inch diameter has a partially quilled top in a floral pattern which is made up of 405 quills alone. The edging adds another 588. The pattern on the sides of the bottom add another 795 which makes a total of 1788 quills!

Stitches

By far, the most used stitch is the typical embroiderer's *satin stitch* (Fig. 6). The quills with their almost even thickness require a design filled in with parallel stitches. The shape of the pattern is created with varying lengths and positions of the stitches. The satin stitch is also used to cover the seam of the top disc and sides of cylindrical boxes. Such stitches are often staggered or stepped on the top to preclude the possibility of splitting the bark. Where a distance of design to be covered is greater than the length of a quill, two or more quills are used.

Fig. 6, Satin stitch.

One reaches from the margin of the design to, say, the center. The next uses this same center hole and then reaches toward the opposite margin. If several such stitches are required, these center holes are staggered. On some lids the stitches are all parallel, thus forming a pleasing all-over texture. On most patterns, however, the direction varies according to each separate design element.

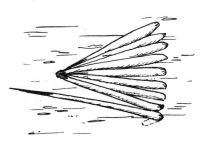

Fig. 7, Fan stitch.

A variation of the satin stitch is found, particularly in the floral patterns, where a radiating *fan stitch* is used (Fig. 7). The quills here spread out in a manner similar to an open fan or wheel spokes. The quills may spread out from a single common hole or holes may be punched closely together near the hub of the design and be spread out more near the rim (to use the analogy of the wheel).

Some satin stitches employ quills in parallels which are grouped at angles to other parallels. This *chevron stitch* (Fig. 8) may be the entire design of the top and is often used on sides as well.

The stitch used for such design elements as plant stems and other linear motifs is called the *outline stitch* (Fig. 9). This is one of two which

Fig. 8, Chevron stitch.   *Fig. 9, Outline stitch.*

can create the impression of a curved line even though it is made of straight quills. A short stitch is taken with one quill. The next stitch is taken about from the middle of, but adjacent to the first and at a slight angle from the first. This method continues so as to build up a curved line composed of a series of short stitches, ever varying in direction.

A simple *running stitch* is a method similar to the above, but each new quill is started in the ending hole made by the previous quill (Fig. 10). Each stitch is done with a separate quill in contrast to the same stitch in yarn embroidery where a single length of yarn is used for several.

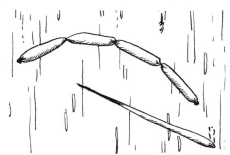

Fig. 10, Running stitch.

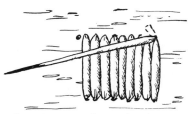

Fig. 11, Satin stitches being hidden by a cover stitch.

Sometimes the holes of design elements are covered with a single quill which may be called a *cover stitch* (Fig. 11). In the case of a long line of holes to be covered, several such stitches may be used.

A *lattice stitch* can be frequently found on box sides, for it fills an area with fewer stitches than others (Fig. 2). A variety of these stitches is possible, but, in general, the lattice stitch is a series of overlapping diagonals which form multiple X's in a kind of cross-hatched linear pattern.

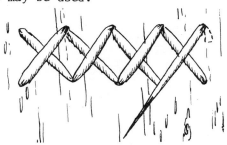

Fig. 12, Lattice stitch.

Finally, an *X-stitch* made with one quill is often
used to attach a liner to a lid or bottom (Fig.
13). Four holes are used in a small square,
and one quill is used in a manner similar to
sewing on a button -- except without the button.
As few of these are used as may be necessary.
This is the only stitch which has a function
other than decorative, for it is used after a
liner is in place. The quill goes through both
the lid and liner.

I have seen only one example on which the quills
were used on the rim proper as a border design.
On this piece, a bark dish, groups of dyed quills
were "whip stitched" around the rim of the bowl
in a technique similar to that of wrapping coiled basketry.

*Fig. 13, X-stitch made
with a single quill.*

A few examples also exist of a kind of woven quillwork. In these cases,
the ends of the quills are stitched into holes as before, but they are
woven over and under quills which they transverse in a true weaving technique. The pattern created gives a checkerboard which is similar to basketry.

Lining and Finishing

At appropriate times during embroidery, the tips inside are cut off on
the inside. Now this process is completed.

If not accomplished beforehand, the box is now completely assembled.

A lid liner, slightly smaller than the original, is cut from a thin
split and pressed into place inside the box. A cylinder or other appropriate shape is cut for the side walls but it is made about 1/4 to 3/8
inch too long. The grain of this liner runs the same direction as the
height of the box. The extra fraction just mentioned is cut into scallops or a saw-tooth edge and is lightly scored to facilitate bending.
This liner, on a cylindrical box is made to bend against the natural
curl of the bark so that it will press against the walls from the inside (Fig. 14). The scallops are bent at right angles to face toward

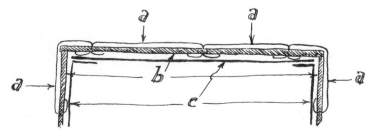

*Fig. 14, Cross section of a quilled box. A, Quills.
B, Box lid and sides. C, Bark liner.*

the center. Placed into position, these scallops will hold the lid **liner** effectively in place. The hem edge of the box is bound with thread **whip** stitching. Almost all Indian work uses a few strands of sweetgrass to hide the layers of bark. Some hems were finished with a fine split spruce root whip-stitched in place.

Conclusion

It seems very unfortunate that the craft of quillwork on birch bark is dying. Indeed, the more popular quillwork on buckskin is almost gone today. Our woods still have a plentiful supply of birch if wisely harvested. Porcupines are in sufficient quantity to anger woodsmen by their feeding habits.

Probably the main reason for the deterioration, if not extinction, of this craft is an economic one. An Indian today can produce many "curios" with a few quills applied in haphazard fashion which can then be sold as "authentic" to indiscriminate tourists. Even with minimal efforts, a wage scale cannot compare with more profitable earnings from other occupations. A really fine piece, well designed and executed, is evidence of much time and care. I would find it difficult to part with my now-treasured attempts at any price.

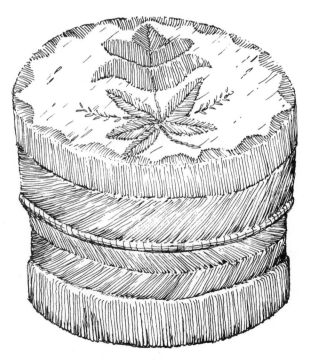

Fig. 15, Micmac porcupine quill embroidery on birch bark. Height: 4 1/2 inch by 5 inch diameter.

REFERENCES

Butler, E., and Hadlock, E.
"Uses of Birch-Bark in the Northeast", *Robert Abbe Museum Bulletin* VII, Bar Harbor, Maine, 1957.

Densmore, Carrie
"Chippewa Customs", *Bureau of American Ethnology Bulletin* No. 86, 1929.

Douglas, Frederick
"Birchbark and the Indian", *Denver Art Museum Leaflet* No. 102, 1941.

————————
"Porcupine Quillwork", *Denver Art Museum Leaflet* No. 103, 1941.

Johnson, F.
"Notes on the Ojibwa and Potowatomi of the Parry Island Reservation, Ontario", *Indian Notes*, Museum of American Indian (Heye Foundation), Vol. VI, No. 3, 1929.

Lyford, Carrie
"Ojibwa Crafts", Dept. of the Interior, Bureau of Indian Affairs, 1942.

Orchard, William
"The Technique of Porcupine Quill Decoration Among the North American Indians", Museum of American Indian (Heye Foundation), Vol. IV, No. 1, 1916.

Seton, Julia M.
"American Indian Arts", Ronald Press, N.Y., 1962.

Watkins, F. E.
"Ottowa Indian Quill-Decorated Birchbark Boxes", *Masterkey*, Vol. IX, No. 4, 1935.

BUILDING A BIRCH BARK CANOE, 1970

What motivates one to build a birch bark canoe at a time when the relative merits of fiberglass and aluminum are argued and the earlier cedar strip and canvas models are all but forgotten?

I doubt if an entirely satisfactory answer can be given; perhaps it is sufficient to say that few others can do it. Another answer might be that the birch bark canoe is the classic prototype for many modern small craft and that one can get a better idea of original design. For persons with a flabby mid-section, building a canoe is a good way to flatten one's stomach. Perhaps also an answer might be that one wishes to understand better the early technology of some parts of the continent. Perhaps one has tired of bead and quillwork and flint flaking and wishes to try a more ambitious project. Or perhaps one merely wishes to kneel on the ribs of a beautifully fashioned canoe, push off silently from shore on a quiet lake and be able to say, honestly, "I, with the help of Nature, did this."

I suppose none of these answers is acceptable to some, but for me they all are true in some measure at least.

In any case, the following are my experiences in building a bark canoe in the summer of 1970. My sources for information were Robert Ritzenthaler's, "The Building of a Chippewa Indian Birch Bark Canoe" which was researched in 1947, and an excellent treatise, "The Bark Canoes and Skin Boats of North America" by Adney and Chapelle. Ritzenthaler's study is based on on-the-spot observation while Chapelle used notes by Edwin Tappan Adney for much of his writing on the bark canoes. As a pragmatist teacher, it seems to me that the greatest understanding of any problem comes from solving the problem in the first person. Anyone wishing to follow this theory is invited to study first these two publications.[1] What follows is my contribution based on one experience.

[1]For those who want a bark canoe without the experience, write Iroqrafts, RR2, Ohsweken, Ontario, Canada. Mr. Guy Spital is acquainted with a few Canadian Indians who can make a canoe for about $20.00 a foot. Such a price, incidentally, approximates that of aluminum and fiberglass.

Gathering the Bark

White Birch (*Betula papyrifera* Marsh.) is abundant in my area of central
Wisconsin where it is cut for paper pulp and firewood. Unfortunately
for me, such trees are generally harvested long before they reach a
size suitable for canoe building. Elbridge Curtis of Merrill graciously
offered me the run of the Merrill School Forest where some large birches
still remain and where some forest management procedures were being
practised. An hour in the forest located some potential trees about 12
inches in diameter. These were forgotten when John Davis, who owns timber in the adjacent area pointed out a "wolf tree" birch on his land.
This tree had apparently been forgotten in earlier cutting and had
created a large shady crown which cut off light from some valuable maple
and basswood trees nearby, hence its nickname. Mr. Davis offered to
let me cut and peel this tree. I greedily accepted.

First point in building a canoe -- don't be greedy. This tree measured
54 inches in circumference a few feet from the base. A slice from this
area showed the bark to be about 1/8 inch thick, but not of the best
quality -- many fine horizontal ridges showed up, all of which were potential splits. Fortunately, however, the bark did not "layer"; i.e., it
didn't separate into many paper-thin layers of bark. Large "eyes" were
evident at intervals up the trunk but the first branch didn't appear until about 12 to 14 feet from the ground. I'd hoped for a longer trunk,
but the diameter was too enticing to look further. Perhaps the "eyes",
the grown-over areas of earlier branches, were not too bad anyway.
Ritzenthaler's notes on the hours spent selecting a tree did not make
an impression at the time. The impression came in the form of lumps and
cracks late in the building.

The first criterion, then, is the selection of the bark. Several trees
should be examined before one is selected to get the thickest bark possible without getting an undue amount of "layering". One can expect the
bark to be thinner near the top of the tree so the height where the sample
is taken should be considered. A thin sliver cut vertically should be
a good test and, if undesirable, will heal in a year or so. The tree
trunk should be as straight as possible, and above all -- no "eyes".
My experience shows clearly that it is wiser to cut a smaller tree of
good quality and add pieces along the gunwales as necessary than to choose
a large tree merely for its size.

On a dreary Memorial Day, then, my wife, son, and I, armed with chain
saw and rope, skidded the VW as far as we could into the logging road
on Davis' property. A novice eye judged the best way to fell the tree,
and a new spark plug made the cutting easy. The tree crashed to a nice
slant -- right into some oaks. On the other hand, the bark was not damaged by dropping the tree completely. A few large branches made an effective cradle and I dropped the long trunk section on them.

A slightly curved cut was made longitudinally. (I forgot to use the line
I had brought for marking this.) A cut is made much better and easier

if the knife is held somewhat at an angle to the tree surface rather
than horizontally. The cork-like white bark creates a strong drag on
the blade; a more slicing cut penetrates much better.

The leaves were well out on the tree's crown, and apparently the sap was
flowing readily. In any case, the cut seemed to release a tension on the
bark, and it almost wanted to peel itself. (Some Ojibwa women in Ontario
reported that they gather bark for their boxes in early June. They claimed that, at the proper time in early summer, the bark peeled off by itself. Our experience substantiated this.) The flat of the hand was
enough to separate the outer, white bark from the inner, thick bark. The

layers were divided by a
noticeably wet zone. A
putty knife helped in a
few difficult places,
but, for the most part,
it was a real pleasure
to peel (Fig. 1). We
rolled the trunk as we
peeled until the bark
was spread out as a long,
shiny, yellow tablecloth
on the forest floor. We
flipped the sheet over
so that the white side
was up, and, with the
aid of some leafy twigs
as a core, rolled it up,
tied it, and packed it
out. We also salvaged
a few sheets from the
larger branches for other
bark projects to be made
later.

Fig. 1, Peeling the bark.

Another tree, about 12 inches in diameter, was also cut, just in case.
Surprisingly, this tree was much more difficult to peel than the first.
I have not been able to discover why at this time, but I expect that it
has something to do with the amount of sap flowing. Much more of the
dark brown inner rind, the "winter bark" spoken of in other writings,
came off. I didn't try hot water to loosen the bark; I didn't have any
and besides, the flies were getting unbearable.

Making the Prow Piece

I acquired some white cedar (*Thuja occidentalis* L.) fence posts which
are commonly found in almost any swamp here. A 14 foot post, about 12
inches in diameter at the butt and tapering to 8 inches, was purchased
for $5.00 for the longitudinal members, and common 7 foot posts were used
for ribs, prow pieces and planking. Some of the cedars grow in a slight
spiral so that in addition to seeking clear wood, I also had to be aware
of the direction of the grain.

Splitting wedges and a 10 pound maul were used for the first split to
halve the posts. Much undesirable splintering occurred. This first
split was the most difficult. Some of the posts had recently been exposed to rain, and it appeared that the dry posts were much easier to
split. Knots, where they occurred near the split, also gave trouble.
Therefore, the second criterion: clear, dry, white cedar logs.

Thicker logs typically have fewer knots. Actually, there may be knots
inside, but the fight for sunlight in the swamp tends to make later
growth layers free from branches which have earlier died and fallen off
-- a characteristic which foresters call "self-pruning". An inch or two
of white sapwood is quite noticeable in comparison with the darker, red-
brown heartwood. The sapwood is usually clearer, but, because it is more
resinous, tends to split less easily. A pleasant aroma accompanies the
splitting, and this makes up for some of the tedium and aches.

The halves were then split, again with wedges and maul, into halves or
thirds, depending on the thickness. I cheated on later logs after I had
ruined some promising billets: I used a portable circle-saw to rip along
the grain on the surface. Actually, some of the logs had already acquired deep, long splits as a result of drying, and all I did was to increase these. These saw cuts saved several logs, I'm sure. Also, it
made the work quicker, although I think, with experience, one could split
just as accurately and quickly with wedges and maul alone.

Now, with several billets split into pie-shaped cross-sections, the wedges
and maul were set aside in favor of a huge "hunting knife". This grand-
father-of-a-bayonet has no real function in hunting, as any woodsman knows.
My weapon was 11 inches overall with a blade thickness of almost 1/4 inch.
It's simply too big and heavy for camping or hunting use except, maybe,
hacking down small trees. For splitting the cedar, however, the wedge-
shaped blade worked fine. The thickness
allowed me to use a wooden mallet (Fig. 2)
to start splits and to get through difficult
spots. The heavy handle also afforded
leverage to twist the blade in the split
to open it up ahead of the cutting edge.

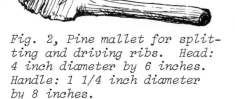

After I had destroyed a few more billets,
I discovered that I was splitting away
the sapwood too easily; i.e., the split
went away from the heartwood. To separate the two, apparently the triangular
inner portion remains stiffer than the
flatter sapwood side, thus causing the
split to open up toward this weaker outside.

*Fig. 2, Pine mallet for split-
ting and driving ribs. Head:
4 inch diameter by 6 inches.
Handle: 1 1/4 inch diameter
by 8 inches.*

Third point to remember: wood splits toward the thinner side. It therefore became important to judge the center of each piece correctly in order to split it evenly. It seemed to me a practical impossibility to
split a thin section off a thicker piece. Thin pieces must be made by

successive halving of larger pieces.

With the successive thinner splitting came the fourth point. Wood splits
toward a curved side. In other words, if a splitting half is bent more
than the other half, the former will probably split completely off. Therefore, to achieve an even split all the way, both pieces must be opened
in an equal-angled "Y". One controls the split by bending one side away
from the other in such a way that the thinnest piece in danger of splitting off is kept straightest.

I achieved this by hold-
ing the billet with one
end pressed on the ground
at about a 30 degree angle
with my knee giving leverage just ahead of the
split as my hands opened
up the crack (Fig. 3).
Don't try the hands alone
too soon on a thick piece.
Pinched fingers are pain-
ful.

Reports of authentic
splitting procedures show
the Indian craftsman standing inside the open split
and pressing away both
legs of the wood on either
side of him.[2] This looks

Fig. 3, Splitting white cedar billets.

good, and I tried it unsuccessfully, but don't try it without someone
else handy. The pressure can get rather strong. It appeared to me that
the end ahead of the craftsman must be pressed against something: a depression in the ground or a tree base. Merely placing the billet anywhere gives no leverage to control the split to right or left.

For the prow pieces, two 4-foot pieces were split in lines radiating from
the center (Fig. 4A). Fur-
ther splitting for the lamination required later can

*Fig. 4. A, Methods of
splitting white cedar. B,
Splitting for prow pieces,
gunwales, outwales. C,
Splitting for ribs, planks,
top plates, thwarts.*

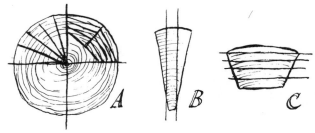

[2]Ritzenthaler, pp. 69-70.

Fig. 5, Crooked knife designed to cut toward the body when handle is held in right hand, palm up, and with thumb along curved part of handle as if it were a one-handled draw-knife. Blade (made from a file): 4 1/4 inches, overall: 8 1/2 inches.

then follow the lines of annular growth. A newly-made "crooked knife" (Fig. 5) was used to shave them down to about 1/2 inch thickness by 3 inches width. These must be perfectly free from knots.

Each piece was split into laminae by first splitting it in half; that is, into two 1 1/2 inch pieces, except that the split is extended only to about one foot from the other end. Each of these sections was then split and re-split until the splits were about 1/8 inch thick and roughly corresponded to the annular growth rings. All splits were made only 3 feet

long so that they all remained joined for the last foot at the bottom (Fig. 6). Two thin nails through this bottom helped to salvage the piece when some of the splits went too far. As will be seen, these splits become laminae for the prow-pieces in the same way that contemporary laminations are made except that, in the Indian method, the wood is all from a single piece of stock.

When both prow-pieces were split (there is no appreciable difference between stem and stern) they were tied to a rope and put into the lake to soak overnight.

Fig. 6, Using a knife to start lamination splits for a prow-piece.

Attention now turned to the *man-boards* or *head-boards* (Ritzenthaler or Adney and Chapelle, respectively) (Fig. 7). These were made of 1/2 by 4 inch splits with the growth rings parallelling the flat of the board (Fig. 4C). I cut these 18 inches long, intending to make the prow-pieces project above them to total some 22-26 inches high. The notch at the bottom was made 1/2 by 3 inches to receive the prow-piece. Side notches 5/8 by 1 1/2 inches were cut to receive the gunwales about 4 inches from the top. Six inches from the top a rectangular hole 1/2 by 3 inches was cut for the top of the prow-piece. The bottom legs were left somewhat blunt so that they would not puncture the bark later. The entire board was shaped to a tear-drop, man-like silhouette.

After almost a full day's soak in the lake, the split prow-pieces were splayed out as a partially opened fan and appeared thoroughly wet. A 6 foot length of thin but strong cord was pinched between one of the splits near the solid end, and a teakettle of boiling water was poured down the vertically held stick -- into a pan, of course. Next point: use plenty of boiling water. One teakettle-full just isn't enough, and one can't wait around to reheat it. In later experiments, I found that a pail of water on a fire was satisfactory. I then used a small can to dip and pour.

When the piece was thoroughly heated (about five minutes of pouring), I slowly bent the split portion into a curve over my knee. Gripping the laminae firmly to keep them from slipping back and with one foot holding the unsplit portion flat on the floor, I slowly created a right-angle curve in the lower end. The split laminae are allowed to slip so that one is bending several 1/8 inch strips rather than a single 3 inch piece. While I held the curve in position a little more curved than desired, my wife spiralled the cord around the piece, pulling as tightly as possible at each turn. The end was pinched in another crack, and more hot water was applied to the remaining straight portion.

Fig. 7, Decorated Man-board.

At a point about 16 inches from the top, the first lamination (the split on the inside of the curve) was bent sharply downward. The wood kinked, but didn't break. When the next in line was bent over the first, the next kink was not so pronounced. Successive bending of the other laminae created a smooth curve 6 inches in diameter, for the bend was made in a 180 degree angle.

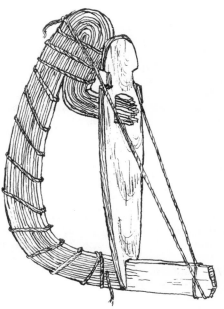

This curve was firmly wrapped with cord, and the man-board was set in place on the lower part about 8 inches from the end. With the man-board at a slight angle from the vertical, I tried to judge the appropriate point at which to begin the final bend which would be at a right angle to the one just made. The laminae were again heated and bent individually to correspond to the rectangular hole cut in the man-board. The bend was bound and as many laminae as could fit were pushed through. Some of the shortest ones did not reach the hole so a few wedges were made and were driven into the cracks between the laminae from the outside. These served to hold the prow-piece to the man-board.

Fig. 8, Laminated and bent prow-piece in place with man-board.

Finally, a temporary cord was fastened diagonally from the prow-piece top to the tip of the bottom sticking out from the man-board. This held the assembly in the proper curve while it was put aside to set and dry (Fig. 8).

Another assembly was made for the stern as exactly alike the first as I could fashion.

Ritzenthaler reports that crayon designs were applied to the man-boards, "to give you something to look at while you are paddling."[3] My search for hematite or ochre had not paid off yet, so I used crayons. Different designs were used for each man-board which served merely as identifying marks. (Later, when the canoe leaked, these marks became handy in identifying the faulty end. Also, I found that one prow-piece was larger than the other. For my one-man canoe, the marks helped to identify this larger end as the stern where the paddler should sit.)

Making the Gunwales

Six pieces about 3/4 by 2 inches by 13 feet were split with the grain (Fig. 4C). These turned out to be not sufficiently clear to be satisfactory, and, rather than take a chance with them or hazard a joint, I found some 3/4 inch spruce siding left over from our cottage. Seldom is this material clear enough, but a thorough search of a lumber yard might prove fruitful if I didn't have just one 14 foot clear piece -- which I did. After several frustrating attempts to use cedar, I finally selected all six pieces from the lumber yard spruce. Fortunately, also, the grain was with the width of the board.

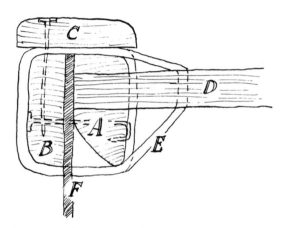

Fig. 9, Cross section of gunwale through center thwart. A, Gunwale. B, Outwale. C, Top plate. D, Thwart. E, Root lacing. F, Bark.

The portable circle saw again saved some time as the pieces could be ripped close to final size. Two gunwales for the inside of the canoe were trimmed with both crooked knife and a small hunting knife. (I got too quickly tired with either one alone.) The gunwales were made 5/8 by 1 5/8 inch in the center and tapered to 1/2 by 1 inch near the ends. The side to be inside was rounded so that the root lacing would not have to be too sharply bent. In my zeal, I rounded the corners too much to make a good, large bevel opposite on the lower edge. This bevel will accept the ribs as they are hammered in place and thus ought to be as large as possible (Fig. 9A). Incidentally, if whittling makes too uneven a piece, a carpenter's plane can even out some irregularities.

Two outwales, 3/8 by 1 5/8 inch were whittled to taper to 1/4 by 1 inch at each end. Here again, I rounded off the outside edges too much. The rounding is fine for the root binding, but not enough flat surface remains on top to make a platform for the top plates (Fig. 9B and 9C).

Both the gunwales and outwales were split into laminae of 1/8-3/16 inch widths for about 18 inches from the ends. The splits are made with the grain. The solid portions bend sufficiently well along the canoe sides, but the sharp upward thrust at stem and stern require the assistance of lamination.

The top plates (Fig. 9C) were made 3/8 by 1 1/2 inch, rounded on the top edges. Although the root binding does not go around the top plates, the rounding is desired here, for these pieces are the top surfaces of the sides which may receive abuse in normal usage of the canoe. The plates were tapered to about 1/4 by 3/4 inch at each end. The ends were split into laminae 18 inches long, again with the grain.

Gunwales and outwales were floated in the lake to soak overnight, for the morrow was to be the day of actual construction, and much was still left to be prepared.

The canoe "form" as an aid to construction appears to be a device peculiar to western Great Lakes techniques. Eastern tribes actually assemble the gunwales and thwarts and use these as a "form" of sorts. I chose the former technique as the most appropriate to my geographic location, and it appeared to be easier to understand.

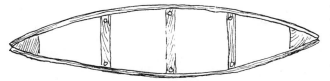

Fig. 10, Canoe form. Length: 10 feet, 10 inches. Beam: 24 inches.

Whereas the "form" would be an expedient in construction and would not be retained, I made no attempt at authenticating techniques. Apparently, these forms were earlier kept and re-used. I, however, made a simple canoe-bottom outline out of 1 X 2's which happened to be 11 feet long. Because I intended to make a 12 foot canoe, this would allow more than 6 inches at either end for the prow-pieces. I made the beam 2 feet, but this was an educated guess. With the 2 foot beam and 11 foot lengths, the actual measurement stem-to-stern was 10 feet 10 inches. The assembly was rudely nailed together with the addition of a few extra crossbars upon which weights could be placed (Fig. 10).

Preparing Lacing

A traditional lacing or binding for bark work is spruce root. Upon more
intensive research, this turns out to be black spruce (*Picea mariana*
Mill.). With more research, one finds that this tree is a very short-
needled swamp spruce often occurring with tamarack, another water-loving
conifer.

So, with hip boots, shovel, and knife, I sloshed into the nearest spruce-
tamarack bog. It's amazing how deep and cold the water is beneath the
sphagnum moss, even in June.

After poking around the bases of some black spruces, I located a few
roots. Quite a few, really, but only a few that I was sure belonged to
the spruces. These roots needed to be rescued inch-by-inch almost, for
the entire bog was a jungle of roots of every description.

After two hours of wallowing and wondering who would find my body when
I became mired, I netted about a dozen roots of 1-4 foot lengths with
1/4-1/2 inch diameter.   Swell! It was apparent that I needed more roots
and help.

On the way home, I recalled that jack pine (*Pinus banksiana* Lamb.) roots
were used.[4] Just then, I passed a grove of small jack pines. Central
Wisconsin is often sandy which is what the jacks like, and, incidentally,
where few other trees can survive. The quality of the soil can be fairly judged by the trees on it, and jack pine means "poor". We have a lot
of jack pine.

The sand was dry, and the chisel blade of my shovel located a root about
6 inches deep in a hurry. A shovelful of sand exposed a 3/4 inch root,
and a blow from the shovel severed it. From then on, pulling the root
was about as difficult as opening a pack of cigarettes. I pulled several about 8 feet long with a dia-
meter of 1 inch at the butt to less
than 1/4 inch before they snapped
off (Fig. 11). I didn't need a
grub hoe to loosen the soil,[5] but
I suspect that this might indeed
be necessary in some soils.

By selecting small trees (10-15
feet high) in fairly open areas,
I quickly gathered about 20 roots
from 4 to 8 feet long. The roots
grow surprisingly straight out
from the trunk, and, by selecting

Fig. 11, Gathering the jack pine roots.

[4]*Ibid.*, p. 66.
[5]*Ibid.*, p. 66.

trees in open areas, there was little interference from crossed roots.
I took only two or three roots from each tree to avoid killing them.

More roots needed to be gathered in days to come, for I had no idea how
many were necessary at the time; but the problem was one of mere incon-
venience, especially after the spruce swamp. I gave up on the spruce
roots entirely.

The roots were coiled in a bundle and tied with a short length of root.
Upon reaching the lake, the bundle was dropped in the water and tied to
the pier to await de-barking.

In days to come, I found that the easiest way to strip bark was to soak
the roots at least overnight although this was not entirely necessary
if they were de-barked soon after gathering. I have stripped bark several weeks after roots were gathered, but they were soaking all the time.
The only noticeable difference was that they had become water-logged and
that the bark had discolored the wood in some places. (Does this suggest a dye?)

The bark can be scraped with the thumbnail, but this wears painful in a
short time. A knife blade accomplishes the same purpose, but I found
that I had insufficient control and scratched the wood as well as incompletely removing the scaly bark.

I finally resorted to a variation of the Tlingit *eena*; a split stick
through which the root is pulled. A split post on our pier was ideal.
By sawing the root back and forth in the split, the bark was stripped
off quite easily, and variations in diameter were serviced by sawing
higher or lower in the split as necessary.

A pleasant concomitant is the pungent, sweet, turpentine odor emitted in
this process. This, and the later splitting, left aromatic residue on
my hands which was objectionable only during dinner.

Fig. 12, Splitting the roots.

I have long tried to split willow in threes by holding one
split in my teeth while the
hands pulled the other two.
No success. With a ready supply of roots available, I set-
tled for a simple split in twain.
A knife started the split at
the butt of the root. By holding the split sections with
thumb and forefinger with the
other fingers guiding the solid
portion, the splitting proceeds
apace (Fig. 12). The principle
of bending toward the thicker
side as with the cedar applies
here also·

Roots over 3/8 inches in diameter after de-barking were re-split to that
width. These were split parallel to the first split, and the inner, rough
piece was discarded. The smooth, curved part of the split is always
stitched to the visible outside. Roots over 1/2 inch in diameter were
also discarded. Fine hair roots were trimmed off. The good lengths,
which were now 1/4 to 3/8 inches wide and 4 to 6 feet long, were returned
to the water to soak further.

Staking Out

Early the next day, the form
was placed on a level piece
of ground which was to be
the building site. I made
no further preparation of
the area except to pick up
stones and other debris.

Stakes of smooth white cedar
posts about 2 inches in diameter and 2 to 2 1/2 feet
long were driven into the
ground at one foot intervals
around the perimeter of the
form. Two extra pairs of
stakes were driven in as a
continuation of stem and
stern so that the stakes
overall created a distance
of some 14 feet.

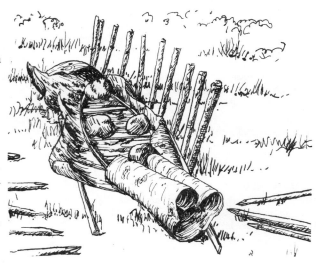

*Fig. 13, Staking out the bark. Form is in
place and is weighted down with stones.*

The stakes were pulled out and laid on the ground at right angles to the
form and a foot or two away from it. Now the form was removed and the
bark carefully centered over the holes left by the stakes. The white
side of the bark was up to become the inside of the canoe. The bark had
already begun to curl upward. It became apparent, when the bark was unrolled, that one end was defective because of excessive "eyes". This
portion was cut off, and, with a simple running stitch, a spare 3 foot
section was attached. This was sewn only in the center portion, thus
leaving the two sides to be stitched up later. Joints of this kind below the water-line are to be avoided if possible. Never is a canoe made
from the bark of two small trees with a seam running the length of the
keel.

The form was replaced in its exact earlier position. About six large
stones were placed on it as weights with care taken that they did not
puncture the bark.

Using long poles under each side of the bark, the stakes were gradually
replaced (Fig. 13). The tendency of the poles was to form a straight

line. Other poles were then required inside the curling bark and were
held in place with shorter stakes inside. These latter were placed in
shallow holes drilled into the form for this purpose. By lashing the
inner stakes to the outer ones, an approximate gunwale curve was created.
The outer stakes were driven in firmly and additional long poles were
slid in, inside and out, as seemed to be required. These were lashed to
the stakes to help them stay in place. Some stakes, particularly those
near the ends, needed to be lashed to opposite stakes to hold them upright. A temporary center thwart, 34 inches long and notched at either
end, was jammed in place.

Fig. 14, Sewing the gores.

Slices were cut 8 to 12
inches long in the bark
sides at about 2 foot intervals or wherever the bark
already had a tendency to
split. These became gores
which are necessary to allow a flat sheet to create
a canoe shape.[6] A long
wedge was driven in between
the bark and the ground to
make a lever to lift the
stem and stern about 6 inches
from the ground to create
a straight bottom with a
curve at either end. As it
turned out, my canoe ended

up with a slightly "hogged" bottom somewhat higher in the center than toward the ends. This was the result of poor gore sewing, but it's a hard
thing to estimate with no experience. Now the slits or gores, including
the one created by the addition of the extra piece of bark, were stitched
up with a horizontal stitch (Fig. 14).

An awl made from a sharpened
triangular file 3/8 inch
across was used to punch the
holes (Fig. 15). A triangular or 4-square awl is best
for this because a normal
round awl tends to begin

*Fig. 15, Triangular Awl. Blade: 3/8 by 3
inches. Length overall: 7 inches.*

a split in the bark which may spread later. The shape of a triangular
awl cuts a hole instead. Stitches were staggered slightly to avoid following the grain of the bark which might rip open later.

The split roots were prepared by cutting one end to a sliver point about
an inch long which usually could be pushed through the awl holes. Actual
experience quickly suggested that an additional strength was needed on

[6]Adney and Chapelle, pp. 29-31.

the seam so I added a scrap piece of bark as a reinforcement to the inside of each gore. This was stitched on at the same time. One drawback
of the reinforcing pieces came later; caulking the seams could not be
done on the inside of the canoe but had to be applied only from the outside.

Placing the Prow Pieces and Gunwales

The prow pieces, which now were "set", were put into position at either
end butted up against the canoe form on the bottom. (A few thin nails,
well placed, helped to hold the "set".) The extra six inches or so
which stuck out in front of the man-board was sawed off to allow only an
inch to protrude. When the prow-pieces were in place, some of the extra
bark was trimmed off the ends.

The gunwales, which had been soaking, were now retrieved and were marked
with 1 1/2 inch crayon bands about 3 1/2 inches apart. The last foot at
either end was left unmarked. The 1 1/2 inch bands were to be left unlaced to keep the bevel open to receive the ribs. By allowing the 3 1/2
inch space at the very center for the center thwart, I ended up with 19
spaces at either side, thus requiring a total of 38 ribs. Both gunwales
were marked at the same time to insure accuracy.

The gunwales were slid into place on the inside of the canoe and into
the notches provided in the man-boards. The height from the ground at
the center was 16 inches. It now became evident that the bark was not
sufficiently wide to reach the gunwales comfortably, so an additional
piece of bark, 2 by 6 feet, was laced to the canoe at the center. The
grain of this piece ran the same as the original. Two smaller pieces
were needed also on one side of each end in order to fit the prow-pieces'
upward curve.

The gunwales were repositioned and then, after the prow-pieces were
checked, were lashed together. Again, though not authentic, a nail
through the gunwales into the man-boards gave me a sense of security.
It turned out that I didn't need the split laminations.

The outwales were taken from the lake and set against the exterior of
the canoe to check for length. A point just inside of the man-boards was
marked as the beginning of the curve upward to meet the curve of the
prow-piece. The outwales were removed, and these curves, with the laminations, were bent upward to about 90 degrees and bound with a split
root.

The outwales were again placed into position opposite to the gunwales
and, after determining the correct position, were nailed through the bark
into the gunwales. Thin, 2 inch "box nails" were used which then pro-
jected some 3/4 inch through the gunwales. A heavy hammer held against
the inside afforded support while the nails were driven. While not absolutely necessary, two C-clamps held the pieces tightly during the pounding. With a pliers, each nail was bent about 3/8 inch from its end.

The hammer then pounded the remainder over and into the gunwales, thus forcing the point back on itself and clinching the nail permanently in place. One nail was used in each 3 1/2 inch section which would be covered with root lacing. Nails do seem out of place, but Chapelle reports that they were probably used before 1850.[7] Certainly the nailing made the lacing much simpler, and it is impossible today to find someone who can made a canoe entirely without nails.

Thwarts

Five thwarts were made out of 5/8 by 2 1/2 inch white cedar stock. The center thwart was 36 inches long. The next thwarts were placed 30 inches away toward each end and were 26 inches long. Short thwarts 10 inches long were made to fit near the man-boards about 58 inches from the center. All thwarts were tapered to 5/8 by 1 3/4 inches, and the edges were rounded off. Note that the normal position of the paddler is kneeling and leaning against the thwart rather than sitting upon it. Therefore these thwarts are not made as heavy as on commercial models.

Two 1/4 inch holes were drilled abut 1 1/2 inch from the end of each thwart. The four shortest thwarts were trimmed on the end to match the angle at which they touched the gunwales. The outline of the end of each thwart was traced on the gunwale position and this area was mortised through the gunwale as deep as the birch bark. The bottom of the mortise is created by the bark and outwale.

By carefully spreading the sides of the canoe, the thwarts were set in their mortises. Any bark protruding above the gunwales was trimmed off flush. The first lacing took place at the center thwart through a hole punched even with the bottom of the outwale and gunwale. A double loop was stitched next to the thwart and the end of the root was pinched behind. Further stitching went thrice through each thwart hole and was pulled tight each time. Each hole punched in the bark below the outwale was used for two turns of lacing although the lace itself was laid side-by-side along the outwales. A last double turn was taken next to the thwart, and the end of the root was pulled through the last loop to secure it. When this became dry, it was quite secure. The remaining thwarts were bound the same way, and the assembly began to look like a canoe.

Lacing the Gunwales

Seated on the ground, we now began the slow work of lacing up the 3 1/2 inch sections. (I have seen canoes of recent manufacture which omit this binding entirely and trust to nails alone.) Most canoes show that the bark which projects up between the gunwale and outwale is bent over

[7] Ibid., p. 66.

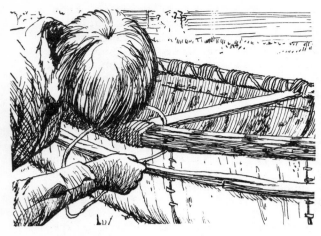

Fig. 16, Lacing the gunwale.

on top toward the inside of the canoe and is trimmed off flush with the gunwale. I trimmed the bark off the top and neglected this folding (Fig. 9F). It would appear best, however, to employ the fold to give better strength when the ribs are driven in as the fold helps to prevent the bark from pulling out.

With two or three persons sewing, the work can begin anywhere along the gunwale as long as each loose end is tucked under previous or new stitches to hold it in place. We took an average of 9 looped stitches in each section with a tenth going diagonally on the outwale into the next section. This created a pleasant design of stitches along the exterior. By holding the awl with one flat side against the bottom of the outwale, the triangular hole was made with the point downward and away from the tendency to split. Lacing went best from exterior into interior, being pulled tight each time. This position is quite a backbreaker with one arm on the inside, the other on the outside, and the head constantly tilted to observe the stitching (Fig. 16).

The root was carefully inserted each time to avoid twists and to keep the half-round portion of the root on the outside. A knife was handy as a new point had to be shaped from time to time. Also, a pail of water was necessary so that the root could be kept moist and pliable. The friction of lacing tended to dry it out. We found that 4 to 6 foot sections of root were most practical. Shorter lengths required too frequent splicing, and longer lengths were too cumbersome.

At each end, near the man-boards, the outwales only were laced to the bark on the upward curve. The bark was, of course, trimmed off to correspond to the curve. To finish, the outwales were lashed together with root on the ends which project up above the man-boards.

Lacing the Prow-Pieces

Beginning as near to the ground as practical for easy working, the prow-pieces were laced in place. Extra bark was carefully trimmed. A staggered whip stitch was used here so that the lacing holes did not align too much with the bark's grain. Five to seven stitches in a group were taken beginning at 3/4 inch from the edge of the curve to about 2 1/2 inches distant, thus giving the lacing a "saw tooth" decorative pattern as well as functioning as a strong fastening (Fig. 17). Such stitching

continued up the curve until the top was reached,
at which time the grain of
the bark no longer was in
danger of being aligned
with the holes.

Each awl hole had to go
through not only the bark
on each side of the canoe,
but had to find a split between the laminae of the
prow-piece. In other words,
an existing crack was en-
larged between the laminae
rather than drilling a hole
through the prow-piece
each time. Drilling, ob-
viously, would have weak-
ened the prow-piece.

Fig. 17, Prow-piece partially laced.

Some recent canoes use a simple X-stitch criss-crossing from side to
side over the prow curve. This would, of course, have been much quicker
and easier because far fewer stitches are required. However, as one of
the least water-tight portions of the canoe and subject to abrasion during use, it seemed to me that the whipped, staggered stitch would be
superior.

Some canoes also use a half-round piece of root along the outside of the
curve from bottom to top. My stitching seemed to make this unnecessary
unless one wanted a sharper prow.

Stitching continued over and down the top curve to the point where the
outwales made further work unnecessary. The other prow-piece was then
stitched. The portion of the curves near the bottom of the canoe which
was not yet laced was left until the canoe was turned upside down.

Finishing the Outside

The top plates which cover the gunwales and outwales had been soaking.
These were removed from the lake, and the ends were bent upward to match
the curve of the outwales. The bends were lashed in place with root.

The top plates, in earlier times, were pegged and lashed in place, but
nails seem to be the only practical way today. Beginning at the center
thwart, the top plate was nailed in place. Nails were staggered to go
into the gunwale and outwale at intervals of about 5 inches.

Because this top plate must be bent in opposition to its normal tendency,
a helper or two was necessary. Care should be taken that the nails do
not go into the unlaced areas reserved for ribs. Nails were used along

the sides until the upward curve was reached at which point the top plate
was nailed to the outwale only. This completed work at this position.

Stakes were now taken out slowly so as not to put undue stress on any portion of the canoe. With the stakes completely removed, the stones holding the form in place were also removed. Because the thwarts were permanently installed, the form could not be taken out whole. I imagine
that authentic canoe forms were tied together and therefore could be removed in pieces. I had to saw mine apart, but I didn't intend to use it
again anyway.

The canoe was then turned upside down on some saw horses so that the
bottom stitching of the prows could be completed. Lower portions of the
gores which could not be reached earlier were also completed.

Making the Ribs

I had been splitting 4 and 5 foot lengths of cedar for ribs intermitten-
ly as my arm permitted. These had been trimmed to 3/8 inch thickness by
2 to 2 1/2 inches wide tapering to 1 to 1 1/2 inch at each end. The edges
were rounded on the side which would be upward when in place in the canoe.
Most of this shaping was done with the crooked knife or hunting knife,

but occasionally a plane simplified mat-
ters. Thirty-eight ribs were required;
I made forty-eight. These were tied securely and sunk in the lake to soak for
a day.

The next day, remembering that a teakettle was insufficient, I brought out what
must be a 40-gallon hog-scalding kettle.
A smaller container could have been used,
but I had none. A good fire and fair
wind brought the water in the kettle to
a boil in less than two hours. I suppose
a larger fire would have done it quicker.
In any case, I used up most of the shav-
ings from the ribs. The fire needed
constant attention during the bending
to follow to keep the water as hot as
possible.

I estimated the bottom of the center of
the canoe to be about 24 inches across
the flat before the curve of the ribs
should start. Several of the longest
ribs were marked with a pencil to locate the beginning of the bend on either

*Fig. 18, Applying hot water
to the ribs.*

end. A rib was placed, one end up, in the boiling water and, with a tin
can, I ladled the hot water over the rib (Fig. 18). The rib was placed
end-over-end several times, each time with hot water ladled over it, for

Fig. 19, Bending ribs.

about 3 or 4 minutes.

I put the hot, wet rib on the ground, rounded side up, placed the outside of my feet at the pencil marks, and began to pull up the ends (Fig. 19). Ritzenthaler notes that the Ojibwa Bob Pine chanted along with the bending.[8] I tried several chants but broke four of the first five attempts. I changed the chant to a more pleading sound and also bent two ribs at a time. I expect that the pressure of one rib against the other had something to do with it and perhaps the new chant was the right one; anyway, this technique seemed to work. Obviously, the inner rib of the pair being bent would be slightly smaller than the other, but smaller ribs are required also, so this is acceptable.

The pair of ribs was bent an inch or two more than was estimated, and my son tied them across the top with baling twine. Finished ribs were hung on a limb to set. Other ribs were bent, shorter ribs with less flat across the bottom, until some were being bent with both feet close together during bending.

Ribs intended to be placed near the pointed ends of the canoe were trimmed to about 1 1/2 inch width and were bent around a fence post to give the desired sharp curve. The very sharpest bends required a reduction in thickness to almost 1/4 inch at the curve. This allowed the curve to be bent easily while the stiffer side still gave strength to the vertical walls of the canoe. The completed ribs could now be temporarily placed in the canoe to check the accuracy of the bends (Fig. 20).

Fig. 20, Ribs placed in approximate position in the canoe.

Planking

By the time all the ribs had been split, I had become quite accomplished in the technique of splitting. Actually, when the billet was split to

1/2 inch or so thickness, I found myself wanting to split them further, even though I needed them for ribs. Now was the time to split further.

Planking should be as wide and as thin as possible. Most of the cedar posts I purchased were already cut to seven feet. Because the canoe would be slightly over 12 feet, two seven-foot lengths would allow a one-foot overlap. Several billets were split and re-split to about 1/8 inch thickness. I tried to keep most of these pieces 3 to 4 inches wide. Some, of course, varied in thickness, width, and, if the split drifted off, length. About 40 of these were made with several additional pieces of shorter length and width.

Crooked knife and hunting knife did some refining, but the use of a plane on a bench did the best work most rapidly. A knife was used to "feather" the ends of the planking where they would overlap smoothly near the center of the canoe. These planks were put in the lake to soak until the next day when the ribs would be set enough also.

Driving the Ribs

Four stakes were driven in the ground in pairs about a foot apart with the pairs about 12 feet apart — roughly the length of the canoe. The canoe was hung just off the ground by tying ropes from these stakes to the small thwarts near stem and stern.

Four temporary ribs were made from 1/4 by 1 inch splits and were roughly bent to fit near the center three thwarts. Beginning at the bottom of the canoe, pointed planks were carefully shoved under the stem and stern pieces so

Fig. 21, Placing planking. Temporary ribs in place.

that the planks overlapped at the center. A rectangle of bark was added below the pointed ends for reinforcement. Pairs of planks were added by overlapping the first slightly and were pushed between the man-boards and bark toward the prow-pieces. More pairs were added, and the temporary ribs were cut short enough to be pressed under the gunwales to hold the planks in place (Fig. 21). A few narrow planks were added where necessary if the main planks did not sufficiently cover the bark. As more planks were placed close to the gunwales, some care was required to keep earlier pieces from shifting. The temporary ribs were removed and replaced as necessary as planking was added.

Fig. 22, Driving stick for ribs.
Length, 15 inches.

When all the planks were in place, the ribs were brought out again, and the twine which bound them was severed. Matching pairs (or nearly so) were arranged in order of size of bend. These were numbered 1 through 19 in pairs and were checked for size in the canoe.

The sizes appeared adequate, so the first rib nearest each end was pressed down into position and was marked level with the top plate. The extra lengths were sawed off, and the ends of the ribs were trimmed to 1 inch width with a bevel cut to correspond to the bevel inside each gunwale. I realized that, if accurate, this length would be too much, but I presumed that I had not forced the rib down completely and that the two inaccuracies would tend to equalize each other. They did, most of the time.

Some hot water had been prepared earlier. The gunwales were dampened with a sponge, and the hot water was carefully poured over the gunwales so as to run down both inside and outside of the canoe. (The canoe leaked profusely at this point, so there was no problem of water collecting inside.) This softened both the root binding and the bark so that they could give slightly as the ribs were driven in. This dampening continued periodically for the next several hours as the ribs were forced in tighter and tighter.

As the ribs were cut and trimmed, they were set in place at a slight angle to the vertical in such a way that their bevelled ends were inserted in the bevelled groove in the gunwale. The wooden mallet and driving stick (Figs. 2 and 22) were used to drive each rib firmly, but incompletely, in (Fig. 23). Successively larger ribs were cut and partially driven in as were the first. The ideal here was that the ribs press on the planking to hold both ribs and planking in place firmly but not with such pressure that the bark skin is burst.

Fig. 23, Preliminary placing of ribs
using driving stick and mallet.

I found that a quick dip in hot water just before inserting them helped the ribs to adjust to the curve of the canoe. Too much soaking, of course, would have caused them to loose the set.

The last ribs, nearest the center thwart, were most difficult to put into position, for they had to overlap slightly in the beginning. They were soon driven apart. In about two hours, all the ribs were in place awaiting final driving.

Some ribs, naturally, had to be removed and trimmed as it was found that they were too long. A few had to be replaced by slightly longer ribs with thanks to the forethought of making extras. Some ribs, especially where the planking came close to the gunwales, resisted driving into the groove which, as has been mentioned, should have been larger. These had to be pinched into the groove by one person while another drove them in. C-clamps again were handy in troublesome places.

Periodically, in the next two hours, more water was poured over the gunwales, and the ribs were driven in a bit more. At the end of this time, all the ribs had been driven in so that they were equidistant from each other and at right angles to the gunwales.

Pitching the Seams

After an enforced rest, we gathered white pine (*Pinus strobus* L.) pitch or gum where we could. We fortunately found some recently-cut stumps which were still oozing pitch. After clearing off the sawdust, we found that we could gather a few ounces every few days. To get the quantity I needed, we should have started weeks ago.

Fig. 24, Gathering white pine pitch.

I blazed some trees Indian-style by chopping a flat horizontal platform about 3 inches deep with the area above it chopped away. This was done mainly as an experiment because I didn't want to disfigure local trees (Fig. 24). I noticed that only the inch or so of white sapwood would exude pitch. The heartwood was inert.

The pitch became quite fluid when heated and burned furiously when it was spilled on the fire. Caution is advised! Some pulverized charcoal was stirred in to give necessary stability to the pitch. The pitch itself is amber; it is the charcoal which accounts for the dark caulking.

This mixture was spread over the seams with a cedar spatula (Fig. 25). Warm pitch can be manipulated with a wet finger. (It sticks to dry skin.)

Fig. 25, Caulking the seams with pitch being applied with a cedar spatula.

A roll of birch bark made into a torch is traditionally used to melt the pitch on the bark and cause it to flow into the seams. Ritzenthaler notes that a gasoline blow torch was used in his observation.[9] I went him one better and used, in addition to the bark torch, a propane torch. By using finger, spatula, and torch, the pitch was smeared into some seams and flowed well, showing good penetration.

All the main seams, at least those below the water-line, should normally be caulked with this mixture. Some Indians used a bit of grease in the mix to keep it from becoming too brittle. I had insufficient pitch to try further mixes.

What I did have (unfortunately, as it turned out) was a quantity of road tar. I melted this in the fire and applied it in the same fashion as the authentic pitch. The suggestions came from a scale model I had seen. On a model it might be satisfactory; on a full-sized canoe, it wasn't. Tar melts at a higher temperature than pitch; it doesn't flow well unless the bark itself is heated to blistering temperatures; it becomes quite brittle at lower temperatures; and it re-softens in the sun. I do not suggest its use. The pitch flowed well and became somewhat glazed over after heating. I wished that I had a more abundant supply.

I have since used common roofing cement which is a gooey, black, asphalt substance which can be purchased in cans. This spreads easily, can be torched, (carefully), and becomes stiffer as time goes on. It's almost as good as pitch and a lot easier to get.

I became increasingly disappointed in my selection of bark because of the large eyes which now appeared as large warts or blisters on the exterior and spoiled the fairness of the curves. The least objectionable eyes were left as they occurred. Some of the worst, however, had to be sliced open. I had to tack these down through the planking, but there was no other choice at this point.

I examined the bottom carefully and patched any tiny splits which were visible, or so I thought. After placing the canoe carefully in the water, a few gallons leaked in in a ten minute voyage. The Indian techniques still had to be used. Once more the canoe was hung from the stakes and water was poured inside. Leaking areas could then be quickly identi-

[9]*Ibid.*, p. 94.

fied and marked on the exterior with a pencil. By tilting the canoe, we
could find leaks above the normal water line which were marked also.

The canoe was turned over to spill the water, and, upon drying, the objectionable parts were pitched -- this time with clear pitch which is
less noticeable on the brown bark exterior. Apparently the black pitch
is desired only on the seams.

At this writing, the canoe is not perfectly waterproof, but nearly so.
I expect that a journey by bark canoe required daily repairs.

Conclusion

Experienced canoeists compliment the handling of the 68-pound craft. I
hesitate to run a rapids just yet and trust only hazard-free lakes. The
high prow and stern catch the wind more than I would like, but, upside-
down, they make a high center which could well be used as a rude shelter
for sleeping.

The paddler's kneeling position requires some practice. Actually, it is
quite a safe position, but my knees don't know it. I recall somewhere
that a cushion of skins or furs would be used in earlier times. The
life preserver cushion required in Wisconsin serves this purpose for me.

The question of time has been asked and is difficult to answer accurately. For instance, some whittling for ribs and planks had begun during
spare hours weeks earlier. I don't recommend that all the work be done
at once as might be implied above. Much of this was done in the three
days following the gathering of the bark, but I'm sure that my arm would
not have lasted had I tried to do it all at once. Working mainly with
my son as helper, and with occasional help from wife and daughter, the
actual construction beginning with the staking out took a week and a day
with some time out for obtaining more cedar and gathering more roots.
Two or three persons who know what to do should be able to do the whole
thing in two weeks.

I still don't know why anyone would want to build a bark canoe today, but,
now that I know how, the next one should be a beauty! The first one
wasn't too bad.

REFERENCES

Adney, Edwin Tappan and Chapelle, Howard I.

"The Bark Canoes and Skin Boats of North America", *United States National Museum Bulletin* No. 230, Washington, 1964.

Ritzenthaler, Robert E.

"The Building of a Chippewa Indian Birch-Bark Canoe", *Bulletin of the Public Museum of the City of Milwaukee*, Vol. 19, No. 2, November, 1950.

Fig. 26, The finished canoe afloat.

SPLINT BASKETRY OF THE WOODLAND INDIANS

Although splint basketry of the Woodland Indian Culture Area appears to be an ancient craft, it seems reasonable to this author that the craft has become more highly developed in the last century and early part of this century as a result of steel tools for increased efficiency and the interest of White buyers. Some fine examples are still being produced today by the few Indians who still pursue it. On the other hand, the low monetary return to the craftsman has often resulted in shoddy work made with short-cuts and little pride in quality workmanship. As with most contemporary crafts, basketry is seldom a full time occupation, for it hardly pays a fair return for the hours involved. It is today about as profitable to the Indian as is the remuneration to a White woman who spends time and money to knit a pair of socks which may be sold for a few dollars to certain individuals who value the hand-knit pair over the 69¢ ones available in stores. In other words, basketry is a labor of love which also produces a few dollars of supplemental income, but it can hardly be the primary source of funds for a full-time enterprise.

Certain Winnebago and Chippewa groups in central and northern Wisconsin still set up tarpaper *wigwams* in summer months along highways in order to sell the spring and summer production of baskets to the tourists. Newer, limited-access roads are, however, forcing these people out of business. The poignant, hand-lettered, "Indian Baskets For Sale" signs are almost invisible to the high-speed traveller. Some Indians are fortunate enough to be able to wholesale their wares through the numerous souvenir shops which are found in Wisconsin's lake regions, but here the mark-up, often 100%, often serves actually to lower the Indian's return. For instance, a basket which would gain the Indian $7.50 would need to be priced in a shop at $15.00 -- a price which is hardly attractive to the souvenir hunter. As an alternative, the Indian is induced to sell his piece to the trader at, for instance, $5.00 so that it could be marked up only to $10.00 which is still too high for tourist consideration. As will be seen later, the time and physical effort involved in gathering materials and producing baskets from them is such that either return to the Indian would still be only a subsistence wage. Another ugly alternative is possible: that of reducing the quality of craftsmanship to cut the time involved thereby increasing the hourly rate.

The Winnebagoes in central Wisconsin still produce splint baskets. Recently, these people have formed the Pot-Chee-Nuk Cooperative near Antigo where their crafts, primarily baskets and beadwork, are sold. It is pleasant to view shelves of well-crafted baskets of many shapes and designs.

Splint basket are also produced today in the Cherokee reservation in
North Carolina and in isolated areas in New England. New York and
Pennsylvania pack baskets are offered for sale in small ads in sports-
man's magazines and are favored by trappers over knapsacks and the like.
Some of these are made with veneer strips rather than the true split
splints. The veneeer is usually obtained from mills as scrap and is,
therefore, simpler to acquire than the splints. The veneer is less easy
to work, is subject to splitting defects, and is generally less satisfactory for the final product. In addition to the United States, most
reserves in Canada are present sources for authentic basketry.

To gain competitive contemporary prices for the investment in time and
money, production methods must be employed. The craft of splint basketry
is such that it must continue to be almost exclusively a hand craft with
little possibility of assembly-line technology. First, a source of
splints must be identified. Oak, hickory, elm, and black walnut have
been used in isolated instances, but by far the favored material is the
wood of the black ash (*Fraxinus nigra* Marsh.), a tree common in the Woodland area. As with most materials, permission must be first obtained
from the owner to search for and take a tree. (Public lands in Wisconsin are public to all, and, as such, no one individual is permitted to
take for his own use what is common property.) Fortunately, the black
ash has little market value as timber or pulpwood. It has little strength
and is not suitable for boards; it rots too quickly for use as fence
posts; it burns quickly with little ash so it has no value for firewood.
It is, however, admirably suited for basketry because it can be split
relatively easily and it accepts rather sharp bends without cracking.

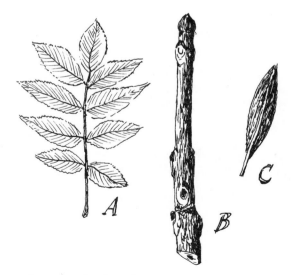

Fig. 1, Black Ash. A, Leaf. B, Twig.
C, Fruit.

Selecting a Tree

When searching for a black ash,
first of all locate a swamp, for
the tree is found in wet locations. Prof. James Newman of
Stevens Point offers this simple identification, "When you
are near a tree which you know
to be an ash, and your feet are
wet, it's a black ash." Black
ash may occasionally be found a-
way from swamps, but it will be
found in these instances that
there is an abundant high ground-
water table available.

The amateur botanist would do well
to identify the tree in summer
for later harvest, for the leaves
offer the next best means of i-
dentification. The leaves are

found growing opposite each other; i.e., leaves are in pairs; one on one side of the twig and the other 180 degrees around on the other side (Fig. 1B). In the absence of actual leaves, the leaf scars from the previous season may be seen in this pattern. All ash species' leaves are compound, with the exception of the terminal leaflet, the others grow in pairs oppositely from the leaf stem. (Palmately compound leaves are different in that all the leaflets grow from a common point on the stem.) The shape of the leaflets is a pointed oval with a serrated or saw-tooth edge. This description is common to all ash species however, so the following further description is important. The leaflets on the black ash are attached directly to the stem. On the white ash, for instance, each leaflet has an individual stem of about 1/2 inch or so. Red ash has a shorter stem, but can be differentiated because of its wool or velvet on new twigs and the underside of the leaflets. Black ash leaflets have hardly any stem and no wool or velvet. The description so far would also identify blue ash, but the blue ash is unique and can be identified by scoring the bark so that the sap appears. The distinctly blue hue which is created when the sap comes in contact with the air gives the blue ash its name.

Other clues for the black ash include stout gray twigs. (Blue ash is somewhat ridged.) The bark of mature trees is ridged and flaky, and never has the deeply-scored diamond pattern of the white, red, or green ash. The clusters of paddle-shaped fruits or seeds which appear in late summer offer another key (Fig. 1C), but the location, leaf shape, twig cross section, and bark are most useful.

Splitting the Splints

The following procedure should be accomplished in reasonably rapid order, for the dampness inherent in fresh wood is necessary for successful splitting of the splints. It is doubtful that this can be accomplished on old wood or logs which have been allowed to dry out. If necessary, the log can be dampened or even stored in a pond or stream for a few days. A fresh, damp log can be wrapped in plastic to keep it moist.

Fig.2, Man's knife or "crooked knife". Length: 12 inches.

The traditional and best time to harvest a tree is in early spring when the sap has loosened the bark from the previous year's growth. A tree is selected for straightness, freedom from knots or branches, and diameter. Billets or logs of about 4-7 feet long will be cut after the tree is felled, so an otherwise crooked tree may be used if certain bad sections are discarded. The normal growth of the tree often provides a relatively clear trunk for 10-20 feet with the branches reserved for the rather scraggly crown. A lumpy trunk indicates knots inside which will

Fig. 3, Hardwood mallet.   Length: 12 inches.

be unusable, for the splints should be straight and clear.

A Winnebago informant, gesturing with her hands, indicated that a diameter of 12-14 inches was her preference. Hoffman[1] calls attention to the "limbs" of the "Black elm" being "3 to 4 inches in diameter." My experience proves that a larger diameter is superior although lesser sizes are satisfactory. The larger log affords the best support for the pounding described later, and splints may be removed of greater width due to the lesser convexity of the greater diameter.

The bark, which is about 3/8-1/2 inch thick is removed. In the spring, it may be possible to peel this by starting it with an ax or drawknife. The Indian man's knife or "crooked knife" is also suited for this purpose (Fig. 2). If cut in the spring, the bark may sometimes be removed in a long, single, cylindrical piece. Cut in half lengthwise, this "peel" can be used as a cushion to preclude dirt and dents on the bottom of the log during pounding.

Splints are made by pounding with a wooden mallet or club about 20 inches long with one end trimmed down to a diameter suitable for a handle.[2] (Fig. 3). Lyford[3] says that the blunt end of an ax was also used, but this seems too light for me. A common nail hammer with a rounded or "bell" face has proven satisfactory in my experience. In any case, the mallet should be heavy enough to strike a hard blow, yet still be comfortable after several hours' work. Care must be taken if a steel tool is used so that the blows are struck flat on the log. Angled blows may dent the wood causing it to break later. The wooden club precludes this problem; further, it can be pounded with no regard for surface for it has no face as such, and is quite easy to make.

The log is pounded in a width about 2-3 inches wide on top of the log and along its length. This first layer may need several beatings before the wood begins to loosen. No short-cuts are possible! Every square inch must be pounded vigorously to accomplish the purpose which is to crush the soft, openly cellular portion of each year's growth to the point where it can be separated from the more closely grained growth. If the pounding has been sufficient, it may be noticed on the cut end of the log that the first layer of wood or annular ring may be a little free from the one beneath it. A blade of some sort can be pried in the crack so that an inch or two can be lifted. Careful pulling (and maybe more pounding) should split off this splint in an even width for the entire length of the log although my experience has been that the first ones tend to taper somewhat (Fig. 4).

[1]Hoffman, pp. 259-60
[2]*Ibid.*
[3]Lyford, "Ojibwa Crafts", pp. 62-63.

Fig. 4, Black ash log with splint being removed.

When one splint has been taken, it is set aside to begin a pile of splints which will be coiled and tied for storage until needed. (Fresh splints may, of course, be used immediately.) The log is then rolled a bit to present a new surface on top; the pounding continues until another splint can be split off. Normally, a single annular ring is taken completely around the circumference of the log before the new ring is begun. Occasionally, several layers may be split as one for use as rim reinforcements and the like. If several layers are taken at once, these may be separated by hand later by starting a split with a knife blade. In any case, the log is kept moist at all times. Work may take place on clean, grassy ground, but care should be taken that the bottom does not become soiled with dirt and grass stain. Saw horses may be more comfortable for persons not customarily sitting on the ground, but here be careful that the wooden horses do not damage the log during pounding.

Small pin knots offer no problem as the splint comes off right over the knot. Larger knots must be by-passed or else the splint may be taken only from the other parts of the log. This becomes more and more of a problem so that the selection of a clear log is appreciated.

The annular rings will not be the same thickness for each year, but are dependent upon the rate of growth for each given year. One may discover variations from about 1/32 inch up to 1/4 inch thickness. Rings representing drought years will, for instance, be thinner than those grown during years of abundant moisture. (This variation in thickness has become the basis for dating the antiquity of wooden objects by counting backwards on the rings. By comparing rings on unknown artifacts with rings on a known-aged wood, this "tree-ring dating" or "dendrochronology" method has given the age of artifacts made centuries ago.) Other variations in thickness may be observed on different sides of a tree in a given year. This is due mainly to the immediate surroundings of the tree which has a tendency to have a richer growth on sides where other trees do not compete for sunlight. Thick and thin splints may be separated into piles -- the thinner for small, delicate work, and the thicker for burden baskets and the like.

It will be noted that the first 6-10 rings will be a white or ivory color known as sapwood. These are kept for the finest baskets and can be dyed to bright hues. Heart rings, those deeper in the trunk, are darker -- a pale walnut hue. While these latter are perfectly good, they are not so highly prized. The difference in hue can have some merits, for designs of light and dark can form subtle, but pleasant, patterns in plaiting.

Rings continue to be split off until the log has become so small in diameter that this becomes impractical. It is generally better to split off
wide pieces, 1-3 inches across, to be re-split later, than to be forced
to use only narrow pieces without this option. The remaining billet may
be split in quarters with an ax in the manner of splitting firewood.
This can yield thicker pieces which may be kept moist to be fashioned into handles. Some people like to score the surface into longitudinal,
deep lines made with a knife blade. In this way, splints of a predeter-
mined width can be obtained which need little trimming thereafter.

It may be unnecessary to state that a rough estimate can be made of the
number of splints to be obtained from a log by measuring the circumference and noting how many splints of a given width can be made from it.
This number, multiplied by the usable annular rings, gives an estimate
of the total. Of course, some splints are ruined and, naturally, the
diminished diameter toward the middle reduces the number. In any case,
it is surprising how many splints are obtained from one log. In earlier
times, one good basket was often given in trade for the log from which
it was obtained.

Obtaining the tree, cutting it, and, to some extent, splitting it was
exclusively men's work according to tradition. Women will now do some
splitting, but further preparation and the actual weaving was women's
work. The division of labor is not so well defined today as in past
times. I recently was told about an aged, 110 pound woman who split an
entire log in one afternoon. "But", it was added significantly, "she
knew just *how* to do it." I don't know how many splints were obtained
nor how much of a "core" remained.

Preparing the Splints

It will be noted that both sides of each splint exhibit the rather rough,
striated texture of the cellular structure of the wood. While this may
be functionally non-objectionable, a finer, smoother surface is generally desired, especially on the outside of baskets. The best baskets are
never made with rough splints. A crooked knife might be used to scrape
one side, but I find that a common paint scraper does a fine job today.
Long, even strokes expose the smooth, fine-grained wood surface. Scraping can best be done while the wood is damp. If allowed to dry, it must
be soaked again first. Scraping can be done on a flat surface with one
hand gripping the splint and the other drawing the scraper. You may wish
to try scraping the splint right on the log before it is peeled. The
pioneer's "Schnitzelbank" or "shaving horse" was adopted by Indians for
gripping splints while scraping them.

Some splints may naturally be the proper thickness for baskets. Occasionally, one may harvest a tree which shows evidence of abundant growth
-- up to 1/4 inch annually. Such thickness is much too heavy for all
except reinforcement rims. (If you have an especially wide thick splint,
you might reserve it for a tom-tom frame.) These may be split and re-
split by starting a crack with a knife at the top wide enough to get your

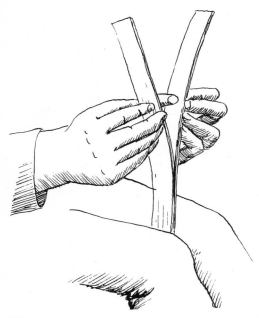

Fig. 5, Splitting a thick splint.

thumbs inside to force the crack open. Hold the lower end between your knees at a convenient distance (Fig. 5). The accuracy of the split can be controlled with the fingers and thumbs by tilting the splint to one side or the other. The wood tends to split toward the side with the most curve. Thus, if the right side, for instance, appears to be getting too thin, hold the splint in a more vertical position and bend the left split more which will cause the crack to drift to the left. Splints split in this manner will exhibit a very nice smoothness which will not require further scraping.

Splints may be dyed by using any of the natural dyestuffs available in the vicinity. Today, however, commercially prepared dyes are used almost exclusively. Unfortunately, the earlier, more organic natural colors seem to be aesthetically better suited to basketry and other native crafts than the modern chemical colors. I have found that adulterating the commercial preparations results in hues more nearly approximating the old hues. For instance, a "Kelly green" may be weakened with brown or orange to dull it. Modern basketmakers still rely primarily on the bright pinks, blues, and other strong colors for their work. When questioned about the absence of the old colors in her work, a Winnebago woman agreed that the old ones were better. "But", she added, "the people (buyers) like the rainbow baskets." Perhaps education should be directed toward the consumer rather than the craftsman.

For dyeing, a large bowl, preferably enamelled (not steel or other bare metal, for these affect the dye), is used. Either dry or liquid dyestuff may be used, but in any case, a strong solution is required. This should be brought to the boiling point and kept there during the dyeing process. Splints to be dyed are immersed singly or tied in a loose coil. Tight coiling and tying causes irregularities in color. Splints are submerged, a few at a time, and simmered until they are a shade darker (stronger) than the desired color. Some color will be lost in rinsing and, besides, the wet splints look darker than dry ones. Stirring during simmering is beneficial. A complete rinsing in cold water washes off the excess dye until the water runs clear. Dyed splints may be used immediately or may be dried for storage.

One final step remains before weaving; namely, to split the splints to the desired widths. Inch widths are generally suitable for bottoms; les-

ser widths for the
weaving elements down
to 1/8 inch for small
baskets. Such split-
ting can be done with
a sharp, thin knife
by eye. A straight
edge is useless, for
the splint slips be-
neath it and the cut
goes awry. Recent
technology has pro-
duced a ripping
knife, in principle
similar to a leather-
cutting tool with a
sharp, thin blade
projecting out a
short distance from
a fixed point on
a handled tool (Fig.
6). A splint is
pushed into the slot
underneath a horizontal
pin which keeps it from

*Fig. 6, Two-
bladed ripping tool
or splitter. Splint
is pulled through in
direction of arrow. Width inside groove: 1 1/2 inches. A,
Pointed knife blades. B, Removable
nail for pressure. C, Clamping screw
for blades.*

slipping out above the blades. After an initial split is made, the pistol-grip handle is pulled with one hand while the splint is pulled through
the blade with the other. Only very thin splints can be split with this
device, but the speed and accuracy of cut is indeed satisfying compared
to freehand cutting. Some Woodland splitters may have several blades
cutting at once. Because the blades are fixed, several such splitters
must be made for different widths. I use a screw or bolt through the
end to clamp the blades firmly; this also allows occasional removal of
the blades for sharpening. Whether a knife is used freehand or a splitter is used, some care must be taken that the cut does not drift.

Splints of the desired width and color are now selected and cut to approximate length. A heavy shears seems to me to be the best tool although
a knife may be used. The length of the splint is determined by the combined lengths of the bottom and two sides including hem or edge allowances.
If the bottom is to be square, all splints will be the same length. If
the bottom is to be rectangular, some splints must be longer because of
the length of the bottom. In the case of a round basket, all splints will
be the length of the diameter of the bottom plus the two sides and hems.

Weaving

It has been said that basketry is the mother of weaving so it is appropriate that weaving terminology be employed here. The longest threads,
those strung on a loom are called *warp* threads. Those which are woven
in-and-out are called *weft* or *woof* threads. (Weft and woof are used

interchangeably, but I prefer the former.) On a rectangular bottom, the longer splints will be called warp and the shorter, weft. On a square bottom, the names are arbitrary. On a round bottom, all the radiating elements may be called warp splints. When the sides of the bottom are bent upward, all bottom splints become *spokes* and the elements to be woven in-and-out are called, simply, *weavers*.

Types of splint weaving are all classed as *plaiting* where all elements are flat, thin strips. These types include *checkeredwork, twilledwork,* and *spoke work.* (Other classes of basketry include wickerwork where elements are more or less round in cross section. Coiled work is used to describe baskets begun with a coil which is stitched together. Twined work is a class made by twisting fibers together in the weave.)

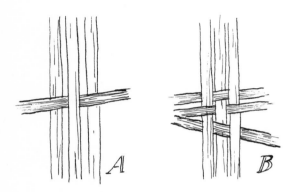

Fig. 7, Beginning a square bottom.
A, First weft splint, B, Additional
weft splints.

Checkeredwork

Checkeredwork, the basic and strongest type of plaiting, is a simple in-and-out weaving of warp and weft. Two warp splints are laid on a flat surface on a vertical axis in front of the craftsman. A weft splint is laid across the center of these on a horizontal axis. A third warp splint is laid between the first two (these should be spread accordingly) and on top of the weft (Fig. 7A). Another weft splint is woven in from the top in a manner just opposite to the first. Whereas the first weft goes over, under, and over the warp, this one goes under, over, and un-der. Another weft splint is woven in from the bottom in the same se-quence as the one on top (Fig. 7B). This results in a simple checker-board pattern from the six splints used so far. This pattern, of course, is most easily seen if contrasting colors are used. Although an inside and outside of the basket are not determined at this point, all smooth sides of the splints should be facing one side which will become the outside when the sides are bent up.

Now, weaving proceeds with two warp splints and two weft splints in se-quence opposite each other to build the mat to the desired dimensions for the entire bottom of the basket (Fig. 8). Naturally, if a rectangu-lar bottom is required, the warp splints were cut longer than the weft, and more weft splints are needed to build the proper dimensions. Check-eredwork may be woven quite tightly by pressing the warp and weft close-ly together. Because of the thickness of the elements, a slight gap re-mains. Occasionally, as in the case of a corn-washing basket which func-tions as a sieve, some distance is permitted between the elements, in which case the weave would be termed open checkeredwork. A general rule-

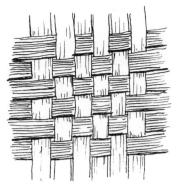

Fig. 8, Checkeredwork.   *Fig. 9, Twilledwork.*

of-thumb in plaited work is to used odd numbers of warp and weft; in this way there is always a center splint which will be handy when a handle is attached.

Twilledwork

Twilledwork is quite similar to the above in the simple right angles of warp and weft. The difference occurs in that the elements are woven over two, under two, etc., in a staggered sequence much as a twilled fabric. This results in a staggered, step-like diagonal pattern across the mat (Fig. 9). Variations of this may occur such as over two, under one, over two, etc. Another pattern, known as *diaperwork*, and more often seen on the sides of baskets from the Cherokee, reverses the step pattern at intervals and results in a diamond or zig-zag configuration. For sturdiness, however, the basic checkeredwork is unsurpassed.

Spoke Work

In the case of a round-bottomed basket, called spoke weaving, all splints are actually functioning as warp splints in the beginning stage. These are laid, in sequence, in a criss-cross arrangement on a flat surface so as to form a radiating or wheel-spoke pattern. A very narrow weft splint (1/16-1/8 inch), narrow because is must be bent quite drastically, is woven over one spoke, under one, over one, etc., back to the beginning (Fig. 10). The ends of this weft splint are cut with a shears to be hidden beneath the spokes, but with an overlap for two or three spokes for strength. Such endings normally occur on the side which will become the inside of the basket. The next weft splint, also narrow, is woven opposite in sequence to the first, and the ends are hidden as before. Beginnings and endings of these weft splints are staggered so that not all of these weak joints occur in line. The beginner may find it easier to begin spoke weaving by pushing a thin awl exactly through the center or hub of the spokes and thence into a board. The entire assembly may then be turned as a wheel, and all weaving can be done in the same position away from the craftsman

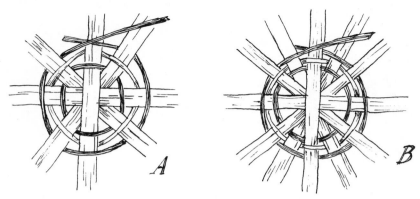

Fig. 10, Spoke bottom for a round basket. A, Eight spokes.
B, Twelve spokes.

as the wheel is rotated. Such a device is not required with experience;
the awl hole may be considered objectionable. Because of the overlapping
of the spokes, the weft splints cannot be woven very close to the center. Normally, the weft is found only near to the outer circumference
of the bottom. Weft splints continue to be woven around until the diameter is increased to the desired size. I find it easiest to weave at
the "top" or 12-o'clock position and to rotate the entire group after a
few spokes have been woven. In this way I can always pull the weft tightly downward with my left hand as I tug on the end of the weft with my
right.

Some large bottoms made in this way create an unusually large space between the spokes some distance from the center. If this is the case, new
spokes cut in half are introduced in these spaces and are tucked in toward
the center. They are then woven in with more weft elements normally.

A basket requiring a normal 8 warp splints
(16 spokes) may be more easily assembled
by dividing this total into two equal parts.
Thus, four splints are criss-crossed 45
degrees apart and are woven together with
two or three weft elements as close to
the center as possible. Then, the next
group of four is laid on top of the first
group so as to fill in the angles, and
the two groups are woven together normally. This results in a somewhat stronger
bottom. Any number of warp splints may
be used; just watch that they are all centered and that the spaces in between are
equiangular.

Fig. 11, Spoke bottom with
tapered spokes.

Another variation of spoke weaving uses

tapered (or actually, double-tapered) spokes (Fig. 11). Wide spokes are trimmed to taper evenly toward the center. Weft weaving can usually be begun closer to the center, and the space between spokes is less pronounced farther out than in the first example.

During all weaving processes above and below, the splints are kept damp. They need not be wet and dripping, but should be well moistened through and through. When stored splints are brought out for use, they must be soaked for a half day (less for thin splints) before weaving commences. Damp splints may be kept damp by wrapping with a wet towel and plastic sheet. Don't keep them damp over a week or so for fear of mildew discoloration. If splints dry out during working, they can be dampened by dunking or with a sponge. Many aboriginal crafts are not conducive to soft, delicate hands. Basket weaving is one of these.

When the bottom measurements are achieved, the splints are bent upward to become the warp or spokes for the sides. Square and rectangular baskets are easily bent over the edge of a table or board as a guide. If the splints are properly prepared, they should bend in quite a small radius. In the instance of a round bottom, each spoke must be bent with the hands although sometimes a disc of wood of the proper diameter may be used as a pattern. Before bending, be sure that the rough sides of the splints will be toward the inside of the basket.

Weaving the Basket Sides

Weft weaving now begins on the sides. Usually a wide first weft or weaver splint helps to hold the spokes vertical. It is probably easiest to hold the basket in one's lap when seated or on a table in front of the craftsman. I like the latter. In either circumstance, weaving is done on the side closest to the craftsman. Checkeredwork is preferred for the initial wefts, for this holds the

Fig. 12, Method of hiding beginning and ending of warp weavers behind spokes. Top view.

sides firmly in position for later work. The basket is rotated as weaving continues around the circumference back to the starting point. The sequence of over-under-over weaving should be related to that of the bottom weaving; i.e., the first side-weaver should be opposite to the last bottom weaver sequence. Cutting and hiding the beginning and ending of the weaver is described above in spoke work. Again, beginnings and endings of weavers are staggered, for they are the weakest places in the weave. All endings occur behind spokes so that they are not visible from the exterior (Fig. 12). On rectangular baskets, all endings should occur on the sides rather than at the corners. The first two weavers are the most difficult to weave, for the spokes try to slip away in all directions, and one wishes for a third hand. If the beginning of the weaver fails to stay in place properly, I strongly suggest using clothespins temporarily to clamp loose ends in place.

Checkeredwork, twilledwork, and diaperwork may be used as the weaving continues up the sides. Openwork is sometimes used, but most weft splints
are pressed closely together to form a closed weave.

Variations in weave may be accomplished by combining weavers of different
colors. Other variations are possible with splints split to varied widths.
Changes in silhouette can be made by weaving loosely, in which case the
basket will tend to bulge outward. Conversely, pulling the weavers tightly around the basket will cause it to diminish in diameter. In this latter case, if the spokes come too closely together after some rows are woven, it may become necessary to taper the remaining portion toward the
top to preserve the space. If a strong, sturdy basket is desired, the
weavers should be pressed down tightly periodically; some shrinkage normally occurs as they dry out, and, if left as is, will make a rather
flimsy basket.

The Basket Rim

When the last weaver has achieved the desired height of the sides, weaving ceases. Starting with the bottom weaver, press all the weavers snugly together with your fingernails to make a tighter basket. Any projecting ends of the weavers may be cut off flush with the last spokes. Two
heavy splints are now cut slightly longer (3-4 inches) than the circumference of the basket lip to allow for overlap. These will form an edge
or rim reinforcement. One of these splints is curled inside the lip;
natural pressure will keep it generally in place. The other is bent
around the outside. (A few clothespins will help to hold this.) If added
strength is required, particularly in a large basket, more than one splint
or a double-thick splint may be used. In any case, the endings are staggered. In the best baskets, the overlapping ends are shaved so that the
overlapped area remains one splint thick. The width of these reinforcements varies -- up to 2 inches wide in the case of some pack baskets.
Some of the better baskets exhibit slightly convex or half-round outer
surfaces which make a nice looking border.

When the basket weaving has been completed and before the rim has been
attached, cut off those spokes which have ended up on the inside of the
basket when the last weaver has been completed. This cutting should be
as close to the last weaver as possible. Cut the other splints (those
which ended up on the outside) to about 3 inches remaining as projections
(Fig. 13A). Cut these to half-widths flush with the weaver second to the top
and split this half off. In most cases, this should split off parallel to the
sides, but some trimming may be necessary. Trim the end to a point (Fig. 13B).
Keep the rim wet and, if necessary, use hot water to bend these half-
splints back downward toward the inside (Fig. 13C). Bend these over the
last weaver so that it is thus held in place and shove them into the
weavers below (Fig. 13D). For the nicest inside, these should be so trimmed that the pointed end is hidden behind a weaver.

When inner and outer reinforcement rims are whipped into place along this

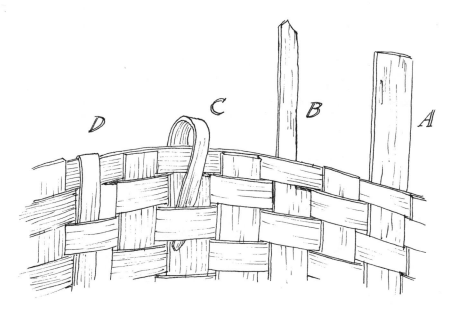

*Fig. 13, Splint basket rim, view from inside of basket. A, In-
side spokes cut off; outside spokes cut to length. B, Outside
spoke split in half and pointed. C, Inserting the spoke.
D, Finished edge before installation of rim.*

edge, this method of finishing affords a simplified technique and strength
where it is necessary.

With the reinforcing in place, a long,
thin splint is selected and is pointed
at one end. This is split to about 1/4
inch width and is stitched through the
space between the last weft splint (including the reinforcing) and a spoke in
such a way that the end of the stitch is
hidden. If weaving was so close that no
ready space exists, one is created with
an awl or small screwdriver. Take care
that the splint does not pull loose nor
twist; it is then brought over the lip
and is stitched through the next opening between weaver and spoke and is
pulled tight (Fig. 14). This whip stitch-

*Fig. 14, Reinforcement rim and
whip stitching.*

ing (or hem stitching, if you prefer) continues around the border to the
beginning. One or two overlapping stitches are advised. The loose end
is tucked in between again and is snipped off. If the stitching splint
is insufficiently long for the entire border, it is terminated and a new
one begun with overlapping as above. If more strength is needed, or a
different decoration is desired, a second whip stitch may be introduced
opposite to the first, thus forming an X pattern along the border. I

prefer to stitch from the exterior inward, but this may be a personal preference.

More expeditious, albeit less aesthetically pleasing, is a nailed border. Thin nails, such as shoe tacks, may be driven through the reinforcement and spokes and weavers to the inside where they are clinched. Long staples may also be used. I recently acquired a pack basket which was rivetted along the rim.

If handles are to be attached, these are usually attached before the reinforcing so that the border and handles are assembled as one with the basket.

A variation of weave, which has become popular in this century, is the use of one weaver, usually about an inch or wider, which, as it is woven to the outside of the basket, is given a twist to the outside before it is woven behind the next spoke. The resulting cone, repeated each time the weaver appears on the outside, creates an interesting, though not functional, pattern in three dimensions. Usually only one weaver is given this treatment, and then customarily near the lip. Occasionally a basket is found with such cones formed around the edge of the bottom where they form small legs upon which the basket may rest. These are known locally as "porcupine baskets", or, if the weaver is dyed red, "strawberry baskets".

Basket lids are made in the same way as the bottoms except that dimensions are more critical and are determined by the measurements of the outside lip of the basket.

Most baskets, because of the flexible nature of the splints, end up with an oval or round rim regardless of the shape of the bottom. In general, this roundness should be retained and, perhaps, accentuated. The opposite alternative is to make a sharp-angled box-like form which seems alien to the medium. In addition to the shape of the rim, the sides of good baskets normally show the bulging curves which contribute to the fullness of the silhouette. In general, a concave shape tends to give a feeling of collapsing.

With experience, other forms can be tried. For instance, some oval bottomed pieces are started with the checkeredwork technique, but the oval is created by tapering some of the elements and bending them upward on a curve rather than a straight line. A hexagonal bottom is made by using elements in a triangular configuration rather than the right-angled checkeredwork or the radiating spoke work to make a pattern similar to that found on caned chair seats. I recently observed an old basket which had designs stamp-printed in each square of the sides, so other possibilities may still be found.

A Pack Basket

One of the most ambitious problems of splint basket-ry is that encountered in making a pack basket (Fig. 15). These are still used today when a light and sturdy pack container is needed.

A good-sized pack basket, with a bottom 8 by 12 inches and 20 inches high, requires 12-20 sturdy 5-foot splints 3/4-1 1/4 inches wide for spokes. Obviously, more narrow spokes are needed to render the desired dimensions than if wider ones are used. The number, of course, can be calculated in advance by totalling the selected widths and allowing about 1/8-1/4 inch between splints. (A bottom can be woven more tightly, but this makes it very difficult to weave the sides.) Some 40 splints,

Fig. 15, Splint pack basket.

1/2 inch or so wide and 4-6 feet long, are required for the weavers for the sides. In addition, two extra-thick strips about 1 inch wide and 4 feet long are needed for reinforcing rims around the top when the weaving is complete. These thicker splints can be obtained by splitting a few splints containing more than one year's growth.

A Pack Basket -- Weaving the Bottom

The 5-foot lengths are soaked for a half hour, removed from the bath, and the excess water wiped off. (Extra splints can be kept wrapped in a damp cloth or plastic until they are needed.) These are woven together in a basic over-under weave beginning at the centers with three vertical and one horizontal splint and weaving in additional splints from the sides. Allow about 1/8-1/4 inch between splints and continue weaving until the desired dimensions are achieved. Care should be taken to assure that all smooth sides of the splints are all on the same side of the weave.

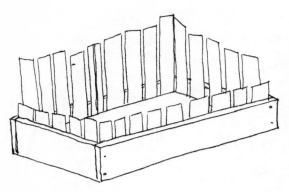

Fig. 16, Basket bottom inserted into mold/form. Pattern board in place in-side. Note split spoke in back.
Spokes are shortened to show inside.

A Pack Basket -- Weaving the Sides

Some people like to use a wood bottom pattern, 8 by 12 inches, cut from 1/4 inch plywood which will remain as reinforcement. The woven basket bottom is at-tached to this pattern with four broad-headed nails driven through the space between the splints near each corner and into the pat-tern board. The nails should be clinched unless one intends to re-move this pattern. The interior or rough side of the weaving should be in contact with the pat-tern.

Place the splints down on a flat surface. They may need to be re-dampened at this point and should be dampened periodically as weaving proceeds. Press down on the wood pattern and bend up each splint at right angles to the bottom. Do not expect the bent splints to remain upright. This bending merely serves to weaken them to facilitate bending them as a group next.

In production basketry, a low basket of the dimensions of the intended bottom is usually handy to be used to mold the sides upward. As a sub-stitute, a rectangular wooden frame with inside dimensions of 8 1/2 by 12 1/2 inches can be nailed together. I used to need such a mold for rectangular baskets, but I seldom require it anymore.

The pattern-splint assembly is placed bottom down on this basket or wood-en mold/form. Carefully press the pattern into the mold/form so that the splints bend upward. Some encouragement may be needed for idividual splints. Press the splints down only far enough to bend them upright (Fig. 16).

Choose one of the long sides of the bottom as the back of the basket and split the center splint vertically from top to bottom. The simple basket weaving to follow requires an odd number of spokes. This split spoke will be considered hereafter as two separate spokes. (Note: an even number of spokes can be used if the weavers are woven in as separate parallel rows by starting a new weaver each time a complete turn is made around the bas-ket as described earlier. Future instructions given below assume that the split-spoke method will be used. Weaving will then be done in a long continuous spiral from the base upward with joints occurring more or less at random dependent upon the length of the weavers used.)

Choose a weaver 1/2 inch or less wide and taper one end for a foot. In-sert this end, smooth side out, in the split-spoke as this side faces you. Note first the weaving of the bottom so that the over-under pattern will be continued with the weaver. Weave this piece in and out, pressing it

downward toward the bottom as it goes. With the actual bottom hidden inside the mold/form, one cannot press this down completely at this point.
Make at least two, and preferably three or four, complete revolutions a-
round the basket. By using the split-spoke as two spokes, the over-under
sequence is assured. (If it doesn't come out this way, you skipped a
place somewhere.)

A 4-6 foot weaver is a practical length to use, but it will weave only
about 1 1/2 revolutions before reaching the end. When this occurs, leave
the loose end behind a spoke to the inside of the basket. Insert a new
weaver to overlap the previous one behind one or two spokes and continue
weaving. Thus the weaving becomes a continuous spiral with joints made
where necessary.

Whether the weaving goes from left to right or vice-versa is, I think, a
matter of custom or personal preference. I am right-handed, and the best
way for me is to proceed from left to right with the basket held on my lap
with the open spokes away from me or on a table top with the spokes point-
ing upward.

When several revolutions have been made, sufficient so that the spokes can
stand vertically, the basket can be removed from the mold/form (if you
used one), and the weavers can be pushed down tightly to meet the bottom.
Some adjustment is usually necessary to make a sharply angled corner all
around. A slight outward slant is desirable, but, if the basket appears
to slant too much, go back and pull the weavers more tightly all around.
If the spokes appear to be coming together at the top of the basket, release the weavers somewhat. The classic pack basket shape calls for a very
slight outward bulge beginning at the bottom, widening out to a shoulder
near the middle, and narrowing again at the top. Further, the back of
the basket (the side with the split weaver) is usually woven as a flat
surface with the remaining three sides woven as a continuous curve. The
basket, as seen from the top, has a D-shaped cross section.

Continue weaving around the basket to create the bulge, then gradually pull
the weavers more tightly when weaving to diminish the diameter of the basket. Press down each row tightly upon the previous row. If your fingers
become too tender, use a small screwdriver or awl for this purpose. Watch
that the spokes remain always in a vertical position. The pulling of the
weavers tends to pull the spokes at an angle. It is far easier to press
the weavers tight and adjust the spokes as weaving progresses than it is
to make changes afterward.

It will be noticed that, as the bulge increases the space between spokes,
the weavers can be pressed down more easily. Conversely, as the bulge de-
creases near the top, the weaving again becomes difficult. If the top
opening of the basket is to decrease appreciably smaller than the base,
it will become impossible to weave, for there will be no space between
the spokes. In this case the spokes themselves must be trimmed gradually
narrower toward the top. This tapering is best left until the weaving
reaches the height at which weaving becomes difficult. Then the appropriate amount of taper can be judged.

If the inward slant near the top is rather pronounced, it may be well
to use gradually narrowing weavers, especially if 1/2 inch widths have
been used. These narrower weavers are necessary if they are to stay
flat against the spokes, for wider ones tend to twist outward and are
harder to press down completely.

Complete the last inch or two of spokes with vertical sides all around.
If the rim of the basket slants inward, it is most difficult to fit the
reinforcing rims tightly against the basket. The final foot or so of
weaver should be tapered to blend in to make a horizontal termination
of the rim. Otherwise, there will be an awkward sudden ending of the
wide weaver.

Because the strains of weaving tend to pull the basket out of shape, adjust the elements as may be necessary to bring the basket back to the desired form.

Pause at this point for a few hours to allow the basket to dry after
which it will be noticed that the weaving has become much more loose
than previously. This is caused by the contraction of the drying elements. The Indian method of compacting the weaving is to jar the bottom of the basket sharply on the ground a few times. I generally prefer pushing each row of weavers down individually with a screwdriver or
awl. In any case, the weavers must be compacted if a firm basket is to
be the result.

A Pack Basket -- Handles

A single handle or pair may be added to the rim at this point. Handles
are handy at times in camp, but they do have a way of getting hung on
twigs when the basket is worn on the back in travels through brush.

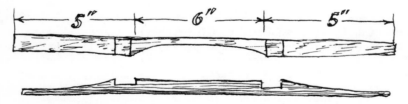

Fig. 17, Handle blank. Note direction of grain.

A single handle can be placed at the center of the basket or one can be
attached at each side. These can be also made from black ash, but white
ash is stronger.

Whittle a piece of wood, green if possible, about 16-18 inches long by
3/4 by 3/4 inch to a handle blank form as shown (Fig. 17). The length
of the notches is determined by the width of the rims to be attached later. Soak the handle overnight, and, if possible, soak it further in hot
water or steam for about a quarter-hour. Hold the middle of the handle

on the ground with a foot and bend up the two
sides as shown (Fig. 18). A wooden post can be
used instead of the foot for the form. Bend
the prongs together a little more than is necessary and tie them with a cord to keep them from
spreading. Allow this to "set" for a day.

When the wood has "set", remove the cord and
weave the two prongs in between weavers on the
outside of the basket and parallel to the spokes.
Press the prongs down far enough so that the
notched sections are outside the basket with
the top of the notch level with the rim. Depend-

Fig. 18, Bent handle.

ing upon the width of the top weavers, you may have to skip a row or
two so that the notches are not hidden.

A Pack Basket -- Reinforcing the Edge

Dampen the top few inches of the basket again. Cut the two double-thick
1 inch wide pieces for the reinforcing rims about 3-4 inches longer than
the circumference of the top of the basket. Shave these ends slightly
so that they blend in at this overlap. Roll one strip, smooth side in,
and press this inside the basket and allow it to unroll, thus pressing
itself against the inside. Roll the other strip, smooth side out, and
wrap it around the outside of the basket. Stagger the joints of the two
strips so that they do not line up. Hold the strips in place with a
clothespin or other device.

Nails do seem out of place on a hand woven basket such as this, but they
have been commonly used for many years. I still prefer a whip stitch.
To nail the rims in place, prepare an anvil or nailing platform by affixing a post securely and horizontally to a sturdy support. Only about 6
inches of post needs to jut out over which the opening of the basket may
be placed. A short length of post may be held in place inside the basket instead if a helper is available for this service.

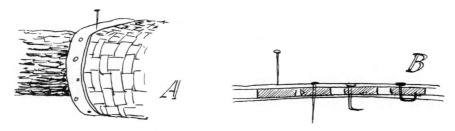

*Fig. 18, A, Nailing with the use of a post anvil. B, Sequence of
clinching nails.*

Select thin nails (I prefer aluminum to prevent rust) about one inch long
with fairly broad heads. Begin nailing near the overlaps of both rims
by placing the basket over the post "anvil", pressing it down, and pounding through from the exterior of the basket rim into the post (Fig. 18A).

Be sure the rims and basket are damp to avoid splitting. Do not nail
through the overlaps because it will be necessary to do this last in
order to press the rims tightly against the basket as nailing continues.
Pull the nailed basket out of the post (a flat tool may be necessary to
pry). With a pliers, bend 1/4 inch of the pointed end of the nail at a
right angle. Press the head of the nail and exterior of the basket on
a hard surface and pound the bent point down back into the rim on the
inside (Fig. 18B). Ideally, this should be at an angle; if the holes
line up too much, the rims may split.

Nail every two inches or every other spoke as may seem necessary, crimp-
ing each nail down and taking care that the two rims fit as tightly on
the basket as possible. The tops of the rims should coincide with the
top of the basket. Finish the nailing all around including the overlapped portions.

A more authentic method of holding the reinforcing is to whip-stitch it
on with a long splint about 1/4-3/8 inch wide stitched over the rims and
between the spokes. This whipping method has the advantage for the beginner in that it may be taken apart and re-done. The nailing method
is final -- good or bad. Another splint stitched in reverse direction
to the first may be added to result in an X or cross-stitch on the exterior of the basket. By calculating correctly, nails can be placed to
become hidden with the whip or cross-stitch.

A tin snips, heavy scissors, or knife can be used to cut off loose ends
projecting to the inside of the basket. Ragged or fuzzy splints can be
trimmed on the outside as well. Careful trimming should complete the
basket. If the basket is dampened slightly first, a torch can be used
to singe away fine fuzz, but I suggest that one practice on a less ambitious basket first. The fine fuzz dries in the torch heat and burns
away while the dampness of the heavier elements makes them less flammable.

A Pack Basket -- Harness

Two methods of back packing are suggested. The *tump line* is traditional,
but is seldom used today. A tump line is simply a wide band or heavy
fabric ribbon, usually woven for this purpose about 3 inches wide at the
center and tapering toward both ends. The ends are fastened to the bottom of the basket away from the carrier's back so that the center of the
line comes across the forehead. A waist strap or belt is usually used
also. If the length is adjusted properly, the carrier can lean forward
slightly with the weight of the loaded basket shared by the back and neck
muscles. Such an arrangement is simple and fool-proof -- once one gets
the hang of it.

A popular method of harnessing is to use web or leather straps around
the basket and over the shoulders (Fig. 19). I prefer leather. (About
10 oz. commercially tanned belt leather is a good weight.) For our basket measuring 8 by 12 by 20 inches high, two wooden cleats, 3/4 by 1 1/2
by 12 inches are required to stiffen the bottom and hold the harness in

place there. Notches are cut
about 1 inch from each end
and about 3/16 inch deep and
slightly wider than the leather to be used. These are
nailed to the basket on the
bottom outside. Nail from
inside out taking care not
to place nails in the notches.
Again, a dampening of the
wood helps to reduce splitting. The nails should be
clinched as for the rim. If
you have used a plywood pattern for the bottom, you can
clinch the nails to this.

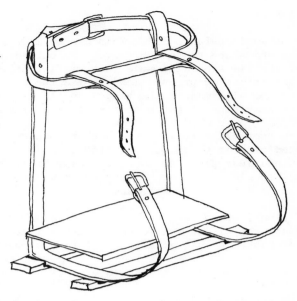

Leather belting is needed as
follows and should be no
less than 1 1/4 inch wide:
     1 piece 5 ft. long for
     the top band
     2 pieces 4 ft. long for
     back straps
     2 pieces 20 in. long for
     shoulder straps.

*Fig. 19, Leather harness. Note position
of notched wooden cleats. Basket is
omitted here to show construction.*

Also needed are three buckles and some leather rivets (unless stitching
is to be used).

Affix a buckle to the top band by doubling the leather over the buckle
and rivetting it together with a two inch overlap. Wrap this belt a-
round the top of the basket just below the rim. Punch holes in the end
of the belt in appropriate places to pull the belt tight. This band
could be rivetted permanently in place, but the buckle allows the harness to be adjusted or removed in the future.

Rivet the 4 foot lengths on either side of the top band. A loop around
the top band allows adjustment later although again, these could be rivetted to the band.

A larger loop is needed for the shoulder straps which are attached between the back straps. Note that these shoulder straps are at right
angles to the flat side of the top band (Fig. 19).

Thread the back straps through the notches in the cleats and buckle up
the top band on the side away from the body. Have someone hold the basket in place on your back while you mark the approximate location of the
buckles. Be sure these don't end up under the arm pits and be sure that
you have enough leather on the shoulder straps to reach comfortably to
the buckles. Allow some extra for times when heavy clothing might be
worn. Rivet the buckles in place and punch corresponding holes in the
shoulder straps.

Final Notes

Some persons prefer a lid. This can be made as a separate low basket of
a size and shape to just fit over the outside rim. If handles have been
used, the lid should be made just smaller than the inside size and shape
so that it can be pressed down inside the basket. A simple flat splint
mat can be also made to be hinged to the basket rim. This generally requires some sort of catch or tie to hold it shut.

Some persons like to give the basket a thorough brushing with shellac
diluted with an equal part of alcohol. This keeps the basket fairly
clean and less prone to lose its shape if it gets soaked. A well-made
basket should stay together anyway, however; and I like the honest dirt
of use so I don't use shellac.

From time to time the leather should be unbuckled and given a dressing
of neatsfoot oil or some other preservative. In general, however, a
splint basket should give years of fine service with minimal care.

The whole basket can be made in one day of hard work (excluding the
splitting) if one's fingers can stand it all at once. A beginner may
need a few days and a jar of hand lotion. Nothing is lost if the basket is not finished in one sitting; all that is required is a thorough
wetting and work can continue.

Having finished such a basket, it is always interesting to contemplate
the possible market value of one's work. For comparative purposes,
veneer pack baskets are commonly sold today -- with harness -- for $7.00
for a 16 inch size to $9.00 for a 20 inch size. Someone ain't getting
rich quick.

You'll have a plentiful supply of cut-off scrap. Just so that these
don't all go to waste, try a small horse (deer, dog, what-have-you)
with a splint about 1 by 3 inches. Be sure that it is well soaked and
split it partially from each end as shown in Fig. 20A. Bend the legs

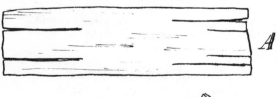

down and neck and tail up,
and finish with the nose bent
down (Fig. 20B). Bend a little too far, for you can expect these to straighten somewhat. Hold them for a while
and check the bends occasionally after you set it aside
to dry. This charming, simple
animal was brought in by an
unknown student from Black River
Falls, Wisconsin. I haven't
seen these anywhere else.

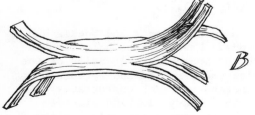

Fig. 20, Toy horse. A, Pattern.
B, Horse bent into shape.

REFERENCES

Harlow, William M.   "Trees of Eastern and Central United States and Canada", Dover, N.Y., 1957.

Hoffman, Walter James   "The Menomini Indians", *Bureau of Ethnology 14th Annual Report*, Washington, 1892-93.

Lyford, Carrie A.   "Iroquois Crafts", Bureau of Indian Affairs, Dept. of Interior, Washington, 1941.

--------   "Ojibwa Crafts", Bureau of Indian Affairs, Dept. of Interior, Washington, 1943.

Mason, Otis T.   "Aboriginal American Basketry", *U.S. National Museum Annual Report*, Washington, 1902.

HANDLES FOR SPLINT BASKETS

Most often used for splint basket handles was the wood of the white ash (*Fraxinus americana* L.), although I have used leftover pieces from black ash (*Fraxinus nigra* Marsh.) which yielded basket splints. Apparently the sapwood was prized, for most handles exhibit the ivory white color of recent growth. The former species is generally used for objects requiring strength such as snowshoe frames and therefore is appropriate for handles which should be thin but need to be strong. I imagine that other wood, such as maple, could be used, but I have not experimented with it. In general, fresh, green stock is easier to cut; dry wood seems to take on added hardness. If old, seasoned wood is used, I suggest that it be soaked for several days before carving.

The most expeditious way to begin any handle is to select a clear billet long enough for your handles. Two to three feet is sufficient for large handles, and I like a piece about 4-6 inches in diameter. Halve and quarter this log and split the sapwood from the heartwood. The flat side of handles should parallel the direction of annular ring growth. This is not only desired for strength and surface finish, but is also conducive to good bends.

Only one tool is needed for most handles, but, at times, others may make the work easier. A sharp jack knife, a small hunting knife, or crooked knife is necessary. A drawknife and Schnitzelbank do an excellent job, often superior to the above. For hinged handles, a drill with a 1/4 inch bit is required.

Two types of handle are most often used; a single-bow, rigid type, and a hinged type which requires more complex cutting and bending and which folds down when the basket is set down. Both handles are begun in similar fashion.

Rigid Handle

Estimate the size of your handle by adding the width of the basket, the height you desire to be above the rim (times two -- one for each side) and add 4-6 inches on each end which will be inserted into the basket sides. Select a straight-grained split of white ash and split and whittle this to about 1/2 inch by 1 inch by the length required (Fig. 1A). Taper the ends to 1/4 inch thickness by 1/2-3/4 inch width (Fig. 1B). Sharpen the ends and round the edges (Fig. 1C).

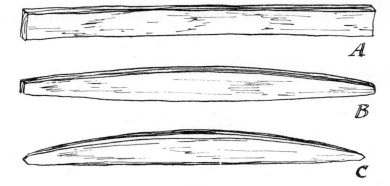

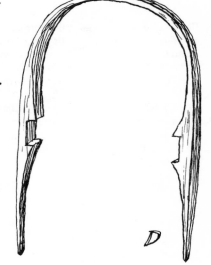

*Fig. 1, Rigid handle. A, Handle blank.
B, Tapered blank. C, Sharpened and
rounded blank. D, Bent handle notched
for installation on inside of basket.*

If the wood is fresh, you may begin to bend it
immediately; otherwise, soak it for a day first.
Heat a pail of water, the larger the better, to
the boiling point. While this is heating, you
might make pencil marks equidistant from the
center at the points where you intend the bend
to be formed if the top of the handle is to be
flat. If, as in the case of small handles, it
is to be a single U-shaped bend, you'll have
to guess at the amount of arc required as you
bend it.

If your water container is deep enough, immerse
the handle in the boiling water for 10-15 minutes; less if the handle is very thin. If the
container is shallow, make a small can into a
ladle and pour the water down over the handle.   If the container is deep
enough for half the handle, simply change it end-for-end a few times.

For the simple U-shaped bend, bend it over your leg (let it cool some
first so that you don't get burned). Curve it in such a way that the
sapwood or bark side of the wood is on the outside of the bend. If it
seems quite resistant, bend it a little first and re-heat periodically.
When the desired bow is achieved, hold the handle between your legs and
tie a loop of string around the ends because it will open up a bit later
anyway. Check the bend for symmetry and make any necessary adjustments.
Then set the handle aside to set for a few days. If you have occasion
to make several handles, you'll find that bending two of them simultaneously serves to make both of them take a more even curve inasmuch as a
possible weakness in one is compensated for by the other.

A more sculptured rigid handle is still being made today and is found
on most old baskets (Fig. 2). In this instance, the flat top is achieved

by allowing extra thickness in the center, usually in the form of a low double-curve on the underside. This allows the handle to be more easily bent to two curved right angles. (It also feels nice when one carries the basket.) The added thickness on both sides is still tapered for insertion into the basket, but it allows for a more pronounced notch for the basket rim and thus makes a more permanent attachment.

Fig. 2, Sculptured double-curve rigid handle. A, Handle blank. B, Bent handle with notches for installation on inside of basket.

When the curve is thoroughly set and dry, remove the binding string and place the handle on the basket where you intend to attach it. Mark the width of the basket rim reinforcement on the handle at the appropriate places. Notch out this space to a depth where about 1/4-3/8 inch remains (lesser amounts for smaller baskets). The deeper this notch can be made, the more permanent the attachment. Of course, if the notch is too deep, the handle will be weakened unduly at this point.

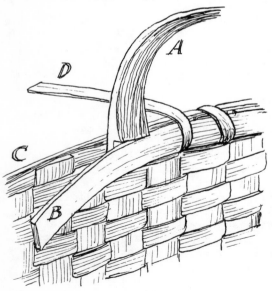

Fig. 3, Typical handle being attached to inside of basket. A, Handle. B, Inner reinforcement rim. C, Outer reinforcement rim. D, Whip lashing.

The handle is usually attached after the basket reinforcing rims have been cut, but before they have been whip-stitched in place. The handle can be inside the basket where it is less visible (Fig. 3), or it can be inserted on the outside. The former is preferable, but there are times when the latter is required. For instance, on a basket where the top portion is contracted to a smaller diameter than the body, a handle may well be pushed into the outside at the largest diameter so that the handle bow and sides clear the rim completely.

Hinged Handle

A hinged handle requires a more complicated bending job and **two**

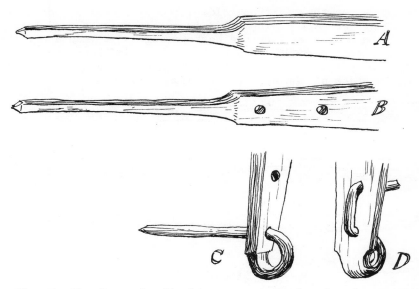

Fig. 4, Shaping a handle hinge. A, A trimmed end. B, 1/4 inch holes drilled. C, First bend. D, Final bend.

bent hinges. Begin as for a rigid handle, but let your measurements include only the length required for the handle above the basket plus 4-5 inches on either end. You can make the length about 2 inches too small anyway, because the hinges will project up from the rim about an inch on either side. Whittle the last 4-5 inches on the ends to about 1/4 inch diameter and make a point on the ends. Make the change in size rather abruptly in order to make this part into a sharp bend (Fig. 4A). Drill two 1/4 inch holes into the handle on each end about 1 inch apart beginning 1/2 inch above the beginning of the thinned portion (Fig. 4B).

Bend the handle bow as above to the proper curve and tie it. Heat the thinned ends in water. Slowly bring one end around toward the inside in an even, small curve until the point can be inserted into the lower hole (Fig. 4 C). Pull or push this through. Use a pliers, if necessary. Keep the area wet and hot, and insert the point through the upper hole. Pull or push this through tightly (Fig. 4D). I've found that putting a smooth, round stick of an appropriate diameter into the first curve helps to make a more pleasing roundness. Bend the other end of the handle also. Excess on the inside can be cut off, but not so close to the hole that it is in danger of slipping out again. Do the same on the other end, but be sure that the direction of the bend is opposite to the first; i.e., both curves should be either toward the inside or toward the outside. If the bends are toward the inside, the handle bow must be a little larger than if they are toward the outside.

Make two basket hinges from two pieces about 1/2-5/8 inch square by about 8-12 inches long (Fig. 5A). Cut a curved notch about 2-3 inches long

out of the center on the heartwood side allowing 1/8-3/16 inch to remain
(Fig. 5B). Shave an edge-grained side in a long taper toward both ends
so that they can be pushed into the basket (Fig. 5C). Round off the edges.
Heat the center sections well with boiling water and bend them into round
curves (Fig. 5D). Again, I think that it's a good plan to bend these a-
round a smooth stick of the appropriate diameter. When both legs of the

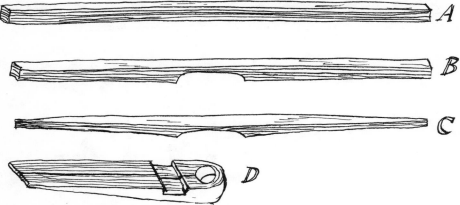

Fig. 5, *Shaping a basket hinge. A, Handle blank. B, Curved notch.
C, Tapered ends. D, Finished hinge.*

curve meet, bind them and allow the hinges to set.

Mark the hinges against the rim of your basket and notch them as for a
rigid handle. To assemble, cut all bindings and spread the basket hinges
just enough so that they can be slipped into the rings on the handle.
Press the hinges into the basket weaving and whip on the rims as before.

Compound Curve Handle

Occasionally, on such items as pack baskets, one may wish a small handle
which is affixed only on one side of a basket. Here, a compound curve
can be used for strength. Whittle the short handle the same as for a
rigid handle, but make the bow only large enough for one hand. Bend
this into a short arc and, while the wood is still hot, twist both legs
so that they are 90 degrees from the original. Obviously, they are
twisted in opposing directions from each other (Fig. 7). Press these
twisted legs into an appropriate crack in a log or other clamping device
until they are set and dry. In this way, one takes advantage of the
strength of the grain of the wood while maintaining the flat cross-section for ease in insertion into the basket. Notch out for the rim as
above and whip the rim in place.

Handle-making increases one's awareness of the strength of wood and the
possibilities of bent wood shapes. One also gains an appreciation of
the skill and ingenuity of Indian technology.

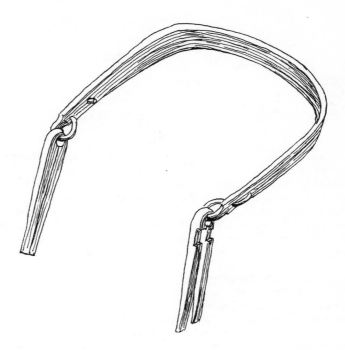

Fig. 6, Assembled hinged handle.   Right hinge notched for inside installation.

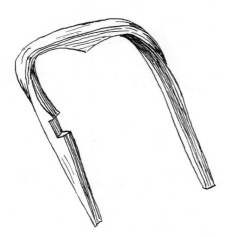

Fig. 7, Compound curve pack basket handle. Right side remains to be notched for installation.

WILLOW WICKERWORK

The name wicker comes from the Anglo-Saxon, *wican*, to bend; and that is just what must be done in this craft -- to bend. Indian wickerwork was common in eastern North American Woodland Culture Areas and in a few pueblos. It was less used in favor of twined or coiled baskets in the Pacific Northwest, Southwest, and Great Basin areas although most tribes resorted to wickerwork for simple, expedient baskets. Today, some of the best work in wicker comes from southeast Asia where vine-like reeds (rattan) are used, and eastern Europe where willow is still popular.

Indian weaving is generally plain over-under-over-under patterning. Asian and European examples today have become quite complex. Wickerwork is similar to checkerwork plaiting except that one of the elements which will be called the warp or spokes, is fairly rigid. (Plaiting is usually done with both warp and weft of similar flexibility.) The weft or weavers are more flexible than the warp and the result of the weave is a sort of ridged pattern over an area of weaving.

Wickerwork is possibly the earliest and most primitive method of weaving. Any group of round twigs woven over and under, in opposing sequence, other round twigs may be classed as wickerwork. Weirs were woven and stuck in shallow water to trap fish. Crude baskets for harvest and transporting were made this way. Mats and sieves could be quickly made, and probably were quickly destroyed in use as well. Today, there are few Woodland peoples who still make willow wicker baskets. The White trade has favored the prettier splint baskets which are still popular. Hopi Indian baskets and mats are of high quality today, nevertheless, and often are excellently designed with dyed fibers in *katchina* patterns. These bring a good return to the basketmaker.

The most popular source of raw material was the willow (*Salix* species) which has so many species, differentiated mainly for botanist's purposes, that it is useless to list them here. Typical is the low-growing bush with greenish-yellow bark which thrives in low areas and sends up annual shoots of about 3 feet. Also native to lowland areas is the Red Osier Dogwood (*Cornus stolonifera*) which is easily recognized by its purplish-red bark which is so attractive against the winter snow. The popular Weeping Willow (*Salix babylonica* L.) tree in residential areas provides shoots up to 6 feet in length. Except in the few cases where thicker pieces must be used for structural strength, shoots of one season's growth are cut for wickerwork. Except in the species cited above, the color of the bark varies even on a single plant to the degree where a shoot may be yellow on one part or side and quite red or brown on another area.

The best time to harvest the willow is in the early spring when a finger-nail test indicates that the sap is running and the bark has loosened so that it can be easily peeled. The budding leaves are also a good indication of the harvest time. Shoots cut in summer have not reached full length, or they are the branched growth of the previous year. Shoots cut in fall or winter are difficult to peel. Willow which is to be peeled is cut in the spring and is peeled within a day or two of cutting, before the shoots dry out. If necessary, they can be soaked for a while before peeling. Bark which has dried on the shoots is best left on permanently. The simplest device for peeling is the Tlingit *eena* made of a split stick stuck in the ground so that the shoot will be stripped clean of bark as it is pulled through the split (See "Containers of Birch Bark".). Peeled shoots may be bundled and dried for future use.

Some shoots may be dried with the bark intact to preserve its color. Dried bark does not retain the exact color of the bark when fresh. The red dogwood becomes almost black; the green willow may turn brownish. Nevertheless, some lovely subtle combinations may be made with peeled and unpeeled contrasting colors.

Peeled willow shoots take a dye quite well. Natural dyes are appropriate, but reasonable substitutes may be made from commercial dyes today. In either case, the shoots should be simmered in the dye bath until a shade of color is reached which is a little darker than the desired final color. A cold water rinse removes some of the color, but the chance for bleeding into neighboring colors is thus lessened.

In any case, whether the shoots are peeled or not, dyed or not, they must be thoroughly soaked until flexible. If they are freshly cut in the spring or have just come out of the dye bath they may be used almost immediately. Otherwise, the period may be up to three days, depending upon their dryness and diameter. Further, it seems that peeled shoots absorb water and become supple more readily than unpeeled ones. I have found that warm water is better than cold for this purpose also.

When they are sufficiently flexible, they should be removed from the water and wrapped in a damp cloth. Soaking them too long or storing them wet for a time may cause a color change and makes no noticeable change in flexibility. A water pail should be handy to the basketmaker at all times. As weaving progresses the shoots must be dampened occasionally with

Fig. 1, Ojibwa Willow "melon basket".

wet fingers to keep them moist.

The Ojibwa half-round or melon shaped basket is typical of Woodland willow basketry (Fig. 1). Tiny baskets are not very practical to try with willow; most of the melon shaped baskets may be about 12 inches in diameter and about 6 inches deep in the middle. These baskets often had a flat lid which may or may not be attached with a hinge.

First, a rim should be made of a sturdy shoot about 1/4-3/8 inch diameter, about 40 inches long which allows a 3 inch overlap for a 12 inch diameter basket. The thickest end of the shoot is pared to become a roughly equal diameter for its entire length.

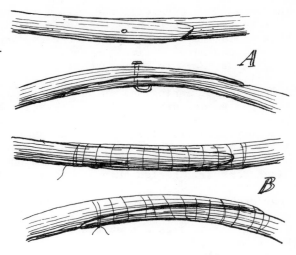

Fig. 2, Rim fastening. A, Bradded. B, Cord wrapped.

The two ends are further tapered, on opposite sides, so that the overlap created when they are brought together does not increase the diameter. Today, a brad or two is driven through and clinched (Fig. 2A). Earlier, this would have to be wrapped with cord (Fig. 2B).

About 11 shoots, about 20 inches long, are required for the warp or spokes on this sized basket. A supple spoke is fastened from one end of the rim in a curve to the opposite side in order to give the proper contour to the basket bottom. The shoot is bent over the rim at each side and returned back on itself. This doubled-back overlap may be temporarily tied, but later weaving will hold it in place so that the tying can be removed as soon as sufficient weft weaving is in place (Fig. 3).

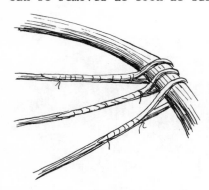

Spokes may be affixed in place at both points on the rim immediately, if desired, or they may be all tied down at one point first before beginning on the opposite side (Fig. 4).

Although the curves of these spokes are not great around the rim, later curves may need to be bent quite sharply. Recently, basketmakers squeeze the point of bending with a narrow pliers such as a round-nosed pliers which do not break the fibers but merely crush them sufficiently for a sharp bend to be made. A cracked bend should be avoided. Probably, the bend around the rim will not need this treatment as the curve is large enough.

Fig. 3, Warp shoots (spokes) wrapped over rim.

At times, also, the area to be bent may be shaved to half thickness which

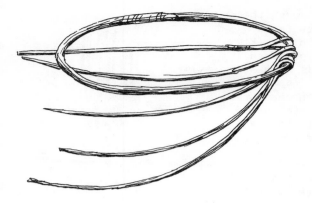

Fig. 4, Spokes radiating from one point.

facilitates the bend further. This is done mainly when heavy shoots are used.

The distance between spokes may be as great as 2 inches at the center of the basket. Naturally, this distance diminishes near the points of attachment. A warp too close together is too hard to weave between; too far apart makes the basket too weak to be functional.

Remaining spokes are bent in place on either side of the center spoke. In this basket design, all spokes radiate from one point on the rim downward and over to a point opposite on the rim. Other variations are possible in different designs. It is not always necessary to tie these temporarily in place, but for the beginner, this procedure is worth the trouble. Often, the area on the rim containing the overlapping spokes is whipped with a fine shoot or cord which, in effect, holds the spokes in place until later weft weaving holds it more firmly.

Now a large number of weft shoots or weavers is needed: some 50–100 depending on their diameters, their lengths, and the size of the basket. These should be as long and with as little taper as possible. For a well-made basket, shoots are chosen as equal in diameter as possible. For a beginner, it is well to start weaving through the center area first. This establishes the spacing between the spokes and determines the curve of the basket itself. Starting in the center does, however, make both ends more difficult to weave later. Starting at one end is simpler in that it requires that only the opposite end will be the difficult one.

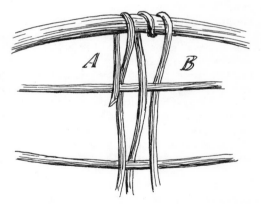

Fig. 5, Wickerwork techniques. A, Beginning a weaver. B, Looping over the rim.

A weaver is bent over the rim in such a way that its end is caught by the nearest spoke. It is then woven under the first spoke, over the second, under the third, and so on as it is pulled through to the opposite rim (Fig. 5A). The "drag" created by this weaver may temporarily disturb the distance between spokes, but this can be adjusted for the first several times after which they fairly well stay in place. These weavers must also be watched to see that they go straight across from side to side, not at some angle. The remaining end of the weaver is now wrapped once around

the rim and then is woven back through the
spokes in a sequence exactly opposite to
the first in a plain weaving technique (Fig.
5B). This weaver is woven back and forth
as far as its length permits until it rests
against the last spoke possible. It is cut
off on a diagonal to blend in with the curve
of the basket so that, normally, the cut-
off end is toward the exterior of the basket.
The location of cut-off varies from basket
to basket dependent upon which surface is
desired to have the best appearance -- exterior or interior. Regardless of which
surface is chosen, all weavers are cut off
for the sake of consistency. Weavers are
not cut off to rest on the rim, but are
rather cut to rest on spokes only (Fig. 6).

Fig. 6, Splicing new weavers.

If the end just finished happens to be the butt or thickest end of the
weaver, the next weaver is started, also butt end first, adjacent to it
so that both butt ends press against the same spoke and project to the
same side. If the end happens to be the tip of the shoot, the next
weaver is started also at the tip. New weavers are added to the weft
-- butt to butt or tip to tip -- as needed to fill the area. The only
possible exception to this rule occurs at the change of one color; in
these cases, the ending is made near the rim rather than at random.

The center area is filled with weft weavers toward the points where the
spokes are attached. It will be soon seen that weaving becomes more difficult near the points of radiation of the spokes. As these points are
approached, the basketmaker must change the method of weaving over one,
under one, to a method of over two, under one, or over two, under two.
This requires some adjustment in the spacing of the spokes to accomodate
this change. The last weavers to be woven in are the most difficult;
the basketmaker may need to open up a hole between shoots with an awl
in order to insert the weaver.

Weavers are usually whipped over the rim once before returning into the
weaving, but some judgement must be made to determine if this is appropriate for an evenness of weave. Occasionally, two whips may be required,
or none may be better, but more often one is used. The determining factor here is simply the shape of the basket and what is best for its form
and strength.

Before completing the ends, a handle should be inserted if such is desired. The handle may be simply a heavy shoot similar to the rim and
bent into a bow. It is pointed at either end so that it can be pressed
into the weft at the ends of the basket. If it is pressed down sufficiently into the curve, it should be strong enough for most purposes. It
is then usually whipped with a length of fine willow around the rim and
handle area and further whipped for its entire length from end to end.
A joint in the whipping, if necessary, is made by pinching the beginning

end of the new piece under the end of the previous one so that succeeding whipping pressure holds the two firmly together.

If two shoots are used side-by-side for the handle, one is usually pressed inside the basket and one outside at each end. If four are used for an especially strong handle, they normally lie flat next to each other on the bow of the handle and are spread at the rim so that the center two are pressed into the basket as above, and the two outer ones are bent parallel to the rim and are wrapped on with the weft or other whipping as the basket is finished.

The willow wickerwork basket is one of the least "finished"-looking of Indian baskets of North America, yet it has a rude honesty which many find charming. Its rugged roughness is quite appropriate for the simple design of the shape and the austere use of banded color areas.

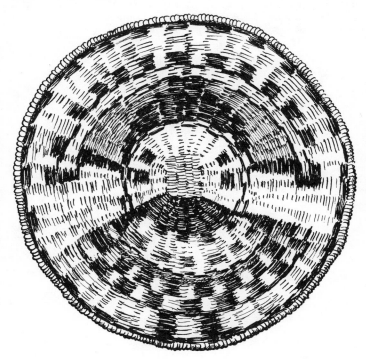

The further mention of Hopi Indian wickerwork may have merits in this paper, for, although the Hopis do not use much willow, their wickerwork trays and mats reach the highest levels of this craft in North America (Fig. 7). If the melon-basket is more than the beginner can manage at first, a flat, round wicker tray in the Hopi method may give him more confidence.

Hopi wickerwork is made only on the third mesa, especially in the old city of Oraibi. For these mats or trays. the warp-spokes radiate from a common center and the weft is woven around this in a gentle spiral. The

Fig. 7, Hopi katchina wicker tray. Diameter: 15 inches.

technique of wicker weaving is similar to that of the melon-shaped basket with some distinct differences -- Hopi baskets employ bright colors woven in designs of animals, bird, and katchina dolls; and willow is not used for the weft. Hopi baskets have spokes of willow or sumac (*Rhus trilobata* -- not the Woodland sumac, *Rhus typhina*) with weavers of one of several varieties of rabbit-bush (*Bigelovia* or *Chrysothamnus*). The rabbitbush

is dyed and selected for even thinness -- a characteristic which is quite
apparent in these baskets. For those who wish to try this method of weaving, I recommend the shoots of the weeping willow because of their length
and even taper.

Two lots of shoots of similar thickness are selected for the spokes.
The length is measured slightly   *Fig. 8, Lot of shoots woven together.*
longer than the diameter of the in-
tended tray. Each of these lots contains two or more groups of from
one to four shoots which are laid flat next to each other. These groups
are woven together with a very fine weaver or a willow split so that
each entire lot forms a flat section of 1-5 inches in width (Fig. 8).

The two lots are laid at right angles to each other and are bound with
a weaver passed over and under the several shoots. For this method of
weaving, the center or hub or the basket is not bound so that a thin
blade may actually pass between them (Fig. 9).

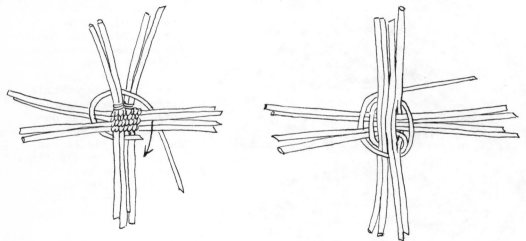

Fig. 9, Two lots being bound,   *Fig. 10, Two lots being bound, Asian*
Hopi method.   *method.*

Asian and European beginnings usually have them bound across the inter-
section. In this method, the weaver often makes several rotations before splitting the spokes. At times, also, one lot of spokes is split
through the middle and the second lot is thrust through this split opening; this entire assembly is then fastened (Fig. 10).

The assembly, now appearing somewhat like a spoked wheel or cross, is
usually placed on a flat surface for the weaving process. Recent basketmakers may press an awl through the center and into the surface to
pin the whole loosely to the surface. The whole can then be rotated as
necessary. Weaving is done either on the side close to or far from the
basketmaker.

The first weaver is woven over-under-over-under each group in each lot of spokes. This requires an opening to be made between each group. The weaver is pressed firmly toward the center of the wheel at all times. An odd number of spokes is necessary so that one group of spokes may need to be "jumped" or divided further to provide this odd number. (An even number of spokes can be woven with the "pairing" or "twining" method, but this is not in the scope of this paper. When a circumference is reached where the spread between spokes is judged to be too great, each group of spokes is again divided into two (except for one group -- to keep the total an uneven number), and each division so made is again considered as a separate group for future weaving. Weaving continues thus until another division is required or until the basket is finished. Asian and European baskets are usually made with an odd number of spokes in the very beginning. When later divisions require an odd number again, a single half-spoke (the length of the radius of the basket) is inserted into some of the already woven weft between existing spokes.

The method of splicing is the same as described for the melon-shaped basket. Changes in color are accomplished in the same way. Pressure from succeeding layers of weft is all that holds the ends in place.

When the desired diameter is reached, the spoke ends may be returned on themselves to be pressed into the weft and so held in place. Hopi baskets normally are finished by cutting off the ends and whipping the rim with split yucca leaf. Split willow could be used in this experiment. Other methods of finishing rims are possible and are readily seen by examining baskets commercially available.

The above description does not purport to be a completely authentic account of Hopi work. Rather, it is intended to give some basic experience in flat round tray weaving which can be expanded into more complex problems as the student desires.

REFERENCES

Douglas, F. H.   "Southwest Twined, Wicker and Plaited Basketry", *Denver Art Museum Leaflet* No. 99-100, 1955.

Griswold, Lester and   "Handicrafts" (10th edition), Burgess, Kathleen   Minneapolis, 1969.

Jeancon, J. A. and   "Hopi Indian Basketry", *Denver Art Museum Douglas, F. H.   Leaflet* No. 17, 1931.

Lyford, Carrie A.   "Ojibwa Crafts", Bureau of Indian Affairs, U.S. Dept. of Interior, 1943.

Mason, Otis T.   "Aboriginal American Basketry", *U.S. National Museum Annual Report*, 1902.

COILED BASKETRY

Among some of the finest baskets ever made are the American Indian coiled baskets which are made more by sewing than by weaving. This method begins with a continuous coil of fibers starting at the center of the bottom of the basket and continues, stitched together, in an ever-increasing circle outward and upward to form the bottom and sides. This coil has a foundation or core of fibers which may be called the warp; these are stitched together with a finer fiber which becomes the weft.

Coiled basketry reached its culmination in the work of the Southwest Culture Area although it was practiced by most tribes all over North America. Some Southwest groups still practice this craft today, mostly in the manufacture of baskets for sale. The same kind of plant fibers have been used for centuries by Hopis, Pimas, Apaches, Navahos, and others. A complete list of plants used for basketry and for dyes is found in Mason's excellent treatise, "Aboriginal American Basketry".

Locally we have used cattail leaves (not stalks) and sedge grass for both foundations and weft. It seems to me that the looseness of these baskets can be attributed to the softness of the foundation of leaves. Leaves are good for the weft, but a more sturdy foundation should be used.

Leafy material should be cured by drying before use and then needs only to be dampened briefly. Fresh material is flexible, but seems to shrink on drying in such a manner that the stitches become loose.

Corn husks can be split into thin lengths for weft material. The inside of the husk is less striated than the exterior. Bleached husks can be dyed nicely. One problem with husks -- they are so short that one is continually splicing in a new piece.

Peeled jack pine root has made the best baskets recently. These are split into half-round cross sections which make a very pleasant surface when used as a weft. The sharpened end of a root becomes its own needle, but needs an awl hole. Fresh root is very flexible, but doesn't dye well. Old roots must be soaked overnight. Unsplit roots work well as a foundation.

Fig. 1, Bundle   *Fig. 2, Rod*   *Fig. 3, Two-rod*   *Fig. 4, Three-*
foundation.   *foundation.*   *foundation.*   *rod foundation.*

Foundations

Foundation types are classed in three: *multiple* or *bundle, rod or slat,*
and *combinations* of the first two. In the first type, grasses, long
leaves, stems, shoots, or roots are split and laid together in a mass
to form the foundation warp of the coil (Fig. 1). Additional fibers are
merely overlapped at random as necessary to lengthen the starting section. Typical fibers include the cattail which is usually gathered in
June, split, and set aside to dry. Willow and cottonwood shoots are also split or shredded into fine slivers for foundation fibers. Yucca is
very popular in the Southwest as it yields long, thin, strong splits.
The local "rabbit bush" of this area was also used for foundations. For
the experimenter, any group of long, thin fibers, either split or used
whole (if they be fine enough) may be used. Bundle foundations often
are oval in cross section, but occasionally are round. Coils of this
type tend to be quite thick and flexible, but, because they are made of
such fine material, they are nevertheless quite light in weight. Some
coils, particularly those for larger baskets, are bundled up to a diameter equal to a finger in cross section; finer baskets use coils about
as thick as a pencil. Some tribes, pariculary those of California,
made tiny baskets -- some smaller than a thimble. These need only a
single thickness of fiber for a warp, but these *tour de force* baskets
apparently were not functional in a practical sense. Papagos today make
miniature baskets as small as 3/4 inch high using horsehair as fibers.
Certain tribes seem to be predisposed to certain diameters and to the
use of certain traditional materials. A good rule of thumb, however,
may be to use large diameters of coils for larger baskets, and small for
smaller baskets in proportion.

Rod or slat foundations are made with walls of single rods set one on
top of the other. Rods enclosed in each stitch of weft are from one to
three, depending on the method of sewing (Figs. 2, 3, 4). Extensions of

rods are accomplished by tapering the ends of the old and the new rod so that the overlapped area is the same thickness as a single rod. Materials for the rod foundations are similar to the first type with the exception of the weaker grasses and other finely shredded materials.

Single wooden slats are also used by some tribes in the same manner as above.

Bundle and rod combinations give the foundation the strength and stiffness of a rod, but with some of the softness and flexibility of the weaker fibers bundled around it.

Bunched rods are probably used in the most solid and long wearing of all coiled basket types. Three or five rods are used in a circular cross section. Three-rod baskets are fairly common, but the five-rod foundation is made only by the Jicarilla Apache.

Other combinations are found in examining any large collection of baskets. For instance, one or two rods and a bundle may be used together; or a slat with a bundle, or any of a number of possibilities.

Sewing

The sewing or stitching is accomplished by wrapping and stitching the foundation coils, layer on layer, one on top of the other, with a weft fiber to interlock the coils together. A long fiber, sometimes very finely shredded or split, may be used for tiny baskets so that individual stitches are difficult to discern. Other weft is made with strips as large as 1/2 inch wide for the largest baskets, but this is the extreme.

As a guide to the beginner, it may be pointed out that both the coils and the stitches vary in measurements. "Old Papago willow pieces averaged four to five coils and nine to ten stitches per inch, while most of the Pima baskets ranged from four to seven coils and ten to twelve stitches to the inch."[1] In this comparison, naturally the Pima baskets would appear to be the finer and tighter of the two. This spacing varied, even within a tribe. Tanner notes that Papago horsehair miniatures exceeded the count of yucca baskets made by either the Pima or Papago, but "Pima baskets had counts of twenty coils and twenty-five to thirty stitches to the inch."[2] To continue the variation between just these two tribes, she notes further that in modern Papago yucca basketry "in a majority, coils ran one and one half to three per inch and stitches six to seven per inch."[3] These contemporary baskets will obviously appear to be heavier and cruder than the older pieces. For the novice, however, the lat-

[1]Tanner, p. 33.
[2]*Ibid.*, p. 34.
[3]*Ibid.*, p. 33.

ter counts will prove less frustrating.
One would do well to attempt finer baskets only after some experience.

A long, fine strong fiber must be found
for the weft. Materials native to the
Southwest are ideal for this purpose
and may offer one reason for the excellence of work from that area. Split
rabbit bush and yucca are quite common
there. Shredded bark, corn husks and
leaves, and certain tall grasses have
been used. Willow and other woody
plants, very finely split, are used.
The beginner should seek out local
materials which will split to an even

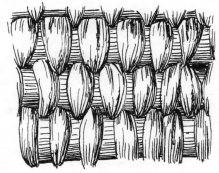

Fig. 5, *Coarse stitching over
bundle foundation.*

thickness and width, will become flexible when dampened, and will not
shred unduly from the friction of stitching.

The foundation fiber is used in its natural color, but the weft is often dyed. Several colors may be used in one basket. Designs are usually geometric, at least to the layman's eye. Superficially geometric designs are, upon close study, often highly stylized representations of
birds, animals, snakes, clouds, and other natural phenomena. Some designs are quite apparently pictorial. Diagonal or curved lines are used,
but close inspection shows that these are not true curves or diagonals,
but a series of "stepped" vertical and horizontal lines caused by the
vertical stitching and the horizontal
coiling.

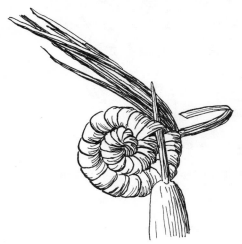

Regardless of the foundation to be
used, it is usually started as a
fairly small diameter which quickly
increases in size in a few turns as
it spirals outward (Fig. 6). If split
fibers or grasses are used, this is
accomplished simply by introducing
more and more fibers or grasses until
the desired thickness is achieved.
If rods are used, the spiral can start
with one and increase to two or more
in a turn or two. If the foundation
is to be the one-rod type, the thin
end of the rod is used as the beginning (presuming that the rod naturally tapers), or it is pared down to a
taper. Generally, the narrow foundation is necessary in the beginning as

Fig. 6, *Starting a coil.*

the initial turns are quite sharp.

The basket is usually held on the lap of the worker who sits on the
ground. Foundation fibers and weft material are on one hand and a bowl

of water is handy on the other. The direction of the spiral in this
working position is not always the same, but some generalizations may
be useful here. In the case of Pima basketry:

> "Bowls have counter-clockwise coils and deep, straight sided bas-
> kets and jars clockwise coils. While being made, bowls are held
> with the inside facing the worker and the sewing is done from the
> inside on the edge farthest from the worker, thus producing the
> finished surface on the inside of the basket. The jars and other
> deep forms are held with the opening facing away from the worker
> and are sewed from the outside on the edge nearest the maker, so
> that the finished surface is on the outside of the basket."[4]

It is easily seen that the side into which the stitch is made will be the
most finished and handsome, although a well-made coiled basket is quite
nice on the opposite side as well. I would encourage the student to use
whichever direction of spiral and stitch he finds most satisfactory to
him.

When the selection of foundation and weft have been made, one needs now
to determine the type of stitch to be used to sew the coils together.
A few tools are necessary also. In all cases, a bone, thorn, or steel
awl is used to open a hole in previous work. A scissors or knife is
needed to cut off unwanted ends.

We may consider one of three basic stitches although investigation and experimentation will suggest alternates and variations.
The simplest is the *lazy stitch*
which alternates a wrapped or whip
stitch and a connecting stitch
(Fig. 7). A few inches of the
tapered beginning foundation is
wrapped with the weft and is bent
into the beginning of the spiral
for the basket bottom. When this
bend has completed the first cir-
cuit of the spiral, the continuing end of the weft is wrapped
over the new part of the spiral

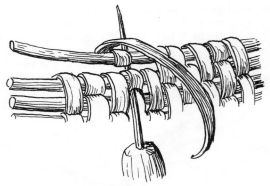

Fig. 7, Lazy stitch.

once and then over both the old and the new parts once. In this manner
the spiral is enlarged. The necessary opening in the previous coil is
made with an awl. A slightly blunt awl is desired to press the fibers
apart. A sharp awl would tend to pierce through the fibers themselves.
The weft end is pushed through this opening and pulled up tightly and
snugly, thus binding the two coils firmly together.

More foundation material is added as needed to continue the coil. A new
weft length can be introduced by pinching the new end under the last

[4]Jeancon and Douglas, p. 9.

stitch or two of the old length. Some of this new weft is then held **in** place **s**ufficiently for stitching to continue.

As long as coils are added outward, the diameter increases. In order to bring the sides upward to make the walls, the coils are stitched more on top of each other. The rapidity of this change of position determines the sharpness of the change of direction from bottom to sides of the basket. Some bowl-shaped baskets with curved bottoms are started almost immediately by sewing new coils just slightly on top of earlier ones.

Another relatively simple method of sewing is the *Figure-8* stitch which

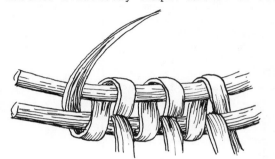

requires a weft with a good surface on both sides such as yucca and some grass leaves (Fig. 8). Split willow, for instance, is not useful here, for it has only one really good side, the peeled side. The Figure-8 stitch can easily be identified in a cross section. In this stitch, as in the lazy stitch, the weft goes under the previous coil. The difference comes when the weft returns between the new and old coils before being whipped over the new one.

Fig. 8, Figure-8 stitch.

The so-called *Apache stitch* is not unique to that tribe, but is very common all over North America. In one sense it too is similar to the lazy stitch, but it does not actually go under the previous coil. Instead, the weft is stitched to the previous coil's weft by being thrust through an awl opening between the weft and foundation of the previous coil (Fig. 9). To this end, a slightly angled opening must be made with the awl.

By comparison, the first two stitches bind coil to coil, while the Apache stitch more accurately binds weft to weft. This stitch is probably most common in coiled basketry.

A few other variations may be mentioned here for the advanced student. In some cases, especially with a grass or other finely shredded foundation, the weft stitches may actually pierce through the previous foundation. Naturally, this is not possible with a one-rod foundation. In a two-rod coil, after the initial spiral beginning, only one rod is added at a time, but two rods are wrapped together -- the top rod from the previous pair is

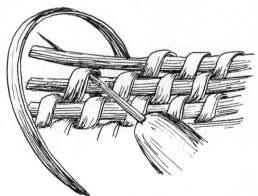

Fig. 9, Apache stitch.

stitched to the new one, thus forming a new pair. This is the basic idea in the description of the lazy stitch and the Figure-8 stitch. A three-rod foundation may be used with the Apache stitch to keep the integrity of the three rods as a group. Sometimes the three rods are stitched as in the two-rod foundation; i.e., only two new rods are added, and the third rod is taken from the top of the previous foundation. For other variations, see Mason's writings on this subject.

As mentioned before, the finest baskets usually are those with the narrowest coils and the smallest stitches (or, the highest count of coils and stitches). However, the quality, evenness, and closeness of the stitchery is important to the beauty of the surface. On a well-made basket, the foundation fibers are almost, if not entirely, covered with weft. Also, the spacing of each stitch is uniform and in keeping with previous stitches.

Colored weft is added in the appropriate places in the same manner as the continuation of other weft. Some baskets, such as those of the Hopis, are made with several bright colors in the design. Other tribes, particularly in the older baskets, often have simpler color patterns of natural fiber and one dark color. These are by far the most common.

As one reaches the rim of the basket, the foundation fibers are decreased in diameter so that the coil, as it completes the rim, becomes quite thin. In this manner, a sharp, noticeable termination of the coiling is not so evident. Sometimes a single, completely round rim is stitched on top of the last coil. The rim is usually finished with a wrapping of weft fibers, normally in the same stitching technique as was used for the rest of the basket. Other stitches, such as a plaited technique, may also be used.

Infinite shapes are possible. By and large, baskets are very similar to pottery forms of the tribe -- mostly low bowls or cylindrical containers. Designs on baskets, while lacking the freedom of brushwork, are also very similar to pottery designs. For suggestions of forms, designs, and materials, the student should research the history of basketry in his vicinity.

*Fig. 10, Sweetgrass. A,
Plant 1/4X. B, Floret 4X.
C, Spikelet 4X.*

Woodland coiled basketry, for instance, has never been very popular, possibly because bark was too plentiful for containers. Some Woodland tribes did make sweetgrass (*Hierochloe odorata*) coiled baskets of a sort. This *Seneca grass, holy grass,* or *vanilla grass*, depending on local terminology, grows to about 2 1/2 feet in isolated marshy areas (Fig. 10). It is usually harvested green from mid-June to early September before it dies and turns light brown. The green hue is prized over the tan so it is dried in the shade to retain this hue. It has little odor while it grows or when first picked, but as it dries, it loses some of the fresh, lush green, and substitutes a pleasant vanilla-like aroma.

Unlike coiled baskets above, the sweetgrass baskets are made with little of the foundation covered. The weft of contemporary baskets is simply heavy black thread. Earlier, native fibers were used.

The grass may be harvested by cutting it off close to the ground. Some tribes gathered it by pulling up the plant whole. In most cases, the leaves are taken off and only the stems, split with the fingernail, are kept. It has been and still is used in certain religious ceremonies as a burned incense.

Baskets are started by knotting the end of a small bunch of grass, perhaps 1/8-1/4 inch in diameter, to form the beginning of the spiral. Stitching proceeds as above, with a blunt needle threaded with the black thread piercing the previous coil and wrapping around the new coil. Stitches are rather far apart to allow the green grass to show. The stitches are noticeably on the diagonal, and usually stitches are taken on top of earlier stitiches so that they tend to line up and further the diagonal direction of the individual stitches. The last coil on the rim is bound with a final whip stitch, usually closer together than the rest.

These coiled baskets often have flat birch bark bottoms and lids. The lids may have scratched, quilled, or beaded designs. Quilled bark mats or coasters were made with sweetgrass coiled borders. Some of these are still produced today, but the time involved in preparing the grass and stitching the baskets does not make this a profitable pasttime.

REFERENCES

Douglas, F. H.	"Basketry Construction Techniques", *Denver Museum Leaflet*, No. 67, 1935.
--------	"Main Divisions of California Indian Basketry", *Denver Museum Leaflet* No. 83-84, 1937.
--------	"Types of Southwestern Coiled Basketry", *Denver Museum Leaflet* No. 88, 1931.
Griswold, Lester and Kathleen	"Handicraft", (10th Ed.) Burgess, Minneapolis, 1969.

Jeancon, Jean, and   "Hopi Indian Basketry", *Denver Museum*
Douglas, F. H.   *Leaflet* No. 17, 1931.

--------   "Pima Indian Close Coiled Basketry", *Denver
                            Museum Leaflet* No. 5, 1930.

Lyford, Carrie A.   "Ojibwa Crafts", Bureau of Indian Affairs,
                            U.S. Dept. of Interior, Washington, 1943.

Mason, Otis T.   "Aboriginal American Basketry", *U.S. Na-
                            tional Museum Annual Report*, Washington,
                            1902.

Seton, Julia M.   "American Indian Arts", Ronald Press, N.Y.,
                            1962.

Tanner, Clara L.   "Southwest Indian Craft Arts", University
                            of Arizona, Tuscon, 1968.

*Fig. 11, Pomo close-coiled basket.   8 3/8 inch diameter
(after Mason).*

PRIMITIVE POTTERY[1]

Why "primitive" pottery? Primarily because of the lack of two important pieces of equipment associated with more advanced technologies:
the potters wheel and kilns. Thus this term refers to the methodology
of the craft, not to its aesthetic qualities. Also, because pottery
techniques as herein discussed are more-or-less common to many cultures,
I hesitate to use a title of "Indian Pottery".

In spite of the lack of potters wheels and high temperature kilns, the
North American Indians, particularly the tribes of the Southwest, ex-
celled in pottery which is equalled, in my judgement, only by tribes in
Central and South America. Some African peoples, for example, still
create wares in primitive fashion, but Indian potters achieved a quality
of design and craftsmanship which is quite unique.

As was the case in many cultures, ceramic cooking and storage wares were
made by women. (It is interesting to observe that cultures which developed a potters wheel also transferred the skill of pottery to a masculine activity.) Until recent decades, the women potters were anonymous
and made wares for household use and occasional tourist trade. Recently,
however, a few native craftsmen have achieved the degree of national reputation that signed wares are becoming more common. Nampeyo of the
Hopi Pueblo and Maria Martinez of San Ildefonso are outstanding examples.
I just heard of a "Maria" pot which sold for $400.00.

Many culture area groups historically produced wares as evidenced by
potshards found in abundance in middens and camp sites as well as burial
sites. Many of these are easily several centuries old, and the quality
of even these fragments suggests that pottery was a well-developed craft
then. Some few tribes have no history of pottery. The Paiutes, for in-

---

[1]Anthropologists prefer *ceramics* as the appropriate term to refer to
non-metallic minerals shaped in a plastic stage and fired to high
temperatures. Unless the ceramic form definitely belongs in the class
of sculpture, I prefer *pottery* as a more precise term when referring
to primarily container shapes such as bowls and jars. Some effigy
figures, pipes, and beads were made of fired clay, but the large proportion of ceramic work was in utilitarian containers. In my definition, *pottery* is an inclusive term encompassing the whole spectrum,
but excluding non-containers.

stance, never acquired the technology. Northwest Coast Indians worked
wood with such skill and imagination that pottery was not required.

Some tribes rapidly lost pottery skills after contact with White trade
goods. Evidences of a well-developed craft are found in central Wisconsin, but these are identified as several hundred years old and pre-date
White contact. Brass and iron kettles and, later, kegs and tin cans,
were adopted instead of fragile ceramic wares. Only in the Southwest
did pottery persist after the time of the White conquerors, although
the quality and quantity of pots declined.

Pottery, unlike more perishable objects of material culture, is particularly valuable for anthropological study. The plastic clay retains much
of the characteristics of its manufacture: finger prints, brush strokes,
tool marks, and the like. This quality gives immediate insight into the
technology regardless of when it was made. Clay, when fired, becomes,
in effect, a metamorphosed rock and acquires the eternity of rock. The
pot itself is, of course, usually fragile, but the shards may well last
thousands of years. The abundance of clay and the relative ease of simple construction provide contemporary seekers with abundant supplies of
these bits and pieces, especially in areas of sedentary populations such
as the Pueblo communities of the Southwest. Because the technology of
primitive pottery is universal, pottery remains give opportunity for the
study of other factors; namely, sources of clay, pot forms, and designs
applied to these forms. The latter is especially interesting in noting
comparisons of modern Hopi wares with those of their ancestors, the ancient Sikyatki peoples. Geologic analysis of shards can identify geographic sources of clay which gives insight into the travels of the potter.
Recent science has developed techniques which can identify the sources
of bits of broken pottery which have been broken up and added to new clay
to make new wares. One can draw conclusions regarding the stability of
a culture. In general, the more sedentary the people, the more likely
the opportunity to work with ceramics and then the more highly refined
the workmanship and the more highly stylized the applied decorations.
Woodland tribes produced deep jars, often with pointed bases, which were
used for cooking. Their designs were limited to impressed and stamped
patterns, and pots often were crude and exhibited textures associated
with construction rather than designs for the sake of decoration. Semi-
nomadic tribes on the Plains made some wares, but as the horse increased
their mobility, the amount of pottery decreased. Pots do not easily survive packing and travelling on horseback. Pueblo cultures, on the other
hand, have populated the same areas for centuries. The Hopi village of
Oraibi is said to have had continuous occupation since 1125 A.D., and the
earlier Basketmaker culture inhabited the vicinity before Christian chron-
ology.

Pottery Shapes

Although Indians relied solely on hand-building (a method which suggests
irregularities to a much greater degree than wheel-thrown pottery), most
pieces were nevertheless designed round as viewed from above. Differences

in shape occurred chiefly in the silhouette as seen from a side. Most
shapes tended to be spherical. Spheroids are stronger for a given size
and thickness than, say, slender or flat shapes or those with projections
or corners (such as narrow necked bottles or rectangular boxes).

Everyday use dictated that wares should be as simple and sturdy as possible. No pieces had legs or a "foot-ring" as provided on contemporary
dishes. Instead, bases were rounded or pointed -- a feature which does
not function well in our table-oriented culture. Rounded or pointed
bases could rest well in a depression in an earthen floor or between rocks
in a fire. Flat bases are produced today by some Pueblo potters, probably on demand by tourist buyers.

Two shapes are common to all primitive cultures: the open bowl for cooking and preparing foods, and the bulging jar for liquids and storage.
One might include a third category -- that of the zoomorphic shapes of
effigies and ritual-oriented artifacts, but I would exclude these from
this chapter as sculpture although some of these did actually function
as pots. One might also include the unique "marriage" or "stirrup" pots
with double necks and a connecting clay strap near the lips, and the
narrow-necked flattened canteens which included small straps for a thong
handle. These latter I would consider exceptions, for the former two
shapes are far more prevalent.

Most wares included wide or open mouths. Extremely narrow necks do not
allow for ease in filling nor cleaning, although there are obvious advantages in carrying and pouring liquids. Further, at least in the early
stages of construction, the opening must be large enough to permit a
hand to finish off the inside of the pot.

Typical wares are quite small -- seldom over 18 inches in diameter or 12
inches tall although 5 and 10 gallon water storage jars have been made
in the past. The characteristic Hopi vessel is a small bowl about 4-10
inches in diameter and a few inches high. Zuni jars are much larger by
comparison. Water vessels or *ollas* (Spanish: *oy'-yahs*) are larger, for
these are to be carried on the head with the aid of a basketry ring for
stability. A woman can obviously carry only one jar at a time, so a
container of several gallons is required to make the trip to the water-
hole worthwhile. A modern straight-sided stoneware crock, by way of contrast, would be useless inasmuch as it is too heavy, could not be balanced
well, and would tend to spill the contents.

Clay Considerations

Clay is quite abundant in the earth's crust and is frequently found on
or near the surface. Areas of erosion are likely hunting grounds. Natural erosion, such as stream gullies or emerging lakeshores often expose strata of clay as might man-made erosion in the form of highway
cuts or building excavations. Some investigation into the history of
your area may result in the location of beds of clay used for bricks.

A knowledge of the geology of your area may offer guides for searching.

Only two requirements exist: the clay must be plastic enough when moist to be easily worked, and it must be refractory enough to withstand the temperatures of firing.

Test the plasticity of your clay by mixing it thoroughly with water to the point where it can be shaped without being so wet that it sticks in globs to your hands. Roll it and stretch it and press it. Some clays are just too "short" to be useful as they crack or deform too easily. Don't be impatient, however; most clays improve with age so that a short clay becomes more plastic in a week or month. *Too* short a clay must be discarded if aging doesn't help.

Regarding refractory qualities -- the proof is in the fire. Depending on the mother rock from which the clay was formed, it may survive temperatures up to 2000 degrees F. or more, which is quite a respectable degree. Some clays may crumble after the firing and cannot be used even though they may be quite plastic. Sometimes one can combine a short refractory clay with a long non-refractory one to make a happy medium. Try some pieces and fire them in the manner described later. In some communities, you may enlist the aid of a local art teacher by asking that a small pot be included in a kiln when student work is being fired. Indian pottery is very "soft" (low-fired); anything over 1500 degrees should be sufficient.

Raw clays may occur in almost any earthy hue: gray, brown, tan, reddish, yellow, and the like. Most clays will "burn" to a light tan to brick red color, depending primarily on the amount of iron oxide it contains. The fired color can only be determined after actual firing. If you are fortunate to find several different clays, keep them for decoration later after you select one for the body clay.

Clays sometimes are happily found which contain few impurities. Others may be full of twigs, gravel, sand, ants, or just plain dirt. Modern potters normally refine such clays by mixing it with sufficient water to make a creamy liquid called "slip". This slip can be strained through sieves. Indian women more likely searched out a bed of relatively clean clay which did not require such straining. Large chunks of rock or root can be removed by hand picking.

Depending on the dampness of the clay as you find it, dig it out by the shovelful or break loose a few chunks. (There is something humbling about taking clay by the handful rather than with the rapacious power shovel used in commercial clay mines.) Indian cultures considered the earth as a Mother who would willingly relinquish required material such as clay if a respectful request was made. Underhill reports that some Pueblo women continue the custom of asking permission and leaving an offering.[2]

[2]Underhill, "Pueblo Crafts", p. 79.

Chunks of clay should be broken or cut into smaller chunks so that **they** can be spread out to dry. In a few days these can be pulverized more. This was done on a stone mortar and pestle (*metate* and *mano*) much as the process of grinding corn meal. Lacking such a grindstone, you can simply whack it with a stick or mallet. If you put the clay in a sturdy cloth sack, you may cut down some of the dust. Just pound right through the bag.

If your clay is especially fine-textured, some gritty material should be introduced as "temper". Some of the Pueblo women used a volcanic sand and others, a pulverized volcanic rock. Zuni and Acoma women typically used ground-up potshards. The Hopi, Taos, and Picuris Indians used a clay which was coarse naturally and needed no further tempering.[3]

Substitutes may be found in the form of sand in your locale -- especially sands originating from feldspathic rocks. You could also break up soft-fired pottery such as the common reddish flower pots. Don't use tableware dishes. These are fired so hard that the effort of crushing them is grossly time-consuming and seldom worth the effort.

An extremely fine clay can accept 5-10 percent temper or more. Experienced women judge by experience or "feel" -- a handful of temper to a bucketful of clay, depending on the amount naturally present in the clay. Use a can or some such measure and keep track for future reference. Better yet, make several batches with different amounts and keep notes on which is superior, both in shaping and in firing.

Tempering tends to reduce shrinkage while drying and also reduces the chance of cracking. Tempering actually seems to improve the plasticity of a clay although excesses, say 25%, will reduce it. Tempering permits a fairly rapid firing and allows for some unevenness in temperatures by keeping the clay somewhat porous. This is because the temper, particularly in the form of pulverized potshards, has already been fired and therefore is not subject to the same stresses as raw clay. For the same reason it helps the pot survive the thermal shock of cooking more easily than a fine clay to the extreme that a pot may even rest directly on a fire. Some modern wares are proudly advertised as "ovenproof", a quality which Indian women accepted as normal. Of course, in the case of the native pots, some of the ability to survive cooking temperatures can be attributed to the fact of very low firing temperatures; modern ovenware is always fired much harder and therefore needs to be more carefully compounded. As will be seen later, coarse tempering does not need to affect the surface texture of the pottery because of the polishing technique used on most pots.

When the clay is judged to be the "right" mixture (no one can give precise proportions), it is mixed with enough water to render it plastic. This "water of plasticity" should be sufficient to allow the clay to be

[3]*Ibid.*, p. 80.

formed easily, but not so much that it
sticks to one's fingers nor slumps too
easily from the desired form. Insufficient water causes the clay to crack.
The amount of water of plasticity is,
obviously, a matter of judgement and
experience.

Mix a good-sized chunk -- melon-size
or larger. Don't chance running out
before your pot is done. The work is
such that it's almost as easy to mix
a large batch as it is for a small one.
This is kneaded, much as bread dough
is kneaded, on a board or rock surface (Fig. 1). This pushing and twist-

Fig. 1, Kneading the clay.

ing evens the consistency of the clay and tends to improve its plasticity. Judicious kneading removes most of the air pockets in the clay
which may otherwise expand in the fire and possibly cause the pot to explode from the pressure. Work the clay for a quarter-hour or so -- the
longer the better. Add water, if necessary, because kneading tends to
dry the mixture. If the clay is too moist and sticky, add more dry clay.

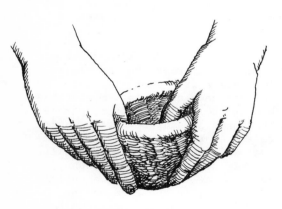

Fig. 2, Pinching a pot.

Building a Pot -- Pinching.

Three, possibly four techniques
of construction are common to
primitive cultures, and most of
these persist to the present day.
A fundamental process, usually
employed by beginners everywhere,
is the pinch method. A ball or
thick slab of clay is cradled in
the fingers of both hands. This
is rotated as the thumbs shape
a depression in the center (Fig.
2). Small pieces, up to 4-5
inches in diameter, may be formed
by this pinching technique alone.
Pinched bases are good beginnings

for later addition of coils. Some cracks normally appear on the rim --
especially if forming is too rapid or the clay is too stiff. Press these
cracks together to re-weld the clay. Don't just smooth them over which
may create dangerous air pockets. If the clay is too stiff, re-knead,
and add more water. It's not worth working when the clay is too dry.
Careful shaping pinches out an even-walled bowl which often needs little
more work. A valuable concomitant of pinching is the acquisition of a
sensitivity to plastic clay and a judgement of thickness.

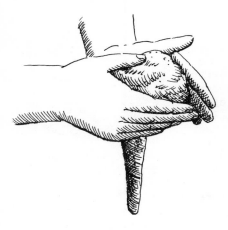

Fig. 3, Rolling a coil.

Building a Pot -- Coiling

The coiling process is universal and seems apparently ageless. In one respect, it is similar to coiled basketry in that a spiralling roll or rope of clay is piled or coiled on top of preceding rolls as the pot is rotated. (There is, of course, no real weaving.) For fairly large pots the women make long coils by rolling a long chunk of clay between the palms of their hands and allowing coils to hang downward as they are formed (Fig. 3). Such coils may be any length and thickness, but they average 2 feet by an inch thick. If you find this procedure awkward, roll a chunk of clay back and forth on a flat surface with the palm of your hand. A fabric-covered board is ideal for this, for it doesn't stick to the clay as quickly as does a smooth piece of wood.

A coil is laid on the circumference of a pinched base and is welded on with short vertical finger strokes (Figs. 4 and 5). Note that the coil is just inside the rim so that it is not only pressed on, but also upward. *Weld*, don't just stick these together, and be sure that you don't accidentally trap air pockets between coils. Several coils are necessary for most pots. As many as are needed are added in this fashion. Sometimes a coil is cut off in order to create a single ring before another is added (Fig. 6). Sometimes a too-long coil is merely continued on top of itself for whatever length it happens to be, thus forming a spiralling coil pattern. Note in the illustrations that

Fig. 4, Beginning a coil pot. A, Pinched base in place on dish form. B, Cross section.

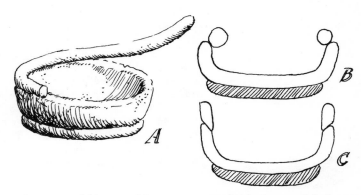

Fig. 5, Adding coils. A, A coil being welded on. B, Placement of the coil on the rim. C, The coil pressed into place and thinned.

no attempt is made to create the curved sides of the final shape; at this point a simple pail shape is sufficient.

The base of the pot is usually supported in a saucer-
like dish which is held in the potter's lap as she
works. This can be placed on a box or table just
as well. This dish enables the potter to turn both
the dish and the pot simultaneously with little danger of distorting the soft clay. Some pots still
retain a change of direction or shallow groove near
their bases as a result of this temporary support.
Broken pottery shapes or pieces of gourd were used
for such dishes. I like ceramic unglazed dishes
because the new work pops off readily. Pueblo pot-

*Fig. 6, Coils welded
on and thinned upward.*

ters may dust on some fine sand or dry clay before the moist base is set
in place to keep it from sticking. Unglazed ceramic dishes also have the
advantage of absorbing moisture from fresh clay which thus helps it to
hold its shape better. If you intend to work on several pots in the future, you would do well to fire some "custom" base dishes. Several pots
are normally being made at one time, so a separate dish for each is desirable.

Continue to add coils until you either achieve the desired size or it
seems apparent that the pot will begin to slump if you continue to add
more weight. In the latter instance, you'll have to allow the pot to
dry partially until it is stiff enough to accept more coils. The time
required may be a few hours or more, depending on the humidity. Try,
nevertheless, to keep the lip soft while the basal area is allowed to
dry. A plastic or damp cloth around the rim may control the moisture
there while you allow circulation to dry the unprotected bottom. Under
no circumstances should you try to add new, moist coils to a rim which
has been allowed to dry somewhat. Such an attempt will surely result
in a crack later as the new clay shrinks more than the drier clay. A
general principle to remember in any ceramic work is to join clays of
equal moisture content. More coils are added again until the shape is
completed or until you must again halt to permit drying.

Somewhere in this coiling process, the bowl's
curves must be modelled. Ideally, this should
be accomplished when all the coils have been
added. Especially on large bowls, this is a
practical impossibility, for clay stiff enough
to support its weight may also be too stiff
to be changed in shape. Therefore a large
piece must be shaped when it is partially coiled
and then allowed to dry before final coils are
added (Fig. 7).

*Fig. 7, Coiled bowl af-
ter shaping. Dotted
line indicates direction
of future coiling.*

A few wooden scrapers, known as "ribs" to potters, are handy tools for shaping. These can
be whittled out of thin wood. A thin, smooth
edge is desired all around. These can be any
size or shape, but a clam size and shape is a

good all-around tool. Curves should approximate curves on the pot and a straight edge
is fine for most convex shaping (Fig. 8).

While the pot is still plastic (and, in the
case of a small-mouthed pot, before the mouth
is made too small to accept your hand) an
appropriate rib is used to press the walls
outward while one's other hand supports the
exterior. The rib is best used in a stroking
fashion, gently bulging the walls. Work
'round and 'round as you stretch the thick
walls toward the desired curve. Continually
check the symmetry of the form as it develops
until you achieve the final form. Some
changing of shape can occur at the rim inward,
but this will thicken the walls which must
then be squeezed upward. Not only does the
shaping rib change the contour of the pot; it

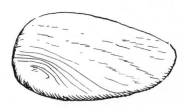

*Fig. 8, Typical wooden
shaping tools.*

also smoothes the surface and removes some of the finger marks and de-
pressions from welding. For some pots, no more finishing is required.
Small-mouthed jars must be imagined in their completion, for the interior must be finished before the top is completed.

For a better bond between coils, modern potters frequently roughen the
surfaces to be joined with a stiff brush or toothed scraper. These areas
are then dampened with a layer of creamy slip. This "slip-and-roughing"
technique is not a substitute for good welds; it merely assures that the
joint is amenable to good welding. Don't try to putty up or fill a bad
joint with slip; shrinkage on drying will cause a crack to appear.

Scraping

When the pot is completed, set it aside in the shade or some draft-free
place to dry more. Don't hurry this drying, for this may cause the piece
to dry unevenly and warp or crack.

When the pot has gotten drier and stiffer, but not dry and stiff, scrape
the surface with a suitable tool. A potshard, broken gourd, bone blade,
or knife is such a tool. Scrape the walls to about 1/4-3/8 inch thickness as uniformly as you can. A good job of shaping earlier makes this
step easier or even unnecessary. Scrape in several directions; a single
direction will usually just increase surface irregularitites. At this
stage of dryness (or dampness, if you prefer) called "leather dry", the
clay should be dry enough to resist further modelling, yet moist enough
to carve or scrape easily. Leather dry clay can easily be cracked, so
support the pot well with one hand on one side as you scrape with the
other.

The tempering in your clay will create a rough texture with the scraping,
but don't fret about that now; concentrate on the shape, the thickness

of the walls, and surface irregularities.

Building a Pot -- Paddling

Some tribes began pots by coiling, but, instead of pinching and
scraping them smooth, used a
paddle to tap or beat them into
the desired shape. This technique has the advantage of com-
pressing the fine clay particles,
thus making the pot stronger. Paddling also makes a refined contour
more readily than scraping alone as the paddle beats down bumps level
with the surface. As with rib-shaping, little or no further scraping is
required so that a coarse clay still retains fine particles on the surface.

Fig. 9, Cord-wrapped paddle.   12 inches.

A simple wooden paddle -- something like a large, flat spoon or spatula
--can be used, but plain wood
quickly becomes damp from the
clay and tends to stick to its
surface. Most tribes wrapped
their paddles with some sort of
cordage (heavy twine is good for
starters) which doesn't stick
unless you really get it wet.
A cord-wrapped paddle creates a
reverse image or print of itself
on the surface of the clay.
This texture is not unpleasant
and is frequently seen on some
primitive pots. Some persons
maintain that they can identify
the raw material of the cordage
by examining the imprint in clay
paddled ages ago and thus gain
insight into the botany of the
area at the time the pot was made.

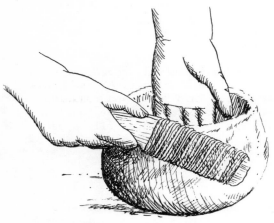

Fig. 10, Paddling a pot.

Leather hard clay, by definition, cannot be shaped by paddling. Soft,
plastic clay may deform from the jarring blows of the paddle. Ideally,
the stage should be somewhere between plastic and leather hard. As is
so often the case, the best time is a matter of experience and judgement.

Building a Pot -- Paddle and Anvil

The method described above is primarily used for refining coiled pots.
By using a paddle on the exterior of a thick pot and an appropriately
shaped stone on the inside (Fig. 11), a pot can be actually shaped and
not merely refined. Here, the coils can be 1 1/2 inches thick or so,

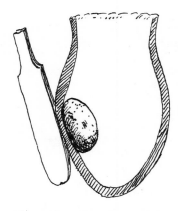

Fig. 11, Cross-section of paddle and anvil shaping.

and the paddle and anvil compress them in thickness as they stretch them in width. The stone anvil tends to refine the inside contour in a manner similar to that used in bumping out fender dents in automobile bodies today.

Some tribes were not troubled by the coil technique for beginning these pots. A lump of clay was simply hollowed out for a beginning and the entire pot was swatted into shape with the paddle and anvil. There is, I think, a limit of size here, because large pots need to dry near the base, as aforementioned. Seldom can one beat a large pot into shape at one time without deforming or slumping. The sharp taps of the paddle are such that the clay can be a little stiffer than for, say, coiling or pinching.

Slipping

If a pot has been scraped, a rough texture is created. Paddling retains the imprint of the cordage in the clay. Both textures are interesting and sometimes may be desirable and may be left as is. The finest pots such as those produced in the Southwest are further surfaced by painting on a thin layer or layers of fine-textured slip. This slip may be made from the clay which was used for the body but without tempering grit. Often, however, the surfacing slip was made from a different clay selected by custom and tradition. Acoma pots are white over a tan clay body; Hopi women use a slip made from the same clay as the body which fires yellow or orange (depending primarily on the placement in the kiln); Zuni pots are slipped with a white clay which seldom extends down to the base which is often slipped with a reddish clay.

Slips may vary from bone-white to tan or brick-red. Pueblo potters have followed tradition so closely that pottery may often be identified by slip color to determine where it was made or when. Some Pueblos produce wares in several colors, usually made by different women who offer statements such as, "That's the way I was taught", or the like. Because of this adherence to tradition, pottery and potshards help to re-create the history of a people.

Pueblo women are known to travel some distance to get just the right clay for slipping and are often understandably cautious about disclosing their sources.

If your body clay is unsuitable for slip or if you seek other colors, some ceramic supply houses today can furnish appropriate substitutes. A "china clay" or "kaolin" is quite refractory and will fire white. An extremely fine material known as "bentonite" has been used also by Indian

women.   Some red-firing clays (*Dalton, Redart*), tan (*Sadler, Albany*), and
brown (*Barnard*) are common in supplier's catalogs. Don't be concerned
about the raw color; remarkable changes sometimes occur in the fire.

A creamy mixture of slip is painted (mopped, really) on the surface of
the pot, inside and out -- sometimes one color inside and another outside. Sometimes the potter may first wipe the surface of the pot with
a damp rag to prepare the surface for the slip. Pueblo women make a
satisfactory brush by chewing yucca leaves on one end to remove the
juicy portion which allows the longer fibers to remain as hairs. Almost
any soft hair paint brush will be satisfactory. A large brush -- 1/2
inch diameter -- will do the job well.

Paint a thin layer on the leather dry pot and allow it to dry until it
loses its wet shine. More layers are painted on and allowed to dry flat
each time. Wet-on-wet layers merely remove earlier layers and cause
streaks. Heavy layers are in danger of shrinking unduly and cracking
off. The slip may also shrink off if it is applied to clay that has been
allowed to dry too much. In spite of these precautions, you may discover some cracking on the surface of the slip due to differences in contraction naturally present in the slip and clay on which it is applied.
Nothing can be done in this latter circumstance except to change either
the slip or the clay.

Polishing

When the pot has again dried to a leather hard stage (moisture from the
slip may soften it somewhat), it may be further polished for the smooth
satin surface which is so lovely on some Pueblo wares. These potters
use a smoothly polished hard stone, agate, for instance, the size of a
walnut or larger. Many of these stones have acquired a polish from use
by generations of potters who have bequeathed these to their daughters.
Today, you might make a purchase from a local "rock hound" who has some
"tumbled" stones. Some sort of hard, shiny surface is required; horn,
bone, glass, metal, if you don't have a good stone. A metal spoon is
convenient because it also has a handle to facilitate gripping as you
press your thumb in the bowl in order to use the convex back for polishing. A rock or other tool is gripped however may be convenient.

If the clay is at the proper stage of leather dryness (which has to be
determined by experience and testing) you should be able to rub the stone
rapidly back and forth over a few square inches of surface. This is
done in different directions to create a very fine, even, shiny surface.
If the clay is too hard, you get powder and a dull finish. If it's too
wet, you dig streaks or grooves. If it's just right, the rubbing will
begin to show a waxy sheen which gets more handsome the longer you rub.
If you've done a good job of preparing the surface with the slip, it
should be quite even with no pits. The heterogenously distributed particles of clay are thus rearranged by the stroking of the stone. The
clay needs just enough water between the microscopic plate-like particles to enable them to slide into a smooth alignment which results in

the burnished gloss.

A good job on a fair-sized pot may take
an hour or more of vigorous and careful rubbing. Older women are concerned
about the lack of patience on the part
of young people who take up this craft.
A half-hour is minimum. Don't add
water; this will destroy the polish
by scattering the clay particles again.
Just rub! Some women like to use a
little grease or oil as an added lubricant, but don't be generous if you
do. Polish until you've gotten as
high a shine as you think possible;
put in another half-hour and you may

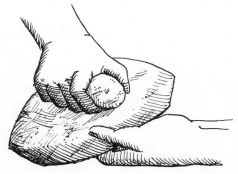

*Fig. 12, Stone-polishing the ex-
terior of a bowl.*

come close to the quality of surface of some of Maria's pots. Not only
is a well-polished pot delightful to see and touch, it also has such a
fine surface that it is almost, though not quite, impervious to water.

Generally, only the finest pots were given this loving polish. Pedestrian pieces for common household use were often left fairly rough.

Decorating

Any decoration to be applied before firing must be mineral in origin to
survive the high temperatures of the kiln. Most paints[4] are made of pigments which lose their hues in the heat, so don't go to a store for poster paint, for instance. Earthy hues, usually with some iron content,
withstand the heat and, fortunately, are compatable with the earthy clay
medium.

As a matter-of-fact, iron oxide in the form of rust can be scraped from
old metal, ground, and strained, to be added to a slip to make a red or
brown-firing slip. Other clays may be found naturally which will fire
to useful shades as mentioned in the section on "Slipping". The Pueblo
women used traditional colors in their designs so that further identification can be determined as to source and period.

[4]I use the term "paint" to refer to any pigment mixed with a medium,
such as oil or gum, which is intended for application to a surface
which is not subjected to intense heat. The paint medium alone holds
the pigment to the surface. Some confusion may exist inasmuch as a
medium may be employed as an expedient to apply a ceramic pigment to
clay, but in this case the medium, being organic, burns away in the
firing and leaves the mineral pigment fired in place. Also, when the
pigment is applied in liquid form with a brush, I shall use the term,
"painting", to refer to the method of application, even though the
ceramic pigment may contain no medium.

Because most pots are slipped with light-firing clay, darker slips are desired for painted decorations. Most often seen are a black and brick-red or brown. These are applied by brushing and, sometimes, stippling, usually in linear, geometric designs although highly stylized bird, insect, and animal designs are quite common at some pueblos. Occasionally, as in the old Hohokam or Mimbres wares, anthropomorphic forms are found. These may have had symbolic significance originally; today, they have a delightful, almost whimsical quality. Certain motifs may have names today such as bird-wing, dragon fly, mountain, and the like. While these also probably had significance in the past, today they seem to be thought of as purely decorative designs and the names are for simple identification. One particularly interesting motif which reoccurs in Zuni designs is the "heart line" which extends as a red line from the mouth to the heart of a black stylized deer.

Pots are usually painted only on the side which most obviously presents the best surface for viewing -- an open bowl, for instance, is decorated on the inside, while a small-mouthed jar would appropriately be decorated on the exterior.

Curvilinear designs, well-suited to pottery surfaces, may be free-standing in the center of a bowl or may be connected to a border line or two near the rim. Exterior designs are most often found in bands around the pot separated by horizontal bands. When viewed from above, the circular shape is often divided into quarters or sixths -- a judgement estimated by eye or, perhaps, with the fingers as measures. Designs within these divisions are often simply repeated. Occasionally the repetitions are precise, but sometimes they are only superficially similar; close examination shows added or subtracted elements between design motifs. Sometimes several design motifs are used in a regular pattern around a pot as with an "a-b-a-b" or "a-b-c-a-b-c" rhythm. Thus, there are regular patterns and irregular patterns in infinite combinations.

Some old Pueblo pots will be observed to have one (sometimes several) broken or incomplete border line, usually near the rim. This device has come to be known as the "life line" or "road of life line" of the pot and is symbolic of the life or spirit of the pot itself or of the potter. This is symbolic of the incomplete or unfinished being or life. In other words, if the line is complete or continuous without beginning nor ending, the life of the pot or potter is also complete; the living spirit has gone full circle from birth to death. It has "died", for its life is as complete as the line.[5]

[5]It is interesting to note that the symbolism of the circle is quite universal, but varies in interpretation. Plains tribes, for instance, symbolized the cyclical nature of life as a complete circle which, if broken, was then ended.

Most Pueblo designs appear to be conceived as black linear outlines filled in sometimes with colored slips. While good potters pride themselves
on filling in these areas neatly and precisely, it is easier, in actual
practice, to go over the black lines again to cover inaccuracies of slop-
py filling in. (This is somewhat like a child's problem in filling the
spaces in a coloring book neatly.) One must still marvel at the accuracy
and fluidity of design, especially when one recalls the yucca leaf brush
which is used.

The coveted black ceramic pigment is created in several ways. Underhill
notes that the Rocky Mountain beeplant (*Peritoma serrulatum*) is boiled
down to form a gluey substance[6] which apparently acts as an acqueous medium or binder. To this is added, at Zuni, for example, a mixture of
iron and manganese mineral matter in pulverized form.

Lacking the beeplant substance, other water soluble media might be used
-- mucilage or syrup is a good beginning for experimentation. Any sort
of water-soluble, organic, sticky or gummy substance might be tried which
will hold the pigment in place before firing after which the pigment will
be fused to the surface of the clay.

You may be able to locate a local source of natural pigment which will
fire black or brown, but this is seldom the case unless you have a knowledge of the history or geology of your area. Certain clay-like minerals
may contain a high percentage of iron or manganese or other dark-burn-
ing oxide. Some stones may be pulverized to yield a fine pigment. It
should be obvious, however, that any pigment needs to be very finely
ground if it is to flow nicely and evenly from the brush.

I have suggested earlier the use of rust as a slip coloring. Manganese
or copper oxide may be obtained from ceramic supply houses. Remember
not to confuse pigments of mineral origin with those of organic origin
or you may discover that your carefully painted design has turned to
ashes after firing.

Oxides may be used alone or in combination with slip as a stain. Mix a
small amount of your medium with the oxide or slip and enough water to
make a liquid which will brush easily yet cover well in one coat. A very
highly polished pot surface will not accept a watery, runny mixture which
beads up as water drops on a waxy surface. The purpose of the gluey medium is to make it sticky enough to overcome this surface tension. Too
gummy a mixture will cover well, but probably will not be able to be
painted on spontaneously; it may also build up too thickly and shrink
off on drying or firing. Designs cannot be painted on an unpolished surface with the expectation that polishing can occur afterward, for the
polishing would destroy the design. Some pots are only lightly polished
which surface then accepts the design more readily.

[6]Underhill, *op. cit.*, p. 86.

A soft hair artist's brush can be used for painting the designs. The
hairs should be as long as possible for smooth, even lines. Pueblo women today may sometimes use modern long handled brushes instead of the
old, shorter yucca brushes which were about 3-4 inches long. Actually,
for the freehand brushwork on the curved pottery surfaces, a short-han-
dled brush might well be preferred. Use whatever you like, but, in general, the diameter of the brush should be about the width of the line you
intend to make with it.

Paint your designs on smoothly and evenly, sufficient to cover the clay
beneath, but not so thickly that the line is raised as a ridge.

Painted designs, depending on the amount of medium, should be handled
cautiously before firing or you may be in the unfortunate circumstance
of painting an excellent design on one side of the pot while you unwit-
tingly smear a design on the opposite side. Notice, too, that the brush
does not have an eraser on its end; bad work will need to be scraped off
and you'll have to slip and polish all over again.

Don't be discouraged if the firing does not fix or fuse the design permanently on the pot. Certainly, it is intended to be permanent, but the
vagaries of pigments and firing may result in something less than that.
Recent Acoma pots sometimes have fragile designs which can be blurred
by rubbing with a finger.

A finished pot should be set aside to dry slowly and completely. Rapid
or uneven drying may cause it to warp or crack. Several days should be
allowed -- more in the case of thick pots or humid weather. If possible,
allow pots to dry slowly in the shade and then set them in the sun for
a day, just to be sure. Some women place them near heat just before firing. No moisture may be present when pieces are placed in the kiln; any
water is a sure way to have them explode as the water turns to steam.

Besides the natural texture of scraped tempered clay and the imprint of
cord-wrapped paddles and slip-painted designs, some other techniques have
been used. Northern tribes often decorated their wares with incised designs which are necessarily linear. A pointed awl or sharpened stick is
an adequate tool. Swirling, interconnected circular patterns are found
on very early potshards as are designs which are more rigidly geometric
such as diamonds or rectangles. The "Greek key" pattern is not unique
with the Grecian culture. Potshards found in the Iroquois area show surface incising of short parallel linear patterns, almost like creative
cross-hatching. Few such pots exist from early times, and none are being made today.

As with the painted designs, the incised patterns appear to be mostly
created as continuous bands around the exterior of pots. Leather dryness
verging on bone dryness seems to be the most propitious stage for scratching designs. Bone-dry work crumbles too much, and soft clay tends to
plow furrows as it is displaced by the tool. I like the clay to be soft
enough to scratch easily, but hard enough so that the dislodged particles
crumble off readily. If you **wait an hour or so** after scratching in your

design, crumbs which still remain on the surface can be brushed off with the hand. Incised designs seldom are scratched deeper than 1/16 inch. Lesser depth is more common. A deep line will weaken the wall too much and really is not necessary. Sometimes you'll find that repeating the incising to deepen it will be superior to making it deep enough in one stroke. The rough lines are quite nice against a polished surface. I know of no pots which combine incising and polychromed slips although this is a technique familiar to contemporary ceramics and dates back to Grecian vases.

A related method of surface decoration today is limited primarily to the Santa Clara and San Ildefonso wares. In this method, areas rather than lines are carved into the surface of the pot (which must be rather thick) so that the result becomes actually a low-relief sculptural pattern. The edges of the relief are normally rounded and the entire pot is polished, including the low areas. When the lowered areas are left rough, the edges can of course, remain more crisp and precise. Although this technique has great possibilities in its three-dimensional quality and combinations of dull and polished textures, the modern work remains traditional.

Julian Martinez is credited with the development of the mat-on-polished ware in 1919 which has been brought to culmination by his wife, Maria.[7] Mat-on-polished ware is fired black and owes its beauty to the contrast of mat and gloss rather than to a contrast in color. At first glance, it would appear that the entire pot is highly polished and then areas are carefully scraped away to expose the dull slip. (This erroneous assumption might, nevertheless, give you a suggestion as another technique.) Actually, Julian (the use of the first name connotes no disrespect) seems to have rediscovered a long-lost technique. He uses a shale-like material which can be ground to a paste on a stone pestle. When thinned with water (and a medium?) it adheres well to even the very highly polished surface of the pots.[8] In this manner, the technique is still a painting procedure, but the result has the initial appearance of scraping. The Martinez' designs use little amounts of the mat surface and rely largely on the polish for the largest areas of the pots. Both San Ildefonso and Santa Clara today produce mat-on-polished wares with designs limited mostly to the *avanyu* or plumed serpent and highly stylized feather patterns.

Firing[9]

Without extreme heat to drive out chemically combined water present in

---

[7]Chapman, p. 34.
[8]*Ibid.*
[9]I prefer the terms *firing* and *kiln* to refer to the process of subjecting clay to high heat and the chamber in which this is accomplished. I prefer to reserve the terms *baking* and *oven* to refer to the process of making cookies.

all clays, pottery would remain very fragile and useless. The superficial water added to clay to make it plastic must be completely dried out,
as mentioned earlier, to a bone-dry stage. Clay which has been dried
but not fired may be re-moistened and will return to a plastic state
again. Fired pottery has been changed chemically and physically so that
superficial water will no longer soften it.

Ceramic studios have modern kilns heated by electricity or combustible
fuel so that they can be easily operated and can be used for many years.
The primitive kiln, if the term is at all appropriate, is created anew
each time firing is done. Modern kilns are almost foolproof, but primitive firing is subject to hazards which may destroy all the labor of
creating a pot. Underhill notes that the Pueblo potters are nervous on
the firing day,[10] understandably so because of the uncertainty of firing.
(Even a modern potter with a precision kiln is somewhat on edge until
the firing is completed and his kiln is opened.)

Firing is usually accomplished early in the morning when diurnal winds
are few. A day predicted to be windless is chosen, if possible, for erratic or high winds may cause local intense heating and thereby breakage. Obviously, a damp or rainy day makes firing impossible.

A preliminary hot fire is built on the ground or in a pit large enough
easily to contain all the pots to be fired. The number of pieces to be
fired may be one or two or dozens. One must decide either to take a
chance on several firings of a few pots each time with all the time and
effort involved in each, or a single large firing which, if poorly accomplished, may break everything inside. Pots to be fired are often set
down gradually closer to the fire to pre-heat them. (Not too close!
You'll have to pick them up again soon.) Turn them frequently to heat
them evenly.

When this fire has burned down,
some supports are placed in the
hot ashes to act as stilts or
posts a few inches above the
bed so that heat can get under
the pots. Stones which have
proved their ability to withstand heat were used in the
past. Broken pieces of large
pots could be used. Today,
women often use tin cans set
on end for these posts. Scrap
iron or grating or a grill are
also good.

Fig. 13, Setting pots in place for firing.

10Underhill, *op. cit.*, p. 86.

Larger pots are usually placed inverted on the supports first. Smaller pots may be placed on or between these. Mottled Hopi ware is produced by random stacking. More uniformed fired color can be expected if pots are stacked more carefully on top of each other or with a space between them. Lip-to-lip or foot-to-foot arrangements usually give good results. Use good judgement to allow for initial expansion from the heat and later contraction as the pot is fired. In other words, pots should be so placed that they will not press against each other tightly. A stack of pots can expand upward, but pots wedged tightly side-by-side may create a strain to the breaking point.

A rude covering of sheet metal is laid gently on the pile of pots so that the fire does not come in actual contact with the wares. Earlier, large potshards performed this function. Some primitive potters neglect this covering or use it minimally. Variations in this covering cause fortuitous variations in the color and hardness of the wares.

In the arid Southwest, dried cakes of cow dung are used for fuel. On the Plains, buffalo dung or "chips" were ideal. Sheep dung, trodden into cakes in corralled areas is almost as good. All these fuels, if completely dried, burn slowly and evenly, thus giving an ideal heat for ceramics. If you use these fuels, you'll probably need a couple of bushelsfull. In Wisconsin, cow dung seldom dries sufficiently to be gathered, and wood must be used. I like hardwood split into thin chunks. Soft wood flares up too quickly and sudden thermal changes are deadly to pottery. Heavy or large chunks burn too long and may collapse the whole kiln. Too thinly split fuels may also flare up too rapidly. I'd suggest pieces about 1-2 inches thick and a few feet long to be piled around and on top of the sheet metal covering in "teepee" fashion. Fuel can be added for ignition on top and more can be placed on later, if necessary. Cakes of dung can be stacked nicely over the sheet metal. Indian potters usually judge the amount to be required and pile this amount on right at the beginning.

Some fine kindling is used to start the pile. Don't use woods which "spit" such as white cedar although its bark is good tinder. Touch the whole thing off all around and shove some fuel underneath the pots for thorough heating. Then hope that the wind doesn't pick up.

The fire must be tended with adjustments made by poking a stick here and there to keep the heat even. More fuel may need to be piled on or pushed underneath. The time of firing varies from an half-hour to several hours. This is dependent upon the size of the pots with the largest or heaviest work requiring the longest time. Good potters try to limit the pieces in each firing to work which needs about the same period of time. In general, ceramics should be fired slowly with the heat being built up gradually. Modern electric or gas kilns are fired in 6-8 hours, but these are usually filled with fine-textured clays which cannot survive the relatively rapid heating of primitive kilns. Coarse, tempered material can resist thermal changes more successfully.

Fig. 14, Interior of kiln. A, Tin can supports. B, Pots. C, Metal sheets. D, Dung fuel. E, Kindling.

A fire slowly elevated to high temperatures is essential. Modern kilns normally fire to a minimum of 1850-1900 degrees F., but seldom does a primitive bonfire kiln achieve 1500 degrees, which is just as well. Dense, high-fired wares are stronger, but are more subject to cracking when they are heated for cooking. Higher temperatures also destroy the sheen of loving polishing as the clay particles shrink closely together.

When the fuel burns down, the firing is complete. Sometimes potters will lift a sheet of metal to observe what's going on inside, but this is dangerous as you may bump the pots unintentionally or allow a sudden draft of cold air to enter the kiln. If you yield to temptation, you should observe that the pots are glowing hot. The degree of incandescence is an indication of the degree of heat and should be observable even in bright sunlight. (Firing at night is fun!) A dull red is observable at about 1000 degrees; 1500 degrees is equal to an orange with lesser temperatures in between.[11] If the pots (not just the coals) are not at least a red-orange, you'd better get more fuel on in a hurry.

Pots are sometimes taken out of the kiln when the fire has first burned down even though some heat remains. I'd urge that the kiln remain unopened until the next day to give it time to cool gradually. Pieces may crack just as easily with sudden cooling as with rapid heating.

When you can't wait any longer, carefully remove the metal coverings, and lift out the pots with some sticks for tongs. (This experience is similar to Christmas morning at our house.) Sometimes these tongs may burn because of latent heat still in the kiln. Set the pots aside to be sure that they are cool enough to handle. Test them gingerly with your bare hands, for hot pots may look cool. When they can be handled, you can brush off the ashes and, for the first time, view your work in permanent form. That's it! The work is now as permanent as we consider permanent to be. The pot may break, but the potshards are forever.

The firing of the black wares of San Ildefonso and Santa Clara is begun as above, but the temperature is generally a little lower to preserve

[11]To get an idea of the temperature you have achieved after the kiln has cooled, you might place a chunk of ordinary bottle glass between the pots and propped up all by itself. Because this glass slumps at about 1500-1600 degrees, you can judge if you have achieved this temperature by the amount of slumping.

the polish better. (This lower firing creates a softer ceramic which tends to crumble if it is soaked with water for some time.) Instead of allowing the fire to burn down normally, the entire kiln is smothered with pulverized or shredded dry manure so as to create a very smoky atmosphere inside the kiln. Because the blackwares are made of a normally red-burning clay which is high in iron oxide, a chemical reaction takes place because of the lack of oxygen to change the red oxide to black iron oxide. This, and, to some extent, the carbon from the excessive smoke cause the clay to acquire a jet black color which penetrates into the walls of the pots as can be observed from shards. This method of firing was developed at San Ildefonso by Maria Martinez who has national reputation for the quality and beauty of her work. If the smothering material is allowed to ignite freely, which can be observed if flame replaces smoke, the resulting burn will return the black color to its red oxide form. Thus, the smoky atmosphere must be continued until the clay is below the temperature when chemical change can occur. Ashes from earlier fires can be used to keep the pots smothered after a smoking period without adding to the combustible fuel. In lieu of smothering dung such as pulverized horse manure, try finely shredded bark or dry, rotten punk. Sawdust may also do the job. A lot is needed, so you'd better stock up with a few boxes-full ahead of time.

Finishing

Nothing remains after cleaning except, perhaps, a thin wiping of grease to bring out the polish, but don't soak it full. American Indians did not develop a technique of glazing, but the fine polish on some wares is just as aesthetically acceptable. A true glaze, however, renders a pot waterproof, and Indian pots were always too low-fired to be impervious to water. Water jars, for instance, became moist on the exterior when they were filled, but this same porosity cooled the contents by evaporation which helped to keep the water sweet and fresh.

Pots used for cooking quickly acquired a greasy film which penetrated the pores of the clay and thereby effectively waterproofed the pots. This may sound to civilized ears as a most unsanitary procedure as may the use of dung for fuel, but many cultures are not as preoccupied with sterility as are contemporary Americans.

Indian-made pots are normally used purely decoratively today anyway, so the porosity of the clay is no problem. If pots *need* to be waterproofed, a coating of oil, grease, or wax warmed into the walls will help, but is not totally efffective. Such a coating also may change the color and finish detrimentally if it is put on heavily. The result is often an ugly "varnished" appearance which looks quite artificial. I suggest that these wares be used just for looking at. If you must put cut flowers in them, place a glazed pot or a glass dish inside as a liner.

Conclusions

Each chapter of Indian crafts closes with a concern about the deterioration and decline of that craft. Pottery may be an exception. Hurriedly-made tourist wares are coupled with the need for a monetary-based economy. There is little time for quality of design and skill in craftsmanship. Fairly nice pieces bring a few dollars, but few tourists will spend $25.00 for large, fine pieces. Some encouragement is offered by art galleries and museums which recognize the beauty of competent work, but this is offset by traders who encourage quickly-made trinkets which can be sold readily and cheaply.

Maria of San Ildefonso and Nampeyo of the Hopi Pueblo have reputations to the degree that a good living is possible from quality pottery as a vocation. Most wares will still be made as an avocation, and, as such, probably will not increase the skills nor beauty of design to a significant degree. Nevertheless, the gratification of pride in one's work and a respectful buying public indicates strong motivation for the perpetuation of the craft.

I have emphasized the techniques of the Southwest potters, because there pottery has been produced continuously to the present day. A few women on the Six Nations Reserve in Ontario have learned the skill of the potters wheel. They find old potshards to be used as design suggestions and are re-creating old shapes and incised patterns with modern wheels and kilns. Their high-fired pieces are glazed on the inside to suit contemporary needs, but they retain the earthy textures of their prototypes on the exterior of the pots. These are finding a market, and the speed of production without sacrificing quality is such that a living wage is potentially possible as full-time work. This may give impetus to other tribes.

Some Indian pots which have been "ritually killed" have been found at burial sites. I have mentioned before the concept of the "life line" symbolizing the spirit inherent in creation. To release this spirit for a life hereafter, some tribes in the past "killed" certain pots by breaking a hole in them intentionally and buried them in graves with deceased persons. It is hoped that new pots will be born, perhaps literally from the dust of their ancestors.

REFERENCES

Bunzel, Ruth L.   "The Pueblo Potter", Columbia, N.Y., 1929.

Chapman, Kenneth M.   "The Pottery of San Ildefonso Pueblo", School of American Research, Univ. of New Mexico Press, Albuquerque, N.M., 1970.

Dutton, Bertha P. (Ed.)   "Indians of the Southwest", Southwestern Association on Indian Affairs, Santa Fe, N.M., 1965.

Fewkes, Jesse W.   "Archeological Expedition to Arizona in 1895", *Bureau of Amer. Ethnology 17th Annual Report*, Vol. 2, 1985-96.

Field, Clark   "Indian Pottery of the Southwest Post Spanish Period", Philbrook Art Center, Tulsa, Okla., 1963.

Fontana, Bernard L., Robinson, William J., Cormack, Charles W., and Leavitt, Ernest E., Jr.   "Papago Indian Pottery", Univ. of Washington Press, Seattle, Wash., 1962.

Lisitzky, Gene   "Four Ways of Being Human", Viking, N.Y., 1966.

March, Benjamin   "Standards of Pottery Description", *Univ. of Michigan, Museum of Anthropology, Occasional Contributions*, No. 3, 1934.

Seton, Julia M.   "American Indian Arts", Ronald Press, N.Y., 1963.

Sides, Dorothy S.   "Decorative Art of the Southwestern Indians", Dover, N.Y., 1961.

Underhill, Ruth   "Pueblo Crafts", Bureau of Indian Affairs, U.S. Dept. of Interior, Washington, D.C., 1944.

————————   "Workaday Life of the Pueblos", Bureau of Indian Affairs, U.S. Dept. of Interior, Washington, D.C., 1946.

Wissler, Clark   "The American Indian", Peter Smith, Gloucester, Mass., 1957.

Wormington, H. M.   "Prehistoric Indians of the Southwest", *Denver Museum of Natural History, Popular Series*, No. 7, 1964.

CORN HUSK DOLLS

Corn husks were not only used for basketry, sandals, masks, and other practical artifacts, they were also used to make children's dolls. Of all the techniques in this book, possibly nothing brings a feeling of commonality with Indians as human beings as the mental picture of a mother pausing in household labors to make a doll for her daughter. If, perhaps, we have been guilty of stereotyped concepts such as bloodthirsty savages, we might do well to close this book on Indian crafts with a chapter on artifacts which are created only for children's amusements.

Few of these dolls are made today. Probably some mothers still make these occasionally for their own children, but their presence as a living craft seems gone. Guy Spittal in Ontario formerly carried these as a stock item in his trading post, "Iroqrafts", but lately he notes that the women who supplied him are gone or have given up this enterprise. This is certainly unfortunate, for we lose not only a small bit of native heritage, but also colonial, because the White settlers soon learned this craft even as they learned maize agriculture.

Corn husk dolls are not difficult to make, although the first dozen or so may appear as rather clumsy attempts. Few tools are necessary. A scissors is handier than a knife for trimming the husks. A few pins -- preferably with large "bead" heads -- are handy for temporary tacking down. A needle and thread are useful, especially to sew hair on the finished doll. Finally, a ball of thin string or thread can be used for making some of the ties.

Preparation

The basic raw material is, of course, corn husk and, maybe, some corn silk for hair. Husks can best be obtained when the corn is ripe; i.e., beginning to dry on the stalk. Green husks may be used. If dried in the shade, these may retain some green hue which might be used for doll clothing. Otherwise, green husks will tend to leach out to a pale tan color on drying. Husks may be harvested in corn fields in autumn, but by that time they will probably show dark spots of mildew stain. These autumn husks can still be used, but one must peel off a few layers to get clean material. Try to find the largest ears because long husks can always be trimmed, but short ones create unnecessary problems of splicing.

Dried husks may be dyed in a strong dye bath. The husks can take a deep color which is quite nice, but their oily surface makes them resist the dye somewhat. This can be overcome by a spoonful or two of detergent. Simmer a few leaves at a time for 10-15 minutes dependent upon the richness of the color desired. Stir them slowly on the fire to distribute the color evenly. When the husks have gotten a little darker (more intense) than is desired, take them out of the dye and rinse them well in cold water until the water runs clear. They may be used immediately or can be spread out to dry for storage for future work.

Fresh husks may be used green, but it is customary to allow them to dry bleached first. If you break off the cob at the base, most of the husk remains joined at the stem. These can easily be hung up to dry. Don't permit these to remain damp for fear of mildew. Save some corn silk, too.

Construction of Head and Body

Fig. 1, Head and body balls.

When you are ready to begin a doll, soak the dried husks in water for a few minutes to soften them. You will notice that the dried husks are quite brittle, so don't try to separate the leaves until they are soaked. Husks are always worked wet, but not necessarily dripping wet. Shake off the excess water and pull off a few leaves. Snip off a bit of the widest butt end so that the husk can be spread out more readily.

Start at the butt end and split off some lengths about 1/4-1/2 inch wide in the middle (You will note that such splits are tapered at each end.) Wind several of these up into a tight ball about 3/4 inch diameter much as one might wind up a ball of string. With a little practice, you'll soon be able to master the simple skill of wrapping down a previous end with a new piece of husk. Start each strip with the pointed end so that the sturdier butt end is last. The strips may be flat or twisted into a rude cord, as you wish, but, when the ball approaches the desired size, wrap the last length flat on the ball's surface. Fasten the end temporarily with a pin (Fig. 1). Make two such balls -- one for the head and one for the body.

Construction of Arms and Legs

Make arms and legs by rolling up or folding a piece of husk 1-1 1/2 inch wide (Fig. 2A). Fold back the ends to help it keep from unrolling so that the total length is about 4-5 inches. The actual length varies dependent upon the intended size of the doll and the method by which the arms and legs will be attached. Pin the folded ends down temporarily (Fig. 2B). About 3/8-1/2 inch from **one end of this rolled core**, begin wrapping a thin

Fig. 2,
Arms and
legs. A,
Rolled core
of husk. B,
Ends folded
back. C,
Beginning the
wrapping. D,
End of wrapper
split and pin-
ned. E, End
is split and
tied.

strip in such a way that its loose end is bound beneath the first wrapping
(Fig. 2C). As before, begin all wrappings with the pointed end of the
strips so that the final knot will be made with the butt end. Wrap tightly
toward the other end in an overlapping spiral, but try not to twist the
rolled core which will then untwist later. About 1/2 inch from the other
end (hopefully, you will have an inch or better remaining on the wrapper)
split the wrapper to create two ends (Fig. 2D), and tie these together
twice -- once on each side of the core (Fig. 2E). Loose ends can be snipped off now or later. As a matter-of-fact, the ends of the core can be
snipped off, if necessary, to even out the ends, but this is best left
for after the assembly.

If necessary, on a particularly long core, a second wrapper can be started
the same as the first and which should also bind down the loose end of
the first. If you have trouble holding the ends firm during this splitting
and tying, try a pin to hold the wrapper in place. Incidentally, a pin is
a good tool to use to split the ends.

Fig. 3, Core wrapped from both ends and tied in the middle.

An alternate method of wrapping is begun the same as before, but, upon reaching the center, stop and pin the wrapper down. Begin now at the opposite end, but wind the wrapper in a spiral opposite to the first. In this way, when you reach the center with this second wrapper, you can tie the two together (Fig. 3). If a single core is to be used for two arms or two legs, the knotted area will be hidden by the body covering.

Fig. 4, Alternate method of creating arms and legs by tying only at the ends of a rolled core.

Another and easier method for making arms and legs is to tie just the ends of the core with a 1/8 inch band of husk. Use the butt end to make a good knot.

Among some White "native" craftsmen, it has recently become popular to roll a pipe cleaner inside the core. This has the obvious advantage of permitting the arm or leg to be bent at the joints more nearly to approximate the human limbs. Makes sense, but it isn't authentic technique.

Assembly

Select a long, clean piece of husk and split out a strip about an inch wide. Lay this over the head ball so that the ends of the piece are of more-or-less equal length. Use this piece of husk in an inside-out position; you will note that the inside surface is smoother than the outside. Twist this piece on top of the head so that the face of the ball is neatly covered, and open the other side to cover the back side of the head. With a heavy thread or a 1/8 inch strip of husk tie this in place as a neck (Fig. 5) (A twisted husk cord is stronger than a flat piece.) Push this tie up tightly under the head and try to smooth out facial wrinkles. If you arranged the cover properly, the pin holding the head ball is still visible and can now be removed, but the wrapper end has been tucked under the head cover.

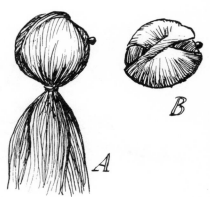

Fig. 5, Method of wrapping the head. A, Front view. B, Top view.

Select a arms-piece and tuck this up to the neck between the ends of the husk (Fig. 6). Insert the body ball below the arms and pinch the husk ends together below this ball. Tie the waist together (Fig. 7).

Select a longer legs-piece and fold it in half. (If the legs were made a

Fig. 6, Inserting the arms.

Fig. 7, Tying the waist af-
ter adding the body ball.

few days earlier, these must be re-dampened.) Tie the legs on to the
body with the remaining husk ends (Fig. 8A). Tie the feet together temporarily. Some doll's feet were bent upward at right angles to the legs.
To do this, kink the core and pin the feet in a bent position until they
dry in place. Whichever way is selected,
cut off the feet evenly, but don't cut into
the wrapping. Cover the waist and hips with
1/2 inch strips to build up an appropriate
width (Fig. 8B). For a boy doll, make a

Fig. 8, Attaching legs. A, Tying on. B, Wrapping the hips.

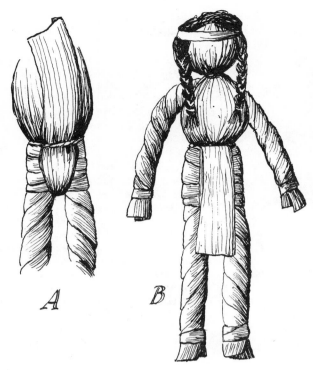

A   *B*

*Fig. 9, Attaching a breech cloth. A,
Breech cloth brought up between the legs
and tied with a belt. B, Breech cloth
folded down on a finished boy doll topped
with braided yarn hair.*

To make a girl doll, you may add legs by
either method above, but forget the breech
cloth. You may also forget the hip wrapping, if you wish. Split several strips
of husk about an inch wide and tie these,
tips upward, at the waist to create a full
skirt (Fig. 11A). Snip off the tips above
the belt (Fig. 11B).

Make a dress from a long husk about 1 1/2
inch wide. Split the butt end about halfway down; fit this over the head and down
the back. By clever folding, you can bring
the solid front portion together to form
shoulders and a bosom to be tied in place
at the waist (Fig. 12A). You can also use
this method backwards to make a *décolleté*

breech cloth of natural or
dyed husk about 1/2 inch wide
by about 4 inches long, and
push this between the legs.
Bring the ends up toward the
head in front and in back,
and tie this on with a 1/8
inch buckskin thong or a
cornhusk belt (Fig. 9A).
Fold the breech cloth down
over the belt (Fig. 9B) and
tie it in place temporarily.
You may also want to tie
down the arms at the sides
for drying. Pins may be
used instead.

If you have made legs which
are too short to be used
doubled, select two legs of
proper length and flare out
one end of each so that the
flare fits against the waist
(Fig. 10A). Tie these on;
then fold down or cut off
any excess to be hidden with
the hip wrapping (Fig. 10B).

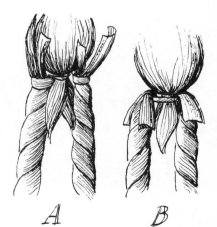

A   *B*

*Fig. 10, Alternate method of
attaching legs. A, Separate
legs with ends flared out a-
gainst the waist. B, Ends
tied and folded down for
covering.*

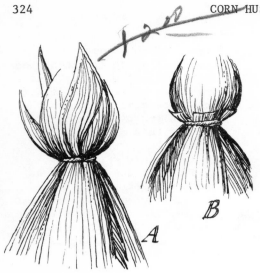

Fig. 11, Attaching "petticoats" for a full skirt. A, Husks tied, tip upward, at the waist. B, Tips cut off.

neckline with the two split ends hanging down as with a shawl (Fig. 12B).

A dress can also be made by cutting a neck hole in the center of a wide husk and putting this on over the head. Pinch this at the waist as above. Obviously, dresses can be made of dyed husks.

Because the skirt hides the legs anyhow, you may omit the legs entirely and merely make a fuller skirt. Enough "petticoats" will permit the doll to stand by herself. (A doll without legs just doesn't seem right to me, nor would it, I'm sure, seem right to a child. There seems to be a simple logic here to include all limbs, covered or not, so that the doll shouldn't be handicapped.)

Hair

Recent dolls have been made with black yarn hair stitched together along a part on the top of the head. I purchased one which used white thread, but it would seem more consistent to use black or, at least, tan thread. Cut about 10-12 lengths of yarn about 4-6 inches long and sew these to the head. A "wig" could be stitched together on a sewing machine, if you prefer. Braid the yarn on either side of the face and tie off the pigtails with a bit of colored yarn. Narrow husk could be used instead. Make a headband of buckskin or husk and tie this on with the knot at the back. I have a doll with

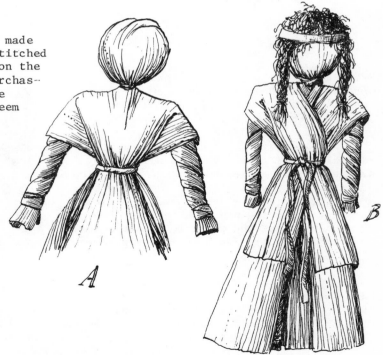

Fig. 12, Girl doll's dress. A, First method with solid front. B, Second method with split front on a finished doll with cornsilk hair.

the headband stitched onto the head in a few places -- just to be sure.

More authentic, but more fragile, hair can be made of some corn silk which may be used as is or may be dyed. Dampen the silk and sew it on as above. If you are really good, you can braid the pigtail, but my hands are too clumsy for this. I just roll or twist the damp silk and tie off the ends.

Finishing

What about facial features? It is interesting to note that primitive dolls universally often neglect facial features but are, nevertheless, quite satisfactory. The last doll I acquired in Canada simply had a spot of orange on each cheek which was quite sufficient. If you insist, eyes and a mouth can be painted on. Use water color or a dye applied with a brush, but test it on scrap husk first to get a consistency which won't run or bleed. I hate to say it, but a felt-tipped pen works fine. Use black for the eyes and red for the lips. (While I'm on the subject, paint can also be used, I suppose, for decorations on the clothing, but I prefer the single natural or dyed color of the husk.)

If you seek further decorations, try buckskin as mentioned earlier. Eighth-inch strips, dyed or not, can be used singly or braided for belts and headbands. Ties at the wrists and ankles can be buckskin or dyed husk. Some dolls could fitted with buckskin or cloth clothing. A string or two of beads could be added as might a tiny feather in the headband. Don't get too gaudy, however. There is a simple charm in the use of un-adulterated natural materials which can be spoiled by overdecoration.

According to Carrie Lyford, "Dolls are dressed as warriors or women and are given all the accessories, bows, tomahawks, baby boards, or paddles, as the sex may require."[1] A pack bag can be made of a folded and tied piece of husk which can be strapped to the back or carried in one arm. A baby can be made with tiny head and arms, but the body and legs can be wrapped completely. Such a baby can be fastened to the back of a girl doll or carried in her arms.

Give a finishing touch with scissors to trim off ragged ends. Tie or pin down parts which project too much. Set the doll aside in a dry place for a day or two after which all such clamps may be removed.

[1]Lyford, p. 67

REFERENCE

Lyford, Carrie A.   "Iroquois Crafts", Bureau of Indian Affairs, Dept. of Interior, Washington, 1941.

.25